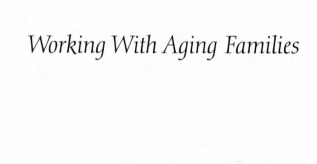
Working With Aging Families

WORKING *with* AGING FAMILIES

Therapeutic Solutions for Caregivers, Spouses, Adult Children

KATHLEEN W. PIERCY

W. W. NORTON & COMPANY

New York • London

For information about permission to reproduce selections from this book,
write to Permissions, W. W. Norton & Company, Inc., 500 Fifth Avenue,
New York, NY 10110

For information about special discounts for bulk purchases,
please contact W. W. Norton Special Sales
at specialsales@wwnorton.com or 800-233-4830

Manufacturing by R. R. Donnelly, Harrisonburg
Production manager: Leeann Graham

Library of Congress Cataloging-in-Publication Data

Piercy, Kathleen W.
    Working with aging families : therapeutic solutions for caregivers,
spouses, & adult children / Kathleen W. Piercy. — 1st ed.
        p. cm. — (A Norton professional book)
Includes bibliographical references and index.
ISBN 978-0-393-73282-5 (hardcover)
1. Social work with older people.   2. Intergenerational relations.   3. Family therapy.   I. Title.
HV1451.P534 2010
362.6—dc22   2010009291

ISBN: 978-0-393-73282-5

W. W. Norton & Company, Inc., 500 Fifth Avenue, New York, N.Y. 10110
www.wwnorton.com
W. W. Norton & Company Ltd., Castle House, 75/76 Wells Street, London
W1T 3QT

1   2   3   4   5   6   7   8   9   0

I dedicate this book to my parents,
Thomas Patrick Walsh III, and the late
Dolores Vivian Walsh.
I also dedicate this book to the many clinical and
research families who taught me so much about
living life and facing death with grace and dignity.

Contents

ACKNOWLEDGMENTS

No book would ever be completed without the love, patience, and hard work of key persons in an author's life. I would like to thank the following persons, who in various ways, contributed to the writing of this book: My mentor, Rosemary Blieszner, for suggesting to Norton that I might be a good choice for this endeavor. Your support and guidance throughout my career has provided me with many opportunities I might otherwise have missed. Two faculty members in my department at Utah State, Thorana Nelson and Linda Skogrand, were instrumental in advising me on how to tackle a book project and what content would be useful to therapists. Teresa Bodrero, staff assistant in our department, was most helpful with the formatting skills that I lack.

On a personal note, I wish to thank my daughter Andrea for her input and careful editing during the writing of the prospectus for this book. My husband, Bill, graciously endured countless hours of solitude during the writing of the manuscript. Several family members and friends shared with me their experiences of caring for older adults in both professional and personal settings, and I am grateful to them. Finally, to my editor, Andrea Costella, I offer my utmost gratitude in seeing me through this process. I could not have done it without any of you.

Working With Aging Families

Introduction

My background includes 18 years as a clinical social worker in both a community mental health center and a private practice. I have spent 15 years as a researcher of aging family issues. As a researcher, I have conducted several studies of older adults and their families. I have interviewed both healthy adults at play, providing care, and doing volunteer work, and disabled seniors who needed daily care from family and paid caregivers. All of them have impressed me with their energy and ability to face life's challenges and difficulties with as much courage as they could muster.

Some of their situations were so striking that I recall them vividly. Early in one study, I spoke with a 93-year-old widower who was being cared for by two daughters and a dedicated home health aide. His voice was not strong enough to be recorded, and his stamina was quite limited because of advanced coronary disease, but he answered my questions as best he could, and smiled. Later, his daughter told me that he had been hospitalized numerous times for heart problems. When I interviewed her afterward, she commented that she always left the room as soon as someone came to visit him (as she had done with me) so that the person would talk to him and not to her *about* him. "He is still a person, and he understands everything you have to say," she said.

I also remember vividly an 80-year-old widow who was a gifted quilter. Her work had won many awards. I was interviewing her to learn more about how this popular leisure activity could be a source of growth and development in late life. I learned so much more. She lived alone. Her faithful companion, a boisterous canary in her living room, chirped happily in response to every answer she gave me. She took great pride in her quilts, but she was even more excited about teaching her skills to others. Producing another generation of creative quilters was what kept her going and, in her words, what kept her young.

Finally, I recall the married man in his mid-60s who had served as a disaster relief volunteer. Encouraged by a friend to get involved in disaster relief following Hurricane Katrina, he was reluctant to go, unsure of what knowledge or skills he had to offer to others. By the time his few weeks of 24/7 volunteer work were over, he had organized the construction of a "tent city" that would be used by other relief workers for months to come. He subsequently became highly trained in disaster preparedness; now, back at home, he was involved in training and assisting others in regional disaster relief efforts. He felt that his volunteer work had benefited him so much more than what he had given to others.

All these examples feature persons who, although in various stages of life and health, were engaged in making the most of their lives. None of them was without scars or health issues. But, not all persons approach the challenges of aging with such positive attitudes and behaviors. Some people fear death and experience despair in their late years, often

brought on by failing health and multiple losses, both expected and unexpected. Their families may or may not provide them with the support they need to address their feelings
and concerns about aging and its challenges. These seniors
and their families often can benefit from professional guidance and knowledge of resources that may assist them in
navigating tough times.

The baby boom generation—fully one-third of the current U.S. population—is aging rapidly. In the U.S., 20% of
the population will be age 65 or older by 2030 (Siegel, 1996).
When all baby boomers have reached their 65th birthday,
20% of Americans will be considered "old," with the fastest
growing segment of the U.S. population composed of persons
age 85 and older (He, Sengupta, Velkoff, & DeBarros, 2005).

But it's important to keep in mind that aging today does
not mean what it did a generation or more ago. Today, ad-
vances in medical treatment, coupled with improved lifestyle
practices, have led to dramatic increases in life expectancy,
which now ranges from 78–82 years (Kinsella & He, 2009).

Moreover, our perception and attitude towards aging has
drastically changed. Old age is socially defined as 65, the age
at which eligible individuals can draw full retirement benefits from the U.S. Social Security system. However, some
adults label themselves "middle-aged" until they are well
into their 70s or 80s. Age is increasingly becoming more a
state of mind and lifestyle than a socially imposed condition.

These aging trends naturally have an effect on the family
structure, so that now, families can include up to four generations of living members. Family members are not limited
to those who have married and borne children. For example,
elderly single persons can play an integral role in the lives of

their siblings, nieces, and nephews. Likewise, many older adults have friends, neighbors, or paid helpers that they refer to as "family," even though they are not related by blood. These "fictive kin" (Gubrium & Buckholdt, 1982) are a rich source of social support for older adults, some of whom provide critical care to these elders in their late life (Piercy, 2000).

The purpose of this book is to bring counselors and therapists who work with aging families timely information about the aging process in both individual and family contexts. Throughout the book, I present case examples of aging couples or families that reflect the complexity of challenges faced by these families and are appropriate for therapeutic intervention. All these cases are composites of various mid- or late-life family problems typically encountered in clinical or research settings, and all names used are pseudonyms.

Working with older adults and their families requires a good deal of flexibility on the part of therapists because of the diverse contexts and ways in which persons seek help from professionals. Clients' health issues may also affect how therapy is conducted, calling for alternatives to the standard 50-minute hour once a week.

Throughout the text, I present situations that often argue for a combination of therapeutic modalities to resolve certain kinds of problems. For example, an elderly couple may seek therapy, but one or both members of the couple may be experiencing grief, depression, or substance abuse. Treatment of these conditions and improvement in the marriage will likely necessitate a combination of individual and couple therapy. Likewise, an older adult may present himself for individual therapy because he is suicidal; however, a lasting resolution of his depressive symptoms may require that a stronger support system of family and friends be activated. If activating this support system is difficult because of family history or current interactive patterns in his family, then family therapy may be indicated. Families are integral to the lives of older adults; thus, an assessment of family relationships should always be part of assessing an individual's situation.

I advocate taking an eclectic approach to working with specific problems experienced by older adults and their families. Like Becvar (2005), I believe that responding in the moment in appropriate ways to each client system is preferable to doing therapy according to a set model or group of techniques. Also, certain therapies, such as cognitive-behavioral therapy for panic attacks and depression, have shown strong efficacy in doing psychotherapy with elderly clients; thus, these methods of treatment are recommended when it seems most appropriate.

Many problems faced by elderly adults lend themselves to a family therapy approach. For example, a renegotiation of roles within families often becomes necessary as elderly parents become less able to function autonomously (Qualls, 1999). Repeated difficult or unproductive interactions among family members over these issues heighten tension and anxiety among family members and suggest a need for improvement in family communication and problem solving. Implementing family therapy among all persons willing to attend sessions, including the older adult whenever possible, is likely to produce the most effective change as it offers families an opportunity to renegotiate family rules and roles in ways that modify old patterns and open up options for new patterns of relating to each other (Qualls, 1999).

Sometimes, key family members are unwilling to participate in therapy. Such situations mean that a therapist may only be able to work with an individual or with a subsystem of the larger multigeneration family. These types of interventions can be productive, however. Systems theory (covered in Chapter 2) posits that changing one part of a family system can lead to changes in other parts (White & Klein, 2008). Carefully targeted change strategies may result in improvements in overall family functioning without the direct participation of all affected family members. Qualls (1999) reminded us that family therapists can also use mechanisms of letters, e-mail, phone calls, and coaching prior to family visits to facilitate family interventions and communication patterns.

In this book, I focus on working with persons in outpatient settings. Offering counseling to those residing in long-term care facilities requires a great deal of knowledge and experience in working with elders who have multiple functional limitations and often moderate-to-severe cognitive impairment, and it is beyond the scope of this book.

As a practicing therapist, I eagerly pursued educational seminars and books that would improve my therapy skills in response to specific problems my clients presented. Being the best therapist I could be is important to me. But, all these tools were of limited value in working with older adults with emotional distress or marital problems. I simply lacked information about the aging process and the special needs and concerns of older adults and their families. While some training programs now offer courses and internships that focus on work with older adults, many in the helping professions still lack sufficient knowledge and experience in working successfully with our elders and their families. A study of practicing marriage and family therapists found that the participants had only an average knowledge of the aging process (Yorgason, Miller, & White, 2009).

Yet, the need to possess this knowledge and experience has never been greater. Working with aging adults and their families is complex, and much must be known to be effective with them. Through up-to-date information about mental health issues such as mild cognitive impairment, dementia, and elder depression, as well as clinical examples of aging persons, couples, and families struggling with various health and family issues, I offer ways to work effectively with these important and growing numbers of families.

CHAPTER 1

The Increasing Complexity of Family Ties: What the Therapist Needs to Know

In the introduction, trends in individual longevity were described that have the potential to add new generations to families as well as greater numbers of older family members with unique needs. In this chapter, other social trends and issues are discussed that complicate family ties and have the potential to make therapy with older adults and their families a more challenging process. Therapists need to be aware of these issues so that they are better prepared to navigate them and offer the most effective therapy possible.

SOCIAL TRENDS THAT AFFECT AGING FAMILIES

There are a number of social trends that affect aging families: divorce, remarriage, and stepfamilies; geographic mobility; working with a culturally diverse population of families; working with both family systems and medical systems; recognizing and working with normal and dysfunctional family processes; exploring family competence; and religious and spiritual factors among older adults and their families. Each of these is discussed in turn, and approaches and clinical suggestions are offered.

DIVORCE, REMARRIAGE, AND STEPFAMILIES

One important trend that has affected family life course behavior is the high rate of divorce and remarriage. Divorce and remarriage have created new family ties while straining ties between many parents and children. Either more strain or adaptation can occur when stepchildren or new half-siblings are added to the extended family or when noncustodial parents gradually lose touch with their children from earlier relationships or marriages.

Divorce and remarriage can affect provision of support in old age by adult children and stepchildren. Generally, it is divorced fathers who are less likely to receive support in their old age from their children, whether in terms of personal care or financial assistance. Divorced mothers are just as likely as widowed mothers to receive support from their adult children (Lin, 2008). There is clearly a process of detachment that occurs between some divorced dads and their children (Silverstein & Bengtson, 1997). Ways to bridge the divide between divorced dads and their children need to be addressed as fathers age and reach out to children for help.

With respect to stepchildren's obligations to their stepparents, relatively little research has been done, and nearly all of it has studied *perceived* obligation to provide support rather than actual support or assistance given (Clawson & Ganong, 2002; Ganong & Coleman, 2006). Interviews with stepparents suggest that few of them expect stepchildren to provide any kind of assistance to them in their later years (Clawson & Ganong, 2002). However, stepchildren saw their willingness to help stepparents in several ways, but the key issue for them was whether they defined the stepparent as kin. Adult stepchildren clearly embraced a sense of obligation to stepparents who were viewed as parents to them, but for those stepparents who were not considered to be kin, perceived obligations to provide assistance were weak or nonexistent (Clawson & Ganong, 2002). Contextual factors such as timing and quality of parental remarriage, along with type of help needed by stepparents, affect perceived levels of obligation (Ganong & Coleman, 2006). Based on these research findings and my clinical experiences, I offer some suggestions for therapists working with families who have experienced divorce and remarriage.

CLINICAL SUGGESTIONS

- Do a brief family history with any clients expressing ambivalence or conflict about helping an elderly parent or other relative. Therapists need to know the history of the client's relationship with a divorced parent, aunt, or sibling, both before and after the divorce, to determine what options are possible for assisting the client and family. Some therapy time may need to be devoted to working through anger or a sense of abandonment to determine whether clients are willing to focus on providing even limited assistance to a divorced or remarried parent.
- While adult children or grandchildren often feel connected to or somewhat responsible for a divorced or remarried parent, their relationships with stepparents may not be close, especially the later in their lives the steppar-

ent entered the family or the more the client sympathized with the other parent in the divorce. Yet, stepparents have to be consulted when they are the primary caregiver to an aging parent. In these instances, brief family therapy that includes the stepparents for several sessions may be more beneficial in moving families to action.

GEOGRAPHIC MOBILITY

Geographic mobility has always been a part of U.S. culture, as in the historical adage to "Go west, young man!" Two groups of Americans may be more likely than others to move from one part of the country to another: the upwardly mobile (those seeking higher socioeconomic status through career moves) and affluent seniors who choose to relocate to the Sunbelt states after retirement. Persons with high levels of education (master's degree and higher) are among those most likely to relocate over 500 miles (Schacter, 2004). The most current movement in 2007–2008 was in the southern and western parts of the United States, two areas that have seen the most population and economic growth since the 1970s (Greenwood, 1988). However, the rate of general mobility has actually declined from 1950 to the present and now is low among older adults. Persons aged 50 and over move at much lower rates than their younger counterparts (less than 8% per year vs. 15% for those aged 35–39; Schacter, 2004). Indeed, it is well documented that most seniors "age in place" either because they prefer to remain near friends and family or because their limited retirement income precludes a move to the Sunbelt states or other location. When senior adults do move, it is usually within the same county or state (Administration on Aging, 2008).

For those families in which parental or child relocation has occurred, transitions into widowhood or physical or cognitive decline present interesting challenges. While provision of emotional support to grieving family members is enhanced by use of cell phones and e-mail or Facebook capability, assisting a parent with declining cognitive or physical abilities is much more challenging from a distance. A growing body of information has developed for so-called long-distance caregivers (Rosenblatt & Van Steenberg, 2003). Also, a relatively new profession, the geriatric care manager, has developed in response to the needs of families who are geographically separated. Usually nurses, gerontologists, or master's level social workers, geriatric care managers provide both customized services to older adults without family to assist them and coordination of services for purchase that the older adult may require to remain independent, such as chore assistance and personal care. The National Association of Professional Geriatric Care Managers has a Web site (http://www.caremanager.org) that includes a locator service for those families who may be seeking additional assistance from professionals who work in the same area as their relative.

CLINICAL SUGGESTIONS

- Encourage adult children and other family members looking after elderly relatives from a distance to know their elderly relatives' neighbors, friends, and other potential helpers, such as a long-time barber, hairstylist, or landlord. Tell your caregiver clients to give those potential helpers their contact information so they can call them at the first signs of any significant change in the elderly relative that might compromise his or her safety.

- Ask your client to use the Eldercare Locator service (http://www.eldercare.gov) or the local Area Agency on Aging (http://www.n4a.org) to become familiar with medical and social services offered in the relative's community. Medical providers sometimes have incomplete information about the array of volunteer and agency services that may help an aging relative remain at home longer than otherwise possible. Thus, relying only on a family physician to link one to services may result in missed opportunities for help.

- Once the elderly relative has developed a relationship with a health or social services provider, encourage your client or family member to visit or telephone the provider to introduce him- or herself and explain the client's care situation. In some cases, the older adult eventually will need to be moved to the long-distance caregiver's community. It may be easier to make the transition when local providers who have trusting relationships with the elder can be supportive of these discussions.

- It is also important to establish ongoing contact with the care recipient's primary care physician so that medical and lifestyle decisions can be made with good lines of communication in place.

- Keep the client focused on finding workable solutions, including finding paid or volunteer services when client caregivers cannot be involved in daily care. Long-distance caregivers may feel guilt about living far away when a parent or other close relative needs care; conversely, they may feel frustrated or angry that their relative refuses to move to be closer to them (and aging in place and remaining independent are of the utmost importance to many older adults). For clients whose relatives have adequate financial resources, hiring a geriatric care manager may be the best option.

WORKING WITH A CULTURALLY DIVERSE POPULATION OF FAMILIES

Most developed countries, including the United States, have become far more racially and culturally diverse than they were a century ago. In America, all ethnic minority groups are growing. Even those groups that consist mostly of new young immigrants, such as political refugees from several African countries and Latinos from Mexico and Central America, will add to the burgeoning number of older adults in the future.

Like the general population, the proportion of older adults who are members of minority groups is also increasing. Projections for 2030 are that 11% of elderly Americans will be Hispanic, 10% will be African American, and 5% will be Asian, up from current percentages of 6%, 8%, and 3% per group, respectively (He, Sengupta, Velkoff, & DeBarros, 2005). Minority elders are more likely to have lived in poverty than their Caucasian counterparts and may experience more illnesses and disabilities in old age along with fewer resources from which to draw for support.

Therapists who work with members of minority racial and ethnic groups are challenged to avoid making assessments of these individuals and families based on white middle-class norms (McGoldrick, Giordano, & Garcia-Preto, 2005; Minuchin, Lee, & Simon, 1996). Exploring the family power structure and extended family interactions is crucial for understanding interaction patterns among many ethnic and racial minority families (McGoldrick et al., 2005; Minuchin et al., 1996). In addition, understanding and addressing the impact of factors such as societal and personal racism are pivotal to working effectively with aged minority group members and their families (Akamatsu, 2008). Finally, an appreciation for the role played by organizations outside the family, such as churches and community groups, coupled with a willingness to build on the connections between families and these organizations can help in the resolution of family dilemmas (Boyd-Franklin, 2008).

Understanding of and responsiveness to the unique cultural factors affecting elderly members of racially and ethnically diverse minority groups are crucial to working with them and their families. According to Fowers and Davidov, a culturally competent therapist is one who "acts knowledgeably and consistently with openness to the other" (2006, p. 582) through a process of acquiring awareness, knowledge, and skills. Other clinicians have argued that multicultural competence extends beyond learning to work well with members of racial and ethnic minority groups. They noted that working with persons who possess sexual orientations, socioeconomic backgrounds, and disability status different from those of their therapists present unique challenges that ideally are met by therapist development of multicultural competence (Hansen, Pepitone-Arreola-Rockwell, & Greene, 2000).

DEVELOPING MULTICULTURAL SKILLS
IN YOUR PRACTICE

Central to training in multicultural competence is personal transformation. As Fowers and Davidov (2006) noted, accepting and embracing cultural difference requires strong character and a sustained commitment to cultivate openness to others. Therapists desiring cultural competence engage in a process of active exploration of their biases and ethnocentrism, leading eventually to acceptance that their worldviews are "part of one worldview among many" (Fowers & Davidov, 2006, p. 585). To achieve these ends, more contact with members of other cultures, races, and ethnicities and acquiring empathy for those whose cultures are different from one's own are needed (Fowers & Davidov, 2006). To those tasks, Hanson and associates (2000) suggested a therapist should gain cultural immersion experiences and supervision provided by therapists who have already developed competence with cultures whose members seek help from the therapist.

The National Center for Cultural Competence (http://nccc.georgetown.edu) offers resources for organizations and practitioners desiring cultural competence or enhancement of their delivery of culturally competent services. Based on assumptions that cultural competence is a developmental process and that practitioners can increase their cultural awareness, knowledge, and skills, this organization offers cultural competence assessment tools for health professionals as well as resources to help increase cultural competence in response to health issues in families.

As part of developing cultural competence, therapists

working with ethnic minorities need to be aware of and sensitive to the unique aspects of life history and cultural practices that influence older adults with minority group status.
The strong prejudice and discrimination experienced currently by African American elderly persons may make them
wary of trusting any counselor who is not a member of their
race. A therapeutic alliance is unlikely to be formed until the
therapist acknowledges and accepts how race has organized
and affected the lives of elderly African American clients
and their families. Therapists of different races who work
with African American families should relinquish the notion
that there is one "reality, one right solution" and work toward solutions that flexibly address the realities of their African American clients (Hardy, 2008). An example of such
differential realities can be found in how African Americans
have constructed their families as a cultural adaptation to
oppression (McAdams-Mahmoud, 2008). Unlike the mainstream U.S. cultural ideal of a two-parent biological family
with children, many African Americans live in single parent
or multigeneration families, each type an adaptation to reduced availability of men, fewer job opportunities for men,
and discrimination experienced by members of both sexes.
Instead of criticizing these family forms, a culturally competent therapist will make the effort to understand the life experiences and challenges that affected how these families
evolved and determine what purposes they serve. With a
nonjudgmental attitude and stance, the therapist can then
help these families to address their problems.

Similarly, Latinas in the United States have cultural expectations that put them at odds with the values and practices
of mainstream U.S. culture. Examples of these differences

are the expectation that young Latinas will stay close to the family until marriage, and that one daughter may remain single to help care for her aging parents (Garcia-Preto, 2008). Therapists need to make a concerted effort to understand specific family expectations and how they affect marital and family behavior. Garcia-Preto asserted that most Latino immigrants adapt to America "only to the extent that it feels safe" (2008, p. 262). Any Latino elder who seeks counseling brings a unique cultural context, set of values, and immigration pattern to his or her life experiences. Understanding and validating these contexts is a prerequisite to providing effective intervention. In addition, the intergenerational family relationships often need to be addressed for issues affecting elders to be satisfactorily resolved. The following clinical suggestions were developed by Jessica Olson, MSW, who worked as a mental health clinician with a diverse population for several years. The last tip is based on my clinical experiences.

CLINICAL SUGGESTIONS

- Become familiar with the demographics of the community in which you work. Then, strive to learn about cultural norms, values, and history (both in general and within your specific geographical area) for the major cultural groups in your community.
- Identify "cultural guides" (Skogrand, 2004) for cultural groups within your community. A cultural guide is someone who represents an identified cultural group who can help you understand important cultural issues.
- Realize that there is often as much difference within groups as between groups. Therefore, you should use cul-

tural knowledge as a guide for understanding individuals and families without blindly applying that knowledge to every member of a group.

- Recognize cultural differences between family generations, especially when working with immigrant families. Younger generations are often more acculturated to American social norms and values than are older generations. This can exacerbate family issues when differences in expectations regarding caregiving and other important factors exist.

- Approach cultures and cultural issues with a stance of eagerness to learn and understand.

- Ask clients questions regarding cultural issues when appropriate. The individuals with whom you work are experts on their own lives and the ways in which they are personally influenced by cultural values and norms.

- Treat everyone with dignity and respect.

- There are several excellent written resources for therapists who wish to better understand family dynamics among families of different ethnicities. One such resource is *Ethnicity and Family Therapy* by McGoldrick et al. (2005). This book is a comprehensive examination of important characteristics in families of all ethnicities who have settled in North America, including families of European origin that we do not think of as "ethnic minorities" (Irish, English, German, Greek, Italian, etc.). Furthermore, chapters in all three editions (McGoldrick et al., 2005; McGoldrick, Giordano, & Pearce, 1996; McGoldrick, Pearce, & Giordano, 1982) emphasized increased knowledge of and sensitivity to the values and customary behavior patterns of each cultural group that are relevant

for therapists: help-seeking, cures, and appropriate interventions. This book can serve as an important reference
for family counselors and therapists who wish to work effectively with persons and families of all ethnicities.

Working With Both Family Systems and Medical Systems

Many older adults have several medical conditions that
may affect their emotional well-being and, in some cases,
their response to various types of therapy and psychotropic
medications. Examples of these conditions are diabetes;
chronic pain from arthritis, injuries, or autoimmune disorders; and heart disease. Clinicians need to be familiar with
the more common conditions and illnesses experienced by
older adults and in many cases may need to work closely
with medical providers to better understand a client's response to psychological treatment strategies. (Chapter 6 provides more information on this topic.)

Working with medical providers is also challenging. Most
seniors have several doctors and take more than a few prescribed medications. Doctors have limited time in which to
coordinate care with social service or mental health providers. There are limited numbers of doctors who are geriatricians, those with specialized knowledge and training in the
care of older adults. Thus, they also may struggle with the
most effective ways to care for their elderly patients.

Innovative models of care have shown some promise in
getting older adults to access therapy for emotional distress
and substance abuse. A study of an integrated model of care

that offered mental health or substance abuse treatment under the auspices of the primary care physician's office reported that 71% of primary care elderly patient referrals engaged in treatment compared with only 49% of elderly patients referred to specialty mental health and substance abuse clinics (Bartels et al., 2004). These results, conducted in a clinical trial format, strongly suggest that mental health practitioners can team with primary care physicians whenever possible to provide timely care in a less-threatening environment.

To make therapy more attractive and less threatening to contemporary elders, counselors can offer psychoeducational seminars in places where seniors congregate and seek health-enhancing information. For example, many older adults enjoy attending health fairs, which provide information about a host of healthy lifestyle options. Short educational seminars about maintaining and enhancing emotional health in late life are often well received. Senior and community centers, as well as churches, are optimal venues for offering such seminars. Yang and Jackson (1998) recommended the use of analogies when offering education to older adults about psychotherapy and family counseling. One such analogy compares psychotherapy with the functional aspects of wearing glasses: Just as one does not think much of wearing glasses to see better, counseling is a tool to help one think or feel better. It is no more of a crutch than wearing glasses to correct vision problems.

When older adults and their family members seek therapy, find out everything you can about the physical health of the older adult and how involved he or she is with the medical system and with individuals in the medical care system. For example, does the individual have several doctors? If so, which one is considered the primary care physician? Is another medical organization involved in serving your aging clients, such as the Veterans Administration?

Second, ask your elderly client to sign a release so that you can access any medical records that might assist you in formulating an appropriate treatment plan. It is not unusual for primary care physicians to prescribe antidepressant medication to patients prior to or in lieu of a referral for counseling, and therapists need to know both what has been prescribed and whether the doctor will work with them on needed changes in medications and other medical care.

Third, older adults and families in counseling may have stories to tell about the efficacy of their medical care. In a study of older adults with depressive symptoms that we conducted, we found that many of our participants were frustrated with the lack of attention they received from one or more of their doctors. Those with complaints often felt hurried and unable to fully discuss their concerns, especially mental health issues (Norton & Piercy, 2010). Our current outpatient medical care system does not offer patients the opportunity for long consultations with their physicians, although some physicians do their best to address both patient and family concerns, even to the extent of calling family meetings when they see a need for family intervention in a patient's deteriorating health (Davis, 2009).

Counselors and therapists can alleviate some anxieties about developing certain conditions by providing education about the chief issues of concern. For example, the National Institute of Mental Health (2007) offers an excellent, succinct fact sheet, *Older Adults: Depression and Suicide Facts.* Other educational materials on memory issues and cognitive impairment (see Chapter 3) and selecting adult day centers (ADCs), assisted living facilities (ALFs), and nursing homes (NHs) (see Chapter 6) can be given to older adult or family member clients.

CLINICAL SUGGESTIONS

- Learn as much as possible about the medical community in your area. In small towns and rural areas, one or two physicians may have many elderly patients in their practices. Try to establish a relationship with those physicians and their nurse practitioners so that treatment can be coordinated when needed.
- Counselors and therapists in locations with geriatricians and geriatric psychiatrists should establish working relationships with them. Often, persons with mild cognitive impairment or dementias with strong psychiatric components, such as Lewy body dementia, will need a specialist to help manage their treatment while you work with their families to help them make important care decisions.
- When a medical school exists in your area, find out if special clinics are available for older persons with depression or dementia. These clinics may offer treatment at low cost and opportunities to participate in cutting-edge research in these important areas of study.
- When consulting with medical professionals, prepare your questions in advance and try to keep conversations as brief as possible. Talk with nurse practitioners when they are involved with your clients; they may be more accessible than physicians and may be having a great deal of face-to-face contact with elderly persons and their families.

Recognizing and Working With Normal and Dysfunctional Family Processes

Some families provide eldercare in a cooperative way. Here is one example.

Ella is 98 years old. She resides alone with a caretaker in the home she has occupied for 65 years. Her two sons, both in their late 60s, and one daughter-in-law oversee her around-the-clock, paid, in-home care. One son visits his mother daily. When these sons and their spouses are out of town, their children lovingly look after their grandmother's welfare. The family runs like a well-oiled machine, with each person connected to the other. They gather for birthdays and holidays, and Ella is always included, even though she has limited strength and ability to comprehend all that goes on around her.

By contrast, some families have more difficult experiences with caregiving based on long-term family dynamics. Consider the following example.

Darlene is 65 years old. She has diabetes and is very timid. She has 6 children and lives with her daughter Emily, who is divorced and in her mid-40s. They have coresided for a year now because Darlene was not managing her diabetes well. She did not follow a proper diet and took her insulin sporadically. Emily works full time to support herself and her mother. She gets no help from her siblings, some of whom are not on speaking terms with their mother. A couple of her siblings are alcoholics. Emily has been stressed by her mother's dependence and demands. She has sought counseling to try to adjust to the caregiver role. Her only support comes from her 25-year-old daughter, who has a 4-year-old and

2-year-old of her own. She wonders aloud how long she can do all she is doing; yet, her mother is far from disabled and likely will be living with Emily a long time. Emily has tried to get her mother involved in activities at a local senior center or her church, but Darlene will not try them.

Why is it that some families pull together in times of difficulty and others split further apart? Although some therapists are reluctant to use the label *dysfunctional family* with the families they encounter, there clearly are some families who have learned to work together well over time to solve intergenerational problems and others who do not collaborate effectively to resolve such difficulties. A therapist needs both a history of family interaction and keen observational skills to assess family function and dysfunction. Without such an assessment, therapeutic intervention is less likely to succeed.

A study of a nationally representative sample of adults with living parents showed that intergenerational families can be characterized into one of five types: tight knit, sociable, obligatory, intimate but distant, and detached (Silverstein & Bengtson, 1997).

- *Tight-knit family relationships* were described by those who reported high levels of all types of solidarity among generations. These families are likely to be functional rather than dysfunctional in the sense that they communicate well with each other and are highly motivated to resolve together any difficulties that arise. They are likely to present for therapy only when a crisis situation has overwhelmed their resources for addressing it.

- *Sociable family relationships* described adult children who interacted with their parents based on geographic proximity, similarity of opinions, emotional closeness and frequent contact but did not exhibit exchanges of assistance between generations. These families may present to therapy primarily when the need for assistance to a member of the oldest generation first arises or when the elderly family member resists needed help from others.
- *Obligatory relationships* were characterized by parental engagement based on geographic proximity and frequent contact but not emotional closeness or similarity of opinions. Some, but not all, children were engaged in reciprocal exchanges with their parents. When these families present for therapy, it is likely that only some members will participate and that the less emotionally close members may opt out of therapy. The exception to this is a family with an only child who must address aging parental decline and who may feel ambivalent about assuming the caregiver role.
- *Intimate but distant family relationships* consisted of children who felt emotionally close and similar in opinions to their parents but lived at a distance from them and had fewer contacts and exchanges of assistance than those who were tight knit. Adult children in these families may be more likely to seek brief individual therapy rather than family therapy when a transition in parent need for care occurs.
- *Detached relationships* were characterized by low or absent levels of solidarity between child and parent. Because contact between the generations in these families is sparse and prior events in family life may have created the dis-

tance or even cutoffs, these families may be dysfunctional. Providing counseling for or conducting therapy with these families is difficult. Family members may feel little motivation to provide assistance to one or both elderly parents, although they may be less emotionally detached from their siblings. Therefore, exploring siblings as resources for therapeutic intervention may be beneficial in working with detached families.

The majority of relationships described by participants in the Silverstein and Bengtson (1997) study fell into the three middle categories rather than in the tight-knit or detached categories, thus suggesting that most parents and children exhibit some, but not all, aspects of solidarity in their relationships with one another. This finding lends support to the notion that most families experience both solidarity and ambivalence among their members (Luscher & Pillemer, 1998). Two other noteworthy findings from the Silverstein and Bengtson (1997) study were that adult children tended to express stronger solidarity with their mothers than their fathers, and that those children with divorced fathers were more likely to report a detached relationship with them (Silverstein & Bengtson, 1997).

EXPLORING FAMILY COMPETENCE

Therapists may find the notion of exploring family competence useful in working with aging families. Using an underlying assumption of families as systems, Beavers and Hampson (2003) developed a method of measuring family competence that relies on both clinical observation and family members' self-reports of their behavior patterns. They focused on family *functioning* in place of symptoms or typologies and family *competence*, which they defined as "how well a family as an interactional unit performs the necessary and nurturing tasks of organizing and managing itself" (2003, p. 551). Family competence is indicated by adults' abilities to negotiate and share leadership and the family's ability to establish clear generational boundaries. They then placed families along a continuum from optimal in their functioning to severely dysfunctional, with the former group most likely to amend and adjust their style of functioning as developmental changes occur, while the latter group tends to operate in a rigid way in response to such alterations. Competent families are more skilled at communicating openly and directly, show a wide range of feelings, and are generally more optimistic than pessimistic in their approaches to problem solving (Beavers & Hampson, 2003).

Beavers and Hampson also developed assessments of family style, which they defined as "the degree of centripetal or centrifugal qualities in the family" (2003, p. 552). *Centripetal* means moving toward a center and in this context describes families who seek satisfaction more often from within their families. By contrast, *centrifugal* refers to forces that direct movement away from a center and describes families who seek gratification from outside the family unit more than within it (Beavers & Hampson, 2003). Families with a combination of these styles were called "mixed." In their studies of family styles, they have found that extreme centripetal-style families are characterized by more internalizing disorders (anxiety and depression), and extreme centrifugal-style families exhibit more externalizing problems, such as conduct disorders (Beavers & Hampson, 1990).

Because older adults may be experiencing aspects of both physical and cognitive decline, a family approach to helping them is frequently the most desirable and effective approach to problem solving. Thus, this volume focuses on the types of issues aging families may confront as well as possible solutions and resources available to assist these families. Assessing a family's competence and style is an important first step to working with aging families. While it is important to recognize that patterns of relating to each other may have been established very early in family life, the presence of crisis or a desire to resolve past wounds equips the therapist with powerful motivation for change, even in dysfunctional family circumstances.

CLINICAL SUGGESTIONS

- Use your observational skills to begin your assessment of family competence and style. Just as Beavers and Hampson (2003) recommended, I look for patterns in communication (who speaks, who is silent, to what extent family members add to each others' thoughts and attempt to speak for each other, and with how much care and respect they talk to and about each other).
- In multigenerational families with elderly members present, how are issues of power and control displayed in both verbal and nonverbal communication? Do children talk to you about their parents as though their parents were not present? Do parents interrupt their children or vice versa when describing problems? Is there a power

struggle occurring over how to *define* the problem (e.g., an adult child thinks it is time for a parental move to assisted living and the parent vehemently disagrees, suggesting that the child or family just needs to step up their help). If an elderly couple attends the session, how do they communicate with each other and with other family members present? How protective are they of each other with other family members?

• One can learn a lot about family flexibility and family style by assessing what has been done to date to address the presenting problem. If the family has been able to accomplish little because of the opposition of one or more members, then the family may need help in developing more flexibility. Be careful, however, to avoid confusing the presence of strong cultural values with a lack of flexibility. A family may have a strong need to "keep it (the problem and its solution) in the family," expressing the more centripital style as described by Beavers and Hampson (2003). Finding a balance between honoring strong cultural values and keeping aging family members secure and safe can be a difficult challenge (see Maria's story in Chapter 4).

• Consider using a written assessment tool, such as the Self-Report Family Inventory (Beavers & Hampson, 2003), to obtain information from all relevant family members about their perceptions of family functioning and independence. These tools offer excellent supplementary data to therapists' observations of and interaction with aging families and may be crucial when some family members say little in sessions or follow cultural prescriptions to remain silent in the presence of more powerful or older family members.

RELIGIOUS AND SPIRITUAL FACTORS AMONG OLDER ADULTS AND THEIR FAMILIES

Many older adults and their families have a strong religious or spiritual orientation. Population studies of U.S. adults showed that older adults attend religious services, pray, read Scripture, meditate, and report having daily spiritual experiences and using religion to cope with life crises more often than their younger counterparts (Idler, 2006). On average, women tend to express higher levels of religiousness than men, and African Americans and Latinos endorse greater levels of religiosity than Caucasian adults. For older members of minority groups, churches provide a crucial support network, offering both emotional and financial support during times of need (Taylor & Chatters, 1986). Indeed, for many African American families, there is little distinction between church and extended family (Johnson & Barer, 1990).

Religious practices have known physical and psychological benefits for those with strong orientations to spirituality or a particular religion. Both health maintenance and recovery from serious health problems can be positively affected by a religious orientation (Contrada et al., 2004; Powell, Shahabi, & Thoresen, 2003). Wink, Dillon, and Larsen (2005) found that in late adulthood, being religious buffered against depression for persons in poor physical health. Engaging in specific religious or spiritual practices also reaps benefits. Benson (1996) determined that active practice of religious rituals, such as prayer, invokes the relaxation response.

When elders with strong religious faith are in need of help, their ministers or church leaders are often the first persons to whom they turn for support, advice, or links to services, and this practice is especially strong among elderly minority group members (Blank, Mahmood, Fox, & Guterbock, 2002). Although Moran and associates (2005) found that depression, serious mental illness, and suicide were the emotional problems that clergy felt least confident to address, these clergy reported rates of consultation with mental health professionals that were quite low. A closer collaboration between clergy and mental health professionals would provide families with access to the benefits that spiritual leaders can provide as well as referral for pastor-endorsed counseling when personal or family difficulties are beyond the abilities of their clergy to help them resolve. For example, with elders and families of some racial and ethnic minority groups, a community clergy member serves as the trusted gateway to their acceptance of secular mental health or family counseling. If the clergy member endorses the counselor's services and refers the family to counseling, then these families may be more likely to follow through. Thus, counselors who work in settings or communities with families who are unfamiliar or uncomfortable with secular counseling should establish relationships with these important clergy members to increase the likelihood of family acceptance of counseling and to increase counselor understanding of both spiritual and cultural values in these families.

SPIRITUAL ASSESSMENT IN THERAPY SETTINGS

When working with older adults and their families, it is potentially useful to seek information from them about their spiritual involvement and religious practices and to validate the positive aspects of clients' religious practice and coping strategies. It is well known that client's religious beliefs and spirituality can affect service or therapy provision, and to deliver both effective and culturally sensitive counseling to elders and their families, understanding those spiritual beliefs and practices is paramount (Hodge, 2006). Acknowledging positive spiritually oriented coping strategies may help to build a relationship between a clinician and an older adult client with a strong religious orientation. It also is consistent with use of a strength-based perspective in therapy as spiritual practice and faith communities are often assets and resources for clients struggling with various issues (Hodge, 2001).

However, not all individuals and family members who seek counseling may practice a faith tradition. Therefore, asking a few questions on an intake form about whether a client observes the practices of any religion or spiritual tradition and to what extent clients see their faith as important in their lives is an appropriate prelude to conducting a spiritual assessment as part of the counseling process. If clients' answers to these intake questions indicate that faith or spiritual traditions are important to them, then consent to conduct a spiritual assessment of the client should be sought (Hodge, 2001, 2006). The goals of spiritual assessment are to improve understanding of how spiritual issues affect clients and their families and to determine the extent to which spiritual beliefs and practices may be drawn on as resources in resolving client problems.

A spiritual assessment may be brief or more comprehensive, depending on the client's or family's willingness to discuss spiritual matters and the salience of spirituality and religious faith in their lives. Next, I discuss how I begin a spiritual assessment and when I expand it from a brief to a more detailed assessment.

I begin by asking a couple of questions on the intake form, as noted:

- Do you observe the practices of any organized religion or spiritual tradition? If so, what is this religion or tradition called?
- To what extent do you consider your faith or spiritual tradition to be important in your life: not important, somewhat important, very important, crucial to life, other?
- Is your current religious affiliation or spiritual practice different from what it was in your youth or earlier adulthood? If yes, then briefly explain what has changed from then to now.

I include the last question for two reasons. First, religious conversion experiences have become more commonplace, and in some multigenerational families, conversion to a faith different from that of one's parents or a decision not to practice one's childhood faith can create lasting relationship tensions. Second, with very old persons or persons who have significant physical limitations or cognitive impairment, the ability to attend church may be compromised and a source of distress to them. Yet, they may not have expressed this distress to anyone for fear of being a burden to others.

Although persons can pray alone and otherwise maintain a spiritual focus, for many adults the rituals involved in the public practice of faith offer an important connection to a deity and faith community. Thus, exploring the personal meaning of being unable to attend religious services and determining whether resources are available to assist an elder in continuing a public practice of faith are important components of a spiritual assessment for some clients.

When an individual, couple, or family indicates on the intake form that a religious faith or spiritual tradition is at least somewhat important, then the following three questions recommended by Hodge (2004) should be asked in an assessment session:

- Do you consider spirituality or religion a personal strength?
- In what ways does your spirituality help you cope with difficulties you encounter?
- Are there certain spiritual beliefs or practices that are particularly helpful to you in dealing with problems?

To these questions, I add:

- To what extent have you used these beliefs or practices recently to help you deal with the problems you have described to me today?

Two additional questions one may ask those clients who are active members of a particular denomination or congregation are as follows:

- To what extent is your faith community or congregation supportive of you?
- Why or why not do you have their support?

These questions are important for several reasons. Persons with religious beliefs or affiliations are not always well integrated into their faith communities and may need help in becoming better connected to them. In addition, some clients may feel guilt over thoughts they have had or actions they have contemplated (like suicide), or they may have acted in ways that met with disapproval from their fellow congregants (like marrying someone of another faith or getting caught in an alcohol-related violation of both church precepts and secular law, as in driving under the influence). Determining the degree of supportiveness of one's congregation affects the kind of interventions a therapist may recommend to clients (G. Culbertson, personal communication, November 1, 2009).

For those whose high levels of spiritual or faith commitment may affect the course of therapy, a more comprehensive spiritual assessment may be a valuable tool for understanding behaviors and shaping future therapeutic interventions. Conducting this assessment also makes the statement that the therapist is willing to try to understand and work with all types of issues and beliefs that are important to clients.

To assist me, I ask clients to explain key values and beliefs of their faith that affect how they view the problems they are having. For example, in some faiths, a divorce or the drug addiction of one's child may bring shame to the older members of a family that may result in their distancing themselves from their faith community. To some members of churches or religions that view homosexuality as sinful, such a disclosure by a close family member may precipitate a crisis of acceptance and create coalitions of support and opposition in the extended family. In these types of circumstances, the use of several verbal and visual means of conducting comprehensive spiritual assessments, including spiritual genograms, spiritual ecomaps, and spiritual ecograms, can be useful (Hodge, 2005). A *spiritual genogram* is a three-generation genogram (McGoldrick, Gerson, & Shellenberger, 1999) that, when drawn, represents "a blueprint of complex intergenerational spiritual interactions" (Hodge, 2005, p. 346). This type of genogram can include other influential nonfamily members, such as a youth pastor or a televangelist, through use of additional geometric shapes. These genograms also incorporate spiritually meaningful events as well as family members' degree of religious practice or their conversion to particular faiths.

An *ecomap* is a diagram of an individual's social relationships, with the client placed in the center of the map and lines drawn to each person named in the client's social network (Rempel, Neufeld, & Kushner, 2007). Lines are drawn in different thicknesses and ways to show relationship strength, and arrows depict the flow of resources (see Chapter 4 for a discussion of a client's ecomap). A *spiritual ecomap* is one that focuses exclusively on the client's spiritual network, including both current and existential relationships (Hodge, 2005). Outside the client's center circle, smaller circles that represent spiritual domains (e.g., pastors, faith communities, and religious rituals) are drawn and linked to the client. The purpose of this type of ecomap is to gain increased understanding of the nature of and contributors to a client's spiritual network as well as the degree of support clients receive from their networks.

A *spiritual ecogram* combines a spiritual ecomap and genogram in one diagram, giving the therapist information about both current and past networks and spiritual experiences. An ecogram may be useful when members of a multi-generation family have changed their religious orientation or practices over time or have experienced conflicts over the practice of one or more faith traditions over time. Cutoffs of certain family members may occur when they have embraced faiths at odds with those of clients or other important family members.

Therapists select assessment tools on the basis of a need to better understand a past history or present experience of spirituality as well as the client's or family's capabilities to change. The visual nature of ecomaps and genograms may be more useful in work with persons who struggle to put ideas into words or who have a complicated history with many important persons or with elders who fatigue easily or have mild cognitive impairment.

Therapists who work with persons with strong commitments to a particular faith or set of spiritual practices need to learn all they can about those beliefs and practices with which they are unfamiliar. For example, before I came to Utah, I had little understanding of the doctrine, beliefs, and traditions of members of the Church of Jesus Christ of Latter-Day Saints (Mormons). I have learned a great deal about those beliefs and practices during my years in Utah. Without such knowledge, I might propose culturally and religiously insensitive interventions in my work with individuals of this faith.

Likewise, it may be difficult or impossible for some therapists to work with members of all faiths. Occasionally, it may become evident to a therapist that an individual's or family's religious beliefs and values are in significant conflict with those of the therapist. When therapists do not feel that they can work with clients of a particular faith or spiritual tradition, referral to another therapist is recommended.

SPIRITUALLY BASED INTERVENTIONS

Broadly defined, *spiritual interventions* are "activities that strengthen, reinforce or promote the spiritual and religious resources of individuals, or that utilize existing spiritual resources present in the individual to address well being and needs regarding spirituality and other life domains" (Brennan & Heiser, 2004, p. 2). Clients may provide clues regarding what types of spiritual interventions may be useful to them. Conversely, after conducting spiritual assessments (as discussed in the preceding section), therapists may suggest specific interventions that draw on the client's faith community or the rituals of their faith. For example, encouraging older adults in poor health and their primary family caregivers to remain connected with their faith communities is often helpful to them. For Protestants, visits from ministers and fellow congregants to pray and read Scriptures together may be meaningful. If struggling with mental or physical health challenges, Mormons may be uplifted to receive blessings from their bishops (Piercy, Norton, & Jones, 2007). Homebound Catholics can benefit from lay ministers who can offer Holy Communion and prayer services as part of the Orders for the Blessing of the Sick (*The Catholic Handbook for Visiting the Sick and Homebound*, 2010). And, members of the Jewish faith are encouraged to visit the sick in a mitzvah called *bikkur cholim* (http://www.bikurcholimcc.org/whatisbc.html).

Another type of therapist-based spiritual intervention with documented efficacy is one that has been incorporated into existing treatment strategies, such as mindfulness-based cognitive therapy (MBCT) for persons with persistent anxiety or depression (Segal, Williams, & Teasdale, 2002). *Mindfulness*, the central tenet of Buddhist meditation, is defined as paying attention to the moment and looking deeply and nonjudgmentally into the self "in the spirit of self-inquiry and self-understanding" (Kabat-Zinn, 1990, p. 12). This type of practice, as a part of cognitive therapies or by itself, is generally taught in eight individual or group sessions, with weekly homework, and incorporates meditation and breathing practices that may induce calmness and a state of relaxation. In MBCT, persons are taught skills to accept and let go of persistent thoughts that contribute to anxiety and depression. Turner (2009) recommended that mindfulness be introduced to clients as nonjudgmental self-awareness, and that the techniques of breathing and meditation be gradually introduced into therapy sessions. Therapists themselves can benefit from a mindfulness practice that helps them to improve skills of attention, affect regulation, attunement, and empathy when working with clients (Turner, 2009). Affect regulation is a crucial skill for counselors and therapists to acquire and practice, particularly when doing grief work and couple therapy with highly volatile clients.

CHAPTER 2

Understanding Family Dynamics

I was 25 years old when I first rafted the raging waters of the Chattooga River, a swift-moving, narrow river on the border of South Carolina and Georgia. I went with a guided tour led by a local outfitter. Each raft was anchored by an employee of the outfitter's company. We were told that these young, tan, fit-looking men and women had much expertise guiding beginners like me in the art of navigating big river rapids, and we were encouraged to view them as our leaders. We were going to run the infamous Section IV of the river, known for its big, churning Class 4 and 5 rapids, with names like Seven Foot Falls, Jawbone, and Sock 'em Dog. People had been killed with some regularity while canoeing, kayaking, or rafting these turbulent waters.

My reaction? Sweat poured out of me. Was it mounting exhilaration and heart-pumping adrenaline from the excitement of the unknown dangers that were ahead? Or, was it just raw fear and anxiety from the prospect of putting myself in harm's way? I suspect it was some of both. I listened carefully to our instructions: Let the guides tell you what to do next, always wear a life jacket, do not panic if you fall into the river, and so forth. I am pretty good at following directions, but I was not fond of the idea of falling into those rushing, boulder-strewn waters (although that was indeed to be my fate that day). I had no prior life experience dealing with rushing rapids; I grew up paddling the peaceful waters of southern Missouri lakes and rivers.

We got into the boat and began paddling. Calm waters met us at the beginning, but when I thoroughly examined my surroundings, I could see how fast the river flowed downstream. Rough water was ahead; there could be no doubt of that. It was not long before we arrived at the first rapids.

Whenever we approached a big rapid that day, our guide asked us to pull into a tranquil pool with an overlook of the roaring waters to come. We then got out of the raft to look at the rapid and get advice on how to position ourselves for a successful run. Such "scouting" became a way that we learned how to develop our approach to the rapid and was often a key to our success in navigating it. Although some in our party wanted just to plow through the unknown waters ahead, scouting was touted by the instructors as a big part of staying safe in turbulent waters. And, it seemed to work for our group, except at Seven Foot Falls. Somehow, our "system" broke down there. I suspect our group's anxiety level had no small part to play in how we approached this rapid. As we scouted it from above, Seven Foot Falls looked all of its name and then some. Murmurs spread around the group. As we went over the falls, into the river I plunged, along with a few others in the raft, including the guide. After a while, we all got back in, fully soaked and very much alive, to continue our journey. No other mishaps occurred in our boat after that event.

A few hours later, with Jawbone and Sock 'em Dog safely

behind us, we paddled peaceful, clear waters for nearly 2 miles. Our adventure was over for that day. My husband and I returned to raft down that river several times, sometimes with outfitters and other times with friends and eventually bought our own white-water canoe. After a few disappointing experiences on our own with the canoe, we took lessons from the pros on how to navigate rapids in a canoe, which required different skills from those of rafting.

White-water canoes and rafts were popular then. But now, canoes have been largely replaced by kayaks, which with their light shells and streamlined designs can be maneuvered through rapids far more adeptly than canoes. Over time, the way families navigate rough waters, and the tools that they use to do so, change, often for better. But, some people still prefer canoes or rafts to kayaks.

The life course of every individual is very much like a river that drops in elevation as it winds its way to the sea: full of both calm periods (life trajectories) and rapids (challenging events and transitions or turbulence) that must be navigated successfully. We come to each bend in the river armed with our prior life experiences as both individuals and members of multigenerational families. These experiences and family members guide us in how to navigate each turn in the river and rapids along the way. The manner in which our families navigated earlier life transitions affects our responses to our own life course decisions in adulthood. Even with scouting, some of our life challenges tax our resources or exceed them altogether. When several challenging situations appear at once, we may struggle to cope with them, particularly by ourselves. Because family members operate like systems and are linked in many ways throughout the life course, I feature two theoretical perspectives in this chapter: the life course perspective and family systems thinking. Each perspective contributes to our understanding of and ability to work with older adults and their families. After a discussion of each theoretical perspective, I tie the perspectives together and provide a case example that illustrates how concurrent transitions in a multigenerational family can strain the resources of the family and require a careful navigational process from all family system members.

THE LIFE COURSE PERSPECTIVE

A principal architect of the life course perspective, Elder (1994), described the life course as

> the interweave of age-graded trajectories, such as work careers and family pathways, that are subject to changing conditions . . . and to short-term transitions ranging from leaving school to retirement. Transitions are always embedded in trajectories that give them distinct form and meaning. (p. 5)

The study of one's life course is the study of development and change over time among individuals and family members (Bengtson & Allen, 1993).

As a developmental theory, the life course perspective makes the following assumptions about human development: (a) that human development does not stop in adulthood but rather is lifelong (Baltes, Lindenberger, & Staudinger, 1998); (b) that individual development is multidimensional, incor-

porating psychological, social, historical, and biological dimensions, among others; (c) that individual development
occurs in multiple life spheres, such as work, education, family, and leisure; and (d) that development includes simulta-
neous occurrence of both gains (growth) and losses (declines)
between dimensions and domains of functioning (Settersten,
2003).

Because aging is a lifelong process, we arrive at our later
years having navigated many transitions in our lives. Some
of these transitions were welcomed, like marriage, but others
were foisted on us, like a sudden death or unwanted divorce.
The choices we have made during sudden crises and life
transitions (how we responded, coped; what we did) affect
the remainder of our life's trajectory. There are consequences,
sometimes positive, other times negative, for "roads not tak-
en." When individuals choose poorly, they and sometimes
their families pay for the rest of their lives with sadness, injury, isolation, cutoffs from family members, and regret.
However, life course theorists maintain that early life experiences, such as abuse or abandonment, are not so constrain-
ing of development and growth, and that some individuals
can move beyond them (Settersten, 2003). In this way, the
life course for some persons can be a story of resilience.

Transitions such as widowhood, remarriage, retirement,
or a diagnosis of diabetes or dementia are periods of considerable turbulence in older adults' lives. Choices must be
made about how to address these life transitions, and those
choices affect their life trajectories as well as those of close
family members. At best, people face their adverse transitions with resolve and resilience. At worst, they approach

these new challenges with bitter and unresolved feelings about things that have occurred earlier in life. They in turn often view the new transition as an unwelcome burden.

When faced with transitions, some people act as scouts: They gather information and discuss their options with others before choosing. Other people ignore warning signs of approaching turbulence and forge ahead blindly. They attempt to adjust to consequences as they occur. Still others try to navigate transitions alone, with little or no help from others. Personality structure, cultural values, plus a lifetime of experience in social interaction with family and others affect how transitions are addressed by individuals at any point in their lives.

Stressful individual transitions may trigger family stressors and conflict. In any case, those transitions must also be navigated, much like the river rapids, to reach the calm waters on the other side. Everyone's life course is unique; yet, we do not navigate most transitions alone. A person's life course always occurs in both historical and social contexts, but contexts that are continually changing, like the move from using canoes to kayaks in white-water river running.

The tenets of life course theory can be used to understand individual and family behavior, especially patterned behavior over time. Some of us are familiar with this perspective through our pleasure reading. Both novelists and biographers have been writing persuasively for many years about the life course of their characters, about how their lives and destinies are linked to each other and affected, sometimes profoundly, by family and historical contexts. Two examples of these writings are John Grogan's (*Marley and Me*) new book, *The Longest Trip Home*, in which he examines his upbringing and family life; and the novelist Lisa See's *Shanghai Girls*, the fictional story of two sisters whose lives are forever entwined during the 1930s, a period of great unrest and social change in China. In addition, one of the best contributions of Mary Pipher's *Another Country*, a book that details her experiences in working with older adults and their families, is the way she links the values, behaviors, and lifestyle preferences of elders with the historical times in which they have lived their lives.

The notion of *timing* is crucial to one's understanding of an individual's or family's life course. Timing is defined as "the age at which experiences occur" (Settersten, 2003, p. 25). In most societies, a certain time period in an individual's life course is assigned to the execution of certain life tasks, such as education, marriage, childbearing, and retirement. When age norms exist in societies, then individuals are considered to be "on time" or "off time" in terms of when they attain a certain status (such as parenthood) or carry out these life tasks. In contemporary American life, notions of on and off time are being blurred by greater acceptance of deviation from traditional age norms. For example, fewer eyebrows are raised now when a man begins having children at age 50 or 60 or a woman continues paid employment well into her 70s or 80s.

Bengtson and Allen pointed out that a life course perspective "emphasizes the importance of time, context, process, and meaning on human development and family life" (1993, p. 471). Thus, development has multiple temporal contexts, with a focus on ontogenetic, family, and historical time as crucial to understanding a person's life course and choices.

The first aspect of time is *ontogenetic time*, which refers to the timing of crucial events in the lives of individuals that have the potential to influence or change their behavioral processes (Bengtson & Allen, 1993). In life course theory, human agency is assumed to operate in individuals' lives. As we age, however, and experience more constraints on our choices because of various types of physical losses or limitations, we face the prospect of what Settersten (2006) called "agency within structure."

The task of older adults is to take action at transition points and create meaning within the parameters imposed by personal constraints, such as declining health, and individual resources, such as supportive friends and family members. One example of these processes occurs when an elderly man diagnosed with cancer faces several choices about what course of treatment he wishes to pursue and what quality of life he wishes to maintain both during and after treatment. Another example of a meaning-making process occurs when a daughter and grandchildren suddenly move in with a middle-aged divorced woman after the daughter's marital separation. If the middle-aged woman attributes a positive meaning to the acquisition of a multigenerational family after years of living alone successfully and decides to integrate them into her life, her growth and development are likely to be enhanced as she ages. As she nurtures her grandchildren, she also acquires some valuable resources for her own late life.

There can be a tendency among some family members to view those individuals who have become more dependent as they age as largely incapable of making good decisions, so they behave in paternalistic ways toward these aging family members. This behavior pattern may be resented by their elders, who see themselves as still capable of making decisions on their own behalf, and may lead the older generation either to withdraw or to resist, actively or passively.

A second element of time that is important for understanding the life course is *family* or *generational time*. What is going on in the multigenerational family at the time a key personal or historical event occurs? At what point is the family in its life course? A key transition, such as parental divorce, affects individual family members differently depending on what shared family history they have experienced, the meaning they have given to that shared family history, and the time in their personal development at which the divorce occurs. When an older couple experiences the divorce of one of their sons, they may experience reduced contact with his children, their grandchildren, a situation that may precipitate a grief process for them and their son.

The timing of key events in the lives of family members and how societies structure norms about the timing of roles affect how families respond to these events. Is an event considered on time or off time in a given family according to its expectations? Elder (1994) defined *social timing* as the incidence, duration, and sequencing of roles, expectations, and beliefs based on age. Expectations in families may closely conform to societal norms, such as norms that call for marriage and childbearing in young adulthood. Families whose expectations mirror those norms would be likely to put more pressure on a single adult to marry if he or she has reached or exceeded age 30, whereas other families with more flexible expectations about marriage and childbearing may be quite tolerant and accepting of a 35-year-old never-married family member.

Stresses in aging families may occur when an event (transition) brings to the forefront conflicting age norms among members of different generations in families. Although remarriage among widowed or divorced older adults, especially men, is not uncommon, it may be viewed negatively by younger generations of family members who were particularly close to the dead or divorced parent or who feel that their remaining parent is "too old" to remarry. These children may feel that their remarried parent has betrayed their deceased or divorced parent. Strong feelings that they have lost their remaining parent to the new spouse are not uncommon. Some adult children may also see their inheritance threatened by the presence of a new spouse and his or her family. In the minds of these adult children, the elderly parents were supposed to remain single until death. Their disapproval may have a deleterious effect on their aged parent's life course and, if not addressed, reduce the available resources for both generations.

The third aspect of time is that of *historical time*. Attention to the influence of historical time is important for understanding the expressed values and the perceived constraints regarding acceptable options for individuals and families during transitional periods. For example, many of today's older adults could not cohabit before marriage without the risk of being ostracized and cut off from their families and societies.

Persons born around the same time progress through life as a cohort, and the social changes that occur during their key life transitions affect their life patterns (Elder, 1994). Those who became young adults during the civil rights and Vietnam war eras experienced profound social changes at a time in their lives when they were making major decisions about marriage, military service, careers, and families. Older or younger members of their families did not experience these social changes at the same points in their lives and thus were likely to view them differently from those young adults. Differences in perceived importance of certain events or the change in norms during a historical period can lead to conflict in families. The so-called generation gap, a phrase coined during the turbulent decade of the 1960s, captures this notion of differential experience and interpretation of experience by different age cohorts (Settersten, 2006).

An example of conflict stemming from differences in historical time occurs when a cohabiting relationship in the young adult generation of an extended family ignites conflict and disapproval among the older generations of family members, who may view cohabitation as morally wrong and detrimental to the family's reputation in the community. A grandparent may then put pressure on a son or daughter to do something to stop it or may directly confront the cohabiting grandchild with his or her displeasure and threats of withdrawal of financial or emotional support.

A life course perspective is a dynamic approach to understanding human development. Rather than viewing life as a set of discreet stages through which individuals pass, it emphasizes active decision making throughout life as people confront events and transitions that occur. Their decisions in turn shape the trajectories of our lives in familial, societal, and historical contexts.

FAMILY SYSTEMS PERSPECTIVE

Thinking of the family as a system is a paradigm: a view of the world and how it operates among the people within it.

Although it is important to understand the individual, it is not sufficient to stop at assessing an individual life course when working with older adults because nearly all individuals are reared in families. Those families operate as systems, exerting their influence on individual members and their life courses, just as those individuals exert influence on families as group and social entities.

What is meant by this idea? To think of families as systems, one focuses on the interrelations (interactions) of the group and the emotional processes that occur among persons who are part of this family group (Gilbert, 2004). The classic approach to family systems theory was articulated by Bowen (1978, 1983), and his ideas are outlined in the following discussion of family systems theory. First, I present some basic assumptions of systems thinking and describe some of the key concepts in a systems approach.

ASSUMPTIONS IN SYSTEMS THINKING

There are several core assumptions that guide systems thinking: interconnectedness, understanding by viewing the whole, reciprocal behavior, and focus on knowing or thinking.

INTERCONNECTEDNESS

All parts of a system are interconnected (White & Klein, 2008). All family members are emotionally connected to each other for life. Even when members of a given family, nuclear or extended, are not in frequent contact with each other, they remain part of the family system. Their behaviors and mental states matter to all family members, and their interactions (or lack thereof) with family members become part of the family system's functional capability.

UNDERSTANDING BY VIEWING THE WHOLE

Understanding is possible only by viewing the whole (White & Klein). A helping professional working with an older adult can benefit greatly by encouraging family participation in the assessment and counseling process. When family members are not readily available, an assessment tool such as a genogram (McGoldrick et al., 1999) may serve to provide understanding of family events and processes. To learn how and why someone acts and reacts in the manner they do or why they approach challenges or transitions with fear and anxiety, a therapist should gather information about the family of origin as well as the family of procreation and when possible meet with as many family members as are available to them. Such exposure to the family system creates an opportunity to validate or reframe an older adult's perceptions of family interaction and support and potentially provides the means to influence familial interactions that do not promote healthy methods of problem solving.

RECIPROCAL BEHAVIOR

A system's behavior affects its environment; the environment also affects the system (White & Klein, 2008). Behavior is a form of feedback, and feedback flows continuously between families and the environments in which they reside. Those environments may be close, such as communities in which they live or churches or schools attended by family members, or more distant, such as the state or larger society in which a family resides.

Focus on Knowing or Thinking

Systems are ways of knowing or thinking about things rather than concrete objects (White & Klein, 2008). We use systems thinking as a way of organizing and interpreting knowledge about the families with which we work in counseling settings.

Key Concepts in Systems Thinking

There are several key concepts in systems thinking: boundaries, variety, subsystems, Bowen's family systems theory, and the family projection process.

Boundaries

A system's boundaries represent the borders between a given family system and its environment. Boundaries affect the flow of information in and out of a system (White & Klein, 2008). Boundaries can be thought of as more or less permeable, meaning that more or less information is exchanged between families and their environments. For example, in some families in which abuse of spouse or children occurs regularly, the information shared with extrafamilial environments is minimal. These types of situations represent closed family boundaries. In other families, information is exchanged regularly with other environments. When a crisis occurs, such as the terminal illness of a parent, a family with open boundaries will inform and rally support from multiple environments, including extended family members, church organizations, and possibly social services offered through the health care system, such as hospice care.

VARIETY

When it possesses the resources, whether financial, emotional, or task oriented, to adapt to changes, a family is said to possess variety (White & Klein, 2008). Family rules may enhance or inhibit its ability to adapt to changes. An example of this concept in an aging context occurs when an elderly couple has failed to make adequate plans for the care of an adult child with mental retardation who lives with them. One or both parents eventually become incapacitated, throwing the family into crisis. Its ability to adjust and continue to provide adequate care for all dependent members will hinge on factors such as whether other family members step up to assume responsibility for care provision, the financial resources of the elderly parents to provide for their own and the dependent child's care, and the family's willingness to involve supportive others, such as social service agencies, in care planning for both parents and child.

SUBSYSTEMS

A *subsystem* is a part of a larger system. All family systems are composed of two or more subsystems, such as parent-child, marital, and sibling subsystems (White & Klein, 2008). These subsystems may vie for control of the family system, especially as the oldest generation ages and becomes more reliant on the children or grandchildren in the family. Subsystems may work well or poorly together, such as often occurs when a sibling subsystem is presented with the challenge of caring for a widowed parent with cognitive impairment. Siblings may work collaboratively to see that their parent receives good care, or part of the sibling subsystem may collaborate while the remainder stays out of care planning or provision. How the sibling subsystem handles such a transition in their family may affect their relationships with other family members for the rest of their own lifetimes.

BOWEN'S FAMILY SYSTEMS THEORY

Psychiatrist Murray Bowen has been credited as the first person to develop a comprehensive theory of family functioning (Doherty & Baptiste, 1993). Viewing nuclear families as *emotional* systems, he saw family interactions as either promoting or curtailing each member's differentiation of self, which refers to an individual's ability to adapt to life challenges by balancing "intellectual and emotional functioning and autonomy and togetherness in social relationships" (Doherty & Baptiste, 1993, p. 510). A well-differentiated self is believed to be necessary for optimal functioning in life.

Autonomy and togetherness are always in varying degrees of tension in families, for when families experience anxiety, they have a tendency to "fuse," that is, to herd or huddle together to deal with problems. When fusion occurs, family members "donate" parts of their individuality or self to the service of the group (Gilbert, 2004). When a family member or family as a whole becomes too fused, the ability to think and function as individuals is compromised, and symptoms such as depression, anxiety, or overly aggressive behavior may emerge in those family members.

Bowen (1978) viewed anxiety as the primary motivational

force in families, as an emotion that affected all parts of a family system once it was experienced by one family member. Families experience both acute and chronic forms of anxiety, and anxiety is additive; that is, as they occur, new stressors add to whatever background level of anxiety already exists in families, thus increasing the overall level of anxiety. Because all families experience life stressors, anxiety exists in all families to varying degrees. It is how families *handle* these anxiety-laden experiences that matters in terms of a family member's ability to differentiate, as well as families' abilities to solve problems they face (Gilbert, 2004). Bowen observed four customary family relationship patterns that emerged when anxiety took place in families: triangling, conflict and distancing, overfunctioning and underfunctioning reciprocity, and cutoffs.

Triangles occur in families when anxiety is passed from two family members to a third member. According to Bowen (1978), all families have triangles; it is a part of the normal family process. One example that illustrates the process is as follows: A couple is arguing, and their young child enters the room. Most often, that child will become anxious as the child realizes that something is wrong and his or her parents are upset. The child may react in several ways to try to break up the argument and discharge the anxiety felt: getting between the parents physically, distracting them by asking a favor, or destroying a toy, any of which is likely to shift the focus to the child and away from the arguing parents. In this way, the child has been triangled into the anxiety occurring in this family. If arguments are frequent and chronic, this child may escalate the strategies to reduce the anxiety felt and the arguments of his or her parents, eventually developing a destructive behavior pattern, such as aggression toward others, that may shift the parents' focus onto the child. In this way, symptoms in families are formed, and the parents' distress is shifted from their marital relationship to the parenting relationship or subsystem (Gilbert, 2004).

I return now to the potential crisis that occurs in multigenerational families when elderly parents do not plan for the care of their child with retardation as the parents become dependent or frail themselves. It is likely that the anxiety created by the special needs of this child, and the way in which these couples responded initially to their anxiety, created a triangle with this child long before the parents reached old age, a triangle in which the child's needs took primacy over those of the marital subsystem. The parents may have dealt with their distress over the birth and rearing of this child by focusing their attention on this child and the child's care, possibly neglecting both their own individuality (differentiation of self) and their marriage. Their customary pattern of devoting considerable attention to this child's needs may have led them to neglect doing any thinking about a time in their lives when they would no longer be able to care for this child. Also, they may have expected this child to precede them in death and, with such an expectation, never believed that such planning would be necessary.

When conflict occurs in families, it raises the intensity level of interactions and, when not resolved, may lead to chronic blaming and in some cases physical violence in marriage and nuclear families (Gilbert, 2004). When conflict is too intense, distancing may occur. Distancing happens when persons no longer trust family members to hear and respond appropriately to their concerns. In a distancing relationship, family members withdraw from each other. Communication occurs less frequently; when it does, it is not at a deep emotional level. According to Bowen (1978), while distancing feels good, it solves nothing and can lead to divorce and relationship cutoffs.

Cutoff is another key concept in the family process, according to Bowen (1978). He defined a *cutoff* as "a process of separation, isolation, withdrawal, running away, or denying the importance of the parental family" (1978, p. 383). Cutoffs in families can occur when two family members have significant conflict, and a decision is made to withdraw from contact with the family, a decision that can be either mutual (both parties want the cutoff and participate in it) or unilateral (one participates in the cutoff but not the other). Cutoffs occur when a familial relationship reaches a state of high emotional intensity (with increasing anxiety, distress, or anger). At some point, a family member will cut off internally or geographically (Gilbert, 2004).

Cutoffs may seem like a good idea in some families, but they are often deleterious to the development and differentiation process of the persons who participate in them. Cutoffs create anxiety, and unresolved anxiety can lead to symptoms. Bowen (1978) observed that those who cut off from their nuclear families have a tendency to carry an exaggerated version of (their) parental family problems into their marriages and may be at great risk of getting involved in a marriage that has its own high level of emotional intensity, with divorce as the final outcome. It also has been observed that when one family member is cut off from the whole family, other members may make attempts to bring that person back into the fold, with increased anxiety for them as their attempts fail.

When overfunctioning or underfunctioning reciprocity occurs in marriage, one spouse will adopt a style of making most decisions for the couple over time; the other spouse adapts to the dominant spouse's decisions. The adapting spouse gradually loses the ability to make decisions for him- or herself and, if stresses become too great, may underfunction or develop symptoms, such as depression or substance abuse. This triggers great efforts on the part of the overfunctioning spouse to help the underfunctioning one "get better." However, these efforts rarely work, and until the pattern is recognized and changed, the process continues.

FAMILY PROJECTION PROCESS

In families with multiple children, we often notice that the individual children function differently. Gilbert asserted that many families "display a wide range of functioning in their offspring" (2004, p. 65). Some are more independent; as they reach adulthood, some are more successful in the major tasks of work and love. In Bowen's (1978) family systems perspective, the term *family projection process* is used to describe the ways in which differentiation of self is passed from parents to children. Here, the triangling process may be instructive; the more a parent or set of parents worries about a particular child, the more anxiety they are likely to pass to that child. A tight triangle is then formed. Conversely, if parents routinely neglect a given child because of their anxieties or concern over another child, the neglected child may struggle with healthy differentiation of self as he or she tries to bond with parents.

Parental neglect or overinvolvement with children may lead to higher levels of fusion between those parents and children, with lower levels of differentiation of self evolving through the projection of anxiety. Higher levels of fusion generally result in less differentiation of self. However, Gilbert (2004) pointed out that in families in which most anxiety is projected onto a single child, some of the other children may experience less fusion and be better able to develop a healthy self that functions well in the world, provided that they have remained flexibly connected to the family system.

The Bowen (1978) systems perspective suggests that both strengths and weaknesses in the forms of fusion and differentiation of self are passed from one generation to the next in families; thus, it is important for family members with high levels of fusion and low levels of differentiation of self to work toward a healthy resolution of these issues. Counselors and therapists working with families can look for certain themes in the handling of the following issues: death, survival of trauma, reproduction, money, religion, and divorce and separation (Gilbert, 2004). They also should ask about significant, watershed-type events, including the entry (birth, adoption) or exit (death) of family members. Physical, functional, or emotional losses test a family's ability to function well, with well-integrated families exhibiting a history of adapting to difficult losses, and less-well-integrated families eventually showing symptoms of physical or emotional illness or maladaptive behaviors.

People who come to counseling need to gain a better understanding of their family heritage to make the decisions and changes in their life that restore an equilibrium and promote differentiation of self. The life review process is one strategy that can be facilitated by having a person complete a genogram. Completing a genogram may provoke anxiety and guilt in some persons as a result of perceived failures and relationships badly handled but, in the hands of a skilled counselor, may prompt an individual or family to work to come to terms with what has occurred in their lives. Forgiving self and significant others for events and behaviors one regrets may lead to a better differentiation of self as well as a sense of ego integrity that Erikson, Erikson, and Kivnick (1986) postulated as the final task of a person's life (Brubaker, 1987).

TYING THE LIFE COURSE AND SYSTEMS PERSPECTIVES TOGETHER

By viewing families as systems and by assessing an individual's life course transitions and trajectories, counselors and therapists develop the understanding needed to assist aging families with difficult life transitions and symptomatic expression, such as depression or physical illness. In some families, members of different generations may be experiencing key life transitions simultaneously. The extended family system may then exhibit increased stress levels as each person strives to meet the needs of self while attending to others. Table 2.1 shows possible concurrent transitions that occur in a multigenerational family.

The likelihood of concurrent transitions may be small in some families, but as elders live longer and family size increases, concurrent transitions, such as widowhood in the oldest generation, remarriage in the middle generation, and

TABLE 2.1
Possible Concurrent Transitions in a Multigenerational Family

Familial Generation		
OLDER	MIDDLE	YOUNGER
Retirement	Divorce, remarriage	Entering high school or college
Illness or disability	Elder care	College graduation, boomerang children
Widowhood	Bereavement	Workforce participation
Dating, remarriage	Retirement, widowhood	Cohabitation, marriage, divorce

a young adult child returning home to live (boomerang child) within a few months of each other, become more common. The degree of differentiation of self and fusion in families affects how these concurrent transitions are navigated.

Life course theory orients practitioners to consider the influence of both past and current transitions occurring for an individual who seeks help. Assessing the impact of recent transitions in persons' life course, as well as their concerns about upcoming or future anticipated transitions, help a therapist understand better how clients handle stress and view the meaning of these transitions in their lives. Transitions are important events or series of events in peoples' lives, and it is at the point of transition, or shortly thereafter, that people are most likely to be motivated to make changes in themselves or their family relationships. Learning about the life course of the nuclear or multigenerational family also gives therapists a window into a client's reaction to making changes that have an impact on other family members as well as themselves.

Systems thinking orients practitioners to obtain information about how family members involved in and affected by key life course transitions customarily interact with each other to facilitate or impede personal and family growth and development. Systems thinking also encourages therapists to involve multiple family members in the therapy process to resolve situations that affect the lives of both the client and the key family members.

The case illustration presented next illustrates the power of multiple concurrent transitions, as well as anticipated transitions, on the symptoms expressed by a woman caught in the middle of them. Through a combination of individual and family therapy, she was able to develop strategies for dealing with her anxiety and the felt responsibilities contributing to this anxiety.

JACKIE: I KNEW THIS DAY WAS COMING, BUT WHY NOW?

Jackie was a 43-year-old divorced woman who presented for therapy because of increased anxiety that was interfering with her sleep and ability to concentrate at work each day. She also had begun having panic attacks, which usually occurred when she planned to shop or go out. A few attacks were bad enough that she had to miss work. She had seen her family physician, who was reluctant to prescribe anti-anxiety medications for Jackie because of the difficulty so many people had in giving them up. He suggested that she see a therapist, to which she agreed.

Jackie came alone to her first session, although her boy-friend was with her in the waiting room. She twisted her scarf and fidgeted constantly while discussing her situation. She told the therapist that the anxiety had been building a while, but the panic attacks had occurred only for a month. She was very worried about them and the damage they might do to her job and relationship with her boyfriend.

Her therapist asked about current stressors in her life. Jackie related several. Her parents were both alive, but their health was declining. Her mother had just completed a treatment regimen for breast cancer, and her dad fractured his femur in several places last year and was slowly adapting to his repaired leg. He could walk with the help of a walker, but his gait was quite unsteady. Whenever Jackie was around them, she watched him closely. When she was away from them, she worried that he would fall again. He had always been the "strong one" and the decision maker in their family. Without him around, Jackie felt her mother would just "give up."

Jackie's oldest daughter, Belinda, age 23, had recently an-nounced her engagement to a young man she met at work. Jackie was quite concerned about this impending marriage as Belinda had only known her fiancé for 4 months. "We just knew right away," she told her mother. Jackie shud-dered as she described to the therapist her own shotgun marriage to Belinda's dad, insisted on by her parents when she became pregnant with Belinda. Belinda, who still lived with Jackie, was pressing her mother to become involved in her wedding plans. She wanted the big wedding her mother never had. Jackie did not know how she would pay for such a wedding. The relationship with Belinda's father, her ex-husband, had grown tense after his remarriage and the birth of Belinda's half-brothers. Jackie and her ex-husband had often quarreled about his failure to pay all the child support he owed while their children were younger. Now, she doubted that he would contribute much, if at all, to Belinda's wedding expenses.

What worried her most, though, was her parent's failing health. Her parents had always looked after her younger sister, Kate, who was mentally ill, and whose entire adult-hood seemingly had been spent in treatment, aftercare, or jail. Kate did not function well in society and had never kept a job for long. Her parents had not pushed Kate to be-come more independent. Jackie dreaded the day she would have to look after her sister. While they got along pretty well, Kate was demanding and would need a lot of Jackie's time. Jackie was concerned that the impending responsibili-ty of looking after Kate would interfere with her work, rais-ing her son at home, and her prospects for remarriage to her current boyfriend, of whom she was quite fond. Jackie and Kate had an older brother, Joe, but he was loosely tied to his family. He communicated by phone only sporadically, un-predictably, and never came home to visit. He lived about 500 miles from the rest of his family.

The therapist suggested that they complete a family genogram, to which Jackie agreed. The genogram revealed a history of cutoffs among males in her family and several alcoholic family members on both her mother's and father's sides. It was this family history of substance abuse that prompted her family physician to suggest therapy instead of medication. Jackie's father's alcoholism had caused a num-ber of problems in his family, including occasional violent outbursts toward his wife and children. Through Alcoholics Anonymous, he had achieved sobriety for about 15 years. Sensing her vulnerability to substance abuse and her minimizing of problems, Jackie's doctor did not want to risk her becoming dependent on prescription medications.

The therapist continued by asking:

Therapist: Can you tell me about the most important events in your and your siblings' lives and how your parents responded to them?

Jackie: Well, Joe's withdrawal from our family is pretty important. My parents have never understood it. When we were kids, my father's expectations of him were always unrealistic. He thought Joe could be both a star athlete and a student. He picked out both the sport [baseball] and profession [lawyer] for him. He put all his energy into Joe's activities when we were kids, and when Joe didn't accomplish what Dad wanted for him, he rode him unmercifully. Joe left home when he was 22, right after college, and he has been back to visit only a few times since then. I am the one who hears from him, if anyone does.

As for me, my dad was and is a real sexist. Dad was much easier on me, but he really didn't expect much of me. He was surprised when I wanted to go to college, but I dropped out when I got pregnant with Belinda. When Kate came along, he doted on her. He was devastated once he realized that she would never live a normal life. He lost his job pretty much around that same time. He was

fired because of too many absences at work. He
was trying to take care of Kate. And he was drinking a lot back then.

Therapist: Tell me how your father responded to Kate's
mental illness.

Jackie: At first, he tried to tell the counselors how to treat
Kate, but as time went by, he withdrew and left
most of the decisions about Kate to my mom.
Mom is a sweetie, but she doesn't ask for much
from her kids. So, Kate has pretty much done as
she pleased. My parents still pay her living expenses. Kate has trouble keeping jobs. They don't
want her to go on disability because it "would
look bad for the family." I really worry about the
future with Kate. On what I make, I would not be
able to support Kate. I do not know what, if any,
plans Mom and Dad have made for Kate's future
once they are gone. Thinking about all this keeps
me awake at night. I really don't know where to
begin with my parents.

Intervention

The therapist commended Jackie for her willingness to
tackle such a broad array of issues and to be proactive in discussing Kate's future with her parents. They agreed that she
needed to get her anxiety under control before facing her
parents and daughter with her concerns about their future.
He began by working with Jackie individually to get her
anxiety and panic under control. He selected cognitive-
behavioral therapy because of its proven efficacy in treat-

ing both panic and generalized anxiety disorders (Craske, Barlow, & Meadows, 2000). The purpose of cognitive-behavioral therapy is to replace maladaptive reactions to stressors with coping strategies that address each dysfunctional area (Newman & Borkovec, 1995). Interventions with Jackie included progressive muscle relaxation training and self-control desensitization, the latter of which teaches the client to apply "relaxation skills to eliminate imagery-induced anxiety cues and worrisome thinking" (Newman & Borkovec, 1995, p. 6). Cognitive restructuring, which involves the identification of automatic and irrational thoughts followed by replacement of those thoughts with alternative perspectives and logical thoughts, was also employed to reduce Jackie's anxiety (Newman & Borkovec, 1995).

When her anxiety had subsided and no panic attacks had occurred for 2 weeks, the therapist suggested that Jackie contact her parents about coming in for family therapy. Her parents accompanied Jackie to the next session, looking nervous and uneasy. Jackie's dad, David, began by praising Jackie, saying, "She's our normal child, the one who looks after all of us." Jackie's mother, Paula, stayed silent.

The therapist asked Paula and David to tell him what was going on in their lives now and what their concerns were for the future. They both said that they were fine, but they worried about Kate. Her dad then launched into a description of all the problems they had with Kate, to which Jackie replied, "Dad, it's easier for you to talk about Kate than yourself. Please tell Mark [the therapist] what is going on with you!"

Over the course of the next two sessions, David and Paula

gradually revealed their fears for their own lives as well as that of Kate's. Paula had not slept well since her cancer treatment, and David was having trouble accepting the lifestyle limitations created by his slowly healing leg. He was angry and irritable about his slow recovery. With some probing, they acknowledged that they were both deeply saddened by their son's withdrawal from his family and ashamed of Kate's mental illness. "If it weren't for Jackie, we would be complete failures as parents," David said. With tears streaming down her cheeks, Paula nodded her head in agreement.

INTERVENTIONS WITH THE FAMILY

The therapist began interventions with the family by noting that both Paula and David were anxious themselves about undergoing life transitions in the area of personal health that—perhaps for the first time—have brought their mortality in full view. The therapist noted that it is normal to get anxious in the face of declining health and shared his perception that this couple had not fully grieved their youngest daughter's problems and their son's distance from them. They concurred with this assessment. Once the therapist had established a trusting relationship with Jackie's parents, he then, over several sessions, outlined the high price they had paid for avoiding their feelings about what had happened with their children. They adopted a largely passive stance toward the adversity they had faced with their children and buried their grief. Paula observed that her guilt and shame about Kate's mental illness may have contributed to her continuous rescuing of Kate from her problems. While the therapist noted that parental guilt is common among parents of children with mental illnesses, he stressed that by enabling Kate's irresponsible behavior, they send the message to her that it is okay to behave in this manner. Because they are aging, they are also in danger of leaving Jackie with a mess with respect to dealing with Kate. The therapist asked them if this is what they wanted to do, to which they both replied, "No."

The therapist saw the elderly couple alone for several sessions to help them come to terms with their grief over the poor relationships they had developed with their two children. With their new understanding of relationship triangles, they saw how the extra energy they put into their relationship with Kate may have contributed to her irresponsible behavior. David realized that his unreasonable expectations of his son contributed to their alienation from each other and Joe's withdrawal from the family. David and Paula also worked toward accepting the idea that they could not change what had occurred with their children and needed to forgive themselves for what had happened. Once this forgiveness occurs, they can begin to explore some options for their future that may be helpful to everyone.

The therapist then invited both Jackie and Kate to join the therapy sessions. Kate refused, but Jackie returned. Jackie reported that she had met with her ex-husband to discuss Belinda's wedding plans. He agreed to contribute a modest amount to the wedding expenses. Together, they met with Belinda and explained the financial realities they both faced. Although disappointed, Belinda accepted their offer and scaled down her wedding plans.

With the three adults present, together over several sessions they developed a plan of how to deal with Jackie's sit-

uation, both presently and in the future. The parents were
willing to discuss assessment for disability with Kate so that
Jackie is not put in a position of having to decide whether to
assume financial responsibility for Kate when they are
gone. They also shared with Jackie what their preferences
were for their own and Kate's care should they become incapacitated. The couple also met with a lawyer who specialized in estate planning so that they could understand what
options they had for their children's inheritance arrangement. They worked with the attorney to draw up living
wills and health care power-of-attorney documents. A letter
was sent to Joe by his parents asking for his forgiveness and
another chance at a relationship with him. With these steps
taken, this family was better prepared to face the future
transitions that awaited them.

CHAPTER 3

Working With Couples' Issues in Late Life

One of the benefits of current longevity patterns is that more couples attain old age, and often very old age, together. Marriage rates of older adults differ by gender and race, with men aged 65 and older more likely to be married than women and whites in this same age group more likely to be married than persons of other races or ethnicities (the exception is Asian/Pacific Islander men, who are married at slightly higher rates than white men) (U.S. Census Bureau, 2005).

Living into old age with a marital partner has potential health benefits for older adults, particularly when the marriage is of good quality (Umberson, Williams, Powers, Liu, & Needham, 2006). In fact, Umberson and colleagues found that negative marital experiences were associated with a decline in self-rated health among married persons over a 9-year period. Thus, simply being married does not confer health benefits; rather, positive marital interaction is necessary to slow the decline in health that inevitably occurs as we age.

In addition, having a spouse as primary caregiver when one's own health is declining can mean more intensive and personalized care and reduced likelihood of institutionalization in a nursing home. Spouse caregivers tend to provide care longer than their adult children, and some spouses still capable of functioning independently have moved into assisted living facilities with their spouses to avoid placement of their loved one in a nursing home (Kemp, 2008).

Different types of old age marriage are prevalent. The "survivors of marriage," those in long-term marriages, may have been married 40 years or longer by the time they reach age 65. However, many marriages, including some long-term marriages among older adults, are remarriages, occurring after one or both partners have been widowed or divorced. Although divorce rates are low among elders aged 65 and over, increasing numbers of them are divorcing (Clarke, 1995).

In addition to marriage, there are couples who cohabit in late life. Although cohabitation rates are low among older Americans, cohabitation has increased among all age groups (Brown, Lee, & Bulanda, 2006). Characteristics of older cohabiters are mixed in valence; for example, they tend to have more depressive symptoms than married elders, but they rate their relationships as more equitable and spend more time alone with partners (Calasanti & Kiecolt, 2007).

Other nonmarital relationships include homosexual partnerships (in states where same-sex marriage is not legal) and couples who live apart, but consider themselves to be "together." Less is known about these relationships, but they appear to be increasing in prevalence (Calasanti & Kiecolt, 2007).

There are many challenges to couple satisfaction and bonds that occur in late life. Chronic or life-threatening illness for one or both members of the dyad can threaten the couple's bond. Severe illness or death of a middle-aged child can precipitate significant grief that challenges couples to find positive and compatible ways to cope with their losses. An older couple's children sometimes divorce, leaving them to deal with the loss of valued sons- or daughters-in-law and grandchildren. Their children may also remarry, creating new relationships for older couples, such as being step-grandparents for the first time. Eventually, one spouse in most couples is widowed and faced with undergoing a process of bereavement and establishment of a new identity as a single person. In some cases, older adults date and remarry, which can affect relationships in their own intergenerational family as well as those of their new spouse's family.

In this chapter, several life transitions that may warrant therapy with couples and their families are discussed in detail. General issues of bereavement, with an emphasis on widowhood and loss of middle-aged children, are discussed first. Next, therapy to help divorced and remarried couples and their families is discussed. Finally, a challenge to couple-hood, such as facing a diagnosis of mild cognitive impairment (MCI), is presented. Clinical case studies are included to illustrate how therapists might approach different problems.

DOING COUPLE THERAPY WITH OLDER ADULTS

The efficacy of couple therapy with older adults is understudied. There are many types of couple therapy that have been found to be useful, but few, if any, focused on work with couples past middle age. As noted, however, new challenges to couple functioning occur as couples age, and some will seek therapy rather than pursue divorce, particularly those in long-term marriages or new remarriages. How should work with these couples be approached by therapists?

First, as in any other type of therapy, a therapist needs to understand the problems the couple presents and what the couple hopes to gain from therapy. Therefore, if elderly clients identify the marriage as a problem or as in jeopardy, the therapist ideally should see both members of the couple together to begin an assessment of the marital bond and the couple's needs for change. As with any older adult, part of the assessment process should include an inventory of health and memory concerns for both parties. An inventory of current medication use should be conducted, and if recent behavior changes are present, brief memory testing may be indicated as memory impairments are related to some types of behavior changes.

In addition, a question should be asked about how much anxiety those health or memory problems have created for the couple. Couples dealing with serious or life-threatening illnesses in one or both members of the dyad usually have considerable anxiety about the future. Couples in which one partner exhibits signs of cognitive impairment may struggle with accepting the changes in the affected spouse and developing helpful strategies to deal with them.

I strongly prefer conducting a thorough assessment of couples by seeing them once together, followed by once separately before formulating a treatment plan with them. Spending individual time with each member of the dyad permits a therapist to understand each partner's story, explore health and psychological histories thoroughly, and create the conditions for a relationship in which both members of the couple feel safe and supported by the therapist. With the advent of managed care and a limited number of sessions permitted under many insurance plans, this three-session assessment process may need to be condensed (Jacobson & Christensen, 1996). However, many elderly couples either will pay for therapy themselves or use Medicare as their primary insurance provider. With passage of the Medicare Improvement for Patients and Providers Act in 2008, parity in payment for outpatient mental health care has been mandated and is being phased in over 6 years. By 2014, the co-pay for mental health services will be the same 20% currently charged for medical outpatient services (New York State Bar Association, Elder Law, 2008). This change should help increased numbers of elderly couples to pay for needed therapy.

Jacobson and Christensen (1996) delineated several roles that stressful circumstances play in the development or exacerbation of couple relationship problems. Developmental life course transitions (e.g., retirement, or parental death) or unexpected transitions or losses (e.g., death of a close family member or financial losses) can complicate the resolution of incompatibilities in couple relations. They also point out that, whether expected or unexpected, stressful events put new demands on people that may not be met by their typical methods of coping. Stressful life transitions also increase each partner's need for help and support while decreasing the partner's ability to provide them. For example, the loss of a child to death provokes a grieving process for both members of the dyad and may lessen the support they are able to provide to each other. Finally, stressful events can create perceptual distortions and a greater focus on oneself, making it more difficult to understand or appreciate the partner's viewpoint (Jacobson & Christensen, 1996). Loss or absence of mutuality or mutual participation in a relationship threatens a couple's ability to function well in marriage (Genero, Miller, Surrey, & Baldwin, 1992).

Many therapists find doing couple counseling to be among the most challenging of counseling endeavors. The emotional intensity brought to therapy by a severely distressed couple caught in a cycle of mutual blame and disparagement can prompt a therapist to fantasize about putting on a black-and-white-striped shirt and blowing a whistle when couples seem to be spinning out of control. Instead, learning and practicing skills in dealing with couples is crucial to success in couple therapy. The following skills were recommended by Jacobson and Christensen (1996) for use in their integrative couple therapy approach but are applicable to therapists working with all couples seeking therapy.

- Good listening skills, as well as awareness of facial and other bodily cues associated with affect.
- A sensitivity to context, which means paying close attention to a partner's most recent remark (attending to the present situation), and being prepared to shift gears and abandon a prescribed agenda if indicated.
- Acceptance, which in this context is the ability to express compassion and sympathy in reaction to each person's story and to respond to even the most provocative of couple behaviors without blame and accusation. This can be a tall order and often requires experience to master. It

also requires knowing oneself intimately, particularly one's prejudices and limitations. Refer to another therapist any couples you cannot work with because of "irreconcilable differences" stemming from differing religious beliefs or past experiences.

- The ability to maintain a therapeutic atmosphere despite severe conflict without becoming confrontational. It is acceptable to separate a couple for individual therapy when they present and maintain highly charged and destructive interaction styles. Effective couple therapists cannot allow themselves to be drawn into taking sides or blaming, and they strive to remain calm so that they might exert a soothing influence on distressed couples.

- Appropriate language use. Use the couple's language rather than jargon in discussing problem assessment and resolution. If you can get the couple to laugh at their situation without belittling it, humor can be helpful in couple therapy.

The remaining sections of this chapter present several problems faced by older individuals and couples that may lead to a need for therapy. They include widowhood and bereavement of spouse and adult child; divorce, dating, and remarriage; and response to MCI in one spouse.

WIDOWHOOD AND BEREAVEMENT

Widowhood is a common experience in old age, particularly for women. Rates of widowhood for women aged 80 and older in the United States are from 65% to 72%, depending on race or ethnicity (U.S. Census Bureau, 2005). Widowhood is regarded as an experience that requires more psychological and social adjustments than any other late-life event (Hatch, 2000). Yet, the majority of persons adjust satisfactorily to widowhood after a period of grieving, although they follow different trajectories in the months after spousal death (Bonanno, Wortman, & Nesse, 2004). Cross-cultural research suggested that widows and widowers received more emotional and instrumental support in the time following their loss of spouses than their married counterparts, but that contact with and levels of support from others returned to preloss levels about 2.5 years after widowhood commenced (Guiaux, Van Tilburg, & Van Groenou, 2007).

Because there is strong evidence that persons follow different trajectories in their handling of partner loss, it is important to understand the characteristics and implications of these trajectories. In a study that followed married persons into widowhood for 18 months after their loss, Bonanno and colleagues (2004) found five trajectories of bereavement outcomes: common grief, chronic grief, chronic depression, depression-improvement, and resilience. *Common grief* was characterized by an increase in distress following spousal loss that abated over time, while *chronic grief* was defined as a "dramatic increase in depression following the loss that remained elevated throughout bereavement" (Bonanno et al., 2004, p. 261). Those with chronic grief in this study tended to be excessively dependent as persons and in their relationship with their spouses.

Those with chronic *depression* had elevated levels of depression before spousal loss that remained elevated in the 18-month bereavement period. Those who were categorized as *depressed-improved* showed high levels of depression prior to spousal death but were significantly less depressed by 6 months into the bereavement period. This group tended to exhibit more ambivalence and negativity about their marriages when still married. Finally, the *resilient* group had low levels of depression both pre- and postloss and constituted the largest group in their sample, 45.6%. This group showed no evidence of denial of grief in additional analyses (Bonanno et al., 2004).

The authors of this study concluded that only those with chronic grief and chronic depression were likely to need psychosocial intervention or therapy (Bonanno et al., 2004). To determine how best to help persons with chronic grief or depression in bereavement, a theoretical model of grief may be instructive. Stroebe and Schut (1999) articulated a dual-process model of coping with bereavement that focuses clinicians on how to assist persons with grief reactions and normalizes some of the behavior seen in widows and other bereaved adults.

The dual-process model focuses on two types of stressors experienced by those who are grieving: loss-oriented stressors and restoration-oriented stressors. *Loss-oriented stressors* are those that relate to an aspect of the loss experience itself, such as the shock of a sudden, traumatic death; *restoration-oriented stressors* are secondary stressors, such as economic or legal problems, that are consequences of the loss. According to Stroebe and Schut (1999), most grieving persons will oscillate between dealing with these two types of losses, and they believe that such oscillation is necessary for adaptation to the loss. For example, a grieving spouse may take respite from coping with the enormity of the actual loss of the marital partner by working on some of the secondary stressors for a while. In later work, Stroebe, Folkman, Hansson, and Schut (2006) postulated that five elements combine in the life of every bereaved person to determine individual differences in bereavement adjustment: (a) the nature of the stressor, (b) interpersonal resources, (c) intrapersonal resources, (d) appraisal and coping processes, and (e) outcomes. Here, I suggest that when persons are struggling with persistent or overwhelming grief, an assessment of all five areas is needed before a therapeutic plan can be developed.

WORKING WITH THE BEREAVED

Interventions with grieving persons can take several forms, including individual or family therapy, support groups, and hospice care (for those with relatives with a terminal illness). It is important to recognize that the expression of grief is highly personal and shaped by cultural beliefs and practices. Therefore, what is helpful to one person may not be helpful to another person, and interventions should be tailored to individual needs (Nolen-Hoeksema & Larson, 1999).

Therapeutic interventions have goals of prevention or treatment of pathological grief, such as the chronic grief found by Bonanno and associates (2004). Grief counseling is complex, emotion laden, and often difficult to carry out. In my practice, I found that grieving persons, especially those grieving the loss of young children or adult children, experienced extremely intense emotional pain that often felt crippling to them and could be difficult to endure at times. Therapists working with grieving adults need a high tolerance for emotional expression, patience to work slowly—sometimes very slowly—with the tasks of grieving, and the ability to maintain a sense of hope in situations that may seem hopeless to clients at the outset of therapy. Nolen-Hoeksema and Larson suggested that persons working with bereaved individuals must guard against a desire to impose one's own "timing or agenda on the grieving person; rather take their cues from the bereaved and allow the mourning process to unfold naturally" (1999, p. 166).

What are the major tasks to be accomplished in a grief process? In terms of mourning one's loss, Worden (1982) suggested four tasks: (a) accept the reality of the loss, (b) experience grief and pain, (c) adjust to an environment that does not have the deceased in it, and (d) withdraw emotional energy and reinvest it in other relationships. For elderly widows, especially women, the final task may encompass investment in new activities or ones enjoyed before the spouse's illness and death rather than investment in a new partner. Widowed women are less likely to date and marry again than their male counterparts (Smith, Zick, & Duncan, 1991).

Attention next turns to two case studies. The first features a widow struggling with chronic grief after the loss of a second spouse; the second features a couple who developed marital problems following the loss of a middle-aged son.

MILLIE: A STRUGGLE WITH CHRONIC GRIEF

Millie was a 75-year-old woman who presented for therapy after referral by her family physician. Millie's mood was not improving substantially after several months of taking antidepressant medication, and her sleep was still sporadic. Her therapist asked her what had precipitated her need for medication, and she said, simply, "I lost my husband. He was everything to me. Even though it's been almost a year since he passed, I still can't believe he's gone." She then reached for the box of tissues nearby, placed them in her lap, and burst into tears.

Millie and Joe had been married a scant 4 years when he was diagnosed with colorectal cancer. He died just short of 1 year after his diagnosis. Although they knew his diagnosis was terminal, Millie and Joe decided to embark on a series of trips together until Joe was too sick to travel. They were determined to make the most of the time they had left together. "I think this has made it harder for me," Millie said. "I have such wonderful memories of us traveling together. I can't get them out of my mind." She added, "I've buried two husbands now. I hate being alone. I just don't know how to be by myself—I feel lost."

The therapist asked Millie what grieving her first husband had been like. She replied, "Not too difficult. He was hard to get along with and very domineering. He had been sick a long time and in a lot of pain. I was tired of caring for him and to tell you the truth, a bit relieved when he died."

Next, the therapist asked her to talk about how she met Joe. Millie quickly replied,

"I started dating Joe about 3 months after I buried Gabe. I met Joe at a dance club, and we hit it off immediately. I married him just a year after I was widowed. Losing Joe was so much more difficult than my first husband."

With a little more exploration, the therapist learned that Millie had depended on men nearly all her life. She described her father as domineering, much like her first husband, Gabe, had been. Although Joe was not controlling, she noted that he also took care of their money, household and auto maintenance, and even bought her clothes and jewelry. He did all their driving when together, although Millie could drive. She could rely on Joe for anything. Millie was aware that she was on her own now, and it terrified her. She resented the fact that she was put in this position. Sometimes, she resented Joe for his unwillingness to see doctors for regular checkups. "The cancer might have been caught if he'd just done the screening," she said. "But I feel so guilty saying anything bad about him; he was a wonderful husband."

When asked what resources she had now, Millie frowned. "I have two children, Adam and Jack, but they're of little use to me. Jack lives out of town. Adam's wife is nice, but I can tell she thinks I should get over Joe and just move on." When asked how she can tell her daughter-in-law feels this way, Millie says, "I don't know; I just think she feels that way." The therapist asks about friends or other family members, and Millie cries. "I neglected my friends when I married Joe. He became my social world." She did say she had a sister who lived nearby: "But she's got her own problems. Her husband is sick. I don't want to bother her."

CASE ANALYSIS

Millie is having a chronic grief reaction precipitated by the loss of her second husband. Because she was married only 4 years, she seemed to feel that she was robbed of her spouse at a time when they were still building closeness and connection to each other. This overwhelming grief was a new reaction to spousal death for Millie. She was not depressed after her first husband died, and her (relatively) quick remarriage to Joe suggests that she was uncomfortable living on her own. Although she may choose to marry again, she needed to accept Joe's loss and, with it, the accompanying pain; adjust to a life without him; and invest her considerable energies in other persons or activities. Following the dual-process model of coping with grief described earlier in this chapter, the therapist will work to provide Millie a safe place to share her painful feelings and memories of the deceased while helping her establish an identity that includes honing some abilities to care for herself. Also needed is reconnection with others, including her family and perhaps her old friends, who can assist her in developing new meaning in life.

These therapeutic goals can only be attained at a pace that Millie sets. If she responds well to the grieving process in individual therapy, a support group specifically for widows may be helpful to establishing new social connections. Connecting with her son Adam and his wife, Joy, may be helpful to Millie. Contacting her sister to see if they could be of help to each other might benefit both siblings.

INTERVENTIONS

Before beginning to involve Millie in processing her grief, her therapist asked her to describe any health conditions she had and any medications she was taking for them. Millie had high blood pressure and cholesterol, and she took medications for these conditions. Otherwise, she was in good health.

Because this therapist was 30 years younger than Millie, it was important for her to establish good rapport and instill confidence in Millie that she could deal with Millie's grief, even though the therapist had not yet lost a spouse. The therapist began by explaining the dual-process model of coping with grief in terms Millie could understand, noting that it was absolutely normal to want to take breaks from the intense emotions she felt to work on other things, like tasks associated with living alone. She asked Millie to prioritize these tasks and to say which ones she believed she could learn without help and which ones she would need help with. Millie also told the therapist who in her social world she believed would be best able to help her with these tasks. For example, Adam was really good with finances and could teach her to balance a checkbook. He might also be willing to manage her savings. Her daughter-in-law, Joy, was handy and could teach Millie how to do simple home repairs. Millie might get her grandsons to help her with yard work. Millie still did not quite understand medical insurance issues and was not sure who could help her with that issue but realized that her sister had probably also had to deal with them. With a phone call to the Area Agency on Aging, her therapist located a nearby senior center that offered consultations and help with medical insurance issues and income taxes.

The therapist asked Millie to bring with her some mementos of her trips with Joe. She did so reluctantly. As she shared them with her therapist, she was asked to tell stories of her and Joe's times together and to explain the meaning of the mementos she brought. These sessions were very emotional and intense for both, but Millie gradually came to realize that Joe was not only a fine companion but also a form of "redemption" to her for all the difficult years spent with her first husband. She felt robbed when Joe died because she looked at him as someone who would make all those painful memories with Gabe "evaporate." Now, she realized that no one could make bad memories "go away," and that she would have to let them go herself. Her therapist asked her to picture her life without both past and current resentments. Millie looked at her with wonderment and said, "I guess I'd feel rather light. I suppose I've been accumulating resentments for a long time."

When she was ready, Millie went to Gabe's grave alone and told him what she wanted to say about their life together. In doing so, she acknowledged that it was not all time lost; Adam and Jack were the good that came out of the marriage. She told her therapist that she went straight from her father's home to marriage with Gabe without any realization of the price of her fears and dependence. She said: "I thought it was what was expected of me." After a few additional sessions, she scattered some of Joe's ashes in their favorite picnic spot; she was not quite ready to give him up completely. This time, she took Joy with her; they had been talking regularly, and she had begun having dinner at Adam and Joy's home once a week.

One of the major tasks of grieving is to help the widow emotionally relocate the deceased (Worden, 1991), which means finding a place in one's current life for the deceased spouse. This task can be done in several ways, including creating a legacy in the deceased's honor, such as a scholarship or a fund-raising event, or wearing an item of the spouse's jewelry (Nolen-Hoeksema & Larson, 1999). Millie decided to purchase a stone that bore Joe's name for the new alumni center of his college alma mater. They had attended alumni events and gone on several tours through the travel office of Joe's college.

The therapist then raised the issue of Millie attending a support group for widows. She saw Millie's potential to provide others with comfort during the grieving process as well as an opportunity to decrease Millie's social isolation through interaction with group members. Millie resisted this idea. They revisited this intervention when Millie felt stuck in moving toward independence; this time, she agreed to go if Joy would go with her a time or two. Much to her surprise, Millie actually enjoyed talking to other widows and became a regular attendee of this group. She decided to contact one or two of her friends and, with a new friend from the support group, formed a card-playing group that met weekly. She also called her sister and began visiting her and her brother-in-law. She would look after him occasionally so that her sister could get her hair done or shopping completed. She was able to discontinue antidepressants and therapy shortly thereafter.

BOB AND VERA: UNSPEAKABLE LOSS OF A SON

Bob and Vera Evans, aged 74 and 69, respectively, came to couple therapy on the recommendation of Vera's brother, who bowled with Bob regularly and had benefited from marriage counseling when his own marriage was in trouble a few years earlier. The therapist was a middle-aged male who specialized in working with couples. The presenting problem was that Bob's drinking had increased substantially since their son Charley's death a year ago from a farming accident. Bob now was drunk nearly every night and withdrew from Vera when she tried to talk with him about anything. Vera worried that Bob, who also was a farmer, would harm himself by drinking and driving heavy farm machinery. She could not bear to lose both her son and her husband, she said. However, she was angry with him for drinking and withdrawing from her.

Bob was stoic and spoke little during the first session. At times, he seemed to be elsewhere. Vera talked and talked, asking the therapist what they might try to do to get things right between them. The therapist wanted to know more about their son and what had happened in the aftermath of his death. The couple looked shocked. "You want us to talk about Charley?" Vera said. "Yes," the therapist replied, "It sounds as though things have come apart for you since he died." Vera's eyes welled up with tears. Bob looked panic stricken.

Vera began by recounting that Charley had gone missing after a day of work with the tractor. His farm was adjacent to theirs; in fact, they had planned to sell their farm to Charley before they died. He was the only farmer among their four children. Bob had found Charley crushed underneath the machinery. Charley was separated from his wife at the time of his death, so it fell to Vera and Bob to make funeral arrangements for their son. He was buried in the family plot in a nearby cemetery after a Catholic funeral mass. Vera visited the grave site every week and talked to Charley there often; as far as she knew, Bob never went there. Of Bob, she said, "He's just crawled into a bottle, and I can't get him out."

The therapist asked Bob what he wished to add to Vera's account of what had happened. Bob replied, "Nothing; I don't want to talk about it." Vera appeared frustrated at this response.

The therapist explained that he liked to meet with each member of the couple at least once before developing a treatment plan. Thus, separate sessions were scheduled for Bob and Vera.

From his session with Vera, the therapist learned that the marriage had been a satisfactory one until this tragedy took Charley from them. However, they were a couple with a traditional division of labor and traditional ways of handling emotions throughout their years together. Vera was highly expressive of feelings and liked to talk; Bob was quiet and almost never revealed how he was feeling to others. Vera had little tolerance for alcoholics; both her father and grandfather had been alcoholic, so Bob's current behavior was unacceptable to her. "I don't know where I'd go, but I won't live with him this way," she said.

Bob's session was a struggle for both men. Bob volunteered no information at first. He maintained a silence about his son. When asked why he came to the sessions, Bob said, "My drinking. I've lost control, and Vera is about ready to kick me out. I want to get control of my drinking."

When asked why he drank, Bob replied swiftly: "I can't sleep on my own. I have terrible nightmares when I drift off to sleep. I see Charley's mangled body morning, noon, and night. I can't function without something to dull my thoughts. Just can't function."

CASE ANALYSIS

This couple suffered a terrible loss. Elderly persons who lose children often struggle with these deaths and maintain that it should have been them rather than the child. In addition, farmers often feel deeply rooted to their land and to farming as a way of life. This couple had pinned their hopes on Charley to continue the family farming tradition, so they had lost not only a child, but also the dream to continue their family farm. Bob also gave hints that he was traumatized by what he saw when he discovered Charley, and it appeared that his drinking was a form of self-medication to cope with a profound sense of loss coupled with both intrusive thoughts and depression.

Research suggests that late-life couples with one depressed partner also show reduced abilities to communicate feelings and problem solve together (Harper & Sandberg, 2009). When both partners are depressed, these abilities are impaired even more. Yet, to process their grief and reestablish equilibrium in their marriage, Bob and Vera will need to address their feelings about Charley's loss and, if possible, find ways to mourn him together. It is a positive sign that they have come to therapy as a couple, but both could benefit from individual work to process their grief and address Bob's alcohol abuse before they can reunite in therapy to make meaning of their loss of a favored son.

INTERVENTION

The therapist referred Bob to an alcohol and drug specialist to get his drinking under control. The couple therapist declined to serve in this capacity for Bob, feeling that he could be more effective as a couple therapist for the Evans if another therapist treated Bob's substance abuse. Having Bob work with someone else on his drinking problem avoided two pitfalls that can impede progress in couple therapy: the temptation to have an "identified patient" and the need for the couple therapist to police the substance abuse (Jacobson & Christensen, 1996, p. 244). Bob declined an opportunity to join a 12-step program, but he did agree to take disulfiram (Antabuse) as prescribed by his doctor after a physical examination showed he was an acceptable candidate for it.

Once Bob had stopped drinking, the couple therapist scheduled individual sessions with Bob and Vera for additional evaluation of the marital problems. He also wished to strengthen his relationship with both of them to assist them in processing their grief and to prepare them for work together (and possibly with other family members present) to make some positive meaning of their loss. He discovered that Vera had suppressed some of her grief because of Bob's behavioral spiral and worked with her on expressing her intense feelings of loss.

As the therapist worked patiently with Bob to gain his trust, he was able to get Bob to talk about Charley and their relationship, which had been a quiet but close one. In addition to farming together, they had enjoyed regular fishing and hunting trips. Bob felt like he had lost a best friend in addition to losing a son. He also learned to let out some feeling as he described this relationship, although he appeared somewhat embarrassed whenever he showed any emotion.

When the couple resumed conjoint sessions, the therapist shared his formulation of their predominant issue. Such formulations, which in integrative couple therapy consist of identification and discussion of a theme, polarization process, and mutual trap (Jacobson & Christensen, 1996), offer couples an explanation for their difficulties and shift the fo-

cus from their preoccupation with differences to their customary methods of handling differences. Methods of
handling differences are more amenable to change; basic
personality differences such as introversion or strong belief
systems are better candidates for acceptance.

The therapist began the formulation by noting that both
Bob and Vera were grief stricken over the loss of Charley
and their dream of keeping the family farm going past their
death. Used to turning to each other during past trials, they
had been unable to do so since Charley's death. Bob held his
sorrow inside and coped primarily through drinking and
other solitary pursuits. Vera tried to turn to Bob for a listening ear and his support, but she had been largely rebuffed.
The more she sought closeness from Bob, the more he withdrew. Their theme was one of closeness-distance, with Vera
trying repeatedly to pursue Bob's support by talking to him
and Bob distancing himself from Vera by getting drunk.
The more Vera tried to reach Bob through talking to him,
the more he withdrew or drank. This was their polarization
process.

Neither Bob nor Vera knew or had tried other ways to
connect with each other. They were trapped in this cycle
of pursuit and distancing. At this point, the couple was
nodding in agreement. "What else can we do?" cried
Vera.

Over a couple of additional conjoint sessions, Bob and
Vera explored their personal experiences of handling loss
and grief and their rationales for reacting as they had. They
also explored what they could change about themselves to
improve their relationship with each other. Bob stopped
drinking, was still taking the medication, and was begin-

ning to spend evenings with Vera, just being together without discussing Charley. Sometimes, they just went for a drive and listened to music. At other times, they took their grandchildren into town for a movie or shopping.

In these conjoint therapy sessions, the couple learned and practiced active listening and validating communication skills with each other. When using validation, the listener not only demonstrates that he or she has understood the speaker, but also expresses that the speaker's point of view is valid and his or her feelings are understandable (Jacobson & Christensen, 1996). Bob might have said to Vera, "You don't like it when I turn away from you when you have something important to tell me about how you are feeling that day. It is understandable that you would want to share your feelings with me when you are excited or upset." The couple was encouraged to increase their positive interactions with each other by listening and responding to each others' daily bids for attention or expressions of affection (Gottman, 2004).

Vera stopped seeking daily support and reassurance from Bob. She was trying out strategies to channel her expressiveness to persons or activities other than her husband, who felt overwhelmed with Vera's need to talk. Vera began some volunteer work at a nearby hospital, with a focus on helping families with sick children. She found this activity rewarding and was increasing her time at the hospital to 3 days a week. She also reconnected with a group of friends who play bridge and other card games over lunch every week.

Once the couple was communicating better with each other, the therapist turned his attention to remaining prac-

tical issues that the couple faced, such as the disposal of
Charley's assets to his estranged wife and children. Bob
wanted to provide for them but worried that if his daughter-
in-law kept the farm that she might sell it to a developer.
With help from Vera, they approached their daughter-in-
law about buying the farm from her, to which she agreed.
They worked out a payment plan that would allow them to
purchase the farm and their daughter-in-law to stay home
with the children until they reached school age. Vera also
offered to watch the children once a week for her daughter-
in-law, thus relieving some of the strain in their relationship that occurred after the marital separation.

When the couple was reunited in therapy, they had improved their ability to talk and share with each other about
daily activities, but they still struggled to make sense together of Charley's loss. The therapist suggested that additional family members join the couple as "consultants" to
this therapeutic process of meaning-making, a process of
collectively making sense of a loss (Nadeau, 2008). Vera and
Bob invited a daughter, a son, and a (different) daughter-in-
law. Nadeau (2008) pointed out that sometimes in-laws may
be more effective consultants in meaning-making processes
because they did not grow up with the same family rules
that may inhibit blood relatives. In family sessions, each
family member shared his or her feelings about Charley's
loss, along with what he or she would remember about him
and what he gave to his family. Carla, sister-in-law to Charley, recalled with a chuckle his off-the-wall sense of humor
and silly practical jokes played on all family members, especially on their birthdays. This recollection prompted Charley's family to develop a new ritual of practical joke playing

on each other on Charley's birthday each year "to honor
Charley's memory." Thus, instead of experiencing only
negative feelings about his loss, the family decided to cele-
brate his life each year with one of his signature activities,
thus honoring his memory in ways that Charley would likely approve of.

Divorce, Dating, and Remarriage: Carving Out a New Life

Although divorce rates are relatively low among older
adults, they are increasing (Clarke, 1995). However, little is
known about later-life divorces. One study of divorces occurring from ages 40 to 69 suggested that mid-late-life divorces
have both up- and downsides for those who experience them.
Participants cited loneliness, depression, dealing with uncer-
tainty, feelings of desertion or betrayal, and feelings of inad-
equacy as difficult aspects of their divorces. On the positive
side, over 75% said that they made the right decision in divorcing their spouses, and those who remarried had a higher
current outlook on life than those who had not remarried
(Montenegro, 2004).

Divorce has some consequences for aging parents' relationships with their adult children. A longitudinal study suggested that divorced fathers experience less contact with
their adult children, but that divorced mothers have more
frequent contact with at least one adult child (Shapiro, 2003).
Other studies showed that divorced elders with functional
difficulties received less help from their children (Pezzin,
Pollak, & Schone, 2008) and perceived less support from kin

(Curran, McLanahan, & Knab, 2003), and that fathers lose more support from kin than mothers. A high level of predivorce solidarity between mothers and children may result in less disruption of affectual and associational solidarity (Nakonezny, Rodgers, & Nussbaum, 2003), but this finding did not hold for divorced fathers. Because men are more likely to remarry after divorce, support may be forthcoming from new wives but not necessarily stepchildren (Clawson & Ganong, 2002; Pezzin et al., 2008). However, men who remain single may have difficulty finding kin to assist them when their health becomes compromised in late life.

Studies of dating and remarriage among older adults are also sparse. Although men are more likely to remarry than women, relatively few do so: only 2% of older widows and 20% of older widowers remarry (Smith et al., 1991). In an interesting study of widows' and widowers' desires to date and remarry, Carr (2004) found that men with low or average levels of social support at 6 months postloss were more likely than women to report interest in remarrying. At 6 months after a spouse's death, men were more likely than women to desire remarriage (30% vs. 16%), to desire dating (17% vs. 6%), and to be dating at present (15% vs. less than 1%). However, at 18 months postloss, men and women did not vary in their desire to remarry, although this desire remained below 30% for both sexes. Men were still more likely to want to date and actually date than women at 18 months postloss. Carr (2004) also found that social support from friends reduced a widower's desire to remarry but increased the odds that widows would seek remarriage. Thus, gender seems to play an important role in response to widowhood in terms of dating and remarriage.

Problems in remarriage may occur when one or both partners has not adequately grieved the lost spouse or continues
a relationship with an ex-spouse following divorce. Also,
problems with adult children, particularly a triangulation of
the adult child in the new marriage, may create conflict between the couple and threaten the success of a late-life remarriage. Unresolved issues of money and inheritance may
also create tensions in late-life remarriages. The following
vignette addresses problems with a dependent adult child
that affected marital conflict and quality in a remarriage.

JACK AND LINDA: A REMARRIAGE TRIANGLE

Jack and Linda Tyler, aged 68 and 64, respectively, had
been married 18 months when they sought marriage counseling. They both were widowed when they met at a church
social and were married after a 6-month courtship. Both
had grown children in their 30s and 40s. Jack's only daughter, Mary, aged 35, had been diagnosed with dysthymia and
dependent personality disorder in early adulthood. She was
single, had low self-esteem, and had difficulty holding a job.
Although living on her own when they met and married,
Mary had since lost her job and car and moved in with Jack
and Linda. The couple agreed to this arrangement on a
temporary basis, but Mary had been with them nearly a
year, and Linda's patience for this arrangement was wearing thin.

Linda, always assertive and successful in her endeavors,
had little tolerance for Mary's sad demeanor and lack of ini-
tiative. She wanted Mary out of the house and back on her
own as soon as possible. She believed that "there's no room

for two grown women in the same household." She also was angry with Jack for withholding information about Mary's problems until she experienced the crisis that led her to move in with them. Jack and Linda's arguments had escalated recently, and Linda was considering separating from Jack. They decided to see Mary's therapist for marriage counseling, expecting that if the counseling was successful, Mary eventually would join them for family therapy. This therapist was found 12 years ago through Jack's work, which had an employee assistance program (EAP) that offered brief therapy to employees and their family members. The EAP counselor referred Jack and his first wife to this therapist for help with Mary when she first began having problems living on her own. Although Linda had some misgivings about seeing a counselor who had already established a relationship with Jack, she could see the potential benefits to working with someone who knew Mary and her difficulties.

The therapist began by asking for their courtship story. They tell of a quick, deep connection and falling in love easily, much to their surprise. Linda had been on her own for several years and had no intention of seeking another husband. But, Jack was "just too good to pass up." Likewise, Jack had been widowed for 3 years and had dated some, but Linda was the "only woman I had met that I could love." They shared a passion for cars, and both held leadership positions in their church. "There are no wallflowers in this marriage," said Linda with a smile. "But neither of us seems to know how to back down once the argument gets started," Jack said with a frown spreading across his face.

Linda was proud of her two daughters, who were both professional women with high-powered careers. They seemed to balance work and family issues effortlessly. "I guess this makes it really hard for me with Mary," Linda noted. "Me and my girls are so assertive, and Mary just seems so dependent and passive! I have no idea of how to help her!" The therapist asked Linda if Mary was looking for her help. Taken aback, Linda said, "Hmm, at this point, I guess not. She looks for ways to leave the room whenever I start asking her questions about a job search."

Jack's children had been less successful than Linda's. His son was an autoworker laid off from his job periodically. Even though Mary had a college degree and a profession in demand, she obtained and lost a series of jobs in her field, usually because of excessive absences from work. Her treatment for depression had also been characterized by successes and failures, usually because she stopped taking medication when she felt really good for a while. Jack realized that he had gotten into a pattern of rescuing Mary, but he did not know what else to do. Jack's first wife was better able to communicate with Mary than he had been; now that she was gone, Jack felt somewhat lost himself when trying to talk with Mary.

Case Analysis

Jack and Linda's marriage had been affected by Mary's emotional problems and inability to live independently. However, this couple was at odds on how to resolve the situation, and neither understood how to de-escalate conflict. Linda saw Mary's independence as the only viable solution to the integrity of the marriage, and Jack saw his daughter

as someone with a mental illness who could not avoid having lapses into dependence and depression. Thus, he was
willing to help Mary until she could get on her feet again,
but he lacked skills in working with his daughter to achieve
that goal.

The therapist needed to get this couple to articulate
workable goals to resolve the situation. Both Jack and Linda's current positions were unrealistic given the depth and
duration of Mary's mental problems, Linda's desire for
Mary to become as independent as her own daughters, and
Linda's desire to be the only woman in the house. Yet, an
indefinite tolerance of Mary's coresidence was likely to lead
to the dissolution of this couple's marriage.

By getting the couple to re-create their courtship, the
therapist gained a sense of how much they still cared about
each other and how motivated they were to work on the
marital relationship. This therapist was encouraged by what
she heard and saw in the first session; Jack and Linda still
bantered playfully and seemed to genuinely like each other.
At this time, both seemed motivated to find a solution other
than divorce.

INTERVENTIONS

Initial interventions consisted of two phases: couple therapy and family therapy.

Phase 1: Couple Therapy

Using a systems approach, the therapist decided to work
with the couple's subsystem first in conjoint therapy. One of
the therapist's goals was to provide information to this couple about dysthymia and dependent personality disorder so

that the couple could develop an improved understanding of Mary's problems and behavior patterns. If better understanding were achieved, then more tolerance of her behavior patterns could be developed as a prelude to setting goals with Mary for her independence. Another goal was to teach the couple communication skills to help them deescalate conflicts and discuss issues more effectively. With these therapeutic goals in mind, additional joint sessions for the couple were scheduled.

The couple worked both in sessions and in homework assignments to improve their communication skills. They made some progress, but Linda's anger at Jack for not being informed of Mary's problems before they married still flared up during arguments at home. When it did, Jack withdrew, and the couple felt that they were backsliding. The therapist asked Jack to talk about why he did not tell Linda about Mary's problems, asking Linda to listen and not respond. Jack revealed that he was afraid of losing her if he told her everything, but that he realized he made a big mistake in withholding information about Mary. He realized that he breached Linda's trust and sold her short with respect to her love for him and their ability to work things out.

He then told Linda how much he loved her, but that he had always been afraid of anger, dating back to childhood when he watched hostile, sometimes out-of-control, exchanges between his parents. Sometimes, he would pick a fight with one of his parents so that they would stop fighting with each other. He would like to be forgiven for his past behavior so that they could move forward in their marriage. He promised to be open and honest with Linda and to work toward getting Mary out of their house. He wanted to earn Linda's trust again.

Linda was visibly moved by these statements. She acknowledged that she would have to forgive Jack if the marriage was to succeed. She stated that some of her toughness was a defense against being hurt by others. She had also wondered whether Jack really loved her given his unwillingness to be forthcoming about Mary and his fierce arguing style. These thoughts had left her feeling quite vulnerable. When she felt vulnerable, she attacked. Linda said that she could see how this made things worse for them. She would work to soften her approach to their discussions, especially those that involved talking about Mary.

The therapist suggested that Jack and Mary work on solutions to Mary's independence without Linda's involvement in this process. Jack was committed to getting Mary to live independently, but when Linda was triangled into the father-daughter relationship, Mary seemed to resent it, and nothing was accomplished. By staying out of their discussions, Linda was also likely to experience less impatience and frustration with Mary, which was good for both her marriage and her relationship with Mary.

Phase 2: Family Therapy

Once Jack and Mary were discussing her situation, the therapist invited Mary to join Jack and Linda for therapy sessions. The therapist began by discussing relationship triangles, noting that they are a normal occurrence in family life. However, in their relationship triangle, it appeared that no one felt content, and anxiety levels had escalated. When anxiety gets too high, people distance themselves from each other, and such distancing leads to discontent in all relationships within the triangle. The therapist asked each person to talk about his or her position in the triangle as currently experienced.

Mary: I'm on the outside looking in. Linda is a powerful lady; she just kind of took over the household when she married Dad. She has strong ideas for how I should live my life, too. I think she compares me to her daughters all the time. I'm not her daughter, and I couldn't live up to her expectations!

Jack: I love both Mary and Linda. I want what is best for both of them. I don't know how to get there, though. I wish they could get along, but I don't think they're at a point where they even like each other. I try to figure out ways we can interact together, but Mary doesn't seem to want Linda around her. I take my cues from them now and just back off.

Linda: I want a happy marriage, and I want Mary to be happy, too. I admit I've had a hard time understanding how Mary can be satisfied living at home with her Dad and stepmom. I would just like to understand Mary better, but I get the feeling that she just wants to be left alone. Lately, I just have backed off and decided to let Mary be.

CASE ANALYSIS

This remarried family had been unable to form positive, loving relationships. Instead of trying to form a friendship with Mary, Linda began trying to problem solve with her once she moved in with Mary and Jack. Mary certainly got the message that she was not wanted in her dad and step-mom's home and understandably resented it. At the same time, Mary's lengthy dependence on her father for financial support was undermining her efforts to be autonomous and regain a healthier lifestyle. Her presence had also put a strain on her dad's marriage as Linda did not see coresidence with Mary as part of the marital bargain.

One goal of family therapy was to see if Linda and Mary would take steps toward building a trusting relationship that was more akin to a friendship than a traditional mother-daughter bond. Healthy stepparent–stepchild relationships are difficult to form and nearly impossible to achieve when the two parties do not spend considerable time getting to know each other in nonthreatening contexts.

Another goal was for Jack to affirm his love and commitment to both women by trying to meet their needs while getting off the sidelines to take a more active role in Mary's future plans. Having recently restored goodwill and better communication in his marriage, he needed to develop a plan with Mary for her to regain some independence.

FOLLOW-UP INTERVENTIONS

The therapist met next with Mary and Jack to help them develop a plan for Mary's independence and eventually move to her own place. Mary was unwilling to include Linda in this process initially. In the past, Mary's mother had done the heavy lifting in helping Mary get back to independence; now, it was time for Jack to take on this role.

Mary began by talking about her deep sadness at her mother's death and her dad's remarriage. She noted that although her dad had waited an appropriate length of time before remarrying, she was disappointed at seeing her mother replaced, especially by someone as aggressive as Linda. She was still trying to get used to the idea that her mother was no longer around to love and help her.

Jack responded by validating Mary's feelings of sadness and noted that he was so happy to have Linda in his life that he did not anticipate Mary's concerns or ask her or her siblings how they felt about the marriage. As for not informing Linda about Mary's mental health issues, he could see that not talking with his children about his marriage plans had created resentment that needed to be addressed. He asked Mary's forgiveness.

In the next session, Jack and Mary informed the therapist that they had begun talking about what Mary needed to get out on her own. Mary wanted to resume medication for depression, and she had promised her father that she would take it faithfully. He agreed to pay for it until she could get work and health insurance again. They were at odds about the timing of her moving out. Mary wanted to move out immediately, but Jack wanted her to actively look for work and get a job before she moved out. He also wanted her to take the medication for a few weeks before moving. With the therapist's help, they reached a compromise.

At that point, Mary resumed brief individual therapy. A few weeks later, she came in with Linda to work on their relationship. They explored common interests and agreed to spend more time together in mutually enjoyable activities in an effort to build a friendly bond. Mary informed the therapist a few months later that she was on her own, working, and having dinner with Jack and Linda weekly. She said, "While Linda and I will never be like Mom and me, she's beginning to show signs of being a pretty good stepmom after all. I'm glad you didn't give up on us."

MILD COGNITIVE IMPAIRMENT AND DEMENTIA

One problem facing increasing numbers of older adults and their close relatives is determining whether the elder is experiencing normal memory loss, MCI, or dementia. It is difficult to decide when the time is right to urge a loved one to see a doctor for an evaluation, and older adults themselves may resist the idea, fearing the worst.

There are many excellent sources of information on normal memory loss with aging as well as dementia and its related disorders. The Alzheimer's Association offers information that makes useful distinctions between normal memory loss and dementia. The American Association of Retired Persons has posted extensive materials on memory-related issues on its Web site (http://www.aarp.org). The Harvard Medical School (2008) offered an excellent publication, *Improving Memory: Understanding Age-Related Memory Loss*. With sections that described normal memory loss in aging and conditions for which seeing a doctor is advised, this publication can assist therapists, older adults, and family members alike in determining whether additional steps are necessary to evaluate the nature of memory problems.

Understanding the nature of cognitive impairment is difficult and takes time. Ideally, consultation with a neurologist, neuropsychologist, or geriatric psychiatrist is needed for a comprehensive assessment before effective strategies for treating cognitive problems can be devised. In the absence of a specialist, a family physician can administer memory tests.

Sometimes, the person with memory difficulties is adept at compensating for them (at least for awhile) or will decline a trip to the appropriate professional for memory testing. In addition, some caregivers I have interviewed see no reason to seek a formal diagnosis, especially in the early stages of a spouse's memory loss. They view it as emotionally detrimental to the elder. Instead, they may desire information on how to respond to certain behaviors exhibited by their loved ones with MCI or dementia. They also may want to know where to go to get assistance with both medical and social needs. Still other caregivers see *some* memory loss as just a natural part of the aging process and may not define what is happening with their friend or relative as problematic. In more than a few families, conflict occurs when an adult child wants to "do something about Dad's failing memory," and the parent wants to delay any assessment or treatment. These are situations for which family counseling may be beneficial. Consider the situation presented next.

JOHN AND JOYCE: SPOUSES DEALING WITH COGNITIVE IMPAIRMENT

After some prodding by their daughter Angela, John (age 72) and Joyce (age 64) Powers agreed to see a therapist about their increasing marital distress. John was retired, but

Joyce was still working. Joyce was extremely frustrated with John's recent behavior changes. Instead of doing his house and yard chores while she was at work, he would sit around and watch TV most of the day. When asked why he had not done the chores, he said that after getting started on them, he would feel fatigued and lie down for a brief nap. Sometimes, he forgot why he was outside and came in to gather his thoughts. Somehow, the time would pass, and nothing would get done. He did not really know why, but he was tired of Joyce's nagging. She accused him of being lazy and had begun calling him several times a day to ask if he had done certain chores yet. It was clear that John resented the phone calls; he felt belittled and hounded by Joyce.

The therapist inquired about John's overall health history, which had been good. There was no history of stroke, cardiac problems, or depression. John did acknowledge some difficulty remembering things, but he assumed it was just part of the aging process. Joyce said that their 40-year marriage had been a good one until recently, but now it seemed as if John was a different person, one with whom she had trouble getting along and saw as undependable.

The therapist recommended a full workup by John's doctor and some memory testing and encouraged them to return to see her when the results were known. She did not hear from the Powers for 6 months. Then, Joyce called and requested an immediate appointment. She was panicked. John had left yesterday for the hardware store and was not home when she returned from work. She knew he had been gone for several hours. After searching for him herself, she called the police, and John was found later in a nearby shopping mall, utterly lost and unaware of the time of day. Joyce acknowledged that the doctor's exam had confirmed "mild cognitive impairment," but she figured that they could just handle things on their own. Now, she knew differently but was not sure of what to do: "I don't want to quit my job; I love it, it is my social world as well as a paycheck. But I just can't leave John alone anymore. What should I do?" Once these words were out of her mouth, Joyce sobbed uncontrollably.

CASE ANALYSIS

A diagnosis of MCI or dementia often turns the world of a couple and family upside down. Many couples, like the Powers, initially deny the implications of the diagnosis, preferring instead to attribute memory problems and apathy to laziness or a lack of focus (Blieszner, Roberto, Wilcox, Barham, & Winston, 2007). For many of these families, it is only when presented with dramatic, undeniable evidence of persistent memory loss or unsafe behaviors that they begin to fashion plans to cope with the problem.

WHAT IS MILD COGNITIVE IMPAIRMENT?

Mild cognitive impairment (MCI) is a newer diagnostic category that refers to "the transitional state between the cognitive changes of normal aging and very early dementia" (Petersen & Negash, 2008, p. 45). Researchers and clinicians have sought to understand MCI primarily to provide early intervention that may prevent or minimize later disability. There are two major types of MCI: *amnestic*, which includes memory impairment, and nonamnestic, with impairments in nonmemory cognitive domains. A good clinical workup will determine a likely cause for the MCI, which can include degenerative processes, vascular problems, psychiatric contributors like depression or anxiety, or medical disorders such as congestive heart failure.

Persons with the amnestic type of MCI progress to Alzheimer's disease at the rate of about 10–15% per year (Petersen et al., 1999). Not all persons with MCI necessarily experience Alzheimer's disease, although some of them will progress to other types of dementia, such as vascular or Lewy body dementias (Petersen & Negash, 2008).

Few treatments are available to persons with MCI at present. Clinical trials with medicines such as donepezil (Aricept) have found that their use *may* delay a diagnosis of Alzheimer's disease in persons with MCI (Petersen et al., 2005). Other research is ongoing.

OPTIMAL CARE MANAGEMENT STRATEGIES AND THERAPEUTIC INTERVENTIONS

Research strongly suggests that caregiver or care partner strategies for managing the lifestyle and actions of persons with cognitive impairment and dementia may affect the care recipient's behavior (de Vugt et al., 2004). In this study, researchers identified three prominent care management strategies based in part on whether the caregiver accepted the situation and problems related to dementia. Those who did not accept the situation were called *nonadapters*, and their characteristic approach to the person with memory loss was to respond with impatience, irritation, or anger. They often tried to manage behavior problems by confronting or ignoring the person with dementia.

Caregivers who accepted the situation were called *adapters* and were divided into two categories: nurturing and supporting. Nurturers took on most responsibilities in their households, tried to protect the person with dementia, and saw the spouse or parent as childlike, no longer regarded as an equal. Supporting caregivers, by contrast, found ways to adapt to demented persons' level of functioning and allowed them to lead the way. These caregivers talked things over with their loved ones, exhibited patience while dealing with behavior issues exhibited by the person with dementia, and tried to stimulate the person to do things, either alone or together. De Vugt and colleagues (2004) found that over a year, caregivers who used nonadaptive strategies saw more hyperactive symptoms in the persons for whom they cared and felt less competent as caregivers than those who were supporters. These nonadapting caregivers also reported higher levels of depression and neuroticism than the caregivers using accepting strategies. Thus, care strategies chosen can play an important role in the well-being of both the caregiver and the person with cognitive impairment.

These findings have important implications for those counseling couples or families with a member who has MCI or dementia. Blieszner et al. (2007) documented that care strategies begin early in the care process, and that in their study, spouses used strategies that were both problematic and reflective of resilience in challenging situations. They recommended interventions early in the care process to optimize the care environment for couples and families facing MCI and possible dementia.

For persons with MCI, there are good days and bad days with respect to memory and functional ability. Such fluctuations can create confusion for couples and families coping with the issues they present, especially when they are in denial or the diagnosis of cognitive impairment is new. Loss of a spouse gradually to dementia or Alzheimer's disease is an example of an ambiguous loss, a condition described by Boss (2007) as an unclear loss in which a person is perceived as physically present but psychologically absent. Such ambiguity presents caregivers with many dilemmas about how best to respond to their spouses, parents, or other loved ones. Frank (2007) labeled ambiguous loss as part of an anticipatory grief process experienced by most caregivers of persons with dementia or Alzheimer's disease. Components of anticipatory grief such as sadness and longing for the person who used to be or worry and felt isolation are named by both spouse and adult child caregivers of those with dementia far more often than hands-on care tasks as the biggest barriers they have faced as caregivers. Anticipatory grief appears to be pervasive throughout the dementia care process (Holley & Mast, 2009), including after institutionalization of the person with dementia (Frank, 2007).

Blieszner and colleagues (2007) recommended that therapists help couples and families come to grips with this form of ambiguous loss so that stress and confusion are normalized, attributions of behavior to *memory loss* instead of other causes are made, and problem solving can commence. Couples and families need information about the disease, strategies for managing it as well as possible, and support from key members of their social networks, including family, friends, neighbors, coworkers, and professional providers. A reconstruction of spouse and family "roles, rules, and rituals" (Blieszner et al., 2007, p. 207) needs to be undertaken as part of that process.

CONTINUED: JOHN AND JOYCE: SPOUSES DEALING WITH COGNITIVE IMPAIRMENT

After John and Joyce Powers reconnected with the therapist following John's wandering episode, the therapist began interventions with them.

INTERVENTIONS WITH THE POWERS FAMILY

The therapist worked for several sessions with John and Joyce Powers together to help them mourn the loss of their prior lifestyle and the dreams they had for Joyce's retirement, such as taking trips abroad. The couple was given basic literature about MCI, and in later sessions, John was encouraged to join a local Alzheimer's Association support group for persons in early stages of dementia or with MCI. Such groups have been highly praised by persons in the early stages of dementia as beneficial to both them and their care partners (Alzheimer's Association, 2008).

Joyce reduced her work hours but did not quit work altogether. Daughter Angela was included later in some family counseling and agreed to take her dad for some outings with his grandchildren while Joyce was at work. Use of other social network members to increase John's daily activities was explored, with the result that a long-time friend of John's took him to a local restaurant for coffee and conversation with a group of friends on mornings when Joyce was working. Neighbors agreed to check on John when he was at home alone.

The therapist also directed Angela and Joyce to a U.S. Department of Health and Human Services Web site, the National Clearinghouse for Long-Term Care Information (http://www.longtermcare.gov). This Web site contains well-researched information on three important areas: understanding long-term care, planning for long-term care, and paying for long-term care. By learning more about long-term care, it was hoped that this family would be able to anticipate future needs for John and Joyce and prepare for the "road ahead."

Finally, the couple developed a realistic plan for John's participation in household chores. He performed chores that were less demanding mentally, such as vacuuming and dusting around the house. At their final therapy session, Joyce expressed relief that she and John were getting along much better than before, and she felt less stress and depression. She felt grateful for the resources they had successfully tapped.

CHAPTER 4

Working With Intergenerational Issues in Late Life

Throughout the life course, care and assistance is often provided by one generation to members of other generations to maintain close intergenerational ties. Though much research and public attention focuses on adult children providing help to their elderly parents, older adults or couples often care for adult children who cannot function on their own, or minor grandchildren whose parents cannot care for them. Here, I present three case studies in which younger generations assist older family members, followed by two case studies in which older parents or grandparents provide care to younger generations.

ADULT CHILDREN CARING FOR AGING PARENTS

Adult children make up 42% of all individuals providing care to elderly persons. The majority of child caregivers are daughters or daughters-in-law to the care recipient. Parent care can be a fulfilling experience, an opportunity to return love freely given to children throughout their lives, but it also can be physically and mentally taxing and can strain relationships with parents and other family members. Regardless of the type of care experience, many children become caregivers because of a strong sense of duty to parents or parents-in-law, a desire to reciprocate for care given by parents earlier in life, or because no one else is available to provide assistance. Elderly parents may be widowed, divorced, or married, but as more couples live well into old age, many who need help have a spouse, but one who is unable to provide help or who is limited in what he or she can do by personal health problems or functional limitations.

Adult child caregivers can experience many stressors. For most, care provision, especially as it intensifies, puts limits on time available for other activities, especially leisure or family activities. These constraints can affect relationships between the generations. In one of my research projects, a caregiver daughter who provided intensive care described these effects on her family:

> My children are jealous of it . . . because I cannot go and do with them. Everything now is done here. . . . We don't go to the beach like we used to; we don't go camping as a big family anymore; everything has to be done on the back patio or in the kitchen type thing. Everything's done from here. They think that it's wearing me out. (personal communication, May 16, 1995)

Some adult children who are tapped as caregivers are still caring for children of their own. There are an estimated 3.5 million potential "sandwich caregivers," representing nearly a quarter of all potential caregivers (Spillman & Pezzin, 2000). Other studies found that anywhere from 17% to 33% of adult child caregivers are also caring for one or more children at home or young adults not yet launched (Grundy &

Henretta, 2006; National Association of Professional Geriatric Care Managers, 2008). These caregivers may find their children's needs competing with time spent in caring for a parent or parent-in-law. On the other hand, such multigenerational households may cooperate, rather than compete, for time and attention. My research suggested that some sandwich caregiver's children offered support to their parents by doing household chores or assisting in hands-on care themselves (Piercy, 2007a). A family's values or the degree of multigenerational family solidarity may influence willingness to offer help to both older and younger generations.

Many adult children who provide care to parents at a distance experience significant challenges to their lifestyles and well-being. Studies suggest that women who live at a distance are more likely to engage in frequent, intense care activities with their parents than men (Joseph & Hallman, 1996). For these caregivers, experience with siblings varies, with some collaborating well with siblings who are providing daily elder care and others assessing sibling contributions as inadequate (Roff, Martin, Jennings, Parker, & Harmon, 2007). What is striking in these studies is that few families had developed a care plan in advance of their entry to the caregiver role. Such planning becomes crucial in situations in which the primary caregiver lives at a distance and has little flexibility in making accommodations with employers (Roff, Toseland, Martin, Fine, & Parker, 2003). For some long-distance caregivers, a geriatric care manager hired to help coordinate parent care in the home can be a lifeline.

Why don't more families plan for elder care needs? Adult children may be reluctant to broach this subject with their parents, and many aging parents prefer not to think about the time when their abilities will be seriously compromised. Years ago, I asked my undergraduate students to ask their parents what they would prefer in terms of late-life caring arrangements. Many of them said their mothers shared specific ideas for their care. However, of their fathers, the students said things like, "He'd just prefer to go into the woods and die," or "He wouldn't answer my question." A study by the Pew Research Center (2009) lent some support to these ideas. The study found that older parents were more likely than their adult children to initiate discussions of future needs, but that the issue they most often discussed was that of wills and estate planning (76% of older adults surveyed). Discussions about what to do if parents could no longer live independently were initiated by only 55% of these older adults. Holding discussions about frailty and care until death does not come easily to a society that promotes individualism and personal responsibility. However, such discussions may prevent family problems later.

Having "the talk" with aging parents, preferably while they are still healthy, is an important step for adult children to take. In addition to estate and will considerations, there is the need to obtain advance directives. While gaining in popularity, advance directives still are not in place for many older adults. Advance directives include giving another family member power over health care and financial decisions when elders are unable to make those decisions themselves. Also, decisions about lifesaving treatments can be addressed in a living will. Finally, there are questions about how elderly relatives wish to be cared for when they develop cognitive or functional limitations. For most persons, financial planning is needed to ensure that the elder's wishes can be carried out to the fullest extent possible. I discuss the option of purchasing long-term care insurance in Chapter 6.

One additional layer of complexity for middle-aged caregivers is employment. Studies show that over half of persons caring for a friend or relative work full time; currently, over 7 million workers provide moderately intense levels of care for an adult over age 18 (MetLife Mature Market Institute & National Alliance for Caregiving, 2006). Employment and caregiving are difficult to balance, with a risk of decreased productivity at work and increased odds of scaling back or relinquishing employment for some caregivers. In one study, Fredriksen-Goldsen and Scharlach (2006) found that caregivers who reported the greatest level of strain were females with primary caregiving responsibilities. They also reported more demanding work conditions and lower incomes. By far, family and work demands contributed the lion's share to caregiving strain. With respect to resources, few companies have formal programs in place for employee caregivers (Yagoda, 2004), although increasing numbers of them are offering resource and referral services, such as the Eldercare Locator service (http://www.eldercare.gov) or employee assistance services that offer brief counseling for employees and their families.

THE ROLE OF EXISTING FAMILY DYNAMICS

When an elder care situation arises in families, existing relationships play a role in decisions made and quality of care provided. Relationships between parents and children often fluctuate throughout the lifetime of both generations. They are influenced by myriad factors, including age, parent and child gender, marital stability in both generations, and important life events at both individual and family levels. Intergenerational relationships can be characterized by solidarity (Bengtson, Giarrusso, Mabry, & Silverstein, 2002), ambivalence (Luscher & Pillemer, 1998), and emotional distance (Silverstein & Bengtson, 1997).

Relationship dynamics have significant implications for those working with aging families. An adult child's willingness to help parents in old age may be compromised by deteriorating relationships between family members or long-time detachment in the parent-child relationship. Conversely, willingness to care may be fostered by a lifetime of tight-knit or sociable interaction. Therapists need to thoroughly assess the nature and closeness of parent-child relationships over the life course as part of a comprehensive strategy to assist either parents or children in negotiating successfully for assistance when needed. Issues of triangulation, emotional cutoffs, and overfunctioning or underfunctioning reciprocity may play a strong role in who is willing to provide care and the type and quality of care that is offered to parents.

The position of adult children in their life course may also factor into decisions about how family care is provided. If one or more of the adult children are in a transition period of their own, they may be more (if at retirement age) or less (because of job promotion and relocation) able to offer assistance. For adult children with very old (over age 85) parents, the children's own health problems may interfere with or prevent them from being able to offer hands-on care. The adult children of centenarians are often in their 60s and 70s. Thus, it sometimes becomes a grandchild, niece, or nephew who looks after an elderly relative.

Sibling relationships also may affect who is willing to participate in parent care and the nature of help that is offered. Although many sibling groups develop a well-regarded system of providing parent care, not all are able to accommodate both care receivers and each other. Siblings who are responsible for the majority of care provision may resent distant siblings who cannot provide daily care to parents. For example, a daughter caring for her father with dementia may feel that all siblings should contribute equally despite the fact that several siblings live more than 1,000 miles away from the father. Siblings may disagree on when a father should stop driving and how to accomplish that goal. In a third instance, one sibling may assume the bulk of care provision, then pressure the parent to amend his or her will to give the caregiver sibling the lion's share of a formerly equally distributed inheritance. These types of situations, left unchecked during the parent's lifetime, can create a wedge in family solidarity that may never be resolved.

CAREGIVER BURDEN, DEPRESSION, AND BURNOUT

Many caregivers who seek professional help are experiencing great burden and possibly burnout in the caregiver role. *Burden* in this context refers to the financial, physical, and emotional effects of caring for someone with a disabling condition (George & Gwyther, 1986). *Burnout* is defined as exhaustion stemming from long-term stress, and symptoms of burnout may include depression, constant fatigue, social withdrawal, feelings of helplessness, and increased use of stimulants and alcohol (Seligson, 2009). Desires to withdraw from or avoid the situation are not uncommon when caregivers experience burnout.

There can be many reasons for these reactions. Some caregivers perform 20 or more hours per week of hands-on care, including personal care as well as management of the person's finances, home, and yard. In addition, as noted, most caregivers have other competing responsibilities. Some caregivers try to do these tasks by themselves because they do not wish to "burden" others. Others have tried to secure support from other family members, to no avail, or may live in a rural area with few resources like support groups or in-home service providers.

Not all care recipients are easy to care for. Some may act ungrateful or resist caregiver assistance. Other persons in the throes of dementia or Alzheimer's disease display behaviors that accompany the cognitive impairment, such as agitation, anger outbursts, delusional thinking, or profound apathy. Such behavioral disturbances, as they are called, are upsetting and burdensome to most family caregivers, and their presence early in the dementia process has been associated with early institutionalization by caregivers (Gaugler, Kane, Kane, & Newcomer, 2005). For family members caring for a person with dementia, aid in the forms of overnight help and assistance with personal care tasks may help to delay nursing home placement of the person with dementia (Gaugler et al., 2000).

Most caregivers who attend counseling are looking for help in dealing with burden and burnout. There are many ways to assist them. These strategies are described next.

GENERAL STRATEGIES FOR
HELPING FAMILY CAREGIVERS

Drawing on the work of Rabow, Hauser, and Adams (2004) and Dunkin and Anderson-Hanley (1998) and my experience of working with and studying caregivers, I suggest that there are seven general issues in working with elders and their family caregivers that deserve special attention.

The first is *acknowledgement of caregiver struggles and triumphs*. Many caregivers need repeated validation of the hard work they do every single day. The world of the caregiver is one of ups and downs, with no 2 days alike, and many caregivers are both physically and emotionally exhausted. For some caregivers, care provision takes 3 months of their lives; for others, it may be as many as 20 years. Their lives often revolve around the caring role, with little attention paid to self. While that focus may not be the healthiest for them in the long run, it is a reality for many caregivers, especially those with few resources, and we must keep it in mind as we respond to caregiver concerns. Be patient with caregivers; their commitments to care provision can be strong. Validate the caregiver's hard work while helping them find creative solutions, including self-care, to their problems or challenges.

Second, *good communication* between helping professional and caregiver is crucial. Choose your words carefully. Some caregivers may not be "ready" to hear what we have to say the first time, especially early in a disease process, when either caregiver denial is present or the enormity of the transition the family is undergoing has not yet sunk in (as is often the case in diagnoses of dementia or a terminal disease, such as certain types of cancer). Whatever message needs to be communicated may need saying again and in different ways by different people before it sinks in and is accepted. A clear, caring patient communication style is imperative.

Third, *provide information about the disease, its customary course, and treatments.* Assess the caregiver's knowledge and understanding of the relative's illness and its prognosis (Dunkin & Anderson-Hanley, 1998). This is important for any illness, but it is crucial to those who care for persons with dementia. Conflict between caregiver and care recipient may stem from a lack of understanding of the illness process and the perceptions by caregivers of the care recipient's degree of control over their symptoms or behaviors. Friction between the care dyad may be reduced when caregivers have accurate and comprehensive information about the illness and its likely course.

The fourth general issue is *assistance with decision making.* In an excellent study of persons with cognitive impairments and their family caregivers, Feinberg and Whitlatch (2002) noted that the everyday care situations at home tend to produce the most conflict among family members, and decisions about those situations, such as when to bathe, whether to engage support services, or whether to accept help from other family members, often require careful negotiation. Sensitive, understanding counselors with established relationships of caregiver trust can assist with those decision processes. An understanding of both what is strongly valued and the existing family dynamics is often necessary to be effective in assisting with decision making.

Regarding the fifth issue, caregivers and elders usually want to preserve the home care arrangement for as long as possible. This is a difficult undertaking as persons with dementia progress in the disease or persons with chronic illnesses experience more functional limitations. Conversely, the primary caregiver's health may be imperiled and new care arrangements needed. When possible, we need to *help families find ways to support caring at home* unless or until the care situation is dangerous for the elderly person and the person's caregiver. To achieve this goal, a thorough understanding is needed of home and community-based services available to older adults and their caregivers. Chapter 6 describes in detail a number of resources that are available to support home-centered long-term care as well as alternatives when home care is no longer feasible.

Family caregivers also need to have these services and their payment mechanisms carefully presented to them so that they make informed decisions about accessing services. Keep in mind that some caregivers, particularly spouses, may be reluctant to use in-home services or services like adult day centers for the following reasons: They fear that their relative will not accept anyone but them as caregivers; they feel that it is *their* responsibility to provide all types of care; or they worry about security issues, such as theft of property or neglect of the care recipient by a nonfamily provider. Help them to find an agency or independent provider with an excellent reputation for providing home and community-based care. Often, the staff of the local Area Agency on Aging will know each of the principal home care agencies or adult day centers and be able to offer their ideas on which agency or center may be best for a given family. If seeking the services of a self-employed home care provider, be sure to encourage families to get references and ask questions about the person's experience and practices. The National Association for Home Care and Hospice (http://www.nahc.org) has an excellent online publication, *How Do I Select the Right Home Care Provider?* (2008b), that can be of great value to therapists and their client families alike. For caregivers living in rural areas, explore telehealth resources, which are described in more detail in Chapter 6.

In addition to services for dependent elders, there are structured interventions for stressed caregivers offered in a number of locations around the country. Consider contacting a nearby medical school or university psychology department to see if there are any intervention programs available for caregivers helping persons with specific diagnoses, such as dementia, cancer, or arthritis. Some intervention programs require that the caregivers travel to a clinic setting, while others may be offered in home settings. Some interventions for persons with dementia also train caregivers to interact more effectively with those for whom they care.

Sixth, providing help with *emotions* may facilitate the resolution of difficult care situations. I have described the mixed emotions, burden, and burnout experienced by many dementia caregivers. Experiencing those emotions needs to be framed to caregivers as a normal reaction to situations of ambiguous loss rather than as a pathological response to stress (Boss, 2006). I have noticed that with married couples, any talk of institutionalization can be perceived as a threat to their identities as couples and may be rejected in an effort to maintain couplehood or maintain the vow "until death do us part." Many caregivers express strong emotions when describing the challenges they have faced or the deterioration of a loved one's health. Validating these emotions and helping caregivers find appropriate support or ways to better utilize available support is crucial to their well-being and, in turn, that of the person for whom they care. Grandparents caring for grandchildren may be angry with the son or daughter whose behavior, incarceration, or death put them in the situation of providing custodial care for young children. Helping caregivers with difficult emotions takes time; not all caregivers recognize that their symptoms of depression and anxiety stem from conflicted feelings about the situation and person for whom they care.

Finally, we need to *acknowledge bereavement* among those caregivers experiencing physical or emotional losses. Dementia caregivers often begin the grieving process before their relative is deceased, in a process known as *anticipatory grief* (Holley & Mast, 2009). Defined as "a complex concept that encompasses grief in anticipation of the future loss of a loved one, in addition to previously experienced and current losses as a result of the terminal illness" (Holley & Mast, 2009, p. 388), anticipatory grief has been shown to be related to levels of caregiver burden (Holley & Mast, 2009). Some caregivers experience a mix of relief and grief when their care recipient dies or enters an institution. In every caregiver support group to which I have spoken over the years, I have met one or more members whose relative has been deceased for months or years. They handle their grief by keeping memories of their loved ones alive as well as by mentoring those who are going through the processes they once experienced. Grief has no time limit, and caring professionals can acknowledge and support the grieving process in many ways.

In some families, the middle generation consists of an only child. What happens when an only child becomes a caregiver? The following case study gives us insight into the challenges of dementia care when an only child is called on to assist with a parent's care and does not always agree with the caregiver parent. It also offers understanding of the influence of cultural values on care decisions.

MARIA: DEMENTIA ONSET AND CARE IN AN EXTENDED FAMILY

STAGE 1

Maria had a promising career as a family law attorney. Married to Antonio during law school, she was well on her way to making partner by age 32. Unexpectedly, she became pregnant. Her daughter, Rosa, was easy to care for and adapted well to Grandma Esperanza's tender care while Maria worked. Then, shortly after making partner at her firm, she became pregnant with Carlos. Carlos was born with Down syndrome. He was significantly disabled and exhibited behavior problems as he grew older. Feeling torn between work and her children's care but well aware from her work of what excess work strain did to contemporary couples and families, Maria quit her career as an attorney to stay home with Rosa and Carlos.

Her plan worked well for awhile. Antonio, a midlevel manager with a local computer firm, did well financially. Rosa enjoyed participating in several extracurricular activities she could easily attend even though the household had only one working parent. Carlos's behavior improved somewhat with his mother's full attention during afterschool hours. In her spare time, Maria threw herself into organizing support groups for families of children with Down syndrome in her area. On the whole, she was happy, although sometimes she felt a bit blue about her lost law career. How could she best put her keen mind to work? As an only child, she had been groomed for success by her ambitious and poorly educated parents, who had made many sacrifices for her education.

Now, Maria's mother was showing signs of dementia, including wandering away from home at night, and her father, Pablo, was in complete denial. Pablo had always relied heavily on his wife Esperanza's charm for their social and church connections. He did not know how to respond to his wife's increasingly strange behaviors. He seemed angry at Esperanza for what was happening to their marriage. He called Maria and asked her to help out with the meals and cleaning, things her mother could no longer do reliably. Maria did not feel she could refuse him because of all the work he had done to educate her and because of strong values she had that family takes care of family. But, she felt stretched thin and constantly stressed. In addition to these new demands, Antonio frequently traveled around the country on business and was not often home. Thus, she had little help with Carlos, and her mother did not interact well with Carlos now, even though they had been close in his younger years.

Despite stereotypes about Latino families, this family did not have a large extended family on which to draw for support. There was only one aunt, Linda, a sister of Esperanza, and she worked full time to support herself. Exhausted, depressed, and in need of help to understand her mother's condition, Maria turned to a family therapist recommended by a caseworker at the local senior center, which her parents had attended on occasion before her mother's symptoms became too difficult to manage. The therapist listened carefully to Maria's story, drawing out her frustration and her sense of commitment to both generations of her family. She perceived the ambivalence Maria felt about giving adequate time to her parents as well as her own family.

Maria was a sandwich generation caregiver, one who provided assistance to aging parents while raising children of her own. One of these children had special needs. Neither she nor her father fully understood what was happening with her mother or what the future would hold for Esperanza. Maria was requesting information about dementia and help in balancing her own family's needs with those of her parents. Balancing personal and nuclear family needs with provision of parent care is one of the chief challenges for sandwich caregivers, one that seems to create the greatest stressors for adult children.

A counselor who worked with Maria and her family needed to view Maria's extended family as a system, a system that had functioned well until recently. Maria felt strongly that she should reciprocate her parents for their commitment to her well-being and that of her children while they were younger. Thus, it was important to validate the concerns of both generations as well as attune closely to cultural norms and values held by Maria and her parents. The counselor also needed a thorough understanding of the family's resources and the services they may need as Esperanza's dementia progressed. This therapist also needed for Maria to set goals for therapy and to encourage Maria to consider family counseling for Maria, her parents, and Antonio. Antonio was an important part of Maria's system, even though he may not have had a great deal of contact with his in-laws week to week.

INITIAL INTERVENTION

After a thorough assessment, the therapist made several
initial recommendations. She suggested that Esperanza see
her family physician for some memory testing or consider
visiting the memory clinic sponsored by a local university.
After consulting with her father, Maria took her mother to
the memory clinic at the university. When a diagnosis of
Alzheimer's disease was made, Maria and Pablo saw the social worker associated with the clinic to obtain more information about the disease and assessment of what to expect
as the disease progressed. Esperanza was prescribed Aricept,
and after some initial reluctance to take the medication, she
accepted it and showed some improvement in memory and
behavior. Both Maria and her father began attending a
caregiver support group sponsored by the memory clinic.
This group had among its members other Latino caregivers,
who offered a great deal of support and normalization of experiences to Maria and her father.

A diagnosis of dementia of any type is a significant loss to
a family and, ideally, should be grieved. Often, caregivers
feel as if they lose their loved one in steps over a long period
of time, which makes the grieving process different from
that of a loss due to death. Ambiguous loss frequently is experienced (Boss, 2006). Esperanza was physically present,
but with progressive dementia her psychological presence
would diminish over time. With this family, the therapist
and social worker at the memory clinic felt that a support
group might help Maria and Pablo with that grieving process and normalize the emotions that they were experiencing. The fact that there were other Latino family caregivers

attending this support group helped them to accept the group and attend it for a while.

Next, the therapist explored with both Maria and Antonio their plans for Carlos when he had completed schooling. They were not fond of the group home option, but they would like him to work in supported employment and perhaps get an apartment of his own when he reached adulthood. They were connected to the vocational agency of the state that worked with developmentally disabled persons and their families. They also explored the sense of distance they were experiencing in their marriage and discussed ways to share both their responsibilities and their mutual interests. Their relationship improved when Antonio became more involved with their children. He found ways to reduce his travel through Internet videoconferencing. After this therapeutic process was completed, the family terminated therapy.

A family therapist with a systems orientation recognized that Maria needed a strengthened marital subsystem to meet her nuclear and extended family responsibilities. Antonio needed to hear his wife's concerns for her parents, the couple's children, and their marriage. Antonio made a greater commitment to his family, and the family reached a point at which all subsystems were functioning adequately. The couple's rejection of a group home placement for Carlos was in keeping with their values, but wisely they made alternate plans. This decision and its execution over the coming years will be likely to help the sibling subsystem, as Rosa will likely become care manager or caregiver to her brother when her parents are no longer able to fill that role.

Stage 2: New Problems

Maria returned again to the therapist about 2 years later. The problem this time was focused on her father's unwillingness to consider nursing home placement for Esperanza, whose dementia had progressed and who now needed help with multiple activities of daily living, like bathing and grooming. Esperanza was unable to communicate her needs effectively and often did not recognize her husband and daughter. Since Maria's last visit to therapy, Pablo had suffered two heart attacks and was much weaker physically than he was at the time of his wife's diagnosis. Maria was worried that her father would suffer greatly if he continued to attempt (with her help) to care for Esperanza at home. The therapist suggested that Maria bring Pablo with her to therapy, and after much cajoling, he agreed to attend.

SECOND-STAGE INTERVENTION

Once in therapy, Pablo made it clear that he wanted to continue caring for Esperanza at home. For him, it was part of his sacred vow of marriage. Maria understood that she could not force her father to do what *she* believed was best for both her parents, but she wondered how long her father could continue his caregiver role. Maria commented that her father seemed on edge most of the time, and that she was worried about his health. Pablo acknowledged that he did not sleep well but insisted that he must be available to his wife no matter what the hour.

The therapist asked about getting additional help to tend to Esperanza's needs. Aunt Linda, a certified nursing assis-

tant, had offered to help her sister with bathing and housekeeping, but she still worked full time and could only be
there on weekends. The therapist suggested that Maria contact the Area Agency on Aging of the state to see if her parents might qualify for the consumer-directed home care
program. This type of program allows caregivers to choose
their own home care staff, including family members, so
that Linda could be hired by them and paid by the program. After an assessment, it was determined that they did
qualify, and Aunt Linda was willing to cut back to part-
time work to work for her sister 20 hours a week. At first,
Pablo rejected this solution, saying that he "wanted no
charity." But, after a particularly difficult experience with
Esperanza leaving the house at night and ending up at a
neighbor's house while Pablo dozed off, he agreed to the additional help.

STAGE 3: PABLO SEEKS HELP

Much to her surprise, a few weeks later, Pablo contacted
the therapist to request a session for himself. He described
himself as a nervous wreck, and despite the added help in
the house, he still was struggling to sleep. The therapist
noted that she had never had the opportunity to hear from
Pablo what his marriage had been like over the years and
how he felt about what had happened to it. With tears in
his eyes, Pablo told her of the couple's 50-year love story
and how proud both he and Esperanza were of Maria's academic and career accomplishments. "I've lost my best
friend and companion. How could she leave me to go
through the rest of my life alone?" After pausing, Pablo
said, "Now I feel bad because I am talking as if she was

already gone, and she's still alive! What kind of husband am I?"

THIRD-STAGE INTERVENTION

The therapist remarked that such thoughts and feelings are normal for persons in Pablo's situation. Dementia, she said, takes people away from us psychologically long before the person is physically gone. Such conflicting emotions on Pablo's part are understandable. "But I feel so guilty," he cried. "I took a vow; why is it so hard for me to keep it?"

Over the next few weeks, the therapist and Pablo worked together to try to reduce his anxiety. As Pablo realized that his mixed emotions and his feelings of guilt about them were normal in situations of ambiguous loss (Boss, 2006), he was able to accept his feelings and begin the process of finding some ways to reduce his anxiety. He returned to woodworking, a hobby that gave him great pleasure and a creative outlet. With Maria's encouragement, he also began to attend Sunday Mass again. He participated in the sacrament of confession, received absolution for his sins, and was encouraged by his parish priest to stay the course.

As Pablo slowly accepted that ambivalent feelings are a part of the lives of spouses of persons with dementia, he began to sleep better and for longer each night. He also started using some relaxation tapes that Maria had given him and found to his surprise that they were helpful in anxiety reduction and preparing him for sleep at night.

CASE SUMMARY

This series of interventions was complicated but effective because the therapist was knowledgeable about community

resources and when to use them, but more important, the
therapist respected her clients' values and wishes and tried
to build on existing family strengths. She viewed Pablo's
initial resistance to change his caregiver role as an extension
of both strongly valuing independence ("I don't want charity") and concerns about abandoning a loved one (marital
commitment). Pablo's life course differed from that of Maria in important ways; yet, they both shared strong family
values and preferred family over nonfamily service providers to assist dependent family members. Maria and Pablo
had a close, trusting, and functional parent-child subsystem
over the years. Had that not been the case, the therapist
would have needed to spend time building connection in
that subsystem before working on Esperanza's dementia
care plans and Pablo's anxiety issues.

However, the challenges for this family may not be over
with this set of interventions. Because dementia is progressive, if Esperanza lives long enough, she may become too
impaired to remain at home, no matter how much her family wants to keep her there. Much will depend on Pablo's
health and available resources to supplement family care.

Should Pablo's health deteriorate while Esperanza is still
at home, Maria may be faced with assisting two dependent
parents and an amount of care needed in excess of the family's available resources. Some of the care outcomes for persons with dementia hinge on the presence, number, and
type of behavioral disturbances they exhibit. Behavior problems such as delusions and aggressive and violent behavior
are among the most common reasons for institutionalizing
persons with dementia (Coehlo, Hooker, & Bowman, 2007).

In this study, higher levels of caregiver depression also were predictive of institutionalization of the persons with dementia.

A therapist should pay close attention to Maria's health and well-being and encourage her to access therapy and resources as needed. Local chapters of the Alzheimer's Association provide both information and support to caregivers through support groups and referrals for respite care and other services (http://www.alz.org/index.asp).

Dementia caregivers tend to report greater amounts of strain, health, and mental health problems than those who care for elders without cognitive impairment or dementias (Ory, Hoffman, Yee, Tennstedt, & Schulz, 1999). Thus, dementia caregivers are at greater risk for burnout and health problems of their own.

The next case examines issues related to caring for cognitively intact elders with chronic physical conditions. This vignette also illustrates some of the challenges faced by families with siblings who share care responsibilities for an elderly parent.

EDWARD AND HIS DAUGHTERS: CARING FOR A COGNITIVELY INTACT ELDER WITH CHRONIC PHYSICAL PROBLEMS

Edward was a 73-year-old widowed male who lived at home alone. He drew a modest pension from his years of working as an auto mechanic and received limited Social Security benefits. He had cardiovascular disease and high blood pressure along with osteoarthritis and diabetes. He

did not have a great deal of energy but refused to consider
moving out of his house despite the fact that he could not
keep it up and it was largely unsuitable for modification
with assistive devices. There were steps both up and down
to various rooms on the main floor. His two daughters, Joan
and Beth, were at odds in their care strategies. Joan spent a
couple of hours a day with her dad and took him to have
coffee with his friends in the morning. She did much of his
housework, and her son, Michael, did his grandfather's yard
work. For the most part, Joan respected her father's independence, but he was often critical of her involvement with
him, insisting that he could do more things for himself. He
frequently told her to go home to tend to her family.

Beth, who was his younger daughter, worked full time
and spent mostly weekends with her Dad. She was married
with two children at home. She hovered over her dad during their visits and would not let him do much for himself.
Despite the fact that she was more protective of him than
Joan, he did not criticize her, instead seeming to enjoy
Beth's attention. Joan had observed this differential treatment of the two of them.

The family was now in crisis. Edward had recently fallen
and broken his hip. He was currently in a nursing facility
for rehabilitation following hip replacement surgery and
was making steady progress. No one, however, could agree
to what should happen when Edward was ready to be discharged. Joan would like him to go to a nearby assisted
living facility, where he could get supervised care but maintain some independence. Edward wanted to return to his
home and the previous arrangement with his daughters.

Several recent family discussions have ended in shouting matches, with Beth often siding with her father against Joan. The charge nurse had recommended family counseling, and after some discussion, they agreed to it.

Initial Case Analysis

Deciding on an acceptable level of independence for an elderly parent with multiple health conditions living alone is a gut-wrenching issue for many families. Major health transitions, such as lifesaving surgeries or a broken hip and subsequent hip replacement, call into question whether persons should live alone, particularly when they have other chronic and potentially life-threatening conditions. Hospitals and rehabilitation facilities can only keep patients for a limited time unless a family is willing to absorb costs beyond the number of days permitted, and those costs are usually prohibitive.

While Edward may be comfortable with taking the risk of dying in his own home, his children may feel that they are shirking their duties to protect him from harm by leaving him in his home largely unsupervised. They also may have other responsibilities that preclude them from taking a more active role as caregivers. Family dynamics such as the ones exhibited in this family may make care decisions nearly impossible. In this family, the crisis and responses to it suggest that Beth and Edward had formed a coalition to resist Joan's ideas; yet, Joan was the person most likely to be able to help her father when he needed it. This family needed to learn to work together to produce an acceptable outcome for all parties, if possible.

INITIAL INTERVENTION

The therapist asked each family member in turn to offer an assessment of the problems they were experiencing. The women deferred to their father first. Edward said that he was in good health, had just had "a bit of a setback" with the broken hip, and was on the mend. He would soon be ready to go home. He was dismissive of the thought of living anywhere but at home. "The girls' mother and I lived there for 45 years. It is my home. I don't understand why they think I need supervision all the time. They treat me like I'm glass; like I'll break at any moment!"

Joan spoke next. While she could understand her father's desire to stay at home, she could not help him there as much as she had in the past. Her husband, Dale, had just lost his job, so Joan, an occupational therapist who was not working, would have to find full-time work. She and Dale had two children still in college and a mortgage to pay. She pointed out that their mother died just a few years ago, and that she would feel terrible if her Dad were to die because he was not looked after sufficiently. She also expressed resentment of how her dad had treated her in the past. "Sometimes I feel like he doesn't care about me. I have tried really hard to be helpful, but I'm told too often to scram; he doesn't need me." She turned to her father and said, "Why do you accept Beth's help when you don't want mine?"

Beth looked bewildered. "I just want to do what's right for dad. I want to honor his wishes. Isn't that what we're supposed to do, to 'Honor thy father and thy mother'? I

can't see putting dad in a home! I certainly wouldn't want
to be in one if it was me."

The therapist asked how long Edward had been at the rehabilitation facility, to which Joan replied 80 days. The
therapist noted that Edward would have a maximum of 20
days left of coverage by Medicare and asked what Edward's
doctor had recommended in terms of discharge options.
Joan replied that to her knowledge, the doctor had not discussed it with anyone in the family, including Edward. He
nodded in agreement with her statement.

ADDITIONAL CASE ANALYSIS

There were challenges to working with this family. An
unwanted life course transition, the job loss of Joan's husband, called into question her ability to maintain a caregiving role with her father. Despite this new information,
Edward remained adamant that he was not leaving his
home. But Joan was certain that she would have to return to
work, and Beth could not afford to give up her full-time job.
If Edward's financial resources were plentiful, he could simply hire help during the day. They were not plentiful
enough to do this, yet, like most senior adults, he made too
much money per month to qualify for Medicaid-funded services.

Another challenge was the alliance of Beth with her father against Joan. When siblings share parent care but do
not work collaboratively as a subsystem, conflict occurs. If it
is not resolved, conflict threatens to break down the subsystem and, in this case, to break down home-based care for
their father. Joan and Beth would be sisters long after their

father is gone, so it was in their best interests to find a way to work together on this care issue.

SECOND INTERVENTION

A family resilience framework was suggested for work with this family (Walsh, 2003). Such a framework views families as systems and looks for ways to "foster positive adaptation within the context of significant adversity" (Walsh, 2003, p. 399). Key processes in this resilience framework are to examine family belief systems, organizational patterns, and communication and problem-solving strategies. For this family, the therapist decided to begin with the Bowenian concept of anxiety (Gilbert, 2004) and help the family examine how the anxiety felt by each member had affected the ability of their family system to function well.

To that end, the therapist pointed out how each family member was presently focused primarily on his or her own anxieties about the care process and the future. Joan appeared to channel her anxiety about her father's deteriorating health into a strong sense of responsibility to protect him, her only remaining parent. Edward seemed anxious about his potential loss of independence and responded to his anxiety by denying any potential problems his health may present for his ability to live alone and by encouraging Beth to join him in a coalition to resist Joan's ideas. Beth was close emotionally to her father and enjoyed his attention. She was anxious about losing his approval, so she agreed with his position, even though she could not provide him with the care he needed to remain at home.

Once the family members saw how their own under-

standable anxieties had contributed to difficulty in focusing
on a mutually beneficial solution, the therapist began to address the issue of family strengths and resources. For one,
they were all present in therapy and appeared invested in
seeing that the issue of Edward's care was resolved. Second,
the therapist noted that families who shout at each other
are still communicating; they are neither cut off nor withdrawn. Although communications had been strained lately,
as long as they were still talking, they could likely come up
with a solution to their problem.

Joan and Beth were asked next to discuss situations of adversity in their family in which they had collaborated in the
past and to relate how they did with them. There had been
several over the years. During their adolescence, Joan con-
tracted a serious illness and had to stay home for several
months during the school year. Beth gave her lots of encouragement to get well and brought her homework and
well wishes from friends. Beth's oldest child, a son, was injured in a car accident a few years ago and needed hospitalization for several months. Joan moved into Beth's home
during his hospitalization and cared for Beth's two other
children, one still a baby, so that Beth could spend her days
at the hospital with her son. The sisters also had worked together well to help their father with their mother's care
when she was ill. Together, they convinced their father to
allow hospice care for their mom in her final weeks.

Third Intervention

Once each family member's anxieties were on the table
and the daughters were reminded of ways that they had
supported each other through past adversity, the therapist

asked each of them to articulate what they wanted for each other and for their father. Joan said that she wanted her dad to be safe and as free of pain as possible in his later years and that she loved Beth and wants to work with her rather than against her. Joan then said that she could accept the idea of Edward staying at home if he had some help during the day. Beth wanted her dad to be home but not at the expense of her and Joan's ability to provide for their own families. Edward wanted to stay at home but did not want to tax his daughters' energies excessively. He also did not want to wreak havoc on their families' lives.

These therapeutic interventions had set the stage for family problem solving to begin. The therapist had prodded the family to think in ways that had the potential to build mutual support to deal with Edward's care problems together rather than in coalitions. Family members had begun to recognize and communicate to each other their concern for each other's well-being rather than just their own. Edward was a tough battler who wanted to be at home, but he now realized that without accepting some help, he put both his daughters in great stress, to the peril of his extended family.

FINAL INTERVENTION

Next the therapist began an examination with the family of potential resources. Money was tight for all three family members, so it would be difficult to pay for help in Edward's home. He was still paying medical bills from his wife's terminal illness but would have them paid off in about 9 months. Joan wondered if he had a friend in his coffee group who could take him to and from the restaurant. Beth and Edward belonged to the same church and congregation. Beth wondered if there were church members who could help by visiting Edward a couple of days a week. The therapist mentioned the senior companion program in his area as a possible way of providing Edward with companionship and ways to run errands while his daughters worked. All these were acceptable options to Edward. However, he still would need help in bathing and moving around for a while after he left rehabilitation. No one was sure how to address this issue.

At the next session, two possibilities were discussed. One was to get Joan's son, Darius, to help his grandfather with his bath, shaving, and other hygiene-related tasks twice a week. Darius's class schedule gave him Tuesday mornings and Thursdays off, so he could help his grandfather on those days, and he was willing to do so. Edward frowned and said that he would like to accept Darius's help but not without paying him in return. He did not have the cash to pay him, however. The other suggestion was to get Edward on a waiting list for a personal care aide and housekeeper help through a state-run program for those with functional limitations. It was not known how long it would be before Edward could receive those services.

Joan suggested that Darius's car is in its final stages of life and wondered if Edward would let Darius use his car since Edward would not be driving for a while. Darius would be responsible for fuel and upkeep of the vehicle. She thought Darius would accept this type of "payment in kind." Edward agreed, saying he much preferred to "keep things in the family" over accepting help from someone outside the family. He did, however, accept the rides of a friend to his coffee socialization time every day. He also accepted an occasional visit from his church minister for prayers and maintaining connections to his faith. Darius installed rails in Edward's bathroom and a sit-down chair for his shower stall to assist him with bathing. Joan and Beth took turns looking in on their father in the evenings and on weekends until his death a few years later.

DEPRESSION IN LATE LIFE: IMPORTANT AND UNDERTREATED

The next case studies deal with elder depression issues. Depression in later life often occurs in response to losses; unwanted transitions, such as going to a nursing home or widowhood; or loss of meaning in one's life. Late-life depression is a serious health problem that is often unrecognized or untreated (Friedhoff, 1994). The prevalence of clinically depressive symptoms among older adults ranges from 0.7% to 30% (Palsson & Skoog, 1997; Steffens et al., 2000), with the highest rates of depression occurring among persons 80 years of age or older (Mirowsky & Ross, 1992). After ages 70–85, both prevalence and incidence of major depression double (Alexopoulos, 2005). Persons living in nursing homes have high rates of depression.

Depression often arises in the context of serious medical conditions, such as cardiovascular illness. Depression also exacerbates illness outcomes, placing the elder at greater risk for future medical problems and death (Alexopoulos, 2005). Psychological traits such as neuroticism also place persons at greater risk of developing depression (Alexopoulos, 2005).

Concerns about the prevalence of elder depression have

prompted studies of risk and protective factors for depression. Among risk factors for late-life depression are living alone (Dean, Kolody, Wood, & Matt, 1992); poorer functional status and more chronic health problems (Barusch, Rogers, & Abu-Bader, 1999; Glass, Mendes de Leon, Bassuk, & Berkman, 2006); declines in cognitive abilities (Barusch et al., 1999; Glass et al., 2006); and the death of a spouse (Stroebe, Stroebe, Abakoumkin, & Schut, 1996). Another important factor in identifying depression in older adults is its presentation as it may look different from that of younger adults and adolescents. Gallo and Rabins (1999) established that many elders deny sadness while exhibiting other clear signs of depression. These elders may report instead feelings of anxiety or an inability to feel pleasure (anhedonia).

There are several barriers to recognition or treatment of depression. Chief among them are attitudes that view depression as a normal response to all the losses of late life. Whether they are held by professionals, family members, or elders themselves, these attitudes may inhibit persons from seeking or following through with help. A second barrier is the cost of treatment: Medicare offers limited reimbursement for outpatient therapy services, and secondary insurance may or may not cover mental health treatment. Coupled with fixed incomes in old age, many older adults simply cannot afford to pay the cost of therapy out of pocket. A third barrier may be the older adult's belief that seeking help from others is socially unacceptable or a threat to their autonomy, discussed at length in Chapter 1. This strong need for autonomy and a sense of personal responsibility for one's own problems can persist despite considerable physical and emotional pain suffered by very old adults.

Nevertheless, there are effective treatments for depression in older adults. Antidepressant medications, especially the SSRIs (selective serotonin reuptake inhibitors) and the SNRIs (serotonin-norepinephrine reuptake inhibitors) are generally considered most effective (Alexopoulos, 2005) in producing remission of symptoms. Psychotherapies, particularly cognitive-behavioral therapies, are also highly recommended (Steinman et al., 2007), as are care management programs. These programs are a collaboration of primary care physicians and psychotherapists trained in treatment of geriatric depression and are generally housed in physician's practices. The physician screens the patient for depression, using a validated screening instrument, and refers the person to a care manager, usually a nurse, social worker, family therapist, or other mental health professional, for delivery of patient education and treatment and tracking of progress (Steinman et al., 2007). Finally, early intervention educational and follow-up programs with depressed older adults have shown promise in being effective in decreasing depression symptoms and improving treatment compliance (Sirey, Bruce, & Alexopoulos, 2005).

Consider the following case example of elder depression and a family's response to it.

Evelyn: When Life Has Lost Its Meaning

Evelyn was an 83-year-old widow who lived alone in a large city apartment complex for seniors. She was referred for outpatient therapy after making a serious attempt on her life with an overdose of pills. After her release from the hospital, she was seen by a psychiatrist, who put her on an antidepressant and referred her to a therapist in his practice for individual and family therapy. Evelyn was accompanied to her first session by her youngest daughter, Tammie, age 52, who was divorced with two children.

Evelyn clearly appeared uncomfortable with this venue. At first, she volunteered little information about herself and her circumstances. She kept her head down, appearing to be ashamed of what had happened. Tammie, on the other hand, was talkative. She wanted to do "whatever it took" to keep Evelyn from trying to kill herself again. She said that her mother had endured a hard life and wondered how much this had influenced what had recently occurred.

INTERVENTION: INDIVIDUAL THERAPY WITH EVELYN

At the conclusion of the first visit, the therapist suggested that Evelyn come alone to the next session. At this session, the therapist began asking her questions about her life in an effort to get to know who Evelyn was and what her life had been like until now.

Evelyn had grown up outside the city on a farm in a rural area that had since become a suburb of the city. As a middle child, she had many farm chores to do and some child care responsibilities. Her mother became ill shortly after the birth of her youngest sister and died when Evelyn was 8 years old. Her father remarried 2 years later. Evelyn had mixed emotions about her stepmother. She stayed in her family home only through high school completion, after which she left to marry her first husband, from whom she was quickly divorced. By the time Evelyn was 25, she had lost both parents. Her father had died of heart failure.

Evelyn wiped a tear from her eye and looked at the therapist, saying, "I don't know why I'm telling you this! I haven't talked to anyone about this in years! What does this have to do with anything, anyway?"

Evelyn then related the story of her marriage to Tammie's father. After a brief marriage to the abusive first husband, Evelyn married George, a steelworker. With him, she had three children, two daughters and a son. Their marriage lasted 48 years. George had earned a comfortable living, and they were looking forward to traveling in an RV after retirement. However, once retired, George seemed lost. He missed his work buddies. His drinking escalated, and he became diabetic. In denial about the disease, he continued to drink and refused to follow a proper diet despite Evelyn's best efforts. He died several years later of renal failure. Despite his flaws, Evelyn had loved him and missed his big belly laughs and bear hugs tremendously. She vowed, however, never to marry again. George had been dead 5 years at the time of her suicide attempt.

In the next session, Evelyn told more of her life story. Her children had given her a mixture of joy and pain and continued to do so now. Her older daughter, Lisa, was estranged from her mother. Although they had always had a contentious relationship, things boiled over when Lisa's son entered rehab for drug addiction after an arrest. Evelyn had commented to Lisa at that time that Lisa had put too much effort into her career as a businesswoman and not enough effort into her responsibilities to her children. Feeling blamed for her son's problems and tired of her mother's nonsupportive comments, she stopped calling and taking her mother's calls. Evelyn was devastated by this cutoff and felt guilty about pushing Lisa too far. Evelyn did not know how to reconcile with her daughter and feared her suicide attempt would only push them further apart: "I wonder what she thinks of me now."

Her relationship with her son Mark was cordial but not close. He lived about 200 miles away. Tammie, the youngest, was closest to Evelyn. In her mother's opinion, Tammie had the hardest life, and her problems as an adult had merited Evelyn's special attention. It was Tammie who had found her mother unresponsive on the floor of her apartment and called emergency services. Evelyn viewed this rescue as a mixed blessing: "I really don't know why I'm still here. Nothing means anything much to me. But I can see that I really scared Tammie. I don't want to hurt her or my grandchildren."

The therapist asked how Evelyn came to live at the apartment complex in the city. Evelyn sighed and said that Tammie had insisted that she move into the city to be near her. Evelyn had fallen a couple of years earlier and injured her back. She had undergone surgery to repair her back but still suffered chronic pain in her middle back region. Her blood pressure was high, and she also had recently been diagnosed with macular degeneration. At the time Evelyn moved into the complex, Tammie felt that its layout and location would be good for her mother in that Tammie could visit often, and there would be ample opportunities for socialization with new friends. However, Evelyn had kept mostly to herself, reading and watching TV in her apartment. Now that her eyesight was failing, she did not know what she would do. "I pray that the Lord will take me soon," she said.

INITIAL CASE ANALYSIS OF INTERVENTION WITH EVELYN

In terms of understanding Evelyn's depression, several issues are noteworthy. Evelyn's life course contained several ill-timed losses of close family members. The emotion with which Evelyn described these losses suggested that Evelyn may not have grieved them adequately. Losing a parent at a young age is associated with depression in children thus affected (Melhem, Walker, Moritz, & Brent, 2008). Losing both parents by young adulthood was traumatic for Evelyn, and losing George (spouse) shortly after his retirement resulted in a lost companion as well as lost dreams (traveling after his retirement). She also faced losing her elder daughter, Lisa, if the cutoff between them was not resolved. Given all these prior losses, the impending loss of her eyesight may have been the precipitant that led to the suicide attempt. Another of her major medical conditions, chronic pain, has also been associated with depression (Von Korff et al., 2005) and mental health treatment (Braden et al., 2008) in older adults.

INTERVENTION WITH EVELYN, CONTINUED

The therapist assessed Evelyn's life story as primarily a grief narrative. Her childhood losses had not been fully grieved and seemed to leave Evelyn with a profound sense of aloneness in facing her current life challenges. The therapist and Evelyn spent several sessions processing her grief over losing both parents and her husband, who had provided the most stability and joy in Evelyn's life. While Evelyn

was aware that she missed her parents and especially
George, she had not explored either the depths of her grief
or the way it left her feeling alone and uncertain of herself.
She also realized that her primary bond in adulthood had
been as spouse and caregiver to George, and that she had
made little effort to develop a meaningful life after his
death. She acknowledged that she was still angry with him
for failing to care for himself after he was diagnosed with
diabetes but felt helpless to influence his self-destructive behavior.

Once Evelyn had made substantial progress in grieving
the losses of parents and spouse, the therapist asked Evelyn
to consider what strengths she had acquired and exhibited
as a result of having to go it alone so early in life. Evelyn replied that she had learned to function independently and
preferred being self-sufficient to depending on others. However, with the diagnosis of macular degeneration, she also
realized that she had come to a point in her life where
maintaining independence would be possible only with the
help of others. Before ending this session, the therapist
asked Evelyn to complete an ecomap with her. An ecomap
is diagrammatic drawing of an individual's social relationships, with the client placed in the center of the map and
lines drawn to each person named in the client's social network. Lines can be drawn thickly or thinly to show relationship strength and flow of resources. A dotted line signifies a
tenuous relationship, and hash marks through lines indicate
stressful relationships (Rempel, Neufeld, & Kushner, 2007).
The purpose of this tool is to give the therapist concrete information on available resources and the relative strength
of those resources. In the therapist's estimation, Evelyn

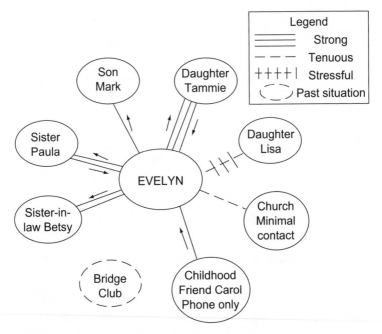

FIGURE 4.1. Evelyn's Ecomap. Arrows indicate the flow of energy.
Adapted from Rempel, Neufeld, & Kushner, 2007. Reprinted by permission of
Sage Publications.

would need to connect with her social network in significant ways as part of her treatment for depression. An example of Evelyn's ecomap is shown in Figure 4.1.

Evelyn's therapist immediately noticed how sparse her
ecomap was in terms of numbers of social contacts but also
noticed that she might have some untapped resources, such
as her childhood friend Carol and her sister and sister-in-
law. Because Evelyn perceived her closest relationship to be
with her daughter Tammie, the therapist requested that
Tammie attend the next session. With the use of the ecomap, the therapist also could explore Evelyn's relationship

to her faith and potential church attendance as well as involvement with her bridge club cronies.

During this and other therapy sessions, Evelyn related that she felt like a fish out of water in the urban apartment complex in which she lived. All her life prior to this move was spent in a rural or suburban environment, where there was air to breathe and land to which she felt connected. Although she made the move to satisfy her daughter's concerns, she had been unwilling to connect socially with fellow residents. Unable to drive anymore, she maintained most of her social contact by telephone or by visits with her daughter Tammie. Her son saw her mostly at holiday gatherings.

FURTHER ANALYSIS OF INDIVIDUAL THERAPY WITH EVELYN

The therapist decided initially to build a relationship of trust with Evelyn in the hopes that she could create an environment in which Evelyn would give insights into how her life history may have shaped her depression and recent suicide attempt. At this point in the therapeutic process, the therapist would like to increase Evelyn's social contacts in an effort to re-create meaningful interactions in her life and to begin, if possible, a family therapy process in which the relationships between Evelyn and her children are strengthened. Research has shown that close family members can affect an older adult's response to and compliance with treatment for depression (Martire et al., 2008). Specifically, these researchers found that depressed elders with caregivers who felt more burdened by the elder's depression are more severely depressed themselves after 6 weeks of treatment than those whose caregivers felt less burdened, even when the elders have complied with taking antidepressant medication. Thus, the therapist believed that Tammie's burden level merited assessment, and the possibilities of healing the rift between Lisa and Evelyn, as well as increasing involvement between Evelyn and her son, Mark, needed additional exploration.

INTERVENTION: FAMILY THERAPY WITH EVELYN AND HER DAUGHTERS

When Tammie and Evelyn come in together, the therapist asked each of them to discuss what they wanted for the other and for their relationship. Tammie wanted her mother to be happy and was open to talking more about how that could occur. She wanted to worry less about her mother.

With some prodding, Evelyn expressed her despair about being socially isolated and about "losing" Lisa: "You never stop loving your children, no matter how much you disagree with them," she said. She then mentioned that she felt terribly alone where she lived. Tammie asked her mother what would help her to feel less isolated and alone. Evelyn said: "I would like to move back to the suburbs, even if it means seeing you less often. I would like to be closer to Carol so we could visit each other. I'd like to see Betsy [sister-in-law] again. They can't visit me here; it's too far away for them to drive." Seeing a disappointed look on Tammie's face, she added that her desire to move had nothing to do with Tammie; she had been a devoted daughter. Evelyn stated: "I'd just like to be closer to my roots and to people my own age that mean something to me." Tammie noted that Evelyn's lease was up in about 4 months, so perhaps they could go to her old neighborhood a few times to find a suitable place for her to live. With George's pension and Social Security benefits, Evelyn could afford several options.

Tammie frowned when the therapist brought up the issue of reconciling with Lisa. Tammie said: "Mother, she was so hurt by what you said that I am not sure she's ready to forgive you. I can talk with her, but. . . ." The therapist asked Evelyn if she was sorry about what she said and if so, was she ready to make amends? Drawing a long breath, Evelyn said, "I feel strongly about Lisa's priorities. I truly believe that she has been absent too much from her kids' lives. But I was wrong to blame my grandson's troubles on her. He's nearly grown up so he should learn to be responsible. I really worry about his future!"

The therapist wanted to know how Evelyn could make amends. Evelyn decided to send Lisa a note expressing an apology for her words and behavior as a starting point. If Lisa did not respond, she would call her. Another session was scheduled for Tammie and Evelyn for 2 weeks later.

When they returned, Lisa was with them. She strode in and said to the therapist: "I decided to come so someone could stop me and Mom from having the same conversation over and over again. Mom says she is sorry and wants to reconcile. I don't know if I can trust her not to say hurtful things again. I also wonder if Mom is just too fragile emotionally to deal with this now. So that is why I'm here."

The therapist asked both Lisa and Evelyn if they wished to work on their relationship now. They both agreed that it was time, but Evelyn expressed the same fear of mistrust as Lisa. The therapist asked for commitment to a specific goal for their relationship. They both set a goal of communicating with each other without defensiveness and criticism. They also committed to a process of exploring their relationship to better understand their pattern of ineffective communication and strong feelings. At this point, Tammie left but promised to return to therapy as soon as she was needed.

INTERVENTION: EVELYN AND LISA

The therapist set ground rules for the session with the goal of each person telling her story without interruption. She used active listening techniques to clarify what was being said and asked the other party periodically to state aloud the messages she was hearing. Lisa began by saying that she had always felt that her mother favored Tammie over Lisa and her brother, Mark, and was not supportive of Lisa's career, even though Lisa's husband did not make enough money by himself to support his family. Lisa did not understand why her mother would give Tammie money when Lisa and her husband could also use this type of support. She framed the problem as Evelyn's favoritism coupled with her criticism of her career.

Evelyn saw things differently. In her view, Lisa had always been a very independent child, often rejecting her mother's advice and following her own course, beginning in childhood. To Evelyn, Lisa did not seem to need or want her in the way that Tammie did. Evelyn felt that Tammie had always been more fragile and had experienced more setbacks in life that necessitated Evelyn's support, both emotional and financial. She added that Tammie's divorce was not of her own making; her ex-husband had deserted her and their children.

In addition, Evelyn thought that Lisa would be insulted by any offers of financial support, so she did not try to offer her money, even when she thought she might be struggling a bit. At this point, Lisa smiled. When asked about this re-action, she said, "Mom, you are probably right. I have a hard time asking anyone for anything, including my hus-band and children." She added that she had only recently become aware of this pattern, which was elucidated during her nuclear family's therapy after her son's hospitalization for drug abuse.

Evelyn then asked Lisa what she wanted from her. Lisa said: "I want your support, Mom. I don't need your money, but I would like you to accept me for what I am and stop complaining about my work. I like what I do. It gives me confidence and a sense of worth. In case you are wondering, I am trying to be a better, more attentive mother to my kids. I have cut back my work hours a couple of days each week to be at home when they arrive from school. John [spouse] is making more money now, so I can do this."

After Evelyn restated Lisa's request in her own words and agreed to work on it, the therapist asked Evelyn what she wanted from Lisa. Evelyn stumbled over this question; she was silent for a while and then grinned: "I guess we are a lot alike. I don't like asking others for things, either. I had to be independent at an early age, and I didn't like asking my stepmom for help. Maybe that's why we argue." The therapist then restated the question, to which Evelyn re-plied, "I want you to tell me what's going on with you.

Don't try to carry the load all by yourself. I promise that I will listen more and speak up less. I also want to spend time with you and your family. I feel like I don't know my grandkids well enough. Perhaps we could get together more often."

Mother and daughter made a commitment to get together every other weekend for dinner at Lisa's home. Lisa also asked Evelyn to attend some of her children's activities, like piano recitals and karate exhibitions: "I know you aren't seeing as well, Mom, and some days the pain gives you fits, but it would mean a lot to us if you would come out to support them."

Case Analysis of Intervention With Evelyn and Lisa

This parent-child relationship had been characterized by ambivalence, with both mother and daughter wanting closeness but pushing each other away instead of acknowledging any need for the other. Luscher and Pillemer's (1998) notion of intergenerational ambivalence argued that parents and children usually experience both conflict and closeness in their adult relationships, and that ambivalence is an ongoing feature of parent-child relationships that is continually renegotiated over the life course. Evelyn desired connection with her children and grandchildren to help her create meaning and a sense of purpose to her final years. She wanted to feel important to them. But, Evelyn now realized that her attempts to mother Lisa by criticizing her just pushed her away. Although still a bit wary, Lisa recognized that her independent persona pushes others away, giving them a sense that they are unwanted. She has resented the special treatment Tammie has received but has left the resentment unspoken until now, perhaps out of fear of her own potential dependence on her mother for support. Both Lisa and Evelyn were judgmental persons, and they would have to work hard to change their communication patterns. But, they understood each other much better and were committed to work on the change process. They understood that there may be setbacks but were resolved to "call each other" on any unhelpful communications or behaviors rather than withdrawing as they had in the past.

INTERVENTION WITH THE FAMILY

The next issue needing resolution was Evelyn's desire to move back to the suburbs. To address this issue, both daughters and son, Mark, attended a session in which they discussed her options. Because Evelyn's eyesight was failing, they agreed that an independent apartment might not be the best choice; instead, they investigated assisted living facilities and located one near where Evelyn and George had lived. It was also close to where Carol and Betsy (her sister-in-law) lived. When her lease was up, Evelyn moved to this facility.

The therapist asked Evelyn about a referral to a pain clinic to work on strategies to manage her pain. Evelyn was ambivalent about this option, stating that she was doing better. She agreed to a follow-up session with her therapist in a couple of months. At this session, Evelyn expressed gratitude for the help she had received. She no longer thought about suicide and had expanded her social network beyond her relatives to include members of her bridge club and a couple of new friends at the facility, with whom she

eats meals and meets for walks around the complex. She
was seeing Lisa and her family regularly and still saw Tammie on weekends. Mark was bringing his mother out to stay
with him and his family one weekend each month. Evelyn
continued to take the antidepressant medication but would
reevaluate this treatment with her physician in a few
weeks. She promised to return to therapy if her symptoms
reoccurred or if she began to withdraw from others again.

WHEN ADULT CHILDREN NEED HELP FROM AGING PARENTS

As noted, there are more aging parents than ever before
caring for adult children and grandchildren well into their
old age. These elders face unique challenges as they attempt
to balance their needs and health issues with those of their
children or grandchildren. Nearly all of the concerns that affect persons caring for dependent or frail older adults apply
to older adults caring for members of younger generations of
their families. Elderly caregivers must adjust to their roles as
caregivers, learn how to provide assistance in the most effective manner possible, and respond to crises and transitions in
the lives of those for whom they are caring as well as their
own. Like all caregivers, they can experience stress, strain,
depression, burnout, and a sense of being overwhelmed by
their responsibilities. They often do so, however, with declining energy levels and serious health concerns of their
own. If they have been caring for a grandchild since the
child's birth or a child of their own with developmental disabilities, they likely have developed patterns of giving care

that they are reluctant to modify, even in the face of their own declining energy or health. They also may worry about burdening their other children with the responsibilities of looking after a dependent sibling, niece, or nephew.

Several types of problems with adult children elicit the help of their parents, including life-threatening illnesses, divorce, mental or physical disabilities, substance abuse and addiction, financial difficulties, and legal problems. While some of these tribulations are crisis oriented and time limited in duration, others become chronic issues that require sustained intervention on the part of elders in multigeneration families. Chronic problems such as drug addiction in the middle generation, for example, may lead elderly family members to assume primary care of one or more of their minor grandchildren. It is to this issue that we turn first. The following case study illustrates the challenges faced by elderly grandparents who assume care of their minor grandchildren.

JAMES AND DESIREE: GRANDPARENT CAREGIVERS

James and Desiree, aged 67 and 55, respectively, were an African American couple living in a suburb of a large Midwestern city, where they have been lifelong residents. James was Desiree's third husband; Desiree was James's second wife. Their daughter Chantell was recently sentenced for a conviction of possession of crack cocaine with intent to distribute. Chantell had been jailed before on drug-related charges but never had to serve time in prison until now. She was given a 5-year sentence and sent to a facility over 2 hours from her hometown. Her two children, Aisha, age 13, and Deion, age 10, have come to live with James and Desiree as there is no one else in the family who could take them. James and Desiree did not want the children to get sent to the foster care system, although they have considerable challenges to deal with in raising these children.

James was retired from the local electric company. His pension and social security benefits were modest as he worked mostly as a custodian in the main corporate office. Desiree worked part time at a local grocery store to help make ends meet. James had heart problems and high blood pressure and was diabetic. He was recently hospitalized for a first bout of congestive heart failure. Desiree also had diabetes and was trying to give up smoking but was struggling with that goal. Desiree was quite anxious about James's deteriorating health.

The children were not without problems of their own. Because of their mother's drug habit, they were frequently neglected and subject to living with a series of their mother's boyfriends, some of whom were also drug addicts. Aisha was rebellious and smart-mouthed. She was interested in boys, and Desiree worried that she might be at risk of becoming sexually active prematurely. Aisha was very bright and a good student at this time. Desiree and James would like to see her go to college.

Deion was withdrawn and sullen. He was not a good student and had taken a lackadaisical approach to his schoolwork. As a result, he was in danger of failing the third grade. He loved sports, though, and spent hours playing basketball with friends after school. He said little to his grandparents, answering their questions with as little feedback as possible.

Desiree had sought professional help for several reasons.

She was not sure how to parent these children. She knew that both were likely reacting to the instability in their upbringing and the loss of their mother, but she felt at a loss of how to respond effectively to their needs. She also was seeking strategies to deal with her husband's disciplinary habits. She worried that James would use the same approach to parenting his grandchildren as he did with Chantell and her siblings in her adolescence, which Desiree described as "my way or the highway." He had already threatened Aisha with "tough love" and foster care if she did not stop mouthing off and staying out past curfew. Desiree wondered if James's parenting style drove Chantell to rebel in a self-destructive way. She worried that history may repeat itself with her grandchildren.

Desiree was also concerned with her grandchildren's academic performance. She told the therapist, "James and I have had a hard life. We didn't get much education. I want these grandchildren to have choices I never had, and I know education is the best way to get those opportunities."

INTERVENTION

The therapist recommended marital counseling followed by family therapy for the four of them. Desiree just shook her head: "James will not come," she said. "He believes in keeping problems 'in the family.'" The therapist decided to begin work with Desiree and to approach the notion of including James at a later time.

CASE ANALYSIS

In a functional sense, James, Desiree, Aisha, and Deion were a newly formed family system at risk for many difficulties. Parenting grandchildren while dealing with one's own declining health and energy levels is an extremely stressful and often undesired life transition, one of those Class 5 rapids that confront some older adults as they round a bend in the river, as described in Chapter 2. This newly formed family system was what is known as a "skipped generation" family, in that Chantell, the mother of the children, was not living in the home with her parents and children. Assuming that this family is able to persevere throughout Chantell's incarceration, a decision about custody of the children will need to be made prior to her release from prison. However, it is unlikely that the children will return to their mother given her history.

Because the two grandparents disagreed on how to parent the grandchildren, there was a risk that relationship triangles would form and inhibit a satisfactory parental alliance, an alliance these children needed. Thus, one challenge for the therapist was to help Desiree find ways to collaborate with James whenever possible to successfully parent their grandchildren. Parenting Aisha and Deion was likely to be difficult, with many ups and downs, because of their prior unstable life with their mother. Children who experience neglect or mistreatment by their parents are at increased risk of behavioral disorders such as aggression or delinquency, mood disorders such as depression and anxiety, as well as problems with academic achievement (Margolin & Gordis, 2004). A close, positive relationship with a caregiving figure can be protective of poor outcomes for these children. However, forming such a close bond is difficult for many grandparents in these situations. In a study of children living in skipped generation households, Keller and Stricker (2003) found that only half of the children surveyed reported optimal relationships with grandparents, and those children whose relationships with their own mothers were nonoptimal were more likely to report nonoptimal relationships with their kin caregivers along with acknowledging their own emotional and behavioral problems.

In addition to addressing the children's need for adequate parenting, Desiree's marital subsystem was being stressed by this additional responsibility. While James and Desiree had been married for over 20 years and had endured much hardship in their lives, the presence of the grandchildren had reopened an old wound about how James disciplined their children. The couple was now in conflict again over how to discipline their grandchildren, and Desiree lacked effective strategies for resolving the conflict on her own. When couples experience such conflict, their ability to support each other is eroded, and such marital support is crucial to their own health and the well-being of the grandchildren.

The relationships between both grandparents and grandchildren must also be addressed as there is evidence that conflict between grandmothers and the grandchildren they are raising predicts poorer health outcomes for grandmothers (Goodman, Tan, Ernandes, & Silverstein, 2008). James's health was already precarious, and Desiree's was at risk because of diabetes and smoking. Thus, it was important that the grandchildren become involved in therapy at some point to work toward strengthening their relationships with their grandparents.

MULTISTEP INTERVENTION

For the first step in the intervention, the therapist began by giving Desiree a brief introduction to the systems approach to family therapy, with a particular focus on the role of anxiety in producing symptoms. Then, together they set goals for Desiree's therapy. Desiree would work on reducing her anxiety level in several ways. She learned some brief relaxation techniques from her therapist, along with the cognitive-behavioral technique of identifying irrational thought processes as they related to her husband and grandchildren, such as overgeneralization and catastrophizing, and working to replace such thoughts with more rational ones.

The therapist also asked her to describe her and James's strengths as a couple, and Desiree identified several of them, including similar values regarding lifestyle practices and a strong work ethic. She was asked to identify ways to build on those strengths as a foundation for a more collaborative parenting style. As homework, she agreed to discuss with James his desires for his grandchildren and to talk about how they could team up to develop strategies to get Aisha and Deion "on the right track."

During the next session, Desiree related that her talk with James did not go well. When asked why, she said that he was vague, negative, and general in his comments. In the face of his responses, Desiree did not know what to do, so she terminated the discussion. The incident did make her realize that she had always deferred to James because his blustery communication style was always easier to handle by appeasement and capitulation. Desiree needed to develop more confidence in talking with her husband, so her therapist worked with her on becoming more assertive. She pointed out that he was not likely to leave her as they had been married a long time and he needed her support in dealing with his health problems. With some additional coaching, Desiree was able to express more of her concerns and feelings to James. They learned that their concerns were similar, but they did not really know how to find solutions comfortable to both of them regarding the children's behavior patterns. Because changes in Desiree's behavior influenced the whole family system and may not last without system change, the therapist wished to bring James into their discussions.

For the second step, the therapist began by raising the question of who was influential with James. Desiree thought a while, then said that their church pastor was one of the few people that James trusted and liked. The therapist encouraged Desiree to ask the pastor if he did any counseling and to explain to him what she was facing. If the pastor did counseling, the therapist suggested that Desiree raise the issue of the therapist and the pastor offering co-counseling sessions to James and Desiree. When Desiree and her pastor discussed the idea, he was amenable to the co-counseling option but wanted James fully informed and willing to participate. He also suggested that James might be more comfortable seeing them in church quarters and offered a room he had set up for counseling his congregation members. He invited James and Desiree to meet with him after church one Sunday.

James at first was taken aback at the suggestion of co-counseling. In a private conversation with the pastor, he reiterated his need to solve things as a family. They talked a little about how difficult this can be with grandchildren who have had the kind of life Aisha and Deion had experienced. The pastor pointed out that little can be accomplished without the cooperation of the children in the matter, to which James reluctantly agreed. James said he would give the counseling a try but wanted it strictly confidential. He preferred meeting at the church.

Through these co-counseling sessions, the couple learned to set goals for parenting their grandchildren. James agreed to back off the threats and the tough love approach in exchange for Desiree's willingness to set some rules and consequences for breaking those rules with Aisha and Deion. She would take the lead in enforcing consequences for rule violations. They also discussed the needs of their grandchildren. Both were quite concerned about Aisha's school environment. They explored other school options and found a magnet school that might provide a more suitable environment for stoking Aisha's intellectual development. After some expressed reluctance to leave her current school, Aisha agreed to this change. James would drive her to school each day and pick her up when school was over.

The counselors and parents agreed that addressing Deion's problems would be harder. After some consultation with Deion's current teacher, they decided on a charter school for him to attend in a nearby neighborhood. He could ride a bus to this school. At this new school, he also would be thoroughly tested for any potential learning disabilities.

The therapist saw Deion both individually for assessment and with his grandparents briefly. They had learned recently from their daughter that he was physically abused by a past boyfriend of hers. James and Desiree were upset but did not plan to press charges. Desiree remarked, "I'm not sure Deion is strong enough for the legal process. I think it would damage him more." Deion was referred to a child therapist for work toward addressing his trust and anger issues related to the abuse and for family therapy when he was ready to discuss his feelings and concerns with his grandparents. The therapist also suggested that James and Desiree look into the process of establishing a legal relationship with their grandchildren and the possibility of receiving some public financial support for the children while they were in their care. They expressed a need for more information about the potential advantages of developing a legal relationship with their grandchildren as they were not sure that being with their mother on her release from prison was in the children's best interest.

ISSUES AND RESOURCES FOR GRANDPARENTS AND OTHER OLDER RELATIVES PROVIDING KINSHIP CARE

Like that of James and Desiree's family, many situations of grandparent care are complex. Grandparents who raise their grandchildren are a heterogeneous group, representing all racial and ethnic groups, middle and older ages, and varying socioeconomic statuses (Hayslip & Kaminski, 2005). The circumstances that require grandparents to step into the caregiver role are also varied, and the grandchildren may have suffered physically and emotionally while in their parents' care (Roe & Minkler, 1998). But, for all grandparents who find themselves in these circumstances, there may be financial, legal, and emotional issues that require adequate decision-making and coping skills for families to adapt to their circumstances. Sometimes, several types of decisions must be made at once. Poverty rates among custodial grandparents, particularly single grandmothers of color, are high. Thus, taking on grandchildren may stretch an already thin budget. The issue of acquiring a legal relationship with one's coresident grandchildren is also a tough decision faced by many grandparents. Finally, nearly all custodial grandparents can benefit from resources to bolster their parenting skills.

Custodial grandparents and their grandchildren are entitled to some benefits programs, but many do not access them. Some grandparents lack knowledge about their availability and eligibility requirements. Even when informed, program requirements, such as becoming a licensed foster care home to receive foster care stipends for children, may be difficult for some grandparent families to achieve. And, while most children in kinship care are eligible for the child-only benefit from the TANF (Temporary Assistance for Needy Families) program, studies showed that the number of families receiving such payments had not increased between 1997 and 2002 (Main, Macomber, & Geen, 2006). Perhaps the stigma associated with receiving welfare benefits or concerns about the intrusion of welfare authorities into family life discourage some grandparents from applying for this benefit.

The study by Main and associates (2006) also showed substantial patterns of difference in financial benefit receipt between grandchildren in private kinship care and public kinship care. *Public kinship care* refers to situations in which child welfare authorities have become involved in removing children from their homes and placing the children with relatives. *Private kinship care* refers to relatives taking on the care of minor children without the involvement of the child welfare system. The latter form of care represents the situation of 78% of all children residing in kinship care, but only about 22% of these families receive some sort of publicly funded benefit to help pay for the cost of care (vs. 70% of families in public kinship care). Because 31% of children in private kinship care live in poverty (Main et al., 2006), such benefits could be helpful to these grandparent caregivers.

Therapists need to explore with these families the circumstances surrounding the acquisition of their grandchildren or other minor-aged relatives and make a determination of whether their client families could benefit from financial assistance. If the answer is affirmative, then therapists need to be acquainted with available options in their state so that they can explain them to family members and facilitate referrals. While therapists can link families to these resources, they also need to respect client decisions to refrain from obtaining public assistance.

In long-term kinship care situations, there can be some advantages to older relatives in becoming foster parents or adopting one's grandchildren or other minor kin. For example, the foster care system can provide child care, financial remuneration, assessments for learning disabilities, and tutoring for children struggling with schoolwork (Dellman-Jenkins, Blankemeyer, & Olesh, 2002). However, taking steps to become a foster or adoptive parent is difficult emotionally for many relatives as it means pursuing the parent's temporary or permanent relinquishment of parental rights and moving in the direction of commitment to raise the children until adulthood is reached (in the case of adoption). In some circumstances, it may be clear that parents will never be able to care adequately for their children, but in other cases, such clarity may not exist, and parents may want to pursue eventual reinstatement of their custodial relationship with their children. It is a judgment call that many grandparents must make, but it is a difficult one with potential long-lasting repercussions for the multigenerational family. However, a study of adoptive grandparents showed that the majority would adopt their grandchildren again if given the opportunity to do so, even in the face of less-positive family functioning (Hinterlong & Ryan, 2008).

Resources for Grandparents Raising Grandchildren

The numbers and types of resources available to grandparents and other kin raising their minor grandchildren or other skipped generation minors have increased dramatically in recent years. Some of these resources address tangible benefits for the children, such as CHIP (Children's Health Insurance Program; formerly SCHIP, State Children's Health Insurance Program) or the child-only grant of the TANF program, but other resources are targeted to improve the knowledge and skills of the older generation. Hayslip and Kaminski (2005) offer a summary of these programs.

Several programs and organizations offer parenting skills training, some of which are in the form of face-to-face training sessions and others that are offered in more individual-friendly formats, such as online. An excellent example of the last type of program is offered by the University of Wisconsin's Extension services, *Through the Eyes of a Child: Grandparents Raising Grandchildren* (Brintnall-Peterson,

Poehlmann, Morgan, & Shlafer, 2009). This program, based on solid child development research and evaluated positively by its users, presents a series of "fact sheets" that address such topics as understanding child development, relationship expectations, child behavior, and the cycle of family patterns (Brintnall-Peterson et al., 2009). Each fact sheet may be downloaded and used by the consumer to increase knowledge and understanding of both grandchildren and important elements of the parenting process. One may access this program by either searching for it on the Internet or going to the University of Wisconsin's Extension Web site (http://www.uwex.edu/ces/flp/grandparent/relationships).

Another resource that may help some grandparents or other kin caregivers is a support group. The American Association of Retired Persons (AARP; http://www.aarp.org) offers links to a nationwide database of such support groups, along with tips on how to start a support group if one is not readily available. Some of these support groups are conducted in person; others are available by telephone or online.

Other organizations with information and support for grandparents raising grandchildren include Generations United (http://www.gu.org/) and Grandparents as Parents (http://www.grandparentsasparents.org/). Some states offer kinship care centers or special comprehensive programs to assist grandparent caregivers. An excellent example of a comprehensive service program is called Project Healthy Grandparents, a multiprong program to assist low-income grandparent family systems with their needs. Services offered to families include health care, social work case management, parenting classes, grandparent support groups, legal assistance, specialized mental health services for grandchildren, and early intervention services. Although it has only been available in Georgia to date, the program is expanding to other states because of its success in improving both grandparents' health and behavioral problems in grandchildren (Kelley & Whitley, 2003).

The next section outlines the issues that can occur as an aging single parent of a child with developmental disabilities struggles to plan for the child's care as her own health and functional abilities decline.

JANELLE AND BRIAN: CARE PLANNING FOR AN ADULT CHILD WITH DOWN SYNDROME

Janelle Smith, aged 72, came to therapy alone, referred by a staff member at the local office of the agency of the state serving persons with disabilities. A petite woman who was quite thin and tired looking, she said that she was having trouble coping with her life: "What is left of it, that is." On her first visit, the therapist learned that Janelle was twice divorced. She had two sons, Wade and Brian, by her first husband, who had died recently. Brian was born with Down syndrome and was now 44 years old. Brian and Janelle lived together in a small house that needed repairs. Wade was living on his own, but he had a "drinking problem" and did not hold a steady job. Brian and Janelle got along well together, so Janelle had not entrusted his care to anyone but herself. She had never taken a vacation on her own. "Brian is my life," she said.

However, Janelle was recently diagnosed with leukemia and would need to begin extensive treatment shortly. The prognosis for her recovery was uncertain. She was terrified of what lay ahead of her. But most of all, she worried about Brian. "What will happen to him? Who will look after him while I'm recovering? If I'm sick from chemotherapy? When I'm gone?"

Janelle was deeply attached to Brian. She had devoted her energies to care for him, to help him adjust to school and to the sheltered workshop and other day services he attended as an adult, and to see after his medical needs, which were considerable. Brian was a big man and had developed diabetes. Janelle watched his diet carefully, dispensed his medications, and consoled him when he got frustrated about his limitations. Brian received Social Security Disability and Medicaid benefits. Janelle received a tiny pension from her work in a textile mill and Social Security benefits. With what they took in together, they could afford to stay in the house but not much more. She wondered if she could meet her expenses with medical bills looming in her future.

The therapist asked Janelle to describe in more detail the ways in which she cared for Brian. "Tell me about a typical day," the therapist said. Janelle said that she generally got Brian up and laid out his clothing for the day, fed him breakfast, and drove him to his day activities. Then, she went home and did as much housework as she felt up to doing, then picked him up. She fixed dinner and did the dishes, and then they usually watched TV together. They had few visitors and went out shopping together occasionally. The therapist asked about Brian's level of functioning. Janelle said, "He's in the moderate range of retardation. We tried sending him out to work once—at a restaurant. He was uncomfortable around all the noise there, so I let him quit." "How was his performance at this job?" the therapist asked. Janelle replied, "Oh, it was OK. They liked him there alright. But *Brian* didn't like it, so I thought it best to get him out of there."

INITIAL INTERVENTION

During Janelle's next session, the therapist asked about Brian's ability to help her around the house when she was undergoing treatment for her cancer. "Well, I suppose I could teach him a few things, like washing dishes and picking out clothes. I don't know if he'll be willing after all this time of me doing it. I guess I've spoiled him a bit." When asked why, she continued, "It was always easier for me to do those things. Then I didn't have to worry about anything going wrong or having to correct his mistakes. I get nervous easily. And I waited on his Daddy all the time, too."

The therapist encouraged Janelle to begin working with Brian on doing some chores, like picking out clothes and helping her with dishes. She then asked about who might come in to help them both while she was receiving treatment. "That's a tough one," she said. "Wade is of no use in a crisis. He'll just drink and take my money." She thought a bit longer, then said, "I've been thinking about asking my niece Brittany to come in and help a while. She's about Brian's age and has always had a special place in her heart for Brian. She does have kids of her own, but she's not working, so maybe she'd come. It's real hard for me to ask anyone for help; I've been independent nearly all my life."

Two weeks later, Janelle returned. She reported some success in getting Brian to carry out his chores, but he was not consistent and whined a lot about doing them. She had talked to Brittany, who was more reluctant to help than Janelle expected her to be. Janelle was not sure why Brittany was so hesitant to come in and watch Brian. Her therapist asked if she had told Brittany the full extent of her illness and that she was in therapy right now to make some decisions about Brian. Janelle stated: "Well, I didn't tell her everything. I'm kind of a private person."

Case Analysis

Janelle appeared to be a parent who had dealt with Brian's mental limitations by sheltering him as much as possible from stressors and real-world issues. As her other close relationships had deteriorated, she put all her energies into her son with Down syndrome and overprotected him. This had created a parent-child subsystem that functioned adequately within the realm of the dyad but not well elsewhere.

Yet, Janelle had reached a life course transition with her cancer diagnosis, one that was both life threatening to her and potentially devastating to Brian. She was faced with treatment that would weaken her and possibly fail, leading to her death; also, it could lead to a need to find immediate help during treatment and eventual placement of Brian somewhere else.

The concerns of elderly parents who care for their children with mental retardation are three-fold: financial, residential, and social and emotional (Brubaker & Brubaker, 1993). Of those areas, social and emotional needs of the person with disabilities were the greatest concern to parents and also the area in which parent caregivers had planned the least. Most caregivers desire continuity of emotional and social support for their children, which is likely why Janelle preferred to involve Brittany instead of nonfamily providers. If Brittany and Brian formed a successful bond, then Brian was likely to be well supported into his old age.

The therapist needed to make an assessment of Janelle and Brian's relationship by seeing both of them together. First, the therapist wanted to test Janelle's willingness to change by asking her to give Brian more responsibility at home. He responded as one might expect of an adult child who has had few responsibilities throughout life. Despite his reluctance, he had begun to do some things that Janelle once did for him. Reinforcement of this change was crucial to success in making Brian more independent.

The therapist also suspected that the niece's hesitation to help may have been because of Brian's lack of independence and Janelle's unwillingness to treat Brian as an adult. She may also have had concerns about Brian's ability to adapt to changes in his routine as routinization is a common strategy used by persons with mental retardation to adapt to life circumstances. Disruption of long-held routines can be perceived as crises by persons with developmental disabilities (Lavin & Doka, 1999). This therapist would also like to invite Brittany to join Janelle for therapy sessions to explore whether some arrangement could be worked out between them. Brian would need a trustee or guardian in place when Janelle dies or becomes incapacitated, and family members are generally preferable to state supervision, provided the family members are willing to serve in this capacity and will not abuse their authority.

Continuing Interventions

Janelle brought Brian to a therapy session. The therapist paid close attention to mother-son interaction. Immediately noticeable was that Janelle tried to answer all questions directed to Brian. After a gentle request from the therapist to allow Brian to answer questions, Brian said that he loved his mother and knew that she was sick. He wanted to take care of her. "But I can't do it by myself," he said. When asked who might help them, he replied, "Brittany. She's my favorite cousin."

Next, the therapist asked Janelle to bring Brittany with her to a therapy session. Also strongly recommended at this time was for Janelle to request a meeting of Brian's support team at the state-sponsored agency that served adults with developmental disabilities. After this meeting, Janelle was to go over her options with her therapist. Janelle was wary of setting up this meeting. When asked why, she said, "I don't think they like me too much over there." When asked why, she said that she has not always taken their advice; instead, she had done what felt right to her. The therapist asked Janelle to envision a situation in which Brian needed immediate help and could not get it because the support coordinator and other staff members did not know what was happening in their lives. Janelle got very fidgety and said, "I see your point. I'll call them later today."

In the first session with Janelle and Brittany, the therapist learned that Brittany was quite fond of Brian but wary of Janelle. Her children were busy with sports after school, and Janelle liked to run the show "her way" according to Brittany. To make matters worse, Brittany's husband had his work hours cut back, and she thought she may have to go to work part time to make ends meet. Still, Brittany was willing to accompany Janelle to a meeting of Brian's support team to see what options were available to this family. "I wouldn't want Brian to get put away in a home because his mom couldn't care for him," she said.

Ten days later, Brittany and Janelle returned for therapy. The support team had laid out various options for Brian's care during Janelle's convalescence. One option was for the state to pay Brittany for Brian's care. If this arrangement was impossible for Brittany, then a home care agency could provide staff to help with Brian's needs, such as bathing, homemaker chores, and medication administration. The staff also encouraged Janelle to begin planning now for Brian's care after her death.

Brittany was still concerned about Janelle's need to control Brian's care. However, Janelle's treatment regimen was to start the next week, and decisions would need to be made soon. The therapist suggested that Brittany take Brian for a few hours one day, then perhaps overnight to see how Brian and Janelle responded to the changes in routine.

Janelle and Brittany returned for therapy the following week. Brittany said that Brian's time with them went well overall, but she became annoyed at Janelle's frequent phone calls and advice giving. The therapist acknowledged that it was no doubt painful for Janelle to surrender some control over Brian's care. Janelle's eyes welled up with tears, and she sobbed: "He's been my job for so many years—the one thing I've done well. I feel like I'm losing everything, my life, my son." The therapist acknowledged that Janelle was entering a difficult part of her life, and that she would struggle with the changes that were needed. However, the therapist pointed out that she must rest to give her treatment a chance to succeed, and that Brian would come to accept her absences if she could accept them herself.

Brittany asked if some simple ground rules between herself and Janelle could be set, such as Janelle not calling when Brian was with her and her children; instead, Brittany would call her once daily with updates about Brian. They also would keep a scrapbook of Brian's activities with his second cousins for him to share with his mother. Brittany also agreed to drive Janelle to treatment sessions if it was necessary and to stay overnight with Janelle and Brian if Janelle's health made her too weak to handle things on her own.

Six months later, Janelle and Brittany returned for a follow-up visit. Brian had adapted well to Brittany's care. However, Janelle's treatment regimen had not been successful, the cancer was progressing, and she had battled pneumonia over the winter, barely surviving. Although weak and sad, Janelle was eager to get a plan completed for Brian because she realized that she might not live much longer.

After working with Janelle to handle her anticipatory grief, the therapist referred Janelle and Brittany again to the support coordinator to discuss guardianship and placement issues. The therapist also suggested that Janelle look into hospice care for her final weeks of life and discuss this option with her doctor. Hospice services would permit Janelle to die at home and would also provide help with Brian's response to Janelle's dying process. Hospice care also offers bereavement services, including counseling for surviving family members. See Chapter 6 for more information about hospice care.

FINAL CASE ANALYSIS

Much of Janelle's self-esteem had been centered on the care of her son Brian. Once she realized that her ability to care for him was in jeopardy, she experienced a life crisis that affected her and other family members. It is understandable that she resisted surrendering authority over Brian's care, but in so doing, she risked alienating the one family member who was most likely to help with Brian and carry out at least some of her wishes. If Brittany, her niece, was less assertive, the therapist would need to help her to set limits with Janelle. Fortunately, Brittany was able to tell Janelle what she needed. By holding a conjoint session with Brian and his mother, the therapist quickly recognized that Brian had more functional potential than he currently exhibited. However, his mother would have to give up some control for him to discover this potential.

The therapist always needs to validate the hard work that the aging adult parent has put into the care of the disabled child as a way of building a therapeutic alliance and acknowledging the pain of letting go of the former identity. Whenever possible, a therapist should allow these parents to acknowledge their limitations as a way to set the stage for relinquishing control over their children, and provide support to help them mourn their upcoming losses. Family therapy is recommended to build a new alliance between the aging parent and the next-generation caregivers. Not having a biological child willing to or capable of assuming care of a disabled sibling can substantially complicate care planning. This family was able to succeed because, ultimately, both mother (Janelle) and niece (Brittany) cared enough about Brian's welfare to make sure that he got the care he needed. Undecided as yet was whether Brittany and her family would take over Brian's care when Janelle dies. They may decide on placement in a group home or other residential arrangement. If they favor residential placement, it is important that Brian be placed on a waiting list for such services as most states have such lists for residential centers.

CHAPTER 5

Working With Siblings and Other Close Family Members in Late-Life Families

The noted gerontologist Victor Cicirelli (1994) called sibling relationships "the longest bond," referring to the fact that we know most of our siblings nearly all our lives. Siblings share a family history as they grow up together, leave home near the time of their siblings' departure from home, and lean on brothers and especially sisters for support in various ways throughout the life span. Although felt closeness to siblings may be lessened somewhat during early and middle adulthood, closeness and interaction among siblings tends to increase in old age, particularly when siblings agree on important life issues (Van Volkom, 2006). Life events such as being widowed and parental disability or death often precipitate an increase in contact and social support among siblings (Cicirelli, 1994; Van Volkom, 2006). Likewise, never-married elders may develop especially close relationships or even coreside with a sibling or a sibling's offspring (Wenger, 2001). Thus, issues of grief may affect the mental health and well-being of older men and women who care for and out-live their siblings.

Sibling relationships in mid- to late life have been far less often studied than sibling relationships in childhood. However, some research has shed light on these relationships. Based on in-depth research with a sample of elderly persons, Gold (1989) developed a typology of sibling relationships in adulthood, characterizing them as intimate, congenial, loyal, apathetic, or hostile. Intimate and congenial sibling pairs experienced mostly positive feelings toward each other, with *intimate* siblings confiding in each other and in frequent contact with each other. *Congenial* siblings are friendly and caring toward each other, but their ties to each other are not as deep or reliable as those who are intimate. *Loyal* siblings have bonds based on their shared backgrounds rather than personal involvement. They respond to a sibling when asked for their help but do not share with each other on a deep emotional level (Gold, 1989).

Apathetic siblings lack solidarity with each other and report minimal contact. They experience no psychological involvement and offer little or no emotional or instrumental support. Hostile siblings will denounce each other and describe each other with disapproval and disdain. Resentment, envy, and psychological involvement are all present in hostile sibling relationships (Gold, 1989). Development of these types of relationships with siblings is affected by many factors that occur throughout the life course, including parental favoritism, sibling rivalry, family trauma, family cohesiveness, and quality of the parents' marriage. The potential for conducting family therapy involving siblings is probably greatest among those with intimate, congenial, and loyal relationships, but apathetic and hostile siblings may be drawn into counseling when there are issues at stake such as financial inheritance or elder abuse and neglect.

Another interesting finding is that negative interactions

between siblings in childhood do not necessarily lead to less-close or strained relationships between siblings throughout the life course. In a study of adults in middle and old age with same-sex siblings, Bedford (1998) found that childhood troubles between siblings, such as conflict, competition, and fights, were often positively reappraised by her participants. They often described benefits from these troubles, such as personal growth through social understanding and improved coping skills. However, some sibling troubles carry over into adulthood, resulting in alienation between siblings and cut-offs (Schulman, 1999). Schulman (1999) recommended that therapists working with aging families conduct an assessment of past and current relationships among siblings to ensure that sibling difficulties are addressed as part of the resolution of family problems.

There are challenges to siblings in mid- and late life that can affect their current and future relationships with each other. Deciding how to provide care for a parent is one of those challenges. In most families with more than one adult child, varying levels of involvement in parent care is the norm. Rare is the family in which all siblings are equally committed to parent care. Sibling groups organize such care based on structure, history of relationships among family members, and extrafamilial ties (Matthews & Rosner, 1988). In sibling groups with brothers and sisters providing assistance to aging parents, the helpful contributions of brothers often are viewed as unimportant by both sisters and the brothers themselves (Matthews, 1995). Moreover, my research suggested that even when parent care is shared between two siblings, there are differences in perceptions of commitment to care and willingness to make similar care decisions, thus creating stress and potential sibling conflict (Piercy, 1998).

Refusal on the part of siblings to help with parent care can strain sibling relationships, creating resentment and distance between them, sometimes for the rest of their lives. For example, when a male sibling who lives nearby absolves himself and his wife of care responsibilities for his parents, leaving it all to his sister to do, resentment between brother and sister may ensue. If these feelings are not addressed while the parents are still alive, it may lessen their bond or create distance between them for the remainder of their lives. Such distance and unresolved conflict reverberate throughout family systems, sometimes causing cousins and other siblings to choose sides and families to fracture.

When sibling groups are entirely male or the sibling living closest to a parent is a son, the hands-on work of parent care frequently falls to his wife. Although many daughters-in-law provide excellent care, they may resent the fact that in some families only blood relatives are permitted input into or to have decision-making power in parent care. The failure to acknowledge daughter-in-law experiences with and investment in the parent-in-law's well-being may lead to schisms in family relations.

It is not surprising that problems can occur when sibling groups are trying to make choices and work out a division of labor over parent care. As siblings mature and leave home, they often have dissimilar life experiences, go through transitions (marriage, childbirth, divorce) that vary by sibling, and may develop value systems at odds with each other. For example, some siblings may continue to practice their childhood religion, while others change religious faiths or decide not to practice any religion. Cicirelli (1994) pointed out that siblings have different personalities and varied experiences while growing up both inside and outside their homes and develop relationships with parents that vary in closeness and degree of conflict. Parents often have different expectations for sons and daughters and may treat them differently.

Some of the most frequent conflicts among siblings are over equity in care provision or major decisions involving parent finances. It is extremely rare that two siblings can share care 50-50, but some try to do so. Tensions can build in these siblings over perceptions of inequity in care provision. It may be better for two or more available siblings to "specialize" in providing assistance to parents. For example, one sibling could handle medical care issues and another sibling supervise the parent's finances. Or, perhaps both siblings attend doctor appointments, but one supervises yard work and the other the indoor housework. Major decisions about parent care often precipitate tension and conflict among brothers and sisters. Rare is the sibling group that completely agrees on when to institutionalize a parent or spend money to hire in-home help. Siblings bring all their prior experiences with their families to their care provision preferences and may be influenced by their spouses, children, and friends. Finding common ground and setting reasonable goals are two challenges all therapists face when working with siblings.

Parent care responsibilities among siblings become even more complicated in situations of parental divorce and remarriage as well as when a remarriage occurs in late life. Clawson and Ganong (2002) found that neither adult stepchildren nor elderly stepparents generally viewed stepchildren as obligated to participate in stepparent care. In this study, those stepchildren who felt some duty or obligation to provide stepparent care were generally ones who grew up with the stepparent, saw him or her as having helped to raise them, and had close relationships with their stepparents. However, if the stepparent had biological children, those children were seen by both generations as primarily responsible to provide parent care.

In a separate study that examined perceived responsibilities of children to assist frail older adults who remarry in late life, Ganong and Coleman (2006) found that perceived responsibilities to help biological parents were greater than responsibilities to assist stepparents. Beliefs about obligations to help were associated with relationship quality and degree of the elderly person's needs. Overall, these researchers concluded that stepparents acquired in later life were usually not viewed as family members; thus, the majority of participants in the study did not apply norms of family obligation to help these late-life stepparents.

These findings have potentially serious, even dire, consequences for aging remarried parents and stepparents who need assistance from their children. The following case study illustrates some of the difficulties aging families encounter when parental divorce and remarriage are combined with a crisis of parent care. Who provides the care in these families when a spouse is unavailable to be caregiver or when both biological and stepchildren are involved, and how are these situations negotiated? Problems can quickly escalate in care situations when stepsiblings have distant relationships with each other. These types of blended family situations will become increasingly prevalent in the future given the rate of divorce, remarriage, and relocation of one or more generations in families in our culture.

HOLLAND FAMILY: PARENT CARE IN A STEPFAMILY

Nora and Darrell Holland were 68 and 80 years old, respectively. They had been together for 30 years and married 22 of those years. Nora had a son, Josh, by a previous marriage who lived in a nearby town. He was married, working, and raising four children, all of whom were still at home. Darrell had been a stepfather to Josh since Josh was 12 years old. Darrell had two children by his first wife; they both lived about a thousand miles from his home and were working full time. Darrell was divorced from their mother when they were teenagers. Although both children, a son and a daughter, were on speaking terms with their father, only the daughter, Sheila, visited him regularly. His divorce from their mother was a bitter one, and Darrell's children did not talk much to their stepmother. Neither had been close to Nora over the years.

Darrell had chronic congestive heart failure. He was so weak that he could not walk without others' assistance or use of a wheelchair. He could still get himself around the house but needed help bathing and dressing each day. He had some memory deficits and frequently forgot instructions from Nora or others. Nora had cared for him daily for 5 years. They did not use any paid services, partly to save money and partly because Darrell did not trust having strangers come into his house. Instead, Nora relied on Josh's teenage son to come by and sit with his stepgrandfather if she needed to be gone more than a couple of hours at a time.

Now, Nora had been seriously injured in an auto accident and was currently hospitalized. It was not known how well she would recover from her injuries. Josh, Nora's son, was distraught and saw himself as unable to care for Darrell while his mother recovered. He called Darrell's daughter, Sheila, and insisted that she come immediately to care for her father. Sheila, while willing to help, was unable to leave town right away for both work and family reasons. She asked Josh if someone could be hired temporarily to care for her father while she tried to make arrangements to take off some time from work. Josh calmly said, "He's your Dad; deal with it!" He then hung up the phone.

Sheila called the local senior center in Darrell's town to explain the situation. The staff person was sympathetic and suggested that Darrell temporarily be moved to a nursing home-based respite program. Because this program was private pay unless a client was Medicaid eligible, Sheila called her brother to see if he could put enough money together to pay for a stay of a few days and the ambulance that would take their father to the nursing home. He reluctantly agreed but did not want to help Sheila beyond a week or 10 days with these expenses. He did not see himself as responsible for Darrell's care.

By the time Sheila arrived at her father's side, it was clear that Nora would live and gradually make a nearly full recovery. However, she would need physical and occupational therapy once she was discharged from the hospital to her home. Darrell was doing poorly at the nursing home. He was upset that Nora was not around and confused about her absence. Once Sheila spoke with him, she realized that neither Josh nor the nursing home staff had explained to him fully what was going on with Nora. Darrell knew that Nora was in a car wreck, but he did not seem to understand the seriousness of her injuries. He continually asked for Nora and became frustrated when she did not appear. Sometimes, he yelled at the staff to get his wife over there.

Sheila took her father's hand and explained to him what had occurred. "The good news, Dad, is that Nora will recover. But it's going to be a while before that happens. So, we have to decide how to do things for you and her once she is released from the hospital."

Sheila later met with Josh to discuss their parents' situations. Josh was less upset than before but maintained that his stepfather's care was not his responsibility, and that he could concentrate only on his mother's well-being right now. He also said his wife could not help out with Nora or Darrell because of child care responsibilities and her need to look after her own mother. Sheila tried to talk to Josh about how they might manage both of them at home together, but Josh dodged a discussion of any realistic solutions. Frustrated, Sheila made an appointment with the social worker at the nursing home where her dad was staying.

The social worker was understanding and suggested that Sheila meet with a local therapist who specialized in working with older adults and their families for brief, crisis intervention therapy. If Josh would join her, any progress made might be quicker. Sheila again talked to Josh, pointing out that both of them had a stake in working out a solution to their problems, and that his mother may recover better knowing that Darrell's care was going well. Reluctantly, Josh agreed to attend a couple of sessions. Sheila would have to pay for the therapy herself as Josh did not have the resources to do so. Sheila contacted her brother, Paul, who agreed to help pay for therapy but declined her invitation to join them for sessions.

CASE ANALYSIS

Although this was a stepfamily that was formed many years ago, close bonds between stepparents and their respective stepchildren did not form. Also, there were no close bonds developed between Josh and his stepsiblings, which complicated problem solving among them when a crisis occurred. Thus, this family was unprepared and minimally equipped to handle a crisis in the life of the spouse caregiver, Nora. Both physical and emotional distance from his biological children further complicated this family's ability to respond fully to Darrell's needs. As a result, Darrell's care was jeopardized immediately, and the respite care procured only a short-term solution for this couple and their families.

In this type of situation, a realistic therapeutic goal is to get the stepsiblings who will participate in therapy to agree to a care plan for both parents and to emphasize that their parents are a system that needs to function as well as possible to facilitate Nora's recovery while minimizing intensive direct involvement among the children. It was unlikely that processing past wounds and unresolved relationship issues would be perceived initially by these stepsiblings as helpful to the current situation. However, it may be necessary if they cannot agree to or cannot execute a workable care plan. Qualls and Noecker (2009) have noted that facilitating such second-order change in families is necessary when poor processes and outcomes for handling prior transitions have created imbalanced structures or problematic relationships among the principal family members. In this family, the failure to reorganize and develop healthy relationships with both the parents and stepsiblings postdivorce and remarriage created distance that must be bridged somehow so that Sheila and Josh could collaborate on a plan for their parents' care. If such work was successful, a new working relationship between Josh and Sheila might be forged, which could be useful when future care transitions occurred.

INTERVENTIONS

The therapist asked both Josh and Sheila to describe their concerns and what they hoped to get out of the therapy sessions. Both wanted a workable solution for their respective parents, but Sheila interjected that she wanted to find solutions that helped *both* her stepmother and father as they both seemed to need each other to be functional. Both parents had told their children that they wanted to go home as soon as possible.

To facilitate Darrell's discharge to home, the therapist began by asking what resources were available to tend to his needs at home. After eliminating several possibilities, they were left with two: Josh said that one of Darrell and Nora's friends had a grown son living with them who was acquainted with Darrell and got along with him okay. This young man was currently unemployed. Josh wondered if he would help Darrell during the day and evening with personal care. The other option was to hire a live-in caregiver until Nora was able to resume some caregiver activities.

Sheila could not stay in town indefinitely. The second option was more expensive; they had priced hiring agency caregivers, and the neighbor was willing to work for less money.

Nora was now well enough to be consulted about these options, so Sheila and Josh agreed to talk with her together. They also agreed to return for one additional session to come up with a final solution.

They returned a week later. Nora strongly favored the neighbor helping out over hiring a stranger and was worried about the financial aspects of both choices. She had asked Josh to talk to the neighbor, which he had done. The neighbor was agreeable to helping for a reasonable amount of money but only until Nora was able to resume care responsibilities. He also would like Saturdays and Sundays off. This meant that Josh and his wife would have to help Darrell on weekends or someone else would need to be hired. Josh had talked to his wife about it, and she was willing to help out but only for a few weeks. She spent many weekends helping her own mother with household chores and bill paying.

At this point, Sheila offered to visit once or twice a month on weekends until Darrell and Nora were able to live on their own again. Although Sheila could not lift her father and might need someone else to bathe him, she could stay with him on those weekends and give Josh and his wife some respite when she was in town. Sheila might be able to get her husband to accompany her on some visits, which would give Josh and his spouse the weekend off altogether, if desired.

They agreed to try this arrangement, and Sheila discussed it with her father. She stayed there long enough to get him back home, meet with the neighbor, and assist him with setting up a routine that would meet Nora and her father's needs. By the time she left to return home, Sheila and Josh appeared to have formed a workable alliance to meet their parents' needs.

However, when Sheila returned for a visit a month later, she observed that Nora and Darrell's home was dirty, and Josh and his wife, Susan, had not come around. She called Josh, who said he was upset with Darrell. Therefore, he decided not to come over to their home for now and sent his son on weekends to bring food and to help Darrell briefly with dressing and bathing. As a result, no cooking or cleaning was done on weekends. Sheila asked Josh what happened with Darrell, and he was evasive. Sheila suggested that they return to the therapist and made arrangements to stay longer so that she and Josh could attend a couple of sessions.

After some prodding by the therapist, Josh shared his disgust with Darrell for being so difficult over the years. His outbursts of anger toward his mother had been painful for him to witness, and he preferred to avoid the situation altogether. Darrell had such an outburst a couple of weeks ago while he was there to help them. Instead of visiting them, he just preferred to talk to his mother by telephone. "Mom says they're getting by," Josh related to Sheila and the therapist.

As Sheila tried to collect herself, she told Josh that she understood his reactions to her father. She had seen her dad's outbursts, and they were tough to endure. She did not like them anymore than Josh, but they could not just ignore the couple's safety and well-being, she insisted.

The therapist suggested a session with the older couple and the stepsiblings together. After some cajoling by Sheila, Nora and Darrell agreed to it, and the therapist made a home visit with the four family members present. The therapist gathered some general information about the older couple's health and medication use. Then, the therapist asked Darrell to talk about his anger outbursts. After hearing Darrell talk about his utter frustration at being so helpless and useless in a wheelchair, Josh was able to tell Darrell that he would no longer tolerate his anger outbursts and noted that they had driven a wedge in his relationship with him and with his mother. Nora began to cry as Josh confronted Darrell.

After Sheila returned home, the therapist worked briefly with Darrell, Nora, and Josh to set ground rules to implement the original care plan. With his permission, the therapist contacted Darrell's doctor with the assessment and asked the doctor about possible treatments for what the therapist believed to be Darrell's depression. Darrell began a new medication for depression shortly afterward, and slowly, things improved in Darrell and Nora's home.

The next case is an example of self-neglect precipitated by unresolved grief and depression over the loss of a close sibling. Self-neglect is a growing problem and can lead to a substantial burden to the state when persons become incapacitated and have no family member or friend to look after their interests (Teaster & Roberto, 2002). Thus, involvement of family whenever possible in resolving problems leading to self-neglect is crucial.

JERRY: SIBLING DEATH AND SELF-NEGLECT ISSUES AMONG OLDER ADULTS

Jerry was an 82-year-old white, never-married male who had lived alone since his sister Pauline died 5 years ago. He had come to the attention of Adult Protective Services (APS) because of the conditions in which he lived and his response to neighbors' efforts to help him. Several neighbors had complained of the stench coming from his home and yard. They had seen Jerry fall several times while walking to the store, but in response to their expressed concern, he always said he was okay. All efforts they had made to talk with him and get him to deal with the odor on his property had failed. State workers from APS were then contacted by local police. When his case was investigated, the workers found rotting newspapers and magazines as well as half-full liquor bottles in his house and similar garbage piled up in his backyard. Jerry himself was unkempt and did not appear to bathe regularly. He walked with the help of a cane but was unsteady on his feet. Although he was upset that APS workers were sent to investigate him, he indicated during an interview that he had been lonely since his sister Pauline had died. He had become a recluse since then, walking only to the closest stores to obtain food and drink.

Jerry owned his home and showed little evidence of being cognitively impaired. Thus, the laws of his state gave him the right to self-determination unless it could be proved that he was a danger to himself or others. Although it was evident that he was neglecting his health and hygiene, there was little that the APS workers could do to effect a change in his habits given that his cognitive functions appeared intact and he still was mobile. They explored his potential support system and learned that he had a 62-year-old nephew named Al who recently moved to the area. Al was Pauline's son. Jerry had no children of his own. His half-brother, Don, had come by occasionally but had not been by in over a year. Jerry thought Don was ashamed of how he lived. "I don't really care," he said. "I wish I could just go like Pauline."

With Jerry's permission, the APS workers contacted Don, who wanted nothing to do with helping Jerry. They then contacted Al, who was concerned about his uncle and indicated a willingness to help if possible. Jerry and Al met with the APS worker and, at Al's insistence, agreed to see a local therapist who specialized in working with depressed older adults. Al got Jerry to clean up and went to sessions with him.

The therapist quickly moved to establish rapport with Jerry and Al. He obtained a history of their relationship with each other and learned that Jerry was a very involved uncle before Pauline died. During Al's childhood, Jerry took him to the family farm and taught him farming skills as well as how to shoot skeet and ride horses. He also helped support Al's college education and an early business venture that eventually paid off. He was present at Al's second marriage 10 years ago. However, Jerry had just withdrawn from all relationships since Pauline's death from lung cancer and had rebuffed all of Al's prior attempts to get Jerry out of the house and back into a social milieu. Al now had two teenage children, so he had tried to get Jerry interested in these children, but without success.

In a second meeting, Al expressed sadness at how much

he had missed his uncle in these past years. He acknowledged also missing his mother. At that point, Jerry broke
down and cried and asked Al to leave the room, embarrassed at his display of emotion. His counselor gave him
plenty of time to compose himself before continuing with
Jerry alone.

INITIAL CASE ANALYSIS

Jerry's self-neglect was likely a product of unresolved
grief and isolation at the loss of his sister, Pauline, to whom
he was close. Support systems for never-married elders, especially men, tend to be smaller than those for married and
widowed persons (Wenger, 2001). Barrett (1999) found that
with increasing age among never-married adults, frequency
of interaction declined significantly with friends and family. Never-married men often have great difficulty adapting
to the loss of sisters who have been close to them or kept
house for them (Wenger, 2001). Jerry had been unable to
reach out to others since his sister died and unwilling or unable to care for himself and his home.

Self-neglect is characterized by the "inability or refusal
to attend adequately to one's own health, hygiene, nutrition, or social needs" (Abrams, Lachs, McAvay, Keohane, &
Bruce, 2002, p. 1724). In many parts of the United States,
self-neglect is the most prevalent problem addressed by
APS agencies, representing as much as half of all APS clients (Dyer, Goodwin, Pickens-Pace, Burnett, & Kelly, 2007;
Teaster, Nerenberg, & Stansbury, 2003). In terms of incidence in the general population, it is estimated that only
one in five cases of elder abuse, neglect, exploitation, or self-
neglect is ever reported to the authorities (U.S. Department

of Health and Human Services, National Elder Abuse Incidence Study, 1998). It can be challenging to help self-neglecting adults because many of them refuse help, and nearly all of them report a deficit in social support networks (Dyer et al., 2007). In the case described here, the presence of a nephew who was willing to help Jerry made it possible to try to get him to change his neglectful behavior.

Research findings on the causes of self-neglect pointed to several contributing factors, including depression and cognitive impairment (Abrams et al., 2002; Dyer et al., 2007). Depression may be manifested as loss of will to live or in self-destructive behavior such as substance abuse or addiction (Lustbader, 1996). Cognitive impairment may stem from damage to the part of the brain that handles executive functions (Dyer et al., 2007). Executive functions of the brain involve the activities needed for goal-directed behavior that include one's ability to start or stop actions, monitor and change behavior, and plan future behavior in response to new tasks or situations (Barry, 2007). Impairment to the executive functions of the brain may lead to difficulties interacting with others, poor judgment, or psychiatric problems such as obsessive-compulsive disorders (Barry, 2007). When attempts are made to assist a self-neglecting person, tests of cognitive functioning as well as assessments of depressive symptoms are crucial for determining what kinds of help are needed.

Physical illnesses and impairments to functional abilities are also common in cases of self-neglect. In the Dyer et al. (2007) study, over half the participants had hypertension, a quarter had diabetes, and 20% had arthritis. More than

70% of both men and women scored in the abnormal range on a test of abilities to perform activities of daily living. Self-neglect likely contributes to the hastening of debilitation and, left without appropriate intervention/assistance, may result in death.

Lustbader (1996) cautioned that resistance to change may be high among self-neglecting elders. She argued that establishing a trusting relationship with helping professionals may take more time and effort than is the norm with other clients and that sufficient time must be allowed to develop a relationship of trust, as well as to troubleshoot many potential solutions (Lustbader, 1996).

INTERVENTIONS

The counselor proceeded slowly with Jerry, seeing him alone for a couple of visits, including a home visit at the counselor's insistence. The counselor built a relationship with Jerry by viewing pictures of Pauline and listening to Jerry's stories of their life together. Pauline had moved into Jerry's home after her husband had died. She kept house for Jerry, shopped for his clothes and groceries, and handled the yard work until she became ill. Jerry had high blood pressure, and Pauline was careful with his diet. Jerry handled their finances. They coresided for nearly 20 years. Thus, the sibling bond was close, and Jerry had become dependent on Pauline. Losing her was terrible, and he had no replacement for her. Always socially awkward, Jerry had dated little and mostly kept to himself.

After several additional sessions in which the therapist gathered this information and explored the meaning of Pauline's loss to Jerry, he convinced Jerry to try an antidepressant medication that, once working, helped them begin to deal with Jerry's grief. He also persuaded Jerry to get a medical checkup, which revealed that Jerry had arthritis and signs of mild cognitive impairment. With Jerry's permission, Al was fully informed of these diagnoses.

Jerry still struggled with establishing a sense of purpose and meaning to his life. At that point, the counselor asked Jerry if Al could begin attending sessions again. Jerry reluctantly agreed to this option. He did not want to impose on Al or be a burden to him. He also liked his counselor and secretly did not want to "share" him with others. The therapist asked Al and Jerry for input on how they would like their relationship to be now. Both wanted to continue their contacts, but Jerry worried about what Al's wife and children would think of him. He questioned the idea that he had anything to offer his great-nephews and -nieces given his age and physical condition. Al reminded Jerry that all kids loved stories, and Jerry had many good ones to tell. He also insisted that the children were proud to have a great-uncle, and they wanted to get to know him. Al also offered to help Jerry clean up his house and yard and to go shopping for or with him to buy some new clothes. This time, Jerry accepted Al's offer.

Al and Jerry continued their relationship through the rest of Jerry's life. As complications from diabetes worsened, Jerry accepted the services of a home health aide, who came in three times a week to attend to Jerry's personal care. Eventually, Jerry's cognitive impairment progressed to early stage dementia, and he agreed to move to assisted living. Later, he was transferred to a nursing facility, where he died at age 86, attended by Al and his family.

CONTINUED CASE ANALYSIS

Success in working with this family stemmed from the early positive life experiences that had forged a bond between nephew and uncle and both men's willingness to attempt a new relationship with each other. The therapist was patient and willing to proceed slowly to build a relationship with a man who trusted few people. The therapist also was willing to do home visits to facilitate a relationship with Jerry and understand his environment. Jerry had to overcome deep depression and substantial doubts about his ability to contribute anything of substance to his family's life; Al had to be kind but persistent with his uncle in getting him to change his stance toward interacting with others.

CHAPTER 6

Support Resources for Aging Families Who Need Long-Term Care

This chapter focuses on supports available to individuals and families who need long-term care. *Long-term care* is defined as "a variety of services and supports to meet health or personal care needs over an extended period of time." (U.S. Department of Health and Human Services, National Clearinghouse for Long-Term Care Information [NCLTCI], 2008). The bulk of long-term care consists of providing personal care activities such as bathing, toileting, eating, dressing, and transferring someone from one place to another. It also may include doing chores and light house-keeping or providing transportation to shopping or doctor's visits. Family caregivers provide most long-term care, but there are well-defined services available to supplement family care at home, and other services are available to those for whom home-based care is no longer possible. Long-term care may be needed by any individual throughout a life span; children and younger adults with significant or severe disabilities may also qualify for long-term care services. However, the majority of persons utilizing the services described in this chapter are aged 65 and over.

Long-term care can be expensive, and relatively few people plan for ways to pay for these services. Many do not realize that Medicare does *not* pay for long-term care. Countless others have spent down their assets and become Medicaid eligible to pay for long-term care in nursing homes. There are other options, however, for middle-income persons who are willing to make plans. Long-term care insurance policies have been available for several years, but relatively few persons have obtained this type of insurance. A study of long-term care services reported that only 7% of long-term care spending in the United States is paid for by private health or long-term care insurance (Feder, Komisar, & Niefeld, 2000).

To some extent, this low rate of private coverage among today's elders is understandable given that it has been both expensive and somewhat limited in the services that it covered in the past. However, now there is a wide variety of policies available for purchase, with coverage of both home and institutional care included. While wealthy persons may be able to cover the costs of long-term care with their assets and retirement income, long-term care insurance may be worth the expenditure for couples or single persons who have or will have limited assets and retirement income or who wish to leave some inheritance for their children. Long-term care insurance is generally available to anyone over age 40, and the younger the age at which the policy is bought, the lower the premiums are. Given that about 70% of all persons over age 65 will need some sort of long-term care services during their lifetime (NCLTCI, 2008) and given the shrinking size of nuclear families and thus available caregivers, making some sort of financial arrangements to pay for one's future long-term care may ensure a better quality of life for oneself and one's family in one's later years.

COLLABORATING WITH THE MEDICAL AND HEALTH CARE SYSTEM

In many, if not most, issues older adults face, our health care system has an important role to play. Most seniors see one or more physicians on a regular basis. As their functional abilities decline or they suffer losses that lead to depression or anxiety, they come to the attention of health care providers, including mental health providers. Despite all the concerns about the way in which our health care system functions presently, there are a number of services offered by health care providers that can be beneficial to older adults and their families. A national study of family caregivers (National Alliance for Caregiving & the American Association of Retired Persons, 1997) documented their use of paid or volunteer services, reporting that nearly 38% of caregivers used personal or nursing care services, almost 16% used homemaker assistance, 14% utilized respite care, and nearly 10% used adult day services to help them with caregiver duties. Among the services most often used were home care services, which are generally provided to homebound persons or individuals who are rehabilitating after an injury or stroke, most of them over age 65 (National Association for Home Care and Hospice, 2008a). In this section, home care services are described first, followed by other supportive and long-term care services: telehealth services, adult day services, assisted living, nursing home care, hospice care, and neighbors, friends, and other social network members.

HOME CARE SERVICES

Among the most frequently used services for older adults who need assistance to remain independent are *home care services*, a term that refers to a variety of services provided by both professional and paraprofessional individuals, including nurses, occupational and physical therapists, social workers, and certified nursing assistants (CNAs). Those persons with acute illnesses recently discharged from hospitals or with long-term health conditions, permanent disability, or terminal illnesses may benefit from home care. For those with acute or rehabilitative needs, the Medicare home health benefit can provide skilled nursing care, personal care, physical and occupational therapy, and social work and counseling services. For those with long-term health conditions or permanent disability, state, private pay, or Medicaid programs may provide personal care and housekeeping or chore services. For persons able to live at home with terminal illnesses, hospice care, usually paid for by Medicare, can provide palliative care services, such as nursing care and spiritual services, as well as family counseling.

In addition to all the help with tasks that these service providers offer to senior adults, many offer social and emotional support to their elderly clients. The nature of the tasks done together (e.g., personal care, counseling, or physical therapy), coupled with the frequency and intensity of care in the home, may enable close relationships to form between home care providers and those who receive their care. In my research, I have found that homebound elderly persons often cherish the companionship and relationships they develop with trusted home care workers. Some of them, as well as their family caregivers, even come to view their professional caregivers as confidants, describing them as friends or "one of the family" (Piercy, 2000). Some caregivers have told me that they valued their home care providers so much that when their relative needed a new episode of home care after hospitalization and rehabilitative care, they asked for the same providers they had before, eschewing all others as "outsiders" (Piercy, 2007b).

Home care services, when of good quality, also offer some benefits to family caregivers. My research suggested that family caregivers benefit in two ways: They feel that their loved one is receiving an enhanced quality of life with home care services, and the paid care providers helped them to improve their performance as caregivers by teaching them important skills and providing opportunities for brief respite from caregiving duties (Piercy & Dunkley, 2004).

Therapists who work with older adults and their families may wish to consider referring their clients to agencies that can assess the need for home-based care and connect them with appropriate, well-respected providers. Persons with acute need for rehabilitation following stroke or other debilitating injury (such as hip fracture or knee replacement surgery) may be eligible for the Medicare home health benefit. A physician must make the referral for this type of home care to a qualified home health agency, whose staff will ascertain the senior's needs and set up a care plan for up to 60 days. If an elderly family member is being discharged from a hospital, a hospital nurse or social worker may be able to coordinate this type of referral with the attending physician.

For those older adults who need *long-term* assistance due to declines in cognitive or physical abilities, the local Area Agency on Aging (AAA) provides staff who can evaluate a senior's need and eligibility for personal care or chore assistance through home care services. Created by the Older Americans Act, AAAs serve the elderly population in all counties of the 50 states, with staff who are extremely knowledgeable about local and regional services for elderly persons. Sometimes housed with a regional Council of Governments organization, these agencies usually serve older adults and their families residing in multiple counties (outside major cities). To find the nearest AAA, go to the Web site for the National Association of Area Agencies on Aging (http:// www.n4a.org/) or to the Eldercare Locator service of the federal government (http://www.eldercare.gov/Eldercare .NET/Public/Home.aspx).

Most states have programs that offer home care services for low-income elders. In addition, Medicaid programs provide home care services such as personal care and housekeeping assistance for senior adults who are Medicaid eligible. When older adults need these services but can afford to pay for them or have long-term care insurance that covers the services, the nearest AAA staff may be able to refer them to qualified home care providers.

Consumer-Directed Home Care

There are newer programs that may pay family members or friends to provide a type of home care; they are called consumer-directed programs, and in some states may be known as "cash-and-counseling" programs. The purpose of consumer-directed care is to permit disabled adults, including seniors, to obtain more control over meeting their care needs, including deciding how those needs will be met and by whom. In consumer-directed programs, the person qualifying for care is permitted to hire and fire his or her caregivers as well as manage the care provided. It is an optional program where offered, rather than a mandated one, but has shown great appeal among those older adults who need care but are capable of managing their affairs as well as those elders who may be uneasy with "strangers" coming into their home to provide services (San Antonio, Eckert, & Simon-Rusinowitz, 2006; Wiener, Anderson, & Khatutsky, 2007). Care recipients who have used these programs are generally satisfied with them (Wiener et al., 2007) and assert that hiring family members is preferable to them because family do more than they are paid for; they provide warm, dependable care; can be trusted; and allow older adults to maintain reciprocity in family relationships (San Antonio et al., 2006). While not available in all states at present, the number of consumer-directed care programs is growing in both size and popularity among senior adults and their caregivers. In my research with family caregivers, I have discovered the existence of such informal arrangements in several families. In these families, the children of a widowed parent recruited a sibling or close friend as care provider, then pooled their money or used the parent's financial resources to pay the designated caregiver, either for several hours a day or to live in with the older family member.

TELEHEALTH SERVICES FOR RURAL OR HOMEBOUND SENIORS AND THEIR CAREGIVERS

The rural population of the United States is often underserved by the programs described in this chapter and by the mental health services that may be needed by caregivers and their families. Issues of accessibility, availability, and acceptability may serve as barriers to receipt of services (U.S. Department of Health and Human Services, 2005). It is for these consumers that telehealth services have been created. *Telehealth* is defined as "the use of communication technology to provide health-related care and information" (Clancy-Dollinger, Chwalisz, & Zerth, 2006, p. 53).

The Veterans Administration has reached out to rural elderly veterans by providing telehealth care services by which nurses may monitor a patient's health signs with the use of technology and provide adjustments to a patient's care at home when indicated. The field of telehealth care, including mental health care services, is growing rapidly in response to the needs of growing numbers of rural elders and their caregivers. The purpose of telehealth services, which include audio, video, telephone, and computerized technologies, is to deliver high-quality care to traditionally underserved populations and to reduce the cost of health care for ill members of those populations. A variety of telehealth services is available around the country, and many have demonstrated both acceptability to consumers and cost savings to care providers and consumers (Buckwalter, Davis, Wakefield, Kienzle, & Murray, 2002). Medicare will pay for a limited number of telehealth services through its Part B plan using approved medical providers, psychologists, and social workers at approved origination sites. Types of services offered include consultations, outpatient visits, individual psychotherapy, medication management, nutrition therapy, neurobehavioral status exams, and follow-up inpatient telehealth consultations (Centers for Medicare & Medicaid Services, 2008).

Two telehealth services illustrate innovative practices that try to address the varied needs of rural persons and caregivers to older adults. In rural southern Illinois, a "telehelp line" for caregivers (TLC) provides professional counseling through a toll-free telephone service to distressed caregivers made aware of the program in a variety of ways (Clancy-Dollinger et al., 2006). Built on a four-component model, counselors work with clients to improve their knowledge, skills, social support, and affect in a structured eight-session block of phone sessions. However, clients can select which of the four areas they wish to address and in what order. Early results comparing clients of TLC with a control group were promising, with the client group showing significant differences from the control group in reduction of psychological distress and increases in social support.

Provision of cognitive-behavioral therapy (CBT) to clinically depressed and anxious women in a rural area of a western state has been accomplished through a technologically assisted psychotherapeutic intervention (TAPI; Openshaw & Pfister, under review). Using state-of-the-art videoconferencing software and equipment, teletherapy of 10 weekly CBT sessions was delivered by two licensed therapists and graduate therapists in training. Results suggested that clients experienced a reduction in depressive or anxious symptoms that was maintained 6 months after therapy ended. Clients rated their satisfaction with therapy at an average of 4.85 of a possible 5 points. Teletherapy has the potential to serve many distressed persons, including older adults, couples, and their families who may have been unable to access therapy services in the past.

Telehealth and mental health services rely heavily on accurate assessment of client problems. Use of multiple measures of health, distress, and other important factors is crucial to accomplishing client goals and delivering high-quality care. To establish trust, a counselor may need to make a home visit before or during service delivery.

ADULT DAY CENTERS/ADULT DAY HEALTH SERVICES

One of the least-understood community-based services for adults needing long-term care is the adult day center. *Adult day care* is defined as "a planned program of activities designed to promote well-being through social and health related services" (Helpguide.org, n.d.). Such centers have become more popular in recent years, with 35% growth in number of centers (to 4,601) nationwide since 2001. There are three major types of adult day centers: social, medical/ health, and specialized. A social adult day center may be most appropriate for ambulatory adults with modest health care needs, a medical/health center is most useful to persons with need for more intensive health and therapeutic services, and a specialized center may be appropriate for persons with specific issues, such as dementia or developmental disabilities.

Most adult day centers are open 5 days a week from about 8 A.M. to 5 or 6 P.M. to accommodate working caregivers. A few operate in the evenings and on weekends. Most centers offer flexible attendance plans for those who use their facilities, with some persons participating 1–3 days or part days and others attending full time.

Good candidates for adult day centers include individuals who can benefit from the friendship and functional help offered at a center, who have physical or cognitive limitations but do not require around-the-clock supervision, or who are in the early stages of dementia or Alzheimer's disease (Helpguide.org, n.d.). Caregivers who need regular respite care or to continue with part- or full-time employment often find that adult day centers meet their needs while offering their relative good-to-excellent care in their absence. Nearly all centers offer the following services: social activities, including large and small group activities; transportation to and from the center; nutritious meals and snacks; personal care (help with activities of daily living); and therapeutic activities, including exercise and cognitively stimulating interactions (National Adult Day Services Association, 2009). Some centers offer intergenerational programming with children from nearby child care centers, a type of activity with appeal to and benefits for many seniors (Jarrott & Bruno, 2003). Adult day *health* centers serve seniors with more health problems and impairments in functioning and usually provide physical, occupational, and speech therapies and have medical professionals, such as a registered nurse (RN), on staff.

A nationwide survey of the costs of long-term care services showed that, on average, adult day center services cost $67 daily. Average daily rates were lowest in Montgomery, Alabama ($27 daily), and highest in Vermont ($150 daily) (Metropolitan Life Inc., 2009). Medicare does not cover the costs of adult day services. However, persons with low income and assets who attend licensed adult day health centers or centers with a focus on serving clients with dementia may have the costs of their day services paid by Medicaid. In addition, some long-term care insurance policies include adult day center care. Other day centers offer scholarships or pay for clients using grants and donations. Still others offer fees on a sliding scale, based largely on a client's ability to pay.

Tips for finding good-quality adult day services are listed on the Web site of the National Adult Day Services Association (NADSA; http://www.nadsa.org). As is the case when deciding on any long-term care service, the first step for therapists is to determine the needs of elders and their caregivers with whom they are working. The next step is to find the adult day centers in the client's area, which can be done through the local AAA. The third step is to call various centers to request information, then develop a set of questions that need to be addressed. When this has been accomplished, then pay a visit to the centers. NADSA offers a checklist of items to help consumers determine the suitability of a given adult day center. They also suggest that potential consumers talk to others who have used the center.

To their suggestions, I would add three additional ones. First, ask about the staff's training in gerontology (defined as the study of aging; more training is usually better for center participants). Second, while observing the center's activities and staff-elder interaction, look for signs of infantilization of participants by the staff. Infantilization is the treatment of old age as a second childhood and includes behaviors, particularly verbal communications (e.g., the use of pet names), or use of child-like patterns of speaking to older participants in the center programs. Center programs whose staff engage in frequent infantilization have been found to provide less autonomy and privacy for their attendees. In addition, older adults involved in these programs may interact less often with peers (Salari & Rich, 2001). Be sure to ask center directors and staff about what they do to help new clients adjust to the center environment. Many caregivers and elderly persons are reluctant to try adult day centers because they do not know what to expect or they fear that a change in the elder's routine will be upsetting and consequently more stressful for caregivers. While these are understandable concerns, a good adult day center staff is experienced in working with reluctant new clients and will be eager to share with anxious caregivers their strategies for making their clients comfortable in new surroundings. I have interviewed several caregivers with relatives in adult day center care, and most were extremely pleased with this option for their relatives. The opportunity to keep a loved one at home for as long as possible is increased by use of good-quality adult day services. The challenges are to find good-quality centers nearby and to find ways to pay for center care.

Next we will discuss other long-term care services, which are available to qualifying senior adults when home-based care is no longer feasible: assisted living facilities (ALFs) and nursing homes. Hospice care, a type of care for persons nearing the end of their lives, is also discussed. Tips are offered for how to select care facilities and hospice programs and work collaboratively with their staff members.

ASSISTED LIVING FACILITIES

The term *assisted living* refers to group residential long-term care facilities that help older or disabled adults maintain as much independence as possible while receiving needed assistance. The philosophy of ALFs is to deliver services that maximize individual choice, dignity, autonomy, independence, and quality of life. Unlike more traditional board-and-care facilities, the newer ALFs offer more privacy and greater resident control over daily activities. Unlike nursing homes, most ALFs do not offer skilled nursing care to frail elderly persons. The intention of most ALFs is to offer care to those adults who need some daily supervision and assistance with activities of daily living but who are not sufficiently impaired to require nursing home care. Services provided to residents are based on an assessment of their needs, and a care plan is written into the resident's contract, which can be modified as an individual's needs change.

Each ALF is required by law to offer the following services: 24-hour awake staff to provide oversight and meet needs, whether scheduled or unscheduled; provision and oversight of personal care and supportive services; health-related services, such as medication management; meals, laundry, and housekeeping; and recreational activities; transportation; and social services. Services are not necessarily limited to those listed (Mollica, Sims-Kastelein, & O'Keeffe, 2007). Some homes will accept persons with more functional limitations than others; for example, some facilities will not permit wheelchairs and walkers in their public spaces. Daily nursing care is permitted at facilities in some states, while other states prohibit this type of service (Hawes & Phillips, 2007). These varying regulations can be confusing to consumers, thus demonstrating a need for potential consumers to review facility policies before deciding on signing a contract for residence.

The ALFs have become a popular long-term care choice among older adults. In 2007, states reported over 38,000 licensed residential care facilities with nearly 1 million beds, a substantial increase since 2004 (Mollica et al., 2007). Of the nearly 1 million residents in ALFs, only 115,000 were Medicaid beneficiaries. Most residents must pay for assisted living from their own funds, thus restricting its use to mostly affluent elders or their families.

States are given leeway in how they define ALFs and in how they regulate them. For example, most facilities do not routinely offer information about criteria for discharging a resident, staff qualifications and training, medication policies, and grievance procedures (Mollica et al., 2007). Instead, an older adult or family caregiver considering a move to an ALF will need to ask for this information, if possible in writing. Some facilities are small and others large, and monthly charges can range from less than $1,000 to over $6,000. Most charge well over $2,000 per month.

Quality of care is important and may differ from one facility to the next. Because states regulate ALFs, there are no national standards for quality of care. Quality of care may mean different things to different stakeholders. For example, most consumers rated highly having an attractive facility, private accommodations, high-quality direct care staff, and ability of the facility to provide services such as medication monitoring and flexibility to provide more or different services as residents' needs arose (Fralich & Hawes, 2004). To the staff of ALFs, quality of care may be tied to adequate number of staff to serve residents as well as technological supports that assist staff in carrying out their duties (Williams & Warren, 2009).

In the absence of uniform standards, elders and their family members can benefit from doing research on ALFs in their area before choosing whether and where to relocate. Organizations such as the American Association of Retired Persons (http://www.aarp.org) and the Assisted Living Federation of America (http://www.alfa.org) provide information helpful to those wishing to learn more about choosing the right facility for their needs. Briefly, their advice is to compare facilities in the elder's area by calling the facilities with questions, visiting them several times, reviewing the contract to make sure it is understandable, and weighing the cost, with an eye toward determining whether the monthly cost is affordable in the long run.

Most people who enter ALFs have experienced a mental or physical disability that required more care than families could provide (Ball, Perkins, Hollingsworth, Whittington, & King, 2009). Residents generally come from their own homes or the caregiver's home, but a few come from hospitals, other ALFs, or nursing homes. Ball and colleagues' (2009) study found that there were three types of decision makers among residents they studied: proactive, compliant, and passive/resistant residents. *Proactive* residents were those elders who decided that their present situation was untenable, took their time to find a facility, and made the decision to move themselves. They generally were happiest with the decision and adjusted well to their new homes.

Compliant persons were those who went along with a family caregiver's decree that they needed to move to an ALF. The decision may have been prompted by a combination of a health care crisis and a desire not to overburden busy family caregivers. Compliant elders made up nearly half the residents in this study (Ball et al., 2009). Those who were *passive* or *resistant* to moving (31% of participants) had no role in making the decision and often opposed it. However, these elders had demonstrated through a series of behaviors that they were no longer capable of caring safely for themselves, so family members arranged for the move to an ALF.

Conditions that cause elderly persons to move into ALFs may affect their adjustment to them as well as their family caregivers' responses. All elderly people, even those who choose assisted living, describe it as an adjustment (Ball et al., 2009). Missing one's home and freedom to do things such as eat when desired are common adjustment issues. Adjustment for compliant or passive/resistant persons may be slow. At the same time, having feelings of guilt may prompt some caregivers to try to hasten their relative's adjustment so that they (the caregivers) feel better about their decision. Therapists can be helpful in pointing out that such adjustments cannot be hastened and to focus on helping caregivers to cope in appropriate ways with guilt feelings. It may also be helpful to remind family members that if their relatives were withdrawn or loners while in their own homes, they are unlikely to behave much differently in group settings, preferring their own company to that of others. At the same time, residents who exhibit depression in their new environment deserve evaluation and treatment.

It is possible for married couples to enter an ALF together, although many ALFs are designed primarily for single adults. Studies of couples in ALFs are rare but suggest that their pathways to entering these facilities resemble those of their single counterparts (Kemp, 2008). However, it is not unusual for one member of the couple to be functioning at a higher level than the other member, a situation that provokes some adjustment issues for the better-functioning spouse. Some well-functioning spouses may find their independence and abilities to socialize with others substantially curtailed by their attention and devotion to the more-impaired spouse (Kemp, 2008). But, for couples who are determined to stay together in the face of functional decline on the part of one or both members and who have the means to pay for an ALF, such facilities may be the optimal choice for them.

NURSING HOME CARE

Nursing homes are probably the best known and most feared of the various types of long-term care facilities. Many an aging person has asked a spouse or adult child to promise never to put them in a nursing home, sometimes with negative consequences for that family member. In an effort to honor this request, some spouse or adult child caregivers persist in providing care to the point that they place their own health or emotional well-being in jeopardy. Balancing the care needs of a frail or demented elderly relative with one's own needs or that of the caregiver's immediate family is a crucial ongoing task that may be made more difficult to achieve when the care recipient's requests for continuing home care become unrealistic. Nursing homes are designed to meet the needs of persons whose cognitive or functional limitations require that they receive medical care and supervision 24 hours per day, 7 days a week.

A study of U.S. nursing homes found that there were over 16,000 facilities that served nearly 1.5 million persons, most of whom were over age 65 (88% of all residents; Jones, Dwyer, Bercovitz, & Strahan, 2009). They were 86% occupied, most were operated for profit (proprietary; 62%), certified by Medicare and Medicaid (87%), with over two thirds located in the Midwest or southern United States (Jones et al., 2009). Most of the staff in nursing homes consists of CNAs, with most other staff made up of licensed practical nurses (LPNs) and RNs. Turnover of staff is problematic for many nursing facilities.

Those who reside in nursing homes report a median length of stay of 463 days, or 1 year and 3 months. The overwhelming number of residents have significant functional limitations, with more than half receiving assistance in five activities of daily living: bathing, dressing, toileting, eating, and transferring (moving from one position to another or one place to another; Jones et al., 2009). Although more elders than ever are using home- and community-based care programs or residing in ALFs, the odds of spending some part of one's later years in a nursing home increase with age. While some residents are in nursing facilities only for a short time (as with rehabilitation of a hip replacement), many enter nursing homes to stay when their cognitive and functional limitations exceed family or paid care resources.

Because Medicare does not cover long-term care in these facilities, payment for nursing home care falls to one of the following resources: private, out-of-pocket pay; long-term care insurance; or Medicaid. To be eligible for Medicaid, an elder must deplete personal assets and have a low monthly income; thus, the majority of persons entering nursing homes do so through private sources (Jones et al., 2009). It is extremely important that care-providing family members know

the elder's financial resources before nursing home care becomes necessary. Financial resources may affect what type of
facility will be best able to accommodate the elder's needs in
the long run. Some nursing homes do not accept Medicaid-
funded residents, so if the older adult needing care will eventually spend down assets to become Medicaid eligible, it is
best to find a facility that can accommodate that shift in payment source.

The decision to place a loved one in a nursing home is a
difficult one. The next three sections address issues of knowing when a nursing home is needed, finding the right home
for one's care recipient or family member, and working with
nursing home staff. Therapists working with families in
these situations will most likely find that they need help
with one or more of these important issues.

How to Determine When Nursing Home Care Is Needed

The answers to the question of how to determine when
nursing home care is needed depend on several factors, including the cognitive abilities of the person receiving care,
the functional limitations of the person receiving care, and
the availability of family or paid caregivers. Sometimes,
family care is available, but the level of supervision needed
by the older adult exceeds what the family is able to offer.

Sometimes, family caregivers have the opportunity to explore nursing home options before they are needed, as when
the elder experiences a gradual loss of cognitive or physical
functioning. However, when the elder has a massive stroke
with complications, quick action may be needed. Whether
decline is abrupt, quick, or gradual, it is usually some event
or series of events that makes caregivers aware that the older

adult can no longer take care of him- or herself or live alone (Caron, 1997).

When decline in the elder is gradual, many family caregivers find it difficult to determine when the time is right for nursing home placement. Putting a spouse, parent, or other loved one in a nursing facility is an emotional experience for many (J. Seefeldt, personal communication, November 15, 2009), in part because placement in a nursing home claims personal autonomy (Caron, 1997). The process can be eased somewhat if all family members with input into the placement decision are on the same page; it can become extremely difficult when the key players have different views on this issue. Thus, therapists may need to work with families who are struggling with making this decision to help them identify and resolve barriers to making the decision. In some families, consensus on nursing home placement may be impossible to achieve. In those cases, consensus among the core caregiver subsystem may be the optimal or only viable solution.

Finding the Right Nursing Home

Another point at which a therapist may be consulted is when family caregivers want to find a suitable placement for their relative. There are several resources for persons looking for nursing home placements. Chief among them is the Centers for Medicare and Medicaid Services *Guide to Choosing a Nursing Home* (2009). This comprehensive document offers suggestions to those looking for nursing homes as well as information about making arrangements to enter the home, paying for care and other costs, and reporting problems with staff or administration. It also contains descriptions of alternative care arrangements, such as home care, retirement communities, assisted living, and hospice care.

Other sources of assistance may be the local AAA or the national Eldercare Locator, which has both a Web site (http://www.eldercare.gov) and a toll-free phone number with coverage on weekdays (1-800-677-1116).

Steps and tips for choosing a nursing home are offered by the Centers for Medicare and Medicaid Services (CMMS; 2008) and are presented here. Following the numbered steps are tips obtained from Julie Seefeldt (personal communication, November 15, 2009), an experienced nurse practitioner who placed both her mother and mother-in-law in nursing homes near the end of their lives. Both placements were deemed successful by family members; neither elder was moved, once placed, and both relatives died comfortably in the nursing home with hospice services.

Step 1: Find nursing homes in your area.

Step 2: Compare the quality of nursing homes you are considering.

Step 3: Visit the nursing homes you are interested in or have someone visit for you.

Step 4: Choose the nursing home that meets your needs.

The following tips address how to accomplish Steps 1–4 successfully:

Tip 1: *Prepare for the next step in care before it occurs.* When one is caring for someone with dementia or gradual physical decline, take the time to look at nursing homes before they are needed. It is always better to do research beforehand (Step 2) rather than make an expedient choice that may need undoing later. The CMMS guide (2008) offers ideas on how to conduct this research. One of their excellent suggestions is to contact the local ombudsperson, whose job it is to visit all nursing homes in the area and ensure quality care by investigating complaints about care provision from residents or family members.

Busy caregivers can do this research with a few phone calls and by using Internet sources. It is best to determine at this stage which nursing homes your family member will be able to afford and eliminate those on the list that are unaffordable or too far away for desired visitation frequency.

Tip 2: *Once you have narrowed the list, visit every facility you are considering.* First impressions can be accurate. Look for a clean, nurturing environment in which residents are treated as people and not just as patients. While there, observe the demeanor of the residents, including how engaged they are with each other, staff, and visitors. If your relative has dementia or Alzheimer's disease, look closely at the dementia unit. How large is it? Where is crucial staff located in the facility—are they in plain view of the residents or tucked away from them? Do both scheduled and unscheduled visits. Do not limit yourself to "the tour" and ask all the questions you have. The CMMS guide (CMMS, 2008) has a comprehensive checklist of things to look for when visiting nursing homes.

Tip 3: *Narrow your choices to about three homes* (perhaps more in urban areas where many facilities have waiting lists). Visit them with your relative if possible (for persons with dementia, such visitation may cause distress, agitation, and fear, so joint visits are usually contraindicated). Get a sense of the elder's reactions and preferences.

The Placement Transition: Family and
Nursing Home Staff Relationships

Once the elderly family member, whether spouse, parent, parent-in-law, or other relative, has been admitted to the nursing home, he or she and the family go through a transition period that can be marked by a great deal of stress, guilt, and anger (usually on the part of the person admitted to the home but perhaps including other family members who did not agree with the placement decision). Caregivers also must adjust to the realities of care provision in a medically oriented institution rather than the home setting (Caron, 1997). Families may need a substantial amount of support during this time, and therapists can provide such support, including normalizing the hostile and withdrawn behaviors on the part of the person admitted to the home and the guilt feelings on the part of caregivers, as well as their frustrations with inevitable changes in long-standing care routines. Because the vast majority of families do not place relatives in nursing homes until they have exhausted their own care resources, they need assurance that their decision was a sound one that benefits multiple family members and provides safety and security for their relative.

Social work staff in nursing homes generally take a personal and family history in an attempt to learn about the new resident. It is helpful for family to offer as much information as possible. Caron (1997) also recommended a biography project in which multiple family members construct a biography of the person being admitted to the nursing home and present it to staff in a care conference or via videotaped recording. The construction of the biography can expose the nursing home staff to the essence of the elderly person as well as improve family relationships through creation of a product that focuses on family history and strength.

Over time, families develop different roles with nursing home residents and staff. Caron (1997) characterized those relationships as disengaged (rare visits), consultants (attend care conferences but do not maintain a relationship with their resident), competitive (try to gain control over staff in how care is delivered), and collaborating (support the staff and act as partners in care). These roles and behaviors have trade-offs. Those who function in disengaged and consultant roles minimize boundary ambiguity by "extruding the elder from the family system" (Caron, 1997, p. 246). However, their relatives may not receive optimal care. By establishing relationships of respect with key staff members from the outset of care and by visiting frequently to observe care provision, family caregivers promote the best possible care for their relative. If one wants good care, then one must engage with both the elderly relative and the nursing home staff (J. Seefeldt, personal communication, November 15, 2009).

Families with realistic expectations of care are likely to maintain positive relationships with staff and administration (Austin et al., 2009). If family members inquire, staff can explain routines, procedures, and other reasons for doing things differently from the way a caregiver did them at home.

It is recommended that when mistakes are made in care provision or problems first occur, the family begins by working with staff at the level at which the error occurred. Most of us appreciate the saying "talk to me, don't tell on me" (J. Seefeldt, personal communication, November 15, 2009). Supervisors should be approached only when the problem cannot be resolved at the level of its occurrence. Serious, persistent problems, particularly safety violations, resident neglect, or abuse, should be reported to the administration and possibly the ombudsperson to investigate.

Therapists can be instrumental in helping families to work through their anxieties about care provision so that they can collaborate with staff as care partners. Care staff generally appreciates a mutual valuing of family and staff expertise (Austin et al., 2009).

HOSPICE CARE

Generally offered to persons with terminal illness and their families, hospice care encompasses medical care, pain management, and emotional and spiritual care that is provided by an interdisciplinary team of medical professionals, social workers, clergy, and volunteers (National Hospice and Palliative Care Organization, 2009). Hospice services offer a compassionate and holistic approach to care near the end of a person's life. They can be delivered in the place that the individual calls home, whether a single-family dwelling, ALF, or nursing home. Hospitals also offer hospice care, and there are free-standing, inpatient hospice facilities as well. In 2008, nearly 1.5 million persons received hospice services, representing 38.5% of all deaths in the United States that year (National Hospice and Palliative Care Organization, 2009). On average, a person uses hospice care for 69.5 days, but over a third of persons served by hospice die or are discharged in a week or less.

The vast majority (83%) of persons receiving hospice care are over age 65; most are women. Whites are far more likely to access hospice care than African Americans, Latinos, or members of other minority groups. People with a variety of diagnoses, including cancer, heart disease, dementia, lung disease, and kidney disease, are currently using hospice care. Hospice care has gained in popularity as people become familiar with what it offers and as determining prognoses for life-ending illnesses has improved. Despite growing popularity, researchers found that many persons are not offered hospice services or are referred only in their last days of life, which limits the services that hospice can provide to them and their families. Barriers to offering this program include a patient's or family's difficulty in accepting a terminal diagnosis, their desire to continue with treatments that prolong life, and difficulty in prognostication (Weggel, 1999).

Hospice services are covered under Medicare Part A, available to all Medicare enrollees. For persons to receive hospice care, a doctor and hospice medical director must certify that the patient is terminally ill and likely to have less than 6 months to live, the patient must sign a statement that asserts choice of hospice care rather than routine Medicare-covered benefits for the terminal illness, and care must be sought from a Medicare-approved hospice program. It is important to note that Medicare will continue to pay covered benefits for any health problems not related to the terminal illness (Centers for Medicare & Medicaid Services, 2009).

Benefits of hospice care can be many for both patient and family. Patients receive intense medical services, with pain management strategies closely monitored by health care providers. Home care aides can perform personal care tasks that are difficult for caregivers to undertake, especially as the end of life nears for the older person. Hospice volunteers are trained to provide compassionate care, and their willingness to sit with the person receiving care offers the primary caregiver an opportunity to attend to other matters both in and outside the home. Volunteers may also reduce the isolation that comes with being homebound, for both patients and caregivers. Clergy provide the spiritual nurturing so important to many dying persons and their families. Finally, hospice services include bereavement care for family members that can extend well beyond the patient's death.

Length of hospice enrollment may make a difference in family caregiver well-being. Bradley and her colleagues (2004) found that family caregivers whose loved ones were enrolled in hospice care for 3 days or less were much more likely to experience major depression at 6–8 months after their relative's death than caregivers with relatives enrolled in hospice for more than 3 days. These researchers were careful to control for the presence of major depression among caregivers prior to their relatives' deaths.

In terms of rating hospice care, most families evaluate services positively. In one study, over 96% of caregivers asserted that the plan of care was clearly explained, 75% of them rated the care received as excellent, 76% felt that the bereavement services met their needs, and 72% felt that the patient's pain was brought to a comfortable level within 2 days of hospice admission (National Hospice and Palliative Care Organization, 2009).

Families caring for frail or very ill elders need information about hospice care, with a focus on the range of services provided and the available options for care in the area they reside. They also need to ascertain the wishes of their elderly relative whenever possible. Doing so may make the "hospice decision" an easier one for families to make in consultation with treating physicians. Sensitive therapists can ask their caregiver clients about their relative's wishes, as well as the desires of the caregiver, for end-of-life care. Doing so before the relative's final days may lead family caregivers to inform their relatives' primary care doctors about their desire to use hospice care when a terminal process has begun.

For those who may balk at the idea of a team of persons coming into their lives at sensitive times, two notions may help them to understand the benefits of hospice care. First, the final days and hours of dying persons can be painful for them, and hospice workers are skilled at pain management for those with terminal illnesses. Persons receiving hospice care generally get more frequent attention than those not receiving such services. Second, use of hospice may avoid hospitalization at the end of a relative's life, which is often in accordance with the wishes of the elderly person. Most elders want to die at home, just as they prefer to age at home.

FAMILY AND LONG-TERM CARE STAFF COLLABORATIONS

An experienced nursing home administrator offered some tips to achieve optimal family-staff collaboration for those who have placed their relatives in nursing homes (M. Canada, personal communication, November 17, 2009). However, I believe that her suggestions could be applied to any paid service provider-family caregiver relationship. They are as follows:

- *Information:* Tell the provider or staff your relative's likes and dislikes. Educate them in your relative's preferences.

For example, "Mom never eats fish" could be helpful to dietary services as they plan menus in a nursing home, day health center, or ALF or to a paid home care worker. Offering the elder's history and any special accomplishments gives the staff a basis for forming positive relationships of respect with the elder.

- *Understanding:* Try to understand and develop an appreciation of long-term care workers and their caseloads. Many have large caseloads, whether they provide home care or care in a residential facility. Some staff are better trained or more experienced in working with older adults than are others and may benefit from your patience and suggestions, tactfully given.

- *Communication:* Spend some time observing how your relative interacts with others when in an adult day center or residential facility. When you observe problems, try to help the staff or home care provider come up with solutions. What has worked with your relative before now?

- *Attitude Matters:* Try to avoid approaching staff or home care providers with anger. Ask them to help you resolve the problem you have identified. If the problem is big enough, talk to a supervisor. In nursing homes and some ALFs, social work staff may be the best resource to mediate difficult problems that have arisen between family members, elders, and staff.

ROLES FOR NEIGHBORS, FRIENDS, AND OTHER SOCIAL NETWORK MEMBERS

Other nonfamily members who can provide assistance to older adults and their families include neighbors, friends, and others with long-time knowledge and contact with older family members, such as landlords, barbers, and hairstylists. Friends can provide socialization opportunities and may also be able to give the primary caregiver short-term respite from care responsibilities. Neighbors and friends often serve as a "first alert" system to families, especially when elders live alone. The types of help both neighbors and friends provide may be similar or different from what is expected of family members or paid caregivers, depending on the situation. For example, neighbors may be able to assist with shopping, transportation to doctor's offices, and socializing activities, such as going to congregate meals at local senior centers or attending plays and sporting events in their communities. Landlords may be able to help with home maintenance issues. All nonkin providers may play important roles as those persons who first notice changes in an older adult's health and behavioral habits. Family members, especially those living at a distance, are wise to cultivate relationships with these nonkin members of their relative's social network as they may be important in coordinating assistance that enables the elderly relative to remain independent and enjoy a good quality of life for as long as possible.

How to Integrate Multiple Sources and Systems of Support for Aging Persons and Couples

There are several ways to integrate various sources of support for individuals or couples who need long-term care. Family care can be supplemented by paid home care services for those who are qualified. Fathers may be particularly uneasy with the notion of their daughters providing personal care such as bathing (as are mothers and sons, usually), so getting a home health aide to perform these tasks may enhance the care provision in the home. Likewise, a caregiver who works full time may benefit from obtaining home care services for a cognitively impaired relative as well as placing the relative in an adult day center during working hours. To supplement the contact provided by neighbors and friends, a long-distance caregiver may want an age-appropriate companion for her elderly parent living alone with some functional limitations. The Senior Companion program, developed as part of the Senior Corps volunteer program and often operated by local AAAs, may be a suitable support resource for elders living alone. The companions furnished are also older adults who can offer transportation and friendly visiting to elders who need assistance with minor chores or wish to reduce their isolation. Having a companion may allow them to live in their own home longer than would otherwise be possible.

Some family caregivers may feel overwhelmed at the thought of using paid home care, adult day health, or ALFs. When these services are of poor quality (e.g., when a home health aide is unreliable or has poor people skills), caregivers may feel more stressed and work even harder to monitor the quality of care provided by others (Piercy & Dunkley, 2004). Thus, it is important that caregivers collaborate to the extent possible as a team with paid or volunteer care providers. It is also important for caregivers to discuss concerns with agency supervisors or directors when services are of low quality. When the supports are informal in nature, as with neighbors or friends, it is useful for caregivers to talk with these individuals periodically to ask about the relationship between them and the care recipient as well as to ask about any changes, physical or otherwise, they have noticed in their relatives.

Working with the staff of the local AAA can also be of enormous help to busy family caregivers. AAA staff members are the local experts on the network of services available to older adults and their families. Their clients have used all the services described in this chapter available in a given location; thus, they know who the best-quality providers are and when a given provider may not be a good fit for a particular elder or a specific set of caregiver needs.

Conclusion

Our future reality is that as people live longer lives, millions of families are going to need and access long-term care services, often progressing from the use of home care and Senior Companions to assisted living or nursing home care and hospice care. It is in the best interest of both families and those professionals who work with them to find ways to integrate services to reduce caregiver burden and simultaneously provide the best quality of life to older adults in their later years.

REFERENCES

Abrams, R. C., Lachs, M., McAvay, G., Keohane, D. J., & Bruce, M. L. (2002). Predictors of self-neglect in community-dwelling elders. *American Journal of Psychiatry, 159,* 1724–1730.

Administration on Aging. (2008). *A profile of aging americans: 2008.* Washington, DC: Department of Health and Human Services. Retrieved May 25, 2009, from http://www.aoa.gov/AoARoot/Aging_Statistics/Profile/2008/docs/2008profile.pdf

Akamatsu, N. (2008). Teaching white students about racism and its implications in practice. In M. McGoldrick & K. V. Hardy (Eds.), *Revisioning family therapy: Race, culture and gender in clinical practice* (pp. 413–424). New York: Guilford Press.

Alexopoulos, G. S. (2005). Depression in the elderly. *Lancet, 365,* 1961–1970.

Austin, W., Goble, E., Strang, V., Mitchell, A., Thompson, E., Lantz, H., Vass, K, et al. (2009). Supporting relationships between family and staff in continuing care settings. *Journal of Family Nursing, 15,* 360–383.

Ball, M. M., Perkins, M. M., Hollingsworth, C., Whittington, F. J., & King, S. V. (2009). Pathways to assisted living: The influence of race and class. *Journal of Applied Gerontology, 28,* 81–108.

Baltes, P. B., Lindenberger, U., & Staudinger, U. (1998). Life-span theory in developmental psychology. In R. M. Lerner (Ed.), *Handbook of child psychology: Vol. 1 Theoretical models of human development* (5th ed., pp. 1029–1143). New York: Wiley.

Barrett, A. E. (1999). Social support and life satisfaction among the never married. *Research on Aging, 21,* 46–72.

Barry, D. (2007). Executive function. In *Encyclopedia of Mental Disorders.* Retrieved October 30, 2009, from http://www.minddisorders.com/Del-Fi/Executive-function.html

Bartels, S. J., Coakley, E. H., Zubritsky, C., Ware, J. H., Miles, K. M., Arean, P. A., . . . PRISM-E investigators. (2004). Improving access to geriatric mental health services: A randomized trial comparing treatment engagement with integrated versus enhanced referral care for depression, anxiety, and at-risk alcohol use. *American Journal of Psychiatry, 161,* 1455–1462.

Barusch, A. S., Rogers, A., & Abu-Bader, S. H. (1999). Depressive symptoms in the frail elderly: Physical and psychosocial correlates. *International Journal of Aging and Human Development, 49,* 107–125.

Beavers, W. R., & Hampson, R. B. (1990). *Successful families: Assessment and intervention.* New York: Norton.

Beavers, W. R., & Hampson, R. B. (2003). Measuring family competence: The Beavers systems model. In F. Walsh (Ed.), *Normal family processes* (3rd ed., pp. 549–580). New York: Guilford Press.

Becvar, D. S. (2005). Families in later life: Issues, challenges, and therapeutic responses. In J. L. Lebow (Ed.), *Handbook of clinical family therapy* (pp. 591–609). New York: Wiley.

Bedford, V. H. (1998). Sibling relationship troubles and well-being in middle and old age. *Family Relations, 47,* 369–376.

Bengtson, V. L., Giarrusso, R., Mabry, J. B., & Silverstein, M. (2002). Solidarity, conflict, and ambivalence: Complementary or competing perspectives on intergenerational relationships? *Journal of Marriage and Family, 64,* 568–576.

Bengtson, V. L., & Allen, K. R. (1993). The life course perspective applied to families over time. In P. G. Boss, W. J. Doherty, R. LaRossa, W. R. Schumm, & S. K. Steinmetz (Eds.), *Sourcebook of family theories and methods: A contextual approach* (pp. 469–498). New York: Plenum Press.

Benson, H. (1996). *Timeless healing: The power and biology of belief.* New York: Scribner.

Blank, M. B., Mahmood, M., Fox, J. C., & Guterbock, T. (2002). Alternative mental health services: The role of the black church in the south. *American Journal of Public Health, 92,* 1668–1672.

Blieszner, R., Roberto, K. A., Wilcox, K. L., Barham, E. J., & Winston, B. L. (2007). Dimensions of ambiguous loss in couples coping with mild cognitive impairment. *Family Relations, 56,* 196–209.

Bonanno, G. A., Wortman, C. B., & Nesse, R. M. (2004). Prospective patterns of resilience and maladjustment during widowhood. *Psychology & Aging, 19,* 260–271.

Boss, P. (2006). *Loss, trauma, and resilience: Therapeutic work with ambiguous loss.* New York: Norton.

Boss, P. (2007). Ambiguous loss theory: Challenges for scholars and practitioners. *Family Relations, 56*, 105–111.

Bowen, M. (1978). *Family therapy in clinical practice.* Northvale, NJ: Aronson.

Bowen, M. (1985). *Family therapy in clinical practice* (2nd ed). Northvale, NJ: Aronson.

Boyd-Franklin, N. (2008). Working with african americans and trauma: Lessons for clinicians from hurricane katrina. In M. McGoldrick & K. V. Hardy (Eds.), *Revisioning family therapy: Race, culture and gender in clinical practice* (pp. 344–355). New York: Guilford Press.

Braden, J. B., Zhang, L., Fan, M-Y. Unutzer, J., Edlund, M. J., & Sullivan, M. D. (2008). Mental health service use by older adults: The role of chronic pain. *American Journal of Geriatric Psychiatry, 16*, 156–167.

Bradley, E. H., Prigerson, H., Carlson, M. D. A., Cherlin, E., Johnson-Hurzeler, R., & Kasl, S. V. (2004). Depression among surviving caregivers: Does length of hospice enrollment matter? *American Journal of Psychiatry, 161*, 2257–2262.

Brennan, M., & Heiser, D. (2004). Introduction: Spiritual assessment and intervention: Current directions and applications. *Journal of Religion, Spirituality & Aging, 17*, 1–20.

Brintnall-Peterson, M., Poehlmann, J., Morgan, K., & Shlafer, R. (2009). A web-based fact sheet series for grandparents raising grandchildren and the professionals who serve them. *The Gerontologist, 49*, 276–282.

Brown, S. L., Lee, G. R., & Bulanda, J. R. (2006). Cohabitation among older adults: A national portrait. *Journals of Gerontology: Social Sciences, 61B*, S71–S79.

Brubaker, E. (1987). *Working with the elderly: A social systems approach.* Newbury Park, CA: Sage.

Brubaker, E., & Brubaker, T. H. (1993). Caring for adult children with mental retardation. In K. A. Roberto (Ed.), *The elderly caregiver: Caring for adults with developmental disabilities* (pp. 51–60). Newbury Park, CA: Sage.

Buckwalter, K. C., Davis, L. L., Wakefield, B. J., Kienzle, M. G., & Murray, M. A. (2002). Telehealth for elders and their caregivers in rural communities. *Family & Community Health, 25*(3), 31–40.

Calasanti, T., & Kiecolt, K. J. (2007). Diversity among late-life couples. *Generations, 31*(3), 10–17.

Caron, W. A. (1997). Family systems and nursing home systems: An eco-systemic perspective for the systems practitioner. In T. D. Hargrave & S. M. Hanna (Eds.), *The aging family: New visions in theory, practice, and reality* (pp. 235–258). Philadelphia: Brunner/Mazel.

Carr, D. (2004). The desire to date and remarry among older widows and widowers. *Journal of Marriage and Family, 66*, 1051–1068.

The Catholic handbook for visiting the sick and homebound. (2010). Chicago: Liturgical Training.

Centers for Medicare & Medicaid Services. (2008). *Guide to choosing a nursing home.* Retrieved November 15, 2009, from http://www.medicare.gov/publications/pubs/pdf/02174.pdf

Centers for Medicare & Medicaid Services. (2009). *Fact sheet: Telehealth services.* Retrieved December 2, 2009, from http://www.cms.hhs.gov/MLNproducts/downloads/ TelehealthSrvcsfctsht.pdf

Cicirelli, V. G. (1994). The longest bond: The sibling life cycle. In L. L'Abate (Ed.), *Handbook of developmental family psychology and psychopathology* (pp. 44–59). New York: Wiley.

Clancy-Dollinger, S., Chwalisz, K., & Zerth, E. O. (2006). Tele-help line for caregivers (TLC): A comprehensive telehealth intervention for rural family caregivers. *Clinical Gerontologist, 30*, 51–64.

Clarke, S. C. (1995). *Advance report of final divorce statistics, 1989 and 1990* [Monthly Vital Statistics Report 43(8)]. Hyattsville, MD: National Center for Health Statistics.

Clawson, J., & Ganong, L. (2002). Adult stepchildren's obligations to older stepparents. *Journal of Family Nursing, 8*, 50–72.

Coehlo, D. P., Hooker, K., & Bowman, S. (2007). Institutional placement of persons with dementia. *Journal of Family Nursing, 13*, 253-277.

Contrada, R. J., Goyal, T. M., Cather, C., Rafalson, L., Idler, E. L., & Krause, T. J. (2004). Psychosocial factors in outcomes of heart surgery: The impact of religious involvement and depressive symptoms. *Health Psychology, 23*, 227–238.

Craske, M. G., Barlow, D. H., & Meadows, E. (2000). *Mastery of your anxiety and panic: Therapist guide for anxiety, panic and agoraphobia (MAP-3).* Boulder, CO: Graywind.

Curran, S. R., McLanahan, S., & Knab, J. (2003). Does remarriage expand perceptions of kinship support among the elderly? *Social Science Research, 32*, 171–190.

Davis, P. K. (2009). *Financing home and community based long term care:*

Adult children caregiver perspectives. (Unpublished master's thesis). Utah State University, Logan, Utah.

Dean, A., Kolody, B., Wood, P., & Matt, G. E. (1992). The influence of living alone on depression in elderly persons. *Journal of Aging and Health, 4,* 3–18.

Dellman-Jenkins, M., Blankemeyer, M., & Olesh, M. (2002). Adults in expanded grandparent roles: Considerations for practice, policy, and research. *Educational Gerontology, 28,* 219–235.

De Vugt, M. E., Stevens, F., Aalten, P., Lousberg, R., Jaspers, N., Winkens, I., . . . Verhey, F. R. (2004). Do caregiver management strategies influence patient behavior in dementia? *International Journal of Geriatric Psychiatry, 19,* 85–92.

Doherty, W. J., & Baptiste, D. A., Jr. (1993). Theories emerging from family therapy. In P. G. Boss, W. J. Doherty, R. LaRossa, W. R. Schumm, & S. K. Steinmetz (Eds.), *Sourcebook of family theories and methods: A contextual approach* (pp. 505–524). New York: Plenum Press.

Dunkin, J. J., & Anderson-Hanley, C. (1998). Dementia caregiver burden: A review of the literature and guidelines for assessment and intervention. *Neurology, 51*(Supplement 1), S53–S60.

Dyer, C. B., Goodwin, J. S., Pickens-Pace, S., Burnett, J., & Kelly, P. A. (2007). Self-neglect among the elderly: A model based on more than 500 patients seen by a geriatric medicine team. *American Journal of Public Health, 97,* 1671–1676.

Elder, G. H., Jr. (1994). Time, human agency, and social change: Perspectives on the life course. *Social Psychological Quarterly, 57,* 4–15.

Erikson, E., Erikson, J. M., & Kivnick, H. (1986). *Vital involvement in old age: The experience of old age in our time.* New York: Norton.

Feder, J., Komisar, H.L., & Niefeld, M. (2000). Long-term care in the United States: An overview. *Health Affairs, 19,* 40–56.

Feinberg, L. F., & Whitlatch, C. J. (2002). Decision-making for persons with cognitive impairment and their family caregivers. *American Journal of Alzheimer's Disease and Other Dementias, 17,* 237–244.

Fowers, B. J., & Davidov, B. J. (2006). The virtue of multiculturalism. *American Psychologist, 61,* 581–594.

Fralich, J., & Hawes, C. (2004). *Results of focus groups interviews with residents and family members in Maine and North Carolina.* College

Station: Texas A&M Health Science Center, School of Rural Public Health, Program on Aging and Long-Term Care Policy.

Frank, J. B. (2007/2008). Evidence for grief as the major barrier faced by Alzheimer caregivers: A qualitative analysis. *American Journal of Alzheimer's Disease & Other Dementias, 22,* 516–527.

Fredriksen-Goldsen, K. I., & Scharlach, A. E. (2006). An interactive model of informal adult care and employment. *Community, Work and Family, 9,* 441–455.

Friedhoff, A. J. (1994). Consensus development conference statement: Diagnosis and treatment of depression in late life. In L. S. Schneider, C. F. Reynolds III, B. D. Lebowitz, & A. J. Friedhoff (Eds.), *Diagnosis and treatment of depression in late life: Results of the NIH Consensus Development Conference* (pp. 491-511). Washington, DC: American Psychiatric Press.

Gallo, J. J., & Rabins, P. V. (1999). Depression without sadness: Alternative presentations of depression in late life. *American Family Physician, 60,* 820–826.

Ganong, L., & Coleman, M. (2006). Obligations to stepparents acquired in later life: Relationship quality and acuity of needs. *Journal of Gerontology: Social Sciences, 61B,* S80–S88.

Garcia-Preto, N. (2008). Latinas in the United States: Bridging two worlds. In M. McGoldrick & K. V. Hardy (Eds.), *Revisioning family therapy: Race, culture and gender in clinical practice* (pp. 261–274). New York: Guilford Press.

Gaugler, J. E., Edwards, A. B., Femia, E. E., Zarit, S. H., Stephens, M. P., Townsend, A., & Greene, R. (2000). Predictors of institutionalization of cognitively impaired elders: Family help and the timing of placement. *Journals of Gerontology: Psychological Sciences, 55B,* P247–P255.

Gaugler, J. E., Kane, R. L., Kane, R. A., & Newcomer, R. (2005). The longitudinal effects of early behavior problems in the dementia caregiving career. *Psychology and Aging, 20,* 100–116.

Genero, N. P., Miller, J. B., Surrey, J., & Baldwin, L. M. (1992). Measuring perceived mutuality in close relationships: Validation of the mutual psychological development questionnaire. *Journal of Family Psychology, 6,* 36–48.

George, L. K., & Gwyther, L. P. (1986). Caregiver well-being: A multidimensional examination of family caregivers of demented adults. *The Gerontologist, 26,* 253–259.

Gilbert, R. M. (2004). *The eight concepts of Bowen theory.* Falls Church, VA: Leading Systems Press.

Glass, T. A., Mendes de Leon, C. F., Bassuk, S. S., & Berkman, L. F. (2006). Social engagement and depressive symptoms in late life. *Journal of Aging and Health, 18,* 604–628.

Gold, D. T. (1989). Sibling relationships in old age: A typology. *International Journal of Aging and Human Development, 28,* 37–51.

Goodman, C. C., Tan, P. P., Ernandes, P., & Silverstein, M. (2008). The health of grandmothers raising grandchildren: Does the quality of family relationships matter? *Families, Systems, & Health, 26,* 417–430.

Gottman, J. M., & Silver, N. (2004). *The seven principles for making marriage work.* London: Orion.

Greenwood, M. J. (1988). Changing patterns of migration and regional economic growth in the U.S.: A demographic perspective. *Growth and Change, 19,* 68-86.

Grogan, J. (2005). *Marley & me: Life with the world's worst dog.* New York: William Morrow.

Grogan, J. (2008). *The longest trip home: A memoir.* New York: William Morrow.

Grundy, E., & Henretta, J. C. (2006). Between elderly parents and adult children: A new look at the intergenerational care provided by the "sandwich generation." *Aging & Society, 26,* 707–722.

Gubrium, J.F., & Buckholdt, D. R. (1982). Fictive family: Everyday usage, analytic, and human service considerations. *American Anthropologist, 84,* 878–885.

Guiaux, M., Van Tilburg, T., & Van Groenou, M. (2007). Changes in contact and support exchange in personal networks after widowhood. *Personal Relationships, 14,* 457–473.

Hansen, N. D., Pepitone-Arreola-Rockwell, F., & Greene, A. F. (2000). Multicultural competence: Criteria and case examples. *Professional Psychology: Research and Practice, 31,* 652–660.

Hardy, K. V. (2008). Race, reality, and relationships. In M. McGoldrick & K. V. Hardy (Eds.), *Revisioning family therapy: Race, culture and gender in clinical practice* (pp. 76–84). New York: Guilford Press.

Harper, J. M., & Sandberg, J. G. (2009). Depression and communication processes in later life marriages. *Aging & Mental Health, 13,* 546–555.

Harvard Medical School. (2008). *Improving memory: Understanding age-related memory loss.* Boston: Harvard Health.

Hatch L. R. (2000). *Beyond gender differences: Adaptations to aging in life course perspective.* Amityville, NY: Baywood.

Hawes, C., & Phillips, C. D. (2007). Defining quality in assisted living: Comparing apples, oranges, and broccoli [Special issue 3]. *The Gerontologist, 47,* 40–50.

Hayslip, B., Jr., & Kaminski, P. L. (2005). Grandparents raising their grandchildren: A review of the literature and suggestions for practice. *The Gerontologist, 45,* 262–269.

He, W., Sengupta, M., Velkoff, V. A., & DeBarros, K. A. (2005). *65+ in the United States: 2005.* U.S. Census Bureau Current Population Reports. Washington, DC: Government Printing Office.

Helpguide.org. (n.d.). *Adult day centers: A guide to options and selecting the best center for your needs.* Retrieved November 30, 2009, from http://www.helpguide.org/elder/adult_day_care_centers.htm

Hinterlong, J., & Ryan, S. (2008). Creating grander families: Older adults adopting younger kin and non-kin. *The Gerontologist, 48,* 527–536.

Hodge, D. R. (2001). Spiritual assessment: A review of major qualitative methods and a new framework for assessing spirituality. *Social Work, 46,* 203–214.

Hodge, D. R. (2004). Spirituality and people with mental illness: Developing spiritual competency in assessment and intervention. *Families in Society, 85,* 36–44.

Hodge, D. R. (2005). Spiritual assessment in marital and family therapy: A methodological framework for selecting from among six qualitative assessment tools. *Journal of Marital and Family Therapy, 31,* 341–356.

Hodge, D. R. (2006). A template for spiritual assessment: A review of the JCAHO requirements and guidelines for implementation. *Social Work, 51,* 317–326.

Holley, C. K., & Mast, B. T. (2009). The impact of anticipatory grief on caregiver burden in dementia caregivers. *The Gerontologist, 49,* 388–396.

Idler, E. L. (2006). Religion and aging. In R. H. Binstock & L. K. George

(Eds.), *Handbook of aging and the social sciences* (pp. 277–300). San Diego, CA: Elsevier.

Jacobson, N. S., & Christensen, A. (1996). *Integrative couple therapy: Promoting acceptance and change.* New York: Norton.

Jarrott, S. E., & Bruno, K. (2003). Intergenerational activities involving persons with dementia: An observational assessment. *American Journal of Alzheimer's Disease and Other Dementias, 18,* 31–37.

Johnson, C., L., & Barer, B. M. (1990). Families and networks among older inner-city blacks. *The Gerontologist, 30,* 726–733.

Jones, A. L., Dwyer, L. L., Bercovitz, A. R., & Strahan, G. W. (2009). The National Nursing Home Survey: 2004 overview. *National Center for Health Statistics. Vital Health Statistics, 13*(167), 1–164.

Joseph, A. E., & Hallman, B. C. (1996). Caught in the triangle: The influence of home, work and elder location on work-family balance. *Canadian Journal on Aging, 15,* 393–412.

Kabat-Zinn, J. (1990). *Full catastrophe living.* New York: Dell.

Keller, S., & Stricker, G. (2003). Links between custodial grandparents and the psychological adaptation of grandchildren. In B. Hayslip Jr. & J. H. Patrick (Eds.), *Working with custodial grandparents* (pp. 27–43). New York: Springer.

Kelley, S. J., & Whitley, D. M. (2003). Psychological distress and physical health problems in grandparents raising grandchildren: Development of an empirically based intervention model. In B. Hayslip Jr. & J. H. Patrick (Eds.), *Working with custodial grandparents* (pp. 127–144). New York: Springer.

Kemp, C. L. (2008). Negotiating transitions in later life: Married couples in assisted living. *Journal of Applied Gerontology, 27,* 231–251.

Kinsella, K., & He, W. (2009). *An aging world: 2008.* U.S. Census Bureau, International Population Reports, P95/09-1. Washington, DC: U.S. Government Publishing Office.

Lavin, C., & Doka, K. J. (1999). *Older adults with developmental disabilities.* Amityville, NY: Baywood.

Lin, I. (2008). Consequences of parental divorce for adult children's support of their frail parents. *Journal of Marriage and Family, 70,* 113–128.

Luscher, K., & Pillemer, K. (1998). Intergenerational ambiguity. *Journal of Marriage & Family, 60,* 413–425.

Lustbader, W. (1996). Self-neglect: A practitioner's view. *Aging, 367*, 51–61.

Main, R., Macomber, J. E., & Geen, R. (2006). *Trends in service receipt: Children in kinship care gaining ground.* Washington, DC: Urban Institute.

Margolin, G., & Gordis, E. B. (2004). Children's exposure to violence in the family and community. *Current Directions in Psychological Science, 13*, 152–155.

Martire, L. M., Schulz, R., Reynolds, C. F., III, Morse, J. Q., Butters, M. A., & Hinrichsen, G. A. (2008). Impact of close family members on older adults' early response to depression treatment. *Psychology & Aging, 23*, 447–452.

Matthews, S. H. (1995). Gender and the division of filial responsibility between lone sisters and their brothers. *Journals of Gerontology: Social Sciences, 50B*, S312–S320.

Matthews, S. H., & Rossner, T. T. (1988). Shared filial responsibility: The family as the primary caregiver. *Journal of Marriage and the Family, 50*, 185–195.

McAdams-Mahmoud, V. (2008). Understanding families in the context of cultural adaptations to oppression. In M. McGoldrick & K. V. Hardy (Eds.), *Revisioning family therapy: Race, culture and gender in clinical practice* (pp. 85–93). New York: Guilford Press.

McGoldrick, M., Gerson, R., & Shellenberger, S. (1999). *Genograms: Assessment and intervention* (2nd ed.). New York: Norton.

McGoldrick, M., Giordano, J., & Pearce, J. K. (1996). *Ethnicity and family therapy* (2nd ed). New York: Guilford Press.

McGoldrick, M., Giordano, J., & Garcia-Preto, N. (2005). *Ethnicity and family therapy* (3rd ed.). New York: Guilford Press.

McGoldrick, M., Pearce, J. K., & Giordano, J. (1982). *Ethnicity and family therapy.* New York: Guilford Press.

Melhem, N. M., Walker, M., Moritz, G., & Brent, D. A. (2008). Antecedents and sequelae of sudden parental death in offspring and surviving caregivers. *Archives of Pediatrics and Adolescent Medicine, 162*, 403–410.

MetLife Mature Market Institute and National Alliance for Caregiving. (2006, July). *The MetLife caregiving cost study: Productivity losses to U.S. business.* Retrieved December 8, 2009, from http://www.MatureMarketInstitute.com

Metropolitan Life Inc. (2009, October). *MetLife market survey of long-term care costs.* Retrieved December 1, 2009, from http://www .MatureMarketInstitute.com

Minuchin, S., Lee, W., & Simon, G. M. (1996). *Mastering family therapy: Journeys of growth and transformation.* New York: Wiley.

Mirowsky, J., & Ross, C. E. (1992). Age and depression. *Journal of Health and Social Behavior, 33,* 187–205.

Mollica, R., Sims-Kastelein, K., & O'Keeffe, J. (2007). *Residential care and assisted living compendium: 2007.* Washington, DC: U.S. Department of Health and Human Services, Office of Disability, Aging and Long-Term Care Policy.

Montenegro, X. P. (2004). *The divorce experience: A study of divorce at midlife and beyond.* Retrieved May 28, 2008, from http://assets.aarp .org/rgcenter/general/divorce.pdf

Moran, M., Flannelly, K. J., Weaver, A. J., Overvold, J. A., Hess, W., & Wilson, J.C. (2005). A study of pastoral care, referral, and consultation practices among clergy in four settings in the New York City area. *Pastoral Psychology, 53,* 255–266.

Nadeau, J. W. (2008). Meaning-making in bereaved families: Assessment, intervention, and future research. In M. S. Stroebe, R. O. Hansson, H. Schut, & W. Stroebe (Eds.), *Handbook of bereavement research and practice* (pp. 511–530). Washington, DC: American Psychological Association.

Nakonezny, P. A., Rodgers, J. L., & Nussbaum, J. F. (2003). The effect of later life parental divorce on adult-child/older-parent solidarity: A test of the buffering hypothesis. *Journal of Applied Social Psychology, 33,* 1153–1178.

National Adult Day Services Association. (2009, November 29). *Adult day services: Overview and facts.* Retrieved November 29, 2009, from http://www.nadsa.org/adsfacts/default.asp

National Alliance for Caregiving and the American Association of Retired Persons. (1997). *Family caregiving in the U.S.: Findings from a national survey* (Final report). Bethesda, MD: National Alliance for Caregiving.

National Association for Home Care and Hospice. (2008a). *Basic statistics about home care.* Retrieved July 3, 2009, from http://www.nahc .org/facts/08HC_Stats.pdf

National Association for Home Care and Hospice. (2008b). *How do I se-*

lect the right home care provider? Retrieved July 3, 2009, from http://
www.nahc.org/consumer/selection.html

National Association of Professional Geriatric Care Managers. (2008, January 21). *Executive summary report: Geriatric care manager/aging study.* Retrieved June 28, 2009, from http://www.caremanager.org/

National Hospice and Palliative Care Organization. (2009). *Facts and figures: Hospice care in America.* Retrieved December 1, 2009, from http://www.nhpco.org

National Institute of Mental Health. (2007). *Older adults: Depression and suicide facts* (NIH Publication No. 4593). Retrieved from http://www.nimh.nih.gov/health/publications/older-adults-depression-and-suicide-facts-fact-sheet/index.shtml

Newman, M. G., & Borkovec, T. G. (1995). Cognitive-behavioral treatment of generalized anxiety disorder. *The Clinical Psychologist, 48*(4), 5–7.

New York State Bar Association, Elder Law Section. (2008, September 3). *New Medicare mental health law.* Retrieved October 17, 2009, from http://nysbar.com/blogs/ Elderlaw/2008/09/new_medicare_mental_health_law_1.html

Nolen-Hoeksema, S., & Larson, J. (1999). *Coping with loss.* Mahwah, NJ: Erlbaum.

Norton, M. C., & Piercy, K. W. (2010). *Physician treatment of elder depression: Elder and physician perspectives.* Unpublished raw data.

Openshaw, D. K., & Pfister, R. (2009). *Mental health services for women diagnosed with depression in rural Utah communities: A pilot study evaluating the clinical effectiveness of a technologically assisted psychotherapeutic intervention (TAPI).* Manuscript submitted for publication.

Ory, M., Hoffman, R. R., Yee, J. L., Tennstedt, S., & Schulz, R. (1999). Prevalence and impact of caregiving: A detailed comparison between dementia and nondementia caregivers. *The Gerontologist, 39,* 177–185.

Ory, M., Hoffman, R. R., Yee, J. L., Tennstedt, S., & Schulz, R. (1999). Prevalence and impact of caregiving: A detailed comparison between dementia and nondementia caregivers. *The Gerontologist, 39,* 177-185.

Petersen, R. C., & Negash, S. (2008). Mild cognitive impairment: An overview. *CNS Spectrum, 13,* 45–53.

Petersen, R. C., Smith, G. E., Waring, S. C., Ivnik, R. J., Tangalos, E. G., & Kokmen, E. (1999). Mild cognitive impairment: Clinical characterization and outcome. *Archives of Neurology, 56*, 303–308.

Petersen, R. C., Thomas, R. G., Grundman, M., Bennett, D., Doody, R., Ferris, S., . . . Alzheimer's Disease Cooperative Study Group. (2005). Vitamin E and Donepezil for the treatment of mild cognitive impairment. *New England Journal of Medicine, 352*, 2379–2388.

Pew Research Center. (2009, June 29). *Growing old in America: Expectations vs. reality.* Retrieved June 30, 2009, from http://pewsocial trends.org/assets/pdf/getting-old-in-america.pdf

Pezzin, L. E., Pollak, R. A., & Schone, B. S. (2008). Parental marital disruption, family type, and transfers to disabled elderly parents. *Journals of Gerontology: Social Sciences, 63B*, S349–S358.

Piercy, K. W. (1998). Theorizing about family caregiving: The role of responsibility. *Journal of Marriage and the Family, 60*, 109–118.

Piercy, K. W. (2000). When it's more than a job: Relationships between home health workers and their older clients. *Journal of Aging and Health, 12*, 362–387.

Piercy, K. W. (2007a). The characteristics of strong commitments to intergenerational family care of older adults. *Journals of Gerontology: Social Sciences, 62B*, S381–S387.

Piercy, K. W. (2007b). Successful collaborations between formal and informal care providers: Paul and Patrice's story. *Generations, 31*(3), 72–73.

Piercy, K. W., & Dunkley, G. J. (2004). What quality paid home care means to family caregivers. *Journal of Applied Gerontology, 23*, 175–192.

Piercy, K. W., Norton, M. N., & Jones, C. (2007). *The utilization of social support by depressed older adults.* Unpublished manuscript.

Pipher, M. (1999). *Another country: Navigating the emotional terrain of our elders.* New York: Riverhead Books.

Powell, L. H., Shahabi, L., & Thoresen, C. E. (2003). Religion and spirituality: Linkages to physical health. *American Psychologist, 58*, 36–52.

Qualls, S. H. (1999). Family therapy with older adult clients. *Journal of Clinical Psychology, 55*, 977–990.

Qualls, S. H., & Noelker, T. L. (2009). Caregiver family therapy for conflicted families. In S. H. Qualls & S. H. Zarit (Eds.), *Aging families and caregiving* (pp. 155–188). Hoboken, NJ: Wiley.

Rabow, M. W., Hauser, J. M., & Adams, J. (2004). Supporting family caregivers at the end of life. *Journal of the American Medical Association, 291,* 483–491.

Rempel, G. R., Neufeld, A., & Kushner, K. E. (2007). Interactive use of genograms and ecomaps in family caregiving research. *Journal of Family Nursing, 14,* 403–419.

Roe, K. M., & Minkler, M. (1998). Grandparents raising grandchildren: Challenges and responses. *Generations, 22*(4), 25–32.

Roff, L. L., Martin, S. S., Jennings, L. K., Parker, M. W., & Harmon, D. K. (2007). Long distance parental caregivers' experiences with siblings: A qualitative study. *Qualitative Social Work, 6,* 315–334.

Roff, L. L., Toseland, R., Martin, J. A., Fine, C., & Parker, M. (2003). Family-social tasks in long distance caregiving. *Geriatric Care Management Journal, 13*(1), 29–35.

Rosenblatt, B., & Van Steenberg, C. (2003). *Long-distance caregivers: An essential guide for families and friends caring for ill or elderly loved ones.* Family Caregiver Alliance. Retrieved December 6, 2009, from http://www.caregiver.org/caregiver/jsp/content/pdfs/op_2003_long_distance_handbook.pdf

Salari, S. M., & Rich, M. (2001). Social and environmental infantilization of aged persons: Observations in two adult day care centers. *International Journal of Aging and Human Development, 52,* 115–134.

San Antonio, P. M., Eckert, J. K., & Simon-Rusinowitz, L. (2006). The importance of relationship: Elders and their paid family caregivers in the Arkansas cash and counseling qualitative study. *Journal of Applied Gerontology, 25,* 31–48.

Schacter, J. P. (2004). *Geographic mobility: 2002 to 2003* (Current Population Reports P20–549). Retrieved May 16, 2009, from http://www.census.gov

Schulman, G. L. (1999). Siblings revisited: Old conflicts and new opportunities in later life. *Journal of Marital and Family Therapy, 25,* 517–524.

See, L. (2009). *Shanghai girls.* New York: Random House.

Segal, Z. V., Williams, M. G., & Teasdale, J. D. (2002). *Mindfulness-based cognitive therapy for depression: A new approach to preventing relapse.* New York: Guilford Press.

Seligson, M. R. (2009). *Caregiver burnout.* Retrieved December 2, 2009, from http://www.caregiver.com/articles/print/caregiver_burnout.htm

Settersten, R. A., Jr. (2003). Propositions and controversies in life-course scholarship. In R. A. Settersten Jr. (Ed.), *Invitation to the life course: Toward new understandings of later life* (pp. 15–45). Amityville, NY: Baywood.

Settersten, R. A., Jr. (2006). Aging and the life course. In R. F. Binstock & L. George (Eds.), *Handbook of aging and the social sciences* (6th ed., pp. 3–19). Amsterdam: Academic Press.

Shapiro, A. (2003). Later-life divorce and parent-adult child contact and proximity: A longitudinal analysis. *Journal of Family Issues, 24,* 264–285.

Siegel, J. (1996). *Aging into the 21st century* (HHS-100-95-0017). Washington, DC: Administration on Aging. Retrieved from http://www.aoa.gov/AoARoot/Aging_Statistics/future_growth/future_growth.aspx#aging

Silverstein, M., & Bengtson, V. L. (1997). Intergenerational solidarity and the structure of adult child-parent relationships in American families. *American Journal of Sociology, 103,* 429–460.

Sirey, J. A., Bruce, M. L., & Alexopoulos, G. S. (2005). The treatment initiation program: An intervention to improve depression outcomes in older adults. *American Journal of Psychiatry, 162,* 184–186.

Skogrand, L. (2004). A process for learning about and creating programs for culturally diverse audiences. *Forum for Family and Consumer Issues, 9*(1). Retrieved from http://ncsu.edu/ffci/publications/2004/v9-n1-2004-march/fa-2-process.php

Smith, K. R., Zick, C. D., & Duncan, G. J. (1991). Remarriage patterns among recent widows and widowers. *Demography, 28,* 361–374.

Spillman, B. C., & Pezzin, L. E. (2000). Potential and active family caregivers: Changing networks and the "sandwich generation." *The Milbank Quarterly, 78,* 347–374.

Steffens, D. C., Skoog, I., Norton, M. C., Hart, A. D., Tschanz, J. T., Plassman, B. L., . . . Breitner, J. C. (2000). Prevalence of depression and its treatment in an elderly population. The Cache County, Utah Study. *Archives of General Psychiatry, 57*(6), 601–607.

Steinman, L. F., Frederick, J. T., Prohaska, T., Satariano, W. A., Dornberg-Lee, S., Fisher, R., . . . Late Life Depression Special Interest Project (SIP) panelists. (2007). Recommendations for treating depression in community-based older adults. *American Journal of Preventive Medicine, 33,* 175–181.

Stroebe, M. S., Folkman, S., Hansson, R. O., & Schut, H. (2006). The prediction of bereavement outcome: Development of an integrative risk factor framework. *Social Science & Medicine, 63,* 2440–2451.

Stroebe, M. & Schut, H. (1999). The dual process model of coping with bereavement: Rationale and description. *Death Studies, 23,* 197–224.

Stroebe, W., Stroebe, M., Abakoumkin, G., & Schut, H. (1996). The role of loneliness and social support in adjustment to loss: A test of attachment versus stress theory. *Journal of Personality and Social Psychology, 70,* 1241–1249.

Taylor, R. J., & Chatters, L. M. (1986). Church-based informal support among elderly blacks. *The Gerontologist, 26,* 637–642.

Teaster, P. B., Nerenberg, L., & Stansbury, K. L. (2003). A national look at elder abuse multidisciplinary teams. In E. Podnieks, J. I. Kosberg, & A. Lowenstein (Eds.), *Elder abuse: Selected papers from the Prague world congress on family violence* (pp. 91–107). Binghamton, NY: Haworth Press.

Teaster, P. B., & Roberto, K. A. (2002). Living the life of another: The need for public guardians of last resort. *Journal of Applied Gerontology, 21,* 176–187.

Trainin, I. N. (2010). *What is Bikur Cholim?* Retrieved from http://www.bikurcholimcc.org/whatisbc.html

Turner, K. (2009). Mindfulness: The present moment in clinical social work. *Clinical Social Work Journal, 37,* 95–103.

Umberson, D., Williams, K., Powers, D. A., Liu, H., & Needham, B. (2006). You make me sick: Marital quality and health over the life course. *Journal of Health & Social Behavior, 47,* 1–16.

U.S. Census Bureau. (2005). *American community survey 2005 questionnaire.* Washington, DC: Author.

U.S. Department of Health and Human Services, Administration for Children and Families and the Administration on Aging. (1998). *National elder abuse incidence study.* Retrieved December 7, 2009, from http://www.aoa.gov/AoARoot/AoA_Programs/ Elder_Rights/ Elder_Abuse/docs/ABuseReport_Full.pdf

U.S. Department of Health and Human Services, Health Resources and Services Administration. (2005). *Mental health and rural America: 1994–2005.* Retrieved December 3, 2009, from ftp://ftp.hrsa.gov/ ruralhealth/RuralMentalHealth.pdf

U.S. Department of Health and Human Services, National Clearinghouse for Long-Term Care Information. Retrieved December 3, 2009, from http://www.longtermcare.gov/LTC/ Main_Site/index.aspx

Van Volkom, M. (2006). Sibling relationships in middle and older adulthood: A review of the literature. *Marriage & Family Review, 40*(2/3), 151–170.

Von Korff, M., Crane, P., Lane, M., Miglioretti, D. L., Simon, G., Saunders, K., . . . Kessler, R. (2005). Chronic spinal pain and physical-mental comorbidity in the United States: Results from the national comorbidity survey replication. *Pain, 113,* 331–339.

Walsh, F. (2003). Family resilience: Strengths forged through adversity. In F. Walsh (Ed.), *Normal family processes* (3rd ed., pp. 399–423). New York: Guilford Press.

Weggel, J. M. (1999). Barriers to the physician decision to offer hospice as an option for terminal care. *Wisconsin Medical Journal, 98,* 49–53.

Wenger, G. C. (2001). Aging without children: Rural Wales. *Journal of Cross-Cultural Gerontology, 16,* 79–109.

White, J. M., & Klein, D. M. (2008). *Family theories* (3rd ed.). Thousand Oaks, CA: Sage.

Wiener, J. M., Anderson, W. L., & Khatutsky, G. (2007). Are consumer-directed home care beneficiaries satisfied? Evidence from Washington state. *The Gerontologist, 47,* 763–774.

Williams, K. N., & Warren, C. A. B. (2009). Communication in assisted living. *Journal of Aging Studies, 23,* 24–36.

Wink, P., Dillon, M., & Larsen, B. (2005). Religion as moderator of the depression-health connection. *Research on Aging, 27,* 197–220.

Worden, J. W. (1982). *Grief counseling and grief therapy: A handbook for the mental health practitioner.* New York: Springer.

Worden, J. W. (1991). *Grief counseling and grief therapy: A handbook for the mental health practitioner* (2nd ed.). New York: Springer.

Yagoda, L. (2004). *Working family caregivers: Issues and opportunities for social work practice.* Retrieved from NASW Web site: http://www.socialworkers.org/practice/aging/aging0804.pdf

Yang, J. A., & Jackson, C. L. (1998). Overcoming obstacles in providing mental health treatment to older adults: Getting in the door. *Psychotherapy, 35,* 498–505.

Yorgason, J. B., Miller, R. B., & White, M. B. (2009). Aging and family therapy: Exploring the training and knowledge of family therapists. *The American Journal of Family Therapy, 37,* 28–47.

INDEX

B

Progress in Mathematics
Vol. 30

Edited by
J. Coates and
S. Helgason

Birkhäuser
Boston · Basel · Stuttgart

Kentaro Yano
Masahiro Kon

CR Submanifolds of Kaehlerian and Sasakian Manifolds

1983

Birkhäuser
Boston • Basel • Stuttgart

Authors:

Kentaro Yano
Department of Mathematics
Tokyo Institute of Technology
Ohokayama, Meguro-ku
Tokyo, 152
Japan

Masahiro Kon
Hirosaki University
Hirosaki
Japan

Library of Congress Cataloging in Publication Data

Yano, Kentaro, 1912-
    CR submanifolds of Kaehlerian and Sasakian mani-
folds.

    (Progress in mathematics ; v. 30)
    Bibliography: p. 198
    Indcludes indexes.
    1. Kahlerian manifolds. 2. Sasakian manifolds.
3. Submanifolds, CR. I. Kon, Masahiro. II. Title.
III. Title: C.R. submanifolds of Kaehlerian and
Sasakian manifolds. IV. Series: Progress in mathe-
matics (Cambridge, Mass.) ; v. 30.
QA649.Y29   1983   516.3'604   82-22752
ISBN 3-7643-3119-4 (Switzerland)

CIP-Kurztitelaufnahme der Deutschen Bibliothek

Yano, Kentaro:
CR submanifolds of Kaehlerian and Sasakian mani-
folds / Kentaro Yano ; Masahiro Kon. - Boston ;
Basel ; Stuttgart : Birkhäuser, 1983
    (Progress in mathematics ; Vol. 30)
    ISBN 3-7643-3119-4
    NE: Kon, Masahiro:; GT

©Birkhäuser Boston, Inc., 1983

ISBN 3-7643-3119-4

Printed in USA

INTRODUCTION

Let $\bar{M}$ be an almost Hermitian manifold with almost complex structure tensor J. We consider a submanifold M of $\bar{M}$ and denote by $T_x(M)$ and
$T_x(M)^{\perp}$ the tangent space and the normal space of M at $x \in M$ respectively. If $T_x(M)$ is invariant under the action of J for each $x \in M$, that is,
if $JT_x(M) = T_x(M)$ for each $x \in M$, then M is called an invariant (or
holomorphic) submanifold of $\bar{M}$. On the other hand, if the transform of
$T_x(M)$ by J is contained in the normal space $T_x(M)^{\perp}$ for each $x \in M$, that
is, if $JT_x(M) \subset T_x(M)^{\perp}$ for each $x \in M$, then M is called an anti-invariant (or totally real) submanifold of $\bar{M}$.

Similar definitions apply to submanifolds of an almost contact
metric manifold.

An invariant submanifold inherits almost all properties of the
ambient almost Hermitian manifold and so the study of invariant submanifolds is not so interesting from the point of view of the geometry
of submanifolds. On the other hand, the theory of anti-invariant submanifolds proved to be a very nice topic in modern differential geometry and has been studied by many authors in 1970's (see our Lecture
Notes [63]).

In 1978, generalizing these ideas, A. Bejancu [2], [4] defined CR
(Cauchy-Riemann) submanifolds of an almost Hermitian manifold as
follows:

Let $\bar{M}$ be an almost Hermitian manifold with almost complex structure tensor J. A submanifold M of $\bar{M}$ is called a CR submanifold of $\bar{M}$
if there exists a differentiable distribution $D : x \longrightarrow D_x$ on M
satisfying the two conditions:

(i) D is invariant, that is, $JD_x = D_x$ for each $x \in M$,

(ii) the complementary orthogonal distribution $D^{\perp} : x \longrightarrow D_x^{\perp} \subset T_x(M)$
of D is anti-invariant, that is, $JD_x^{\perp} \subset T_x(M)^{\perp}$ for each $x \in M$.

Similar definition applies to submanifolds of almost contact metric manifold, or more generally to those of Riemannian manifolds endowed with a tensor field of type $(1,1)$.

The study of CR submanifolds has been started quite recently, but as the "Bibliography" of this book shows, already many papers on these submanifolds have been published and are going to be published proving that the topic is a very interesting one in modern differential geometry.

The purpose of the present lecture notes is to gather and arrange the results on CR submanifolds of Kaehlerian and Sasakian manifolds obtained up to now and invite the readers to the study of this very interesting topic of modern differential geometry which has just been started.

In Chapter I, we first recall fundamental ideas, definitions and formulas in the theory of Riemannian, Kaehlerian and Sasakian manifolds, which will be necessary later. We also give some general results on the so-called f-structures which appear when we consider CR submanifolds of Kaehlerian or Sasakian manifolds. (See Kobayashi-Nomizu [28], Sasaki [42] and Yano [56], [57], [58]).

In Chapter II, we first of all state general formulas on submanifolds. The formula on Laplacian of the second fundamental form will play very important rôles in the following discussions. We then consider submanifolds of Riemannian space forms, especially those of spheres and prove various theorems under conditions that submanifolds are minimal, have parallel mean curvature vector, the normal connection is flat or the second fundamental form is parallel. These theorems will be usefull when we study contact CR submanifolds of a unit sphere or CR submanifolds of a complex projective space. (For the contents of this

Chapter, see Chen [11], Kobayashi-Nomizu [28;Vol.II], Simons [43] and Yano-Ishihara [61]).

In Chapter III, we consider submanifolds of Sasakian manifolds and give some fundamental formulas and important results. We then define contact CR submanifolds and give some examples of contact CR submanifolds. We consider contact CR submanifolds with parallel mean curvature vector or minimal contact CR submanifolds and prove theorems on properties of these submanifolds. We also give an integral formula containing the second fundamental form and consider its applications.

In Chapter IV, we consider submanifolds of Kaehlerian manifolds and first give fundamental formulas and results. We then define CR submanifolds of Kaehlerian manifolds and give some examples. Here we need the method of Riemannian fibre bundles. Moreover, we consider the normal connections of CR submanifolds and introduce the idea of semi-flat normal connection. We prove some theorems under the assumption that the normal connections of CR submanifolds of a complex projective space are semi-flat. We also give theorems on CR submanifolds with parallel mean curvature vector and those on minimal CR submanifolds. We give also an integral formula on the second fundamental form and consider its applications.

In Chapter V, applying the method of Riemannian fibre bundles to submanifolds, we investigate the relations between submanifolds of Sasakian manifolds and those of Kaehlerian manifolds. Thus the relations between the second fundamental forms and those between mean curvature vectors of these submanifolds are made clear and consequently relations between various ideas on submanifolds of Sasakian manifolds and those on submanifolds of Kaehlerian manifolds, for example, to be totally contact umbilical and to be totally umbilical, or to be totally contact geodesic and to be totally geodesic also become clear. We also give, as an application, a theorem on real submanifolds of a complex projective space.

In the last Chapter VI, we consider real hypersurfaces of complex space forms. We first state fundamental formulas and results on real hypersurfaces and then we give a theorem on pseudo-Einstein real hypersurfaces. We then give some theorems on generic minimal submanifolds of complex projective spaces. These are theorems on the reduction of codimension to one and so characterize certain kinds of real hypersurfaces by the restriction on Ricci curvature or sectional curvature.

Finally we give some theorems on hypersurfaces of Sasakian space forms.

The authors wish to express their sincere gratitude to Professor S. Helgason who suggested that we include this book in the series "Progress in Mathematics".

The authors are also very grateful to the reviewers of Birkhäuser whose suggestions were very useful to improve the first draft of the book.

Our hearty thanks also go to Birkhäuser Verlag who took all possible care in production of the book.

August 15, 1982

Kentaro Yano

Masahiro Kon

CONTENTS

Chapter I

STRUCTURES ON RIEMANNIAN MANIFOLDS

§1. Riemannian manifolds

Let M be an n-dimensional connected differentiable manifold of class C^∞ covered by a system of coordinate neighborhoods $\{U; x^h\}$, where U denotes a neighborhood and x^h local coordinates in U. If, from any system of coordinate neighborhoods covering the manifold M, we can choose a finite number of coordinate neighborhoods which cover the whole manifold, then M is said to be compact. If we can cover the manifold M by a system of coordinate neighborhoods in such a way that the Jacobian determinant $|\partial x^{h'}/\partial x^h|$ of the coordinate transformation

$$x^{h'} = x^{h'}(x^1, \ldots, x^n)$$

in every non-empty intersection of two coordinate neighborhoods $\{U; x^h\}$ and $\{U'; x^{h'}\}$ is always positive, then the manifold M is said to be orientable.

We denote by $\mathfrak{X}(M)$ the set of all vector fields on M. A <u>Riemannian metric</u> on M is a tensor field g of type $(0,2)$ which satisfies the following two conditions:

(i) it is symmetric: $g(X,Y) = g(Y,X)$ for any X, Y $\in \mathfrak{X}(M)$,

(ii) it is positive-definite: $g(X,X) \geq 0$ for any X $\in \mathfrak{X}(M)$ and $g(X,X) = 0$ if and only if X = 0.

A manifold M with Riemannian metric g is called a <u>Riemannian manifold</u>. A Riemannian metric gives rise to an inner product on each tangent space $T_x(M)$ of M at x. The inner product g can be extended to an inner product, denoted also by g, in the tensor space T_s^r at x for each type (r,s).

When a Riemannian manifold M is orientable, we can define the volume element of M by

$$*1 = \sqrt{\mathcal{G}}dx^1 \wedge dx^2 \wedge \ldots \wedge dx^n,$$

where $\mathcal{G} = |g_{ij}|$, g_{ij} being components of g, and $\wedge$ denotes the exterior product, and we can define the integral

$$\int_D f(x)*1$$

of a function f over the domain D of M.

Let M and N be Riemannian manifolds with Riemannian metrics g and h respectively. A mapping f: M $\longrightarrow$ N is said to be isometric at a point x of M if $g(X,Y) = h(f_*X,f_*Y)$ for all $X,Y \in T_x(M)$, where f_* is the differential of f. In this case f_* is injective at x of M. A mapping f which is isometric at every point of M is thus an immersion, which we call an <u>isometric immersion</u>. If, moreover, f is 1:1, then f is called an <u>isometric imbedding</u> of M into N.

An affine connection on a manifold M is a rule ∇ which assigns to each $X \in \mathfrak{X}(M)$ a linear mapping ∇_X of $\mathfrak{X}(M)$ into itself satisfying the following two conditions:

$$\nabla_{fX+gY} = f\nabla_X + g\nabla_Y, \qquad \nabla_X(fY) = f\nabla_X Y + (Xf)Y$$

for f,g ∈ 𝒥(M), X,Y ∈ 𝔛(M), where 𝒥(M) denotes the set of all differentiable functions on M. The operator ∇_X is called the covariant differentiation with respect to X.

On a Riemannian manifold M there exists one and only one affine connection satisfying the following two conditions:

(i) the torsion tensor T vanishes, i.e.,

$$T(X,Y) = \nabla_X Y - \nabla_Y X - [X,Y] = 0,$$

(ii) g is parallel, i.e., $\nabla_X g = 0$.

Such a connection on a Riemannian manifold M is called the Riemannian connection or the Levi-Civita connection.

Let M be an n-dimensional Riemannian manifold with the Riemannian connection ∇. If we put

$$R(X,Y) = \nabla_X \nabla_Y - \nabla_Y \nabla_X - \nabla_{[X,Y]},$$

then we see that R(X,Y) is a tensor field of type (1,1) which is linear in X and Y. We call R(X,Y) the curvature (transformation) tensor on M. It can be easily verified that

(1.1) $$R(X,Y) + R(Y,X) = 0,$$

(1.2) $$R(X,Y)Z + R(Y,Z)X + R(Z,X)Y = 0$$

(The first Bianchi identity).

The Riemannian curvature tensor R of M is the tensor field of type (0,4) defined by

(1.3) $$R(X_1,X_2,X_3,X_4) = g(R(X_3,X_4)X_2,X_1), \quad X_i \in T_x(M), \ i=1,\ldots,4.$$

We can verify that the Riemannian curvature tensor R satisfies

$$R(X_1,X_2,X_3,X_4) = -R(X_2,X_1,X_3,X_4) = -R(X_1,X_2,X_4,X_3),$$

(1.4) $\quad R(X_1,X_2,X_3,X_4) + R(X_1,X_3,X_4,X_2) + R(X_1,X_4,X_2,X_3) = 0,$

$$R(X_1,X_2,X_3,X_4) = R(X_3,X_4,X_1,X_2).$$

If $E_1,\ldots,E_n$ are local orthonormal vector fields, then

(1.5) $$S(X,Y) = \sum_{i=1}^{n} g(R(E_i,X)Y,E_i)$$

defines a global tensor field S of type $(0,2)$. S is called the <u>Ricci tensor</u> of M. From S we define a global scalar field

(1.6) $$r = \sum_{i=1}^{n} S(E_i,E_i).$$

The scalar function r is called the <u>scalar curvature</u> of M.

For each plane p in $T_x(M)$ spanned by orthonormal vectors X_1 and X_2, the <u>sectional curvature</u> K(p) for the section p is defined by

(1.7) $$K(p) = R(X_1,X_2,X_1,X_2) = g(R(X_1,X_2)X_2,X_1).$$

The sectional curvature K(p) is independent of the choice of an orthonormal basis X_1, X_2 and the set of values of K(p) for all sections p of $T_x(M)$ determines the Riemannian curvature tensor at x of M. If K(p) is a constant for all sections p in $T_x(M)$ and for all point x of M, then M is called a space of constant curvature. The following theorem due to Schur is well known.

Theorem 1.1 (Schur). Let M be a connected Riemannian manifold of
dimension n > 2. If the sectional curvature K(p) depends only on the
point x, then M is a space of constant curvature.

A Riemannian manifold of constant curvature is called a Riemannian
space form. We denote by M(c) a space of constant curvature c. If M is
of constant curvature c, then we have

(1.8) $$R(X,Y)Z = c[g(Y,Z)X - g(X,Z)Y].$$

If the Ricci tensor S is of the form

(1.9) $$S = \lambda g,$$

λ being a constant, then M is called an Einstein manifold. If $S = \lambda g$,
λ is a function, and if n > 2, then λ is a constant. If R = 0, then
the Riemannian manifold M is said to be locally flat. A Riemannian
manifold M is called a locally symmetric space if its curvature tensor
is parallel, that is, $\nabla R = 0$. A complete locally symmetric space is
called a symmetric space.

A q-dimensional distribution on an n-dimensional manifold M is a
mapping D defined on M which assignes to each point x of M a q-dimensional linear subspace D_x of $T_x(M)$. D is said to be differentiable if
there exist q differentiable vector fields on a neighborhood of x, for
each point y in this neighborhood of x, which form a basis of D_y. The
set of these q vector fields is called a local basis of D. A vector
field X belongs to D if $X_x \in D_x$ for any point x of M. We denote this
fact by $X \in D$. A distribution D is said to be involutive if, for all
vector fields X, Y in D, we have $[X,Y] \in D$. By a distribution we shall
always mean a differentiable distribution.

A submanifold N imbedded in M is called an <u>integral manifold</u> of the distribution D if $f_*(T_x(N)) = D_x$ for all x of N, where f_* denotes the differential of the imbedding f of N into M. If there exists no integral manifold of D which contains N, then N is called a <u>maximal integral submanifold</u> of D. A distribution D is said to be completely integrable if, for every point x of M, there is a unique integral manifold of D containing x. We have

<u>Theorem 1.2 (Frobenius)</u>. An involutive distribution D on M is integrable. Moreover, through every x ∈ M there passes a unique maximal integral manifold of D and every other integral manifold containing x is an open submanifold of this maximal one.

A vector field X on a Riemannian manifold M is called an <u>infinitesimal isometry</u> (or, a <u>Killing vector field</u>) if the local 1-parameter group of local transformation generated by X in a neighborhood of each point of M consists of local isometries. X is an infinitesimal isometry if and only if X satisfies the following Killing equation

$$L_X g = 0, \quad \text{i.e.,} \quad (L_X g)(Y,Z) = g(\nabla_Y X, Z) + g(\nabla_Z X, Y) = 0$$

for any vector fields Y and Z on M, where L_X denotes the Lie differentiation with respect to X. Let $\{e_i\}$ be an orthonormal frame of M. For any vector field X of M we have

$$\text{div}(\nabla_X X) - \text{div}((\text{div}X)X)$$

$$= S(X,X) + \sum_{i,j} g(\nabla_{e_j} X, e_i) g(e_j, \nabla_{e_i} X) - (\text{div}X)^2,$$

where S is the Ricci tensor of M. On the other hand, we have

$$\sum_{i,j} (g(\nabla_{e_j}X,e_i) + g(\nabla_{e_i}X,e_j))^2$$

$$= 2\sum_{i,j} (g(\nabla_{e_j}X,e_i)g(\nabla_{e_i}X,e_j) + g(\nabla_{e_j}X,e_i)^2).$$

Thus we have

$$\sum_{i,j} g(\nabla_{e_j}X,e_i)g(\nabla_{e_i}X,e_j) = -|\nabla X|^2 + \frac{1}{2}|L_Xg|^2,$$

where $|\ |$ denotes the length with respect to the Riemannian metric of a tensor field on M. We have therefore (Yano [55])

(1.10) $\text{div}(\nabla_X X) - \text{div}((\text{div}X)X)$

$$= S(X,X) + \frac{1}{2}|L_Xg|^2 - |\nabla X|^2 - (\text{div}X)^2.$$

§2. Kaehlerian manifolds

An almost complex structure on a differentiable manifold M is a tensor field J of type (1,1) which is, at every point x of M, an endomorphism of $T_x(M)$ such that $J^2 = -I$, where I denotes the identity transformation of $T_x(M)$. A manifold M with an almost complex structure J is called an almost complex manifold. Every almost complex manifold is of even dimension and orientable.

We define the torsion of J to be the tensor field N of type (1,2) called the Nijenhuis torsion, given by

$$N(X,Y) = ([JX,JY] - [X,Y] - J[X,JY] - J[JX,Y])$$

for any vector fields X and Y. If N vanishes identically, then an almost complex structure is called a complex structure and M is called a complex manifold.

A Hermitian metric on an almost complex manifold M is a Riemannian metric g such that

$$g(JX,JY) = g(X,Y) \quad \text{for } X,Y \in \mathfrak{X}(M).$$

An almost complex manifold (resp. a complex manifold) with Hermitian metric is called an almost Hermitian manifold (resp. a Hermitian manifold). We notice that every almost complex manifold M with a Riemannian metric g admits a Hermitian metric. Indeed, for any almost complex structure J on M, putting

$$h(X,Y) = g(X,Y) + g(JX,JY) \quad \text{for } X,Y \in \mathfrak{X}(M),$$

we obtain a Hermitian metric h.

A Hermitian manifold M is called a Kaehlerian manifold if the almost complex structure J of M is parallel, that is, $\nabla J = 0$.

The curvature tensor R of a Kaehlerian manifold M satisfies

$$(2.1) \qquad R(X,Y)J = JR(X,Y), \qquad R(JX,JY) = R(X,Y).$$

Let K(p) be the sectional curvature of a Kaehlerian manifold M for a section p in $T_X(M)$ spanned by orthonormal vectors X and Y. If p is invariant by J, then K(p) is called the holomorphic sectional curvature by p. If p is invariant by J and X is a unit vector in p, then X, JX is an orthonormal basis for p and hence $K(p) = R(X,JX,X,JX)$.

If K(p) is a constant for all sections p in $T_x(M)$ invariant by J and for all points x of M, then M is called a space of constant holomorphic sectional curvature. We have

Theorem 2.1. Let M be a connected Kaehlerian manifold of complex dimension $n \geq 2$. If the holomorphic sectional curvature K(p) depends only on $x \in M$, then M is a space of constant holomorphic sectional curvature.

A Kaehlerian manifold of constant holomorphic sectional curvature is called a complex space form. We denote by $M^n(c)$ a complex space form with constant holomorphic sectional curvature c and complex dimension n. The curvature tensor R of $M^n(c)$ is given by

(2.2) $R(X,Y)Z = \frac{1}{4}c[g(Y,Z)X - g(X,Z)Y + g(JY,Z)JX$

$- g(JX,Z)JY + 2g(X,JY)JZ].$

We denote by C^n the complex number space, CP^n a complex projective space and D^n the open unit ball in C^{n+1} of complex dimension n. It is well known that a simply connected complete Kaehlerian manifold of constant holomorphic sectional curvature c can be identified with CP^n, D^n or C^n according as $c > 0$, $c < 0$ or $c = 0$.

§3. Sasakian manifolds

Let M be an odd-dimensional differentiable manifold of class C^∞ and ϕ, ξ, η be a tensor field of type (1,1), a vector field, a 1-form on M respectively such that

$$\phi^2 X = -X + \eta(X)\xi, \qquad \phi\xi = 0, \qquad \eta(\phi X) = 0, \qquad \eta(\xi) = 1$$

for any vector field X on M. Then M is said to have an almost contact structure (ϕ,ξ,η) and is called an almost contact manifold. We denote by N the Nijenhuis torsion formed with ϕ. The almost contact structure is said to be normal if

$$N + d\eta \otimes \xi = 0.$$

If a Riemannian metric tensor field g is given on an almost contact manifold M and satisfies

$$g(\phi X, \phi Y) = g(X,Y) - \eta(X)\eta(Y), \qquad \eta(X) = g(X,\xi)$$

for any vector fields X and Y on M, then (ϕ,ξ,η,g) is called an almost contact metric structure and we call M an almost contact metric manifold. If $d\eta(X,Y) = g(\phi X,Y)$ for any vector fields X, Y, then an almost contact metric structure is called a contact metric structure. If moreover the structure is normal, then a contact metric structure is called a Sasakian structure (normal contact metric structure) and M is called a Sasakian manifold. In a Sasakian manifold M with structure tensors (ϕ,ξ,η,g) we have

$$\nabla_X \xi = \phi X, \qquad (\nabla_X \phi)Y = -g(X,Y)\xi + \eta(Y)X = R(X,\xi)Y,$$

where R denotes the curvature transformation tensor of M. Moreover, we have

(3.1) $R(X,Y) = -\phi R(X,Y)\phi + X \wedge Y - \phi X \wedge \phi Y,$

where $(X \wedge Y)Z = g(Y,Z)X - g(X,Z)Y.$

A plane section p in $T_X(M)$ of a Sasakian manifold M is called a ϕ-section if it is spanned by a unit vector X orthogonal to ξ and ϕX. The sectional curvature K(p) with respect to a ϕ-section p determined by X is called a ϕ-sectional curvature. It is verified that if a Sasakian manifold has a ϕ-sectional curvature c which does not depend on the ϕ-section at each point, then c is a constant in M. A Sasakian manifold M is called a Sasakian space form and is denoted by M(c) if it has the constant ϕ-sectional curvature c. The curvature tensor R of a Sasakian space form M(c) is given by

(3.2) $R(X,Y)Z = \frac{1}{4}(c+3)[g(Y,Z)X - g(X,Z)Y] - \frac{1}{4}(c-1)[\eta(Y)\eta(Z)X$

$- \eta(X)\eta(Z)Y + g(Y,Z)\eta(X)\xi - g(X,Z)\eta(Y)\xi$

$- g(\phi Y,Z)\phi X + g(\phi X,Z)\phi Y + 2g(\phi X,Y)\phi Z].$

Example 3.1. Let S^{2n+1} be a (2n+1)-dimensional unit sphere, i.e.,

$$S^{2n+1} = \{z \in C^{n+1} : |z| = 1\}.$$

For any point $z \in S^{2n+1}$ we put $\xi = Jz$, where J denotes the almost complex structure of C^{n+1}. We consider the orthogonal projection

$$\pi : T_z(C^{n+1}) \longrightarrow T_z(S^{2n+1}).$$

Putting $\phi = \pi \cdot J$, we have a Sasakian structure (ϕ, ξ, η, g) on S^{2n+1}, where η is a 1-form dual to ξ and g the standard metric tensor field on S^{2n+1}. We see that S^{2n+1} is of constant ϕ-sectional curvature 1, that is, of constant curvature 1.

Let S denote the Ricci tensor of a Sasakian manifold M. If S is of the form

$$S(X,Y) = ag(X,Y) + b\eta(X)\eta(Y),$$

where a and b are constants, then M is called an η-Einstein manifold. If $b = 0$ in the equation above, M is an Einstain manifold.

§4. f-structure

Let there be given, in an n-dimensional connected differentiable manifold of class C^∞, a non-null tensor field f of type (1,1) and of class C^∞ satisfying

$$f^3 + f = 0.$$

If we put

$$l = -f^2, \qquad m = f^2 + I,$$

then we have

$$l + m = I, \qquad l^2 = l, \qquad m^2 = m, \qquad lm = ml = 0,$$

where I denotes the unit tensor. These equations show that the operators l and m applied to the tangent space at each point of the manifold are complementary projection operators. Then there exist in the manifold M two distributions L and T corresponding to the projection operators l and m respectively. Moreover, the rank of f is constant, say r, everywhere (see [45]) and L is r-dimensional and T is (n-r)-dimensional. We call such a structure an f-structure of rank r [56]. For the tensors f, l and m, we have

$$fl = lf = f, \qquad fm = mf = 0, \qquad f^2l = -l, \qquad f^2m = 0,$$

which tell us that f acts on L as an almost complex structure and on T as a null operator.

If the rank of f is n, then f satisfies $f^2 + I = 0$, and consequently an f-structure of rank n is an almost complex structure. Thus n must be even. If the rank of f is n-1, then L is (n-1)-dimensional and T is one-dimensional. When the manifold is orientable, an f-structure of rank n-1 is an almost contact structure. Thus the dimension n must be odd.

The Nijenhuis tensor N(X,Y) of f is given by

$$N(X,Y) = [fX,fY] - f[fX,Y] - f[X,fY] - l[X,Y].$$

As is well known, the distribution T is integrable if and only if $l[mX,mY] = 0$ for any vector fields X and Y. We have [59]

Proposition 4.1. A necessary and sufficient condition for the distribution T to be integrable is that $N(mX,mY) = 0$ or equivalently $lN(mX,mY) = 0$ for any vector fields X and Y.

The distribution L is integrable if and only if $m[lX, lY] = 0$ for any vector fields X and Y. Thus we have

Proposition 4.2. A necessary and sufficient condition for the distribution T to be integrable is that $mN(X,Y) = 0$, or $mN(lX, lY) = 0$, or $mN(fX, fY) = 0$ for any vector fields X and Y.

Because of $l + m = I$, the Nijenhuis tensor $N(X,Y)$ can also be written in the form

$$N(X,Y) = lN(lX, lY) + mN(lX, lY) + N(lX, mY)$$

$$+ N(mX, lY) + N(mX, mY).$$

Taking account of this relation, we have from Propositions 4.1 and 4.2 the theorem

Theorem 4.1. A necessary and sufficient condition for both of two distributions L and T to be integrable is that

$$N(X,Y) = lN(lX, lY) + N(lX, mY) + N(mX, lY)$$

for any two vector fields X and Y.

If the distribution L is integrable and moreover if the almost complex structure f' induced from f on each integral manifold of L is integrable, then we say that the f-structure is partially integrable. We denote by N' the Nijenhuis tensor of f'. Then

$$N(lX, lY) = N'(lX, lY)$$

for any vector fields X and Y on M. Since $N(lX, lY) = 0$ if and only if $N(fX, fY) = 0$, we have [59]

Theorem 4.2. A necessary and sufficient condition for an f-structure to be partially integrable is that one of the following equivalent conditions be satisfied:

$$N(lX, lY) = 0, \qquad N(fX, fY) = 0$$

for any two vector fields X and Y.

Corollary 4.1. In order that the distribution T be integrable and the f-structure be partially integrable, it is necessary and sufficient that

$$N(X, Y) = N(lX, mY) + N(mX, lY)$$

for any two vector fields X and Y.

When two distributions L and T are both integrable, we can choose a local coordinate system such that L's are represented by putting n-r local coordinates constant and T's by putting the other r coordinates constant. We call such a coordinate system an adapted coordinate system.

We now assume the following:

(1) The structure f is partially integrable.

(2) The distribution T is integrable.

(3) The components of the structure f are independent of the coordinates which are constant along the integral manifolds of L in an adapted coordinate system.

In this case we say that the f-structure f is <u>integrable</u>. We have [59]

<u>Theorem 4.3</u>. A necessary and sufficient condition for the structure f to be integrable is that $N(X,Y) = 0$ for any two vector fields X and Y.

Chapter II

SUBMANIFOLDS

§1. Induced connection and second fundamental form

Let M be an n-dimensional manifold isometrically immersed in an m-dimensional Riemannian manifold $\bar{M}$. We put $m = n+p$, $p > 0$. We denote by $\bar{\nabla}$ the operator of covariant differentiation in $\bar{M}$ and by g the Riemannian metric tensor field in $\bar{M}$. Since the discussion is local, we may assume, if we want, that M is imbedded in $\bar{M}$. The submanifold M is also a Riemannian manifold with Riemannian metric h given by $h(X,Y) = g(X,Y)$ for any vector fields X and Y on M. The Riemannian metric h on M is called the induced metric on M. Throughout this book, the induced metric h will be denoted by the same g as that of the ambient manifold $\bar{M}$ to simplify the notation because it may cause no confusion. Let $T(M)$ and $T(M)^{\perp}$ denote the tangent and normal bundle of M respectively. The metric g and the connection $\bar{\nabla}$ on $\bar{M}$ lead to invariant inner products and the connections on $T(M)$ and $T(M)^{\perp}$. We will define a connection on M explicitly.

Let X and Y be vector fields on M. For each point x of M, we put

$$(\nabla_X Y)_x = (\bar{\nabla}_X Y)_x^T,$$

where $(\ )^T$ denotes the orthogonal projection of $(\ )$ on $T_x(M)$. Then ∇ is an affine connection on M. Since we have

17

$$\nabla_X Y - \nabla_Y X - [X,Y] = (\bar{\nabla}_X Y - \bar{\nabla}_Y X - [X,Y])^T = 0,$$

∇ has no torsion. Moreover, we see that $\nabla g = 0$. Thus ∇ is the Riemannian connection on M.

The connection in the normal bundle $T(M)^{\perp}$ is defined similarly. Let X be a vector field tangent to M and V be a vector field normal to M. For each x of M we put

$$(D_X V)_x = (\bar{\nabla}_X V)_x^{\perp},$$

where $(\ )^{\perp}$ denotes the orthogonal projection of $(\ )$ on $T_x(M)^{\perp}$. Then we easily see that D defines an affine connection on the normal bundle $T(M)^{\perp}$. Moreover, for normal vector fields U and V, we have

$$Xg(U,V) = g(\bar{\nabla}_X U, V) + g(U, \bar{\nabla}_X V) = g(D_X U, V) + g(U, D_X V),$$

which shows that D is a metric connection in $T(M)^{\perp}$.

We define two vector bundles over M associated with $T(M)$ and $T(M)^{\perp}$. Let S(M) be the bundle whose fibre at each point is a symmetric linear transformations of $T_x(M) \longrightarrow T_x(M)$. Let us put $H(M) = Hom(T(M)^{\perp}, S(M))$. For a normal vector field V on M and for a tangent vector field X on M, we put

$$(A_V X)_x = -(\bar{\nabla}_X V)_x^T$$

at each point x of M. Then A is well defined, that is, $(A_V X)_x$ depends only on X_x and V_x. We obtain

$$g(A_VX,Y) - g(X,A_VY) = -g(\bar{\nabla}_XV,Y) + g(X,\bar{\nabla}_YV)$$

$$= g(V,\bar{\nabla}_XY) - g(\bar{\nabla}_YX,V) = g(V,[X,Y]) = 0.$$

Consequently, $A_V\colon T_x(M) \longrightarrow T_x(M)$ is a symmetric linear transformation. Clearly A is linear in all variable and therefore $A \in H(M)$. We call A the second fundamental form of M. It will sometimes be more convenient to regard the second fundamental form as a symmetric bilinear form on $T_x(M)$ with values in $T_x(M)^\perp$. That is, for $X,Y \in T_x(M)$, we define $B(X,Y) \in T_x(M)^\perp$ by

$$g(B(X,Y),V) = g(A_VX,Y).$$

Since we have

$$g(B(X,Y),V) = g(A_VX,Y) = -g(\bar{\nabla}_XV,Y) = g(\bar{\nabla}_XY,V),$$

it follows that

$$B(X,Y)_x = (\bar{\nabla}_XY)^\perp_x$$

at each point x of M. Thus we have proved the first set of basic formulas for submanifolds, namely,

(1.1) $$\bar{\nabla}_XY = \nabla_XY + B(X,Y),$$

(1.2) $$\bar{\nabla}_XV = -A_VX + D_XV.$$

The equation (1.1) is called the Gauss formula and (1.2) the Weingarten formula.

A normal vector field V on M is said to be parallel in the normal bundle, or simply parallel, if $D_X V = 0$ for all vector fields X tangent to M. A submanifold M is said to be totally geodesic if its second fundamental form vanishes identically, that is, A = 0 or equivalently B = 0. For a normal vector field V on M, if $A_V = aI$ for some function a, then V is called an umbilical section on M, or M is said to be umbilical with respect to V. If the submanifold M is umbilical with respect to every local normal section in M, then M is said to be totally umbilical.

Let $e_1, \ldots, e_n$ be an orthonormal basis in $T_x(M)$. The mean curvature vector μ of M is defined to be $\mu = \frac{1}{n}(TrB)$, where $TrB = \sum_i B(e_i, e_i)$, which is independent of the choice of a basis. We obtain $\mu = \sum_a [(TrA_a)/n] e_a$, where $e_{n+1}, \ldots, e_m$ is an orthonormal basis in $T_x(M)^\perp$, and we denote A_{e_a} by A_a for simplicity, $a = n+1, \ldots, m$. If $\mu = 0$, then M is said to be minimal.

We notice that any submanifold M which is minimal and totally umbilical is totally geodesic.

§2. Equations of Gauss, Codazzi and Ricci

For the second fundamental form A we define its covariant derivative $\nabla_X A$ by

(2.1)
$$(\nabla_X A)_V Y = \nabla_X (A_V Y) - A_{D_X V} Y - A_V \nabla_X Y$$

for any vector fields X, Y tangent to M and any vector field V normal to M, which is defined equivalently by putting

(2.2) $\qquad (\nabla_X B)(Y,Z) = D_X B(Y,Z) - B(\nabla_X Y,Z) - B(Y,\nabla_X Z).$

If $\nabla_X A = 0$ for all X, then the second fundamental form of M is said to be parallel, which is equivalent to $\nabla_X B = 0$ for all X.

Let $\bar{R}$ and R be the curvature tensor fields of $\bar{M}$ and M respectively. Then the Gauss and Weingarten formulas imply

$$(2.3) \qquad \bar{R}(X,Y)Z = R(X,Y)Z - A_{B(Y,Z)}X + A_{B(X,Z)}Y$$
$$+ (\nabla_X B)(Y,Z) - (\nabla_Y B)(X,Z)$$

for any vector fields X, Y and Z tangent to M. For any vector field W tangent to M, (2.3) gives equation of Gauss

$$(2.4) \qquad g(\bar{R}(X,Y)Z,W) = g(R(X,Y)Z,W)$$
$$- g(B(X,W),B(Y,Z)) + g(B(Y,W),B(X,Z)).$$

Taking the normal component of (2.3), we obtain equation of Codazzi

$$(2.5) \qquad (\bar{R}(X,Y)Z)^{\perp} = (\nabla_X B)(Y,Z) - (\nabla_Y B)(X,Z).$$

We now define the curvature tensor $R^{\perp}$ of the normal bundle of M by

$$(2.6) \qquad R^{\perp}(X,Y)V = D_X D_Y V - D_Y D_X V - D_{[X,Y]}V.$$

From the Gauss and Weingarten formulas we see

(2.7) $g(\bar{R}(X,Y)U,V) = g(R^{\perp}(X,Y)U,V) + g([A_V,A_U]X,Y)$

for any vector fields X, Y tangent to M and any vector fields U, V normal to M, where $[A_V,A_U] = A_V A_U - A_U A_V$. Equation (2.7) is called equation of Ricci. If $R^{\perp} = 0$, then the normal connection of M is said to be flat. When $(\bar{R}(X,Y)V)^{\perp} = 0$, the normal connection of M is flat if and only if the second fundamental form of M is commutative, that is, $[A_V,A_U] = 0$ for all U, V. Particularly, if $\bar{M}$ is of constant curvature, $(\bar{R}(X,Y)V) = 0$, and hence the normal connection of M is flat if and only if the second fundamental form of M is commutative. If $\bar{R}(X,Y)Z$ is tangent to M, equation of Codazzi (2.5) reduces to

(2.8) $(\nabla_X B)(Y,Z) = (\nabla_Y B)(X,Z),$

which is equivalent to

(2.9) $(\nabla_X A)_V Y = (\nabla_Y A)_V X.$

Particularly, if $\bar{M}$ is of constant curvature, $\bar{R}(X,Y)Z$ is tangent to M.

§3. Normal connection

We now give a necessary and sufficient condition for a submanifold to have a flat normal connection (see [11]).

Proposition 3.1. Let M be an n-dimensional submanifold of an m-dimensional Riemannian manifold $\bar{M}$. Then the normal connection D of M in $\bar{M}$ is flat if and only if there exist locally m-n mutually orthogonal unit normal vector fields e_x such that each of the e_x is parallel.

Proof. Suppose that there exist locally m-n mutually orthogonal unit normal vector fields e_x such that $De_x = 0$. Then (2.6) gives $R^{\perp}(X,Y)e_x = 0$, which shows that the normal connection of M is flat.

Conversely, suppose that the normal connection of M is flat. Then we have

$$D_X D_Y e_x - D_Y D_X e_x - D_{[X,Y]} e_x = 0$$

for any m-n mutually orthogonal unit vector fields e_x of M. If we put

$$D_X e_x = \omega_x^y(X) e_y,$$

then we see that $\omega_x^y = -\omega_y^x$ and

$$0 = [X\omega_x^y(Y) - Y\omega_x^y(X) - \omega_x^y([X,Y])]e_y$$
$$+ [\omega_x^z(Y)\omega_z^y(X) - \omega_x^z(X)\omega_z^y(Y)]e_y,$$

that is,

$$d\omega_x^y = -\omega_x^z \wedge \omega_z^y, \qquad \omega_x^y = -\omega_y^x.$$

Thus we know that there exists an (m-n,m-n)-matrix $A = (a_x^y)$ of functions satisfying

$$dA = -A\Omega, \qquad {}^t A = A^{-1},$$

where $\Omega = (\omega_x^y)$. This equation has the local expression

$$da_x^z = \sum_y a_x^y \omega_z^y = - \sum_y a_x^y \omega_y^z.$$

We put $e_x' = a_x^y e_y$. Then e_x' are also m-n mutually orthogonal unit normal vector fields of M and we have

$$\omega'^y_x a_y^z = da_x^z + a_x^y \omega_y^z = 0,$$

where ω'^y_x are defined by $De_x' = \omega'^y_x e_y'$. This shows that each of e_x' is parallel in the normal bundle. This proves our assertion.

Let M be an n-dimensional submanifold of an m-dimensional Riemannian manifold $\bar{M}$. For $x \in M$, the <u>first normal space</u> $N_1(x)$ is the orthogonal complement in $T_x(M)^\perp$ of the set

$$N_0(x) = \{V \in T_x(M)^\perp : A_V = 0\}.$$

If, for any vector field V with $V_x \in N_1(x)$, we have $D_X V \in N_1(x)$ for any vector field X of M at x, then the first normal space $N_1(x)$ is said to be parallel with respect to the normal connection. We have the following reduction theorem of codimension (see [17]).

<u>Theorem 3.1.</u> Let M be an n-dimensional submanifold of an m-dimensional complete simply connected space form $\bar{M}^m(c)$. Suppose the first normal space $N_1(x)$ has constant dimension k, and is parallel with respect to the normal connection. Then there is a totally geodesic (n+k)-dimensional submanifold $M^{n+k}(c)$ of $\bar{M}^m(c)$ which contains M.

§4. Laplacian of the second fundamental form

Let M be an n-dimensional submanifold of an m-dimensional Riemannian manifold $\bar{M}$. Let $e_1,\ldots,e_n$ denote an orthonormal frame in $T_x(M)$. We denote by the same letters local, orthonormal vector fields on M which extend $e_1,\ldots,e_n$, and which are covariant constant with respect to ∇ at x. Let $X,Y \in T_x(M)$. We denote by the same X, Y local extensions which are also covariant constant with respect to ∇. Let $e_{n+1},\ldots,e_m$ be an orthonormal basis in $T_x(M)^{\perp}$. We use the convention that the ranges of indices are respectively:

$$i,j,k,\ldots = 1,\ldots,n; \qquad x,y,z,\ldots = n+1,\ldots,m.$$

We now compute the Laplacian of the second fundamental form of M (see [43]).

First of all, from equation of Codazzi (2.5), we have

$$
(4.1) \quad (\nabla^2 B)(X,Y) = \sum_i (\nabla_{e_i} \nabla_{e_i} B)(X,Y)
$$

$$
= \sum_i [(R(e_i,X)B)(e_i,Y) + (\bar{\nabla}_X(\bar{R}(e_i,Y)e_i)^{\perp})^{\perp}
$$

$$
+ (\bar{\nabla}_{e_i}(\bar{R}(e_i,X)Y)^{\perp})^{\perp}] + D_X D_Y(\mathrm{Tr}B),
$$

where $\mathrm{Tr}B = \sum_i B(e_i,e_i)$.

On the other hand, we have

$$
(4.2) \quad \sum_i (R(e_i,X)B)(e_i,Y) = \sum_i [R^{\perp}(e_i,X)B(e_i,Y) - B(R(e_i,X)e_i,Y)
$$

$$
- B(e_i,R(e_i,X)Y)],
$$

(4.3) $\quad \sum_i (\bar{\nabla}_X (\bar{R}(e_i,Y)e_i)^\perp)^\perp = \sum_i [(\bar{\nabla}_X \bar{R})(e_i,Y)e_i + \bar{R}(B(X,e_i),Y)e_i$

$$+ \bar{R}(e_i,B(X,Y))e_i + \bar{R}(e_i,Y)B(X,e_i)]^\perp$$

$$- \sum_i B(X,(\bar{R}(e_i,Y)e_i)^T),$$

(4.4) $\quad \sum_i (\bar{\nabla}_{e_i}(\bar{R}(e_i,X)Y)^\perp)^\perp = \sum_i [(\bar{\nabla}_{e_i}\bar{R})(e_i,X)Y + \bar{R}(B(e_i,e_i),X)Y$

$$+ \bar{R}(e_i,B(e_i,X))Y + \bar{R}(e_i,X)B(e_i,Y)]^\perp$$

$$- \sum_i B(e_i,(\bar{R}(e_i,X)Y)^T).$$

For any vector V normal to M, (4.1), (4.2), (4.3) and (4.4) imply

(4.5) $\quad g((\nabla^2 B)(X,Y),V) = g(D_X D_Y(TrB),V) + \sum_i [g((\bar{\nabla}_X \bar{R})(e_i,Y)e_i,V)$

$$- g((\bar{\nabla}_{e_i}\bar{R})(e_i,X)Y,V)] + \sum_i [g(R^\perp(e_i,X)B(e_i,Y),V)$$

$$+ 2g(\bar{R}(e_i,Y)B(X,e_i),V) + g(\bar{R}(e_i,B(X,Y))e_i,V)$$

$$+ g(\bar{R}(B(e_i,e_i),X)Y,V) + g(\bar{R}(e_i,X)B(e_i,Y),V)$$

$$- g(A_V X,\bar{R}(e_i,Y)e_i) - g(A_V e_i,\bar{R}(e_i,X)Y)]$$

$$- \sum_i [g(R(e_i,X)e_i,A_V Y) + g(R(e_i,X)Y,A_V e_i)],$$

where we used the first Bianchi identity. Moreover, we see that

(4.6) $- \sum\limits_{i} [g(R(e_i,X)e_i,A_VY) + g(R(e_i,X)Y,A_Ve_i)]$

$$= - \sum\limits_{i} [g(\bar{R}(e_i,X)e_i,A_VY) + g(A_{B(X,e_i)}e_i,A_VY)$$

$$- g(A_{B(e_i,e_i)}X,A_VY) + g(\bar{R}(e_i,X)Y,A_Ve_i)$$

$$+ g(A_{B(X,Y)}e_i,A_Ve_i) - g(A_{B(e_i,Y)}X,A_Ve_i)]$$

$$= - \sum\limits_{i} [g(\bar{R}(e_i,X)e_i,A_VY) + g(\bar{R}(e_i,X)Y,A_Ve_i)]$$

$$- \sum\limits_{X} [g(A_VA_XA_XX,Y) - TrA_Xg(A_VA_XX,Y) + TrA_XA_Vg(A_XX,Y)$$

$$- g(A_XA_VA_XX,Y)],$$

(4.7) $\sum\limits_{i} g(R^{\perp}(e_i,X)B(e_i,Y),V) = \sum\limits_{i} g(\bar{R}(e_i,X)B(e_i,Y),V)$

$$+ \sum\limits_{X} [g(A_XA_VA_XX,Y) - g(A_XA_XA_VX,Y)],$$

where we have used the notation $A_X = A_{e_X}$ for simplicity.

Substituting (4.6) and (4.7) into (4.5), we obtain

(4.8) $g((\nabla^2B)(X,Y),V) = g(D_XD_Y(TrB),V) + \sum\limits_{i} [g((\bar{\nabla}_X\bar{R})(e_i,Y)e_i,V)$

$$- g((\bar{\nabla}_{e_i}\bar{R})(e_i,X)Y,V)] + \sum\limits_{i} [2g(\bar{R}(e_i,Y)B(X,e_i),V)$$

$$+ 2g(\bar{R}(e_i,X)B(e_i,Y),V) - g(A_VX,\bar{R}(e_i,Y)e_i) - g(A_VY,\bar{R}(e_i,X)e_i$$

$$+ g(\bar{R}(e_i,B(X,Y))e_i,V) + g(\bar{R}(B(e_i,e_i),X)Y,V)$$

$$- 2g(A_Ve_i,\bar{R}(e_i,X)Y)] + \sum\limits_{X} [TrA_Xg(A_VA_XX,Y) - TrA_XA_Vg(A_XX,Y)$$

$$+ 2g(A_XA_VA_XX,Y) - g(A_XA_XA_VX,Y) - g(A_VA_XA_XX,Y)],$$

from which we have

Proposition 4.1. Let M be a submanifold of a locally symmetric Riemannian manifold $\bar{M}$. If the mean curvature vector of M is parallel, then we

$$
(4.9) \quad g((\nabla^2 B)(X,Y),V) = \sum_i [2g(\bar{R}(e_i,Y)B(X,e_i),V) + 2g(\bar{R}(e_i,X)B(Y,e_i),V)
$$

$$
- g(A_V X,\bar{R}(e_i,Y)e_i) - g(A_V Y,\bar{R}(e_i,X)e_i) + g(\bar{R}(e_i,B(X,Y))e_i,V)
$$

$$
+ g(\bar{R}(B(e_i,e_i),X)Y,V) - 2g(A_V e_i,\bar{R}(e_i,X)Y)]
$$

$$
+ \sum_X [\mathrm{Tr}A_X g(A_V A_X X,Y) - \mathrm{Tr}A_X A_V g(A_X X,Y) + 2g(A_X A_V A_X X,Y)
$$

$$
- g(A_X A_X A_V X,Y) - g(A_V A_X A_X X,Y)].
$$

Proposition 4.2. Let M be a submanifold of a locally symmetric Riemannian manifold $\bar{M}$. If M is minimal, then

$$
(4.10) \quad g((\nabla^2 B)(X,Y),V) = \sum_i [2g(\bar{R}(e_i,Y)B(X,e_i),V)
$$

$$
+ 2g(\bar{R}(e_i,X)B(Y,e_i),V) - g(A_V X,\bar{R}(e_i,Y)e_i)
$$

$$
- g(A_V Y,\bar{R}(e_i,X)e_i) + g(\bar{R}(e_i,B(X,Y))e_i,V)
$$

$$
- 2g(A_V e_i,\bar{R}(e_i,X)Y)] + \sum_X [2g(A_X A_V A_X X,Y) - \mathrm{Tr}A_X A_V g(A_X X,Y)
$$

$$
- g(A_X A_X A_V X,Y) - g(A_V A_X A_X X,Y)].
$$

If the ambient manifold $\bar{M}$ is a space form or a complex space form, then $\bar{M}$ is locally symmetric. But, if a Sasakian space form is locally symmetric, then it is a space form.

We now assume that $\bar{R}(X,Y)Z$ is tangent to M for any vector fields X, Y and Z tangent to M. Then (4.1) reduces to

(4.11) $\qquad (\nabla^2 B)(X,Y) = \sum_i (R(e_i,X)B)(e_i,Y) + D_X D_Y(\mathrm{Tr}B).$

From (4.2) and (4.11) we have

Proposition 4.3. Let M be a submanifold of a Riemannian manifold $\bar{M}$. If $\bar{R}(X,Y)Z$ is tangent to M for any vector fields X, Y and Z tangent to M, then

(4.12) $\qquad (\nabla^2 B)(X,Y) = \sum_i [R^{\perp}(e_i,X)B(e_i,Y) - B(R(e_i,X)e_i,Y)$

$$- B(e_i,R(e_i,X)Y)] + D_X D_Y(\mathrm{Tr}B).$$

§5. Submanifolds of space forms

In this section we give applications of the expression for Laplacian of the second fundamental form. Let M be an n-dimensional submanifold of a space form $\bar{M}^m(c)$. Suppose that the normal connection of M is flat and the mean curvature vector of M is parallel. Then (4.12) implies

(5.1) $\qquad (\nabla^2 B)(X,Y) = - \sum_i [B(R(e_i,X)e_i,Y) + B(e_i,R(e_i,X)Y)].$

On the other hand, we have

(5.2) $\qquad g((\nabla^2 B)(X,Y),V) = g((\nabla^2 A)_V X,Y)$

for any vector field V normal to M. From (5.1) and (5.2) we obtain

(5.3) $g((\nabla^2 A)_V X, Y) = - \sum_i [g(A_V Y, R(e_i, X)e_i) + g(A_V e_i, R(e_i, X)Y)],$

from which

(5.4) $g(\nabla^2 A, A) = \sum_{x,i} g((\nabla^2 A)_x e_i, A_x e_i)$

$\qquad\qquad = - \sum_{x,i,j} [g(A_x A_x e_j, R(e_i, e_j)e_i) + g(A_x e_i, R(e_i, e_j)A_x e_j)].$

Since the normal connection of M is flat, we see that the second fundamental form of M is commutative. Thus we can choose $e_1, \ldots, e_n$ such that $A_x e_i = \lambda_i^x e_i$ for all x. Thus (5.4) becomes

(5.5) $g(\nabla^2 A, A) = \sum_{x,i,j} K_{ij}(\lambda_j^x \lambda_j^x - \lambda_i^x \lambda_j^x) = \frac{1}{2} \sum_{x,i,j} K_{ij}(\lambda_i^x - \lambda_j^x)^2,$

where K_{ij} denotes the sectional curvature of M for the section spanned by e_i and e_j. On the other hand, we have

$$g(\nabla^2 A, A) = - g(\nabla A, \nabla A) + \frac{1}{2}\Delta g(A, A).$$

Thus we obtain

(5.6) $\frac{1}{2}\Delta g(A, A) = g(\nabla A, \nabla A) + \frac{1}{2} \sum_{x,i,j} K_{ij}(\lambda_i^x - \lambda_j^x)^2.$

Therefore we have the following results (see [18], [61]).

Lemma 5.1. Let M be an n-dimensional submanifold of $\bar{M}^m(c)$ with flat normal connection and parallel mean curvature vector. If M is compact orientable and M has non-negative sectional curvature, then the second fundamental form of M is parallel.

Lemma 5.2. Let M be an n-dimensional submanifold of $\bar{M}^m(c)$ with flat normal connection and parallel mean curvature vector. If $g(A,A)$ is constant on M, and M has non-negative sectional curvature, then the second fundamental form of M is parallel.

We now give a few examples of n-dimensional submanifolds discussed above in an m-dimensional Euclidean space R^m with usual inner product (x,y) (see [61]).

Example 5.1. For integers $p_1,\ldots,p_N \geq 1$, $p_1+\cdots+p_N = n$, consider R^m as $R^{p_1+1} \times \cdots \times R^{p_N+1}$, where $N = m-n$. We put

$$S^{p_i}(r_i) = \{x_i \in R^{p_i+1} : (x_i,x_i) = r_i^2\}, \quad i = 1,\ldots,N.$$

Then the pythagorean product

$$\Pi S^{p_i}(r_i) = S^{p_1}(r_1) \times \cdots \times S^{p_N}(r_N)$$
$$= \{(x_1,\ldots,x_N) \in R^m : x_i \in S^{p_i}(r_i), i = 1,\ldots,N\}$$

is an n-dimensional submanifold M^n of essential codimension m-n in R^m. The mean curvature vector μ of M^n is given by

$$\mu = \frac{1}{n}(p_1 r_1^{-2}x_1 + \cdots + p_N r_N^{-2}x_N)$$

at $(x_1,\ldots,x_N) \in M^n$, which is parallel in the normal bundle of M^n and the function $g(A,A)$ is given by

$$g(A,A) = 1/r_1^2 + \cdots + 1/r_N^2,$$

which is constant on M^n. Moreover, the normal connection of M^n is flat.

For integers $p_1, \ldots, p_N, p$ such that $p_1, \ldots, p_N, p \geq 1$, $p_1 + \cdots + p_N + p = n$, consider R^m as $R^{p_1+1} \times \cdots \times R^{p_N+1} \times R^p$, where $N = m-n$. Then the pythagorean product

$$S^{p_1}(r_1) \times \cdots \times S^{p_N}(r_N) \times R^p$$

$$= \{(x_1, \ldots, x_N, x) \in R^m : x_i \in S^{p_i}(r_i), \ i = 1, \ldots, N, \ x \in R^p\}$$

is an n-dimensional submanifold M^n of essential codimension $N = m-n$ in R^m. M^n has parallel mean curvature vector and flat normal connection. Moreover, $g(A,A)$ is constant.

Using Lemmas 5.1 and 5.2, Yano-Ishihara [61] obtained the following theorems (see also [18]).

Theorem 5.1. Let M be an n-dimensional complete submanifold of R^m with non-negative sectional curvature. Suppose that the normal connection of M is flat and the mean curvature vector of M is parallel. If $g(A,A)$ is constant, then M is a sphere $S^n(r)$, n-dimensional plane R^n, a pythagorean product of the form

$$(5.7) \quad S^{p_1}(r_1) \times \cdots \times S^{p_N}(r_N), \quad p_1, \ldots, p_N \geq 1, \ \Sigma p_i = n, \ 1 < N \leq m-n,$$

or a pythagoren product of the form

$$(5.8) \quad S^{p_1}(r_1) \times \cdots \times S^{p_N}(r_N) \times R^p, \quad p_1, \ldots, p_N, p \geq 1,$$
$$\Sigma p_i + p = n, \ 1 < N \leq m-n.$$

If M is a pythagorean product of the form (5.7) or (5.8), then M is of essential codimension N.

Theorem 5.2. Let M be an n-dimensional compact orientable submanifold of R^m with non-negative sectional curvature, and suppose that the normal connection of M is flat. If the mean curvature vector of M is parallel, then M is a sphere $S^n(r)$ or a pythagorean product of the form (5.7), which is of essential codimension N.

Remark. Suppose that a submanifold M of dimension n immersed in R^m satisfies the conditions of Theorem 5.1 or 5.2, and is of essential codimension s less than m-n. Then M is contained in a plane $\bar{R}^{n+s}$ of R^m, and satisfies the same conditions as those mentioned in Theorem 5.1 or 5.2 and satisfied by M considered as a submanifold in R^m (see Theorem 3.1).

Example 5.2. In R^{m+1} we consider an m-dimensional sphere of radius $a > 0$:

$$S^m(a) = \{x \in R^{m+1} : (x,x) = a^2\}.$$

For mutually orthogonal unit vectors $b_1, \ldots, b_{m-n}$ in R^{m+1}, a submanifold $\Sigma^n(r)$ in $S^m(a)$ defined by

$$\Sigma^n(r) = \{x \in S^m(a) : (x,b_t) = d_t, \ t = 1, \ldots, m-n\}$$

is called an n-dimensional small sphere of $S^m(a)$ with radius r if $(d_1, \ldots, d_{m-n}) \neq (0, \ldots, 0)$, where $r^2 = a^2 - d_1^2 - \cdots - d_{m-n}^2 > 0$ and $1 < n < m$. $\Sigma^n(r)$ is called an n-dimensional great sphere of $S^m(a)$ if

$(d_1,\ldots,d_{m-n}) = (0,\ldots,0)$, i.e., if $r = a$. If $r \neq a$, the $\Sigma^n(r)$ is a totally umbilical submanifold of essential codimension $m-n$ in $S^m(a)$, and the mean curvature of $\Sigma^n(r)$ is given by

$$|\mu| = d/(a(a^2-d^2)^{1/2}), \quad d^2 = d_1^2 + \cdots + d_{m-n}^2 \quad (d > 0).$$

A great sphere $\Sigma^n(a)$ is totally geodesic in $S^m(a)$ and of essential codimension 0.

Example 5.3. For integers $p_1,\ldots,p_N$ such that $p_1,\ldots,p_N \geq 1$, $p_1 + \cdots + p_N = n$, consider R^{m+1} as $R^{p_1+1} \times \cdots \times R^{p_N+1}$, where $N = m-n+1$. Then

$$(5.9) \quad S^{p_1}(r_1) \times \cdots \times S^{p_N}(r_N)$$

$$= \{(x_1,\ldots,x_N) \in R^{m+1} : x_i \in S^{p_i}(r_i), \ i = 1,\ldots,N\},$$

where $S^{p_i}(r_i) \subset R^{p_i+1}$ $(i = 1,\ldots,N)$, is an n-dimensional submanifold M^n of essential codimension $m-n$ imbedded in $S^m(a)$ if $\Sigma r_i^2 = a^2$. The mean curvature vector μ of M^n relative to $S^m(a)$ is given by

$$\mu = \frac{1}{n}(p_1 r_1^{-2} x_1 + \cdots + p_N r_N^{-2} x_N) - a^{-2}(x_1 + \cdots + x_N)$$

at $(x_1,\ldots,x_N) \in M^n$, which is parallel in the normal bundle of M^n relative to $S^m(a)$. We also have

$$g(A,A) = r_1^2(r_1^{-2}-a^{-2})^2 + \cdots + r_N^2(r_N^{-2}-a^{-2})^2 + N(N-1)a^{-2},$$

which is constant in M^n. It is easily verified that the connection of the normal bundle of M^n is flat.

Let $\Sigma^{m-1}(r)$ be an $(m-1)$-dimensional small sphere of $S^m(a)$ $(0 < r < a)$. For integers $p_1, \ldots, p_{N'}$ such that $p_1, \ldots, p_{N'} \geq 1$, $p_1 + \cdots + p_{N'} = n$, $N' = m-n$, in $\Sigma^{m-1}(r)$ consider an n-dimensional submanifold M^n of the form

$$(5.10) \qquad \Sigma^{p_1}(r_1) \times \cdots \times \Sigma^{p_{N'}}(r_{N'}) \subset \Sigma^{m-1}(r),$$

where $r_1^2 + \cdots + r_{N'}^2 = r^2 < a^2$, $\Sigma^{p_i}(r_i)$ $(i = 1, \ldots, N')$ is a p_i-dimensional sphere with radius r_i, and $\tilde{M}^n$ is constructed in $\Sigma^{m-1}(r)$ in the same way as that used in constructing in $S^m(a)$ a submanifold M^n of the form (5.9). Then $\tilde{M}^n$ is an n-dimensional submanifold of essential codimension $m-n-1$ in $\Sigma^{m-1}(r)$ and therefore $m-n$ in $S^m(a)$. The mean curvature vector of M^n relative to $S^m(a)$ is parallel, $g(A,A)$ relative to $S^m(a)$ is constant and the normal connection of $\tilde{M}^n$ relative to S^m is flat.

In view of Lemmas 5.1 and 5.2, Theorems 5.1 and 5.2, Yano-Ishihara [61] proved the following theorems.

Theorem 5.3. Let M be an n-dimensional complete submanifold of $S^m(a)$ with non-negative sectional curvature. Suppose that the mean curvature vector of M is parallel and the normal connection of M is flat. If $g(A,A)$ is constant in M, then M is a small sphere $\Sigma^n(r)$, a great sphere $\Sigma^n(a)$ or a pythagorean product of a certain number of spheres. Moreover, if M is of essential codimension $m-n$, then M is a pythagorean product of the form (5.9) with $r_1^2 + \cdots + r_N^2 = a^2$, $N = m-n+1$, or of the form (5.10) with $r_1^2 + \cdots + r_{N'}^2 = r^2 < a^2$, $N' = m-n$. If M is a pythagorean product of the form (5.10) with $r_1^2 + \cdots + r_N^2 = r^2 < a^2$, $N = m-n$, then M is contained in a small sphere $\Sigma^{m-1}(r)$ of $S^m(a)$.

Theorem 5.4. Let M be an n-dimensional compact orientable submanifold of $S^m(a)$ with non-negative sectional curvature. Suppose that the normal connection of M is flat and the mean curvature vector of M is parallel. If M is of essential codimension m-n, then we have the same conclusion as that in Theorem 5.3.

Remark. If M^n in $S^m(a)$ satisfies the condition of Theorem 5.3 or 5.4 and if M^n is of essential codimension s less than m-n, then M^n is contained in a great sphere $S^{n+s}(a)$ of $S^m(a)$.

When a submanifold M is minimal, we have [61]

Theorem 5.5. Let M be an n-dimensional complete minimal submanifold of $S^m(a)$ with non-negative sectional curvature, and suppose that the normal connection of M is flat. If $g(A,A)$ is constant in M, then M is a great sphere of $S^m(a)$ or a pythagorean product of the form

(5.11) $S^{p_1}(r_1) \times \cdots \times S^{p_N}(r_N)$, $p_1,\ldots,p_N \geq 1$, $p_1 + \cdots + p_N = n$,

$$1 < N \leq m-n+1$$

with essential codimension N-1, where $r_i = a(p_i/n)^{1/2}$ $(i = 1,\ldots,N)$.

Theorem 5.6. Let M be a compact orientable n-dimensional minimal submanifold of $S^m(a)$. If M has non-negative sectional curvature and the normal connection of M is flat, then we have the same conclusion as that in Theorem 5.5.

§6. Parallel second fundamental form

In this section we consider an n-dimensional submanifold M of an m-dimensional space form $\bar{M}^m(c)$.

First of all, we prove the following (Yano-Kon [66])

Theorem 6.1. Let M be an n-dimensional submanifold of $\bar{M}^m(c)$ $(c \geq 0)$ with flat normal connection. If the second fundamental form of M is parallel, then the sectional curvature of M is non-negative.

Proof. Since the normal connection of M is flat, the A_x's are simultaneousely diagonalizable at each point of M. Let λ_i^x $(1 \leq i \leq n,$ $n+1 \leq x \leq m)$ be the eigenvalues of A_x corresponding to eigenvectors $e_1, \ldots, e_n$. We can choose a local field of orthonormal frames $e_{n+1}, \ldots, e_m$ in the normal bundle such that $De_x = 0$ $(x = n+1, \ldots, m)$. Since the second fundamental form of M is parallel, we have

$$A_x R(e_i, e_j)e_i = R(e_i, e_j)A_x e_i = \lambda_i^x R(e_i, e_j)e_i.$$

Thus the eigenspace T_i^x corresponding to λ_i^x has the property that

$$R(e_i, e_j)T_i^x \subset T_i^x \quad \text{for all } x = n+1, \ldots, m.$$

If $\lambda_i^x \neq \lambda_j^x$ for some x, then we have

$$g(R(e_i, e_j)e_i, e_j) = 0,$$

which means that the sectional curvature K_{ij} of M with respect to the section spnned by e_i, e_j vanishes. On the other hand, from the equation of Gauss (2.4), the sectional curvature K_{ij} of M is given by

$$K_{ij} = c + \sum_x \lambda_i^x \lambda_j^x.$$

If $\lambda_i^x \neq \lambda_j^x$ for some x, then $K_{ij} = 0$, and if $\lambda_i^x = \lambda_j^x$ for all x, then $K_{ij} \geq 0$. Thus the sectional curvature K_{ij} with respect to the section spanned by e_i, e_j is non-negative.

In the following, we prove that the sectional curvature $g(R(X,Y)Y,X)$ for any orthonormal vectors X and Y is non-negative.

From (2.4) we have

$$g(R(X,Y)Y,X) = c + \sum_x g(A_x X,X) g(A_x Y,Y) - \sum_x g(A_x X,Y)^2.$$

We now put $X = \Sigma_i \alpha_i e_i$ and $Y = \Sigma_i \beta_i e_i$. Then we see that

$$g(R(X,Y)Y,X) = c + \sum_{x,i,j} \alpha_i^2 \beta_j^2 \lambda_i^x \lambda_j^x - \sum_{x,i,j} \alpha_i \alpha_j \beta_i \beta_j \lambda_i^x \lambda_j^x$$

$$= c + \sum_{i,j} (K_{ij} - c)\alpha_i^2 \beta_j^2 - \sum_{i,j} (k_{ij} - c)\alpha_i \alpha_j \beta_i \beta_j.$$

Since we have $\sum_{i,j} \alpha_i^2 \beta_j^2 = 1$ and $\Sigma_i \alpha_i \beta_i = 0$, the equation above becomes

$$g(R(X,Y)Y,X) = \sum_{i,j} K_{ij} \alpha_i^2 \beta_j^2 - \sum_{i,j} K_{ij} \alpha_i \alpha_j \beta_i \beta_j$$

$$= \sum_{i>j} K_{ij} (\alpha_i \beta_j - \alpha_j \beta_i)^2.$$

We have already seen that $K_{ij} \geq 0$, and hence $g(R(X,Y)Y,X) \geq 0$. Therefore, the sectional curvature of M is non-negative.

Proposition 6.1. Let M be an n-dimensional minimal submanifold of $\bar{M}^m(c)$ with parallel second fundamental form.

   (i) If $c \leq 0$, then M is totally geodesic.

   (ii) If $c > 0$ and $g(A,A) \geq n(m-n)c$, then $R^\perp = 0$.

Proof. From (I.1.8), (4.10) and (5.2) we have

$$(6.1) \qquad \tfrac{1}{2}\Delta g(A,A) = ncg(A,A) - \sum_{x,y}(TrA_xA_y)^2 + \sum_{x,y}Tr[A_x,A_y]^2 + g(\nabla A,\nabla A).$$

Since the second fundamental form of M is parallel, we see that $g(A,A)$ is constant. Thus (6.1) reduces to

$$(6.2) \qquad 0 \le -\sum_{x,y}Tr[A_x,A_y]^2 = ncg(A,A) - \sum_{x,y}(TrA_xA_y)^2.$$

We consider the symmetric $(m-n,m-n)$-matrix (TrA_xA_y). Then we can choose a suitable basis $e_{n+1},\ldots,e_m$ for which the matrix (TrA_xA_y) can be assumed to be diagonal. Thus we have

$$(6.3) \qquad 0 \le -\sum_{x,y}Tr[A_x,A_y]^2 = ncg(A,A) - \frac{1}{m-n}(\sum_x TrA_x^2)^2$$

$$- \frac{1}{m-n}\sum_{x>y}(TrA_x^2 - TrA_y^2)^2$$

$$\le \frac{1}{m-n}[n(m-n)c - g(A,A)]g(A,A).$$

If $c \le 0$, (6.3) implies that $g(A,A) = 0$ and hence M is totally geodesic. If $c > 0$ and $g(A,A) \ge n(m-n)c$, then (6.3) shows that $[A_x,A_y] = 0$ for all x and y, which means that the normal connection of M is flat, that is, $R^\perp = 0$.

<u>Theorem 6.2</u> (Yano-Kon [66]). Let M be a complete minimal submanifold of dimension n of S^m with parallel second fundamental form. If $g(A,A) \geq n(m-n)$, then M is a pythagorean product of the form

$$S^{p_1}(r_1) \times \cdots \times S^{p_N}(r_N), \quad r_t = (p_t/n)^{1/2} \ (t = 1,\ldots,N),$$

where $1 \leq p_1,\ldots,p_N < n$, $p_1 + \cdots + p_N = n$, $m-n = N-1$.

<u>Proof</u>. From Theorem 5.5 the essential codimension of M is N-1. On the other hand, by (6.3), we have $\mathrm{Tr}A_x^2 = \mathrm{Tr}A_y^2$ for all x, y. Since $g(A,A) = n(m-n)$, M is not totally geodesic and hence $\mathrm{Tr}A_x^2 = \frac{1}{m-n} g(A,A)$ $\neq 0$ for all x. Thus we must have m-n = N-1. The other statements are trivial consequences of Theorem 5.5, Theorem 6.1 and Proposition 6.1.

<u>Theorem 6.3</u>. Let M be a complete n-dimensional submanifold of S^m with flat normal connection. If the second fundamental form of M is parallel, then M is a small sphere, a great sphere or a pythagorean product of a certain number of spheres. Moreover, if M is of essential codimension m-n, then M is a pythagorean product of the form

$$S^{p_1}(r_1) \times \cdots \times S^{p_N}(r_N), \quad r_1^2 + \cdots + r_N^2 = 1, \ m-n = N-1,$$

or a pythagorean product of the form

$$S^{p_1}(r_1) \times \cdots \times S^{p_{N'}}(r_{N'}) \subset S^{m-1} \subset S^m, \quad r_1^2 + \cdots + r_{N'}^2 = r^2 < 1,$$
$$m-n = N'.$$

<u>Proof</u>. This is a trivial consequence of Theorems 5.3 and 6.1.

In the following we give some applications of equation (6.1).
Let M be a compact orientable n-dimensional minimal submanifold of
S^m. For any symmetric (n,n)-matrices A and B we have [16]

$$-\text{Tr}(AB - BA)^2 \leq 2\text{Tr}A^2\text{Tr}B^2,$$

from which

$$-\sum_{x,y} \text{Tr}[A_x,A_y]^2 \leq 2\sum_{x\neq y} \text{Tr}A_x^2\text{Tr}A_y^2.$$

Thus we have, for suitable $e_{n+1},\ldots,e_m$,

$$(6.4) \quad \sum_{x,y}(\text{Tr}A_xA_y)^2 - \sum_{x,y}\text{Tr}[A_x,A_y]^2 \leq \sum_x(\text{Tr}A_x^2)^2 + 2\sum_{x\neq y}\text{Tr}A_x^2\text{Tr}A_y^2$$

$$= 2(\sum_x\text{Tr}A_x^2)^2 - \sum_x(\text{Tr}A_x^2)^2$$

$$= (2 - \frac{1}{m-n})(\sum_x\text{Tr}A_x^2)^2 - \frac{1}{m-n}\sum_{x>y}(\text{Tr}A_x^2 - \text{Tr}A_y^2)^2$$

$$\leq (2 - \frac{1}{m-n})(\sum_x\text{Tr}A_x^2)^2.$$

Therefore (6.1) and (6.4) imply that

$$(6.5) \quad 0 \leq \int_M g(\nabla A,\nabla A)*1 \leq \int_M[(2 - \frac{1}{m-n})g(A,A) - n]g(A,A)*1.$$

From this we have a theorem of Simons [43]:

Theorem 6.4. Let M be a compact orientable n-dimensional minimal
submanifold of S^m. Then either M is totally geodesic, or $g(A,A) = n/q$,
or at some point of M, $g(A,A) > n/q$, where $q = 2 - 1/(m-n)$.

When $g(A,A) = n/q$, Chern-do Carmo-Kobayashi [16] proved the following

Theorem 6.5. The veronese surface in S^4 and Clifford minimal hypersurface $S^k((k/n)^{1/2}) \times S^{n-k}((n-k/n)^{1/2})$ in S^{n+1} are the only compact minimal submanifold of dimension n in S^m satisfying $g(A,A) = n/q$.

If the normal connection of a minimal submanifold M of S^m is flat, then we have

$$\tfrac{1}{2}\Delta g(A,A) = ng(A,A) - \sum_{x,y} (\mathrm{Tr} A_x A_y)^2 + g(\nabla A, \nabla A),$$

from which, if M is compact orientable,

$$\int_M [g(A,A) - n]g(A,A)*1 \geq 0.$$

Using this, Kenmotsu [25] proved

Theorem 6.6. Let M be an n-dimensional compact orientable minimal submanifold of S^m with flat normal connection. If $g(A,A) = n$, then there exists an (n+1)-dimensional sphere S^{n+1} containing M as a Clifford minimal hypersurface.

Chapter III

CONTACT CR SUBMANIFOLDS

§1. Submanifolds of Sasakian manifolds

Let $\bar{M}$ be a $(2m+1)$-dimensional Sasakian manifold with structure tensors (ϕ,ξ,η,g). We consider a Riemannian manifold isometrically immersed in $\bar{M}$ with induced metric tensor field g.

First of all, we prove

Proposition 1.1. Let M be an n-dimensional submanifold of a $(2m+1)$-dimensional Sasakian manifold $\bar{M}$. If the structure vector field ξ is normal to M, then M is anti-invariant with respect to ϕ, that is, $\phi T_x(M) \subset T_x(M)^\perp$ for each point x of M, and $m \geq n$.

Proof. Since ξ is normal to M, the Weingarten formula implies

$$g(\phi X,Y) = g(\bar{\nabla}_X \xi,Y) = -g(A_\xi X,Y)$$

for any vector fields X and Y tangent to M, $\bar{\nabla}$ denoting the covariant differentiation in $\bar{M}$. Since A_ξ is symmetric and ϕ is skew-symmetric, we get $A_\xi = 0$ and ϕX is normal to M. This proves our assertion.

In the sequel, we assume that M is an $(n+1)$-dimensional submanifold, tangent to the structure vector field ξ, of a $(2m+1)$-dimensional Sasakian manifold $\bar{M}$. We denote by ∇ the operator of covariant differentiation in M.

For any vector field X tangent to M, we put

(1.1) $\qquad\qquad\qquad \phi X = PX + FX,$

where PX is the tangential part of ϕX and FX the normal part of ϕX. Similarly, for any vector field V normal to M, we put

(1.2) $\qquad\qquad\qquad \phi V = tV + fV,$

where tV is the tangential part of ϕV and fV the normal part of ϕV. For any vector field Y tangent to M, from (1.1), we have $g(\phi X,Y) = g(PX,Y)$, which shows that $g(PX,Y)$ is skew-symmetric. Similarly, from (1.2), we have $g(\phi V,U) = g(fV,U)$ for any vector field U normal to M, which shows that $g(fV,U)$ is skew-symmetric. We also have, from (1.1) and (1.2),

(1.3) $\qquad\qquad\qquad g(FX,V) + g(X,tV) = 0.$

Now, applying ϕ to (1.1) and (1.2), we respectively obtain

(1.4) $\qquad\qquad P^2 = -I - tF + \eta \otimes \xi, \qquad FP + fF = 0,$

(1.5) $\qquad\qquad Pt + tf = 0, \qquad f^2 = -I - Ft.$

If we put $X = \xi$ in (1.1), we have

$$\phi \xi = P\xi + F\xi = 0,$$

from which

(1.6) $\qquad P\xi = 0, \qquad F\xi = 0.$

We define the covariant derivatives of P, F, t and f by

$(\nabla_X P)Y = \nabla_X(PY) - P\nabla_X Y$, $(\nabla_X F)Y = D_X(FY) - F\nabla_X Y$, $(\nabla_X t)V = \nabla_X(tV) - tD_X V$

and $(\nabla_X f)V = D_X(fV) - fD_X V$ respectively.

For any vector field X tangent to M, we have

$$\bar{\nabla}_X \xi = \phi X = \nabla_X \xi + B(X,\xi),$$

from which, using (1.3),

(1.7) $\qquad \nabla_X \xi = PX, \qquad FX = B(X,\xi), \qquad A_V \xi = -tV.$

Especially, we have

(1.8) $\qquad B(\xi,\xi) = 0.$

Let X and Y be vector fields tangent to M. Then we obtain

(1.9) $\qquad (\nabla_X P)Y = A_{FY}X + tB(X,Y) - g(X,Y)\xi + \eta(Y)X,$

(1.10) $\qquad (\nabla_X F)Y = -B(X,PY) + fB(X,Y).$

For any vector field X tangent to M and any vector field V normal to M, we have

(1.11) $\qquad (\nabla_X t)V = A_{fV}X - PA_V X,$

(1.12) $(\nabla_X f)V = -FA_V X - B(X,tV)$.

Let M be an $(n+1)$-dimensional submanifold, tangent to the structure vector field ξ, of a Sasakian space form $\bar{M}^{2m+1}(c)$. Then the
curvature tensor R of M is given by

$$R(X,Y)Z = \frac{1}{4}(c+3)[g(Y,Z)X - g(X,Z)Y] + \frac{1}{4}(c-1)[\eta(X)\eta(Z)Y$$

$$- \eta(Y)\eta(Z)X + g(X,Z)\eta(Y)\xi - g(Y,Z)\eta(X)\xi + g(\phi Y,Z)\phi X$$

$$- g(\phi X,Z)\phi Y + 2g(X,\phi Y)\phi Z] + A_{B(Y,Z)}X - A_{B(X,Z)}Y$$

$$+ (\nabla_Y B)(X,Z) - (\nabla_X B)(Y,Z).$$

Comparing the tangential and normal parts of the both sides of this
equation, we have, following equations of Gauss and Codazzi respectively:

(1.13) $R(X,Y)Z = \frac{1}{4}(c+3)[g(Y,Z)X - g(X,Z)Y] + \frac{1}{4}(c-1)[\eta(X)\eta(Z)Y$

$$-\eta(Y)\eta(Z)X + g(X,Z)\eta(Y)\xi - g(Y,Z)\eta(X)\xi + g(PY,Z)PX$$

$$- g(PX,Z)PY + 2g(X,PY)PZ] + A_{B(Y,Z)}X - A_{B(X,Z)}Y,$$

(1.14) $(\nabla_X B)(Y,Z) - (\nabla_Y B)(X,Z)$

$$= \frac{1}{4}(c-1)[g(PY,Z)FX - g(PX,Z)FY + 2g(X,PY)FZ].$$

Moreover, we have equation of Ricci

(1.15) $g(R^{\perp}(X,Y)U,V) + g([A_V,A_U]X,Y)$

$$= \frac{1}{4}(c-1)[g(FY,U)g(FX,V) - g(FX,U)g(FY,V) + 2g(X,PY)g(fU,V)].$$

If the second fundamental form B of a submanifold M , tangent to the structure vector field ξ, of a Sasakian manifold $\bar{M}$ is of the form

(1.16) $B(X,Y) = [g(X,Y) - \eta(X)\eta(Y)]\alpha + \eta(X)B(Y,\xi) + \eta(Y)B(X,\xi)$

for any vector fields X and Y tangent to M, α being a vector field normal to M, then M is said to be <u>totally contact umbilical</u>. The notion of totally contact umbilical submanifold of Sasakian manifolds corresponds to that of totally umbilical submanifolds of Kaehlerian manifolds. Moreover, if $\alpha = 0$, that is, if B is of the form

(1.17) $B(X,Y) = \eta(X)B(Y,\xi) + \eta(Y)B(X,\xi),$

then M is said to be <u>totally contact geodesic</u>. The notion of totally contact geodesic submanifolds of Sasakian manifolds corresponds to that of totally geodesic submanifolds of Kaehlerian manifolds.

<u>Proposition 1.2.</u> Let M be a submanifold, tangent to the structure vector field ξ, of a Sasakian manifold $\bar{M}$. If M is totally umbilical, then M is totally geodesic.

<u>Proof.</u> By the assumption, we have $B(X,Y) = g(X,Y)\mu$. From (1.8) we see that $\mu = 0$, that is, M is minimal in $\bar{M}$. Therefore, M is totally geodesic. In this case, $FX = B(X,\xi) = 0$. This shows that M is an invariant submanifold of $\bar{M}$ with respect to ϕ.

Definition. Let M be a submanifold tangent to the structure vector field ξ isometrically immersed in a Sasakian manifold $\tilde{M}$. Then M is called a <u>contact CR submanifold</u> of $\tilde{M}$ if there exists a differentiable distribution $D : x \xrightarrow{\hspace{2cm}} D_x \subset T_x(M)$ on M satisfying the following conditions:

(i) D is invariant with respect to ϕ, i.e., $\phi D_x \subset D_x$ for each $x \in M$, and

(ii) the complementary orthogonal distribution

$D^{\perp} : x \xrightarrow{\hspace{2cm}} D_x^{\perp} \subset T_x(M)$ is anti-invariant with respect to ϕ, i.e., $\phi D_x^{\perp} \subset T_x(M)^{\perp}$ for each $x \in M$.

In the sequel, we put dim $\tilde{M}$ = 2m+1, dim M = n+1, dim D = h, dim $D^{\perp}$ = q and codim M = 2m-n = p. If q = 0, then a contact CR submanifold M is called an <u>invariant submanifold</u> of $\tilde{M}$, and if h = 0, then M is called an <u>anti-invariant submanifold</u> of $\tilde{M}$ tangent to ξ. If p = q, then a contact CR submanifold M is called a <u>generic submanifold</u> of $\tilde{M}$. If h > 0 and q > 0, then a contact CR submanifold M is said to be <u>non-trivial</u> (proper).

If M is an invariant submanifold of a Sasakian manifold $\tilde{M}$, then M is also a Sasakian manifold with respect to the induced structure. Then we have F = 0 and t = 0, and $\phi X = PX$ for any vector field X tangent to M and $\phi V = fV$ for any vector field V normal to M. From (1.2), (1.10) and (1.11) we have

Lemma 1.1. Let M be an invariant submanifold of a Sasakian manifold $\bar{M}$. Then

(1.18) $$B(X,\xi) \doteq 0, \qquad A_V\xi = 0,$$

(1.19) $$B(X,\phi Y) = B(\phi X,Y) = \phi B(X,Y),$$

(1.20) $$\phi A_V X + A_V \phi X = 0,$$

(1.21) $$A_{\phi V} X = \phi A_V X.$$

From (1.18) and (1.19) we have

Proposition 1.3. Let M be an invariant submanifold of a Sasakian space form $\bar{M}^{2m+1}(c)$ with constant ϕ-sectional curvature c. Then M is totally geodesic if and only if M is of constant ϕ-sectional curvature c.

If the second fundamental form of an invariant submanifold M is parallel, then $0 = (\nabla_X B)(Y,\xi) = -B(Y,\phi X) = -\phi B(X,Y)$. Thus we have

Proposition 1.4. If the second fundamental form of an invariant submanifold M of a Sasakian manifold $\bar{M}$ is parallel, then M is totally geodesic.

Example 1.1. Let S^{2m+1} be a unit sphere with standard Sasakian structure. An odd-dimensional unit sphere S^{2n+1} (m > n) with induced structure is a totally geodesic invariant submanifold of S^{2m+1}.

Example 1.2. The circle bundle (Q^n,S^1) over a hyperquadric Q^n in a complex projective space CP^{n+1} is an invariant submanifold of S^{2n+3} which is an η-Einstein manifold.

If M is an (n+1)-dimensional anti-invariant submanifold of a (2n+1)-dimensional Sasakian manifold $\bar{M}$, then $\phi T_X(M) = T_X(M)^\perp$. Since, from (1.7), $\nabla_X \xi = 0$, by (I.3.1), (II.2.7) and (1.9), we have the following

Proposition 1.5. Let M be an (n+1)-dimensional anti-invariant submanifold, tangent to the structure vector field ξ, of a (2n+1)-dimensional Sasakian manifold $\bar{M}$. Then the normal connection of M is flat if and only if M is flat.

Similarly, we can prove the following

Proposition 1.6. Let M be an n-dimensional submanifold, normal to the structure vector field ξ, of a (2n+1)-dimensional Sasakian manifold $\bar{M}$. Then the normal connection of M is flat if and only if M is of constant curvature 1.

Proposition 1.7. Let M be an (n+1)-dimensional anti-invariant submanifold, tangent to the structure vector field ξ, of a (2m+1)-dimensional Sasakian manifold $\bar{M}$, then M is not totally umbilical.

Proof. If M is totally umbilical, then $B(X,Y) = g(X,Y)\mu$. Since $B(\xi,\xi) = 0$, we get $\mu = 0$. Thus M is minimal in $\bar{M}$, and then M is totally geodesic in $\bar{M}$. This contradicts the fact that $\phi X = B(X,\xi) \neq 0$. Thus the proposition is proved.

§2. f-structure on submanifolds

Let M be a contact CR submanifold of a Sasakian manifold $\tilde{M}$. We denote by l and $l^{\perp}$ the projection operators on D and $D^{\perp}$ respectively. Then we have

(2.1) $l + l^{\perp} = I, \quad l^2 = l, \quad l^{\perp 2} = l^{\perp}, \quad ll^{\perp} = l^{\perp}l = 0.$

From (1.1) we have

$$\phi l X = P l X + F l X,$$

from which, the distribution D being invariant, we have

(2.2) $l^{\perp}Pl = 0, \qquad\qquad Fl = 0.$

From (1.1), we also have

$$\phi l^{\perp}X = P l^{\perp}X + F l^{\perp}X,$$

from which, the distribution $D^{\perp}$ being anti-invariant, we have $Pl^{\perp} = 0$, and consequently

(2.3) $Pl = P,$

by vertue of $l^{\perp} = I - l$.

Now applying l from the right hand side to the second equation of (1.4) and using the second equation of (2.2) and (2.3), we find

(2.4)   FP = 0

and consequently, using the second equation of (1.4),

(2.5)   fF = 0.

Thus, remembering the skew-symmetry of f and the relation (1.3), we have

(2.6)   tf = 0

and consequently, from the first equation of (1.5), we have

(2.7)   Pt = 0.

Thus, from the first equation of (1.4) we find

(2.8) $P^3 + P = 0,$

which shows that P is an f-structure in M and from the second equation of (1.5), we have

(2.9) $f^3 + f = 0,$

which shows that f is an f-structure in the normal bundle $T(M)^{\perp}$.

Conversely, for a submanifold M, tangent to the structure vector field ξ, of a Sasakian manifold $\bar{M}$, we assume that we have (2.4).

Then we have (2.5), (2.6), (2.7) and consequently (2.8) and (2.9).
We now put

(2.10) $\qquad l = -P^2 + \eta \otimes \xi, \qquad\qquad l^{\perp} = I - l.$

Then we can easily verify that

$$l + l^{\perp} = I, \qquad l^2 = l, \qquad l^{\perp 2} = l^{\perp}, \qquad ll^{\perp} = l^{\perp}l = 0,$$

which mean that l and $l^{\perp}$ are complementary projection operators and consequently define orthogonal distributions D and $D^{\perp}$ respectively.

From the first equation of (2.10), we have

$$Pl = P$$

because of $P^3 = -P$ and $P\xi = 0$. This equation can also be written as

$$Pl^{\perp} = 0.$$

But $g(PX,Y)$ is skew-symmetric and $g(l^{\perp}X,Y)$ is symmetric and consequently the equation above gives

$$l^{\perp}P = 0,$$

from which we have

$$l^{\perp}Pl = 0.$$

From the first equation of (2.10) we have

$$F\mathit{l} = 0,$$

because of FP = 0 and $F\xi$ = 0.

The equations above show that the distribution D is invariant and $D^{\perp}$ is anti-invariant with respect to ϕ. Moreover, we have

$$\mathit{l}\xi = \xi, \qquad \mathit{l}^{\perp}\xi = 0$$

and consequently the distribution D contains ξ.

On the other hand, putting

$$(2.11) \qquad \mathit{l} = -P^2, \qquad \mathit{l}^{\perp} = I + P^2,$$

we still see that l and $\mathit{l}^{\perp}$ define complementary orthogonal distributions D and $D^{\perp}$ respectively since P is an f-structure. We also have

$$P\mathit{l} = P, \qquad \mathit{l}^{\perp}P = 0, \qquad F\mathit{l} = 0, \qquad P\mathit{l}^{\perp} = 0$$

and see that D is invariant and $D^{\perp}$ is anti-invariant with respect to ϕ and also that

$$\mathit{l}\xi = 0, \qquad \mathit{l}^{\perp}\xi = \xi,$$

which mean that $D^{\perp}$ contains ξ. Thus we have (Yano-Kon [73])

Theorem 2.1. In order for a submanifold M, tangent to the structure vector field ξ, of a Sasakian manifold $\bar{M}$ to be a contact CR submanifold, it is necessary and sufficient that FP = 0.

Theorem 2.2. Let M be a contact CR submanifold of a Sasakian manifold $\bar{M}$. Then P is an f-structure in M and f is an f-structure in the normal bundle of M.

§3. Integrability of distributions

We study the integrability of the distributions D and $D^{\perp}$ of a contact CR submanifold M of a Sasakian manifold $\bar{M}$.

Let X, Y $\in D^{\perp}$. Then PX = PY = 0, and hence

$$g((\nabla_Z P)X,Y) = g(\nabla_Z(PX),Y) - g(P\nabla_Z X,Y) = 0$$

for any vector field Z tangent to M. Therefore, (1.9) implies

$$0 = g((\nabla_Z P)X,Y) = -\eta(Y)g(Z,X) + \eta(X)g(Z,Y)$$
$$+ g(A_{FX}Z,Y) + g(tB(Z,X),Y),$$

which then implies

$$g(A_{FX}Y,Z) - g(A_{FY}X,Z) = \eta(Y)g(Z,X) - \eta(X)g(Z,Y).$$

Thus we have

(3.1) $\qquad A_{FX}Y - A_{FY}X = \eta(Y)X - \eta(X)Y \qquad$ for X,Y $\in D^{\perp}$.

Theorem 3.1. Let M be an (n+1)-dimensional contact CR submanifold of a (2m+1)-dimensional Sasakian manifold $\tilde{M}$. The distribution $D^\perp$ is completely integrable and its maximal integral submanifold is a p-dimensional anti-invariant submanifold of $\tilde{M}$ normal to ξ or a (p+1)-dimensional anti-invariant submanifold of $\tilde{M}$ tangent to ξ, where p = dim $D^\perp$.

Proof. Let X, Y $\in D^\perp$. Then we have, from (1.1),

$$\phi[X,Y] = P[X,Y] + F[X,Y] = -(\nabla_X P)Y + (\nabla_Y P)X + F[X,Y]$$

$$= A_{FX}Y - A_{FY}X - \eta(Y)X + \eta(X)Y + F[X,Y] = F[X,Y],$$

from which $\phi[X,Y] \in T(M)^\perp$. Thus we have $[X,Y] \in D^\perp$.

Theorem 3.2. Let M be an (n+1)-dimensional contact CR submanifold of a (2m+1)-dimensional Sasakian manifold $\tilde{M}$. Then the distribution D is completely integrable if and only if

$$B(X,PY) = B(Y,PX)$$

for any vector fields X, Y $\in D$, and then $\xi \in D$. Moreover, the maximal integral submanifold of D is an (n+1-p)-dimensional invariant submanifold of $\tilde{M}$, where p = dim $D^\perp$.

Proof. Let X, Y $\in D$. Then we have, from (1.1) and (1.10),

$$\phi[X,Y] = P[X,Y] + F[X,Y] = P[X,Y] + (\nabla_Y F)X - (\nabla_X F)Y$$

$$= P[X,Y] + B(X,PY) - B(Y,PX).$$

Thus we see that $[X,Y] \in D$ if and only if $B(X,PY) = B(Y,PX)$ for any X, $Y \in D$. If D is normal to ξ, then we have $g([X,Y],\xi) = 2g(X,PY)$ for X, $Y \in D$. Thus, if D is completely integrable, we have $g(X,PY) = 0$, which shows that $\dim D = 0$. This proves our assertion.

§4. Totally contact umbilical submanifolds

Let M be an $(n+1)$-dimensional submanifold, tangent to the structure vector field ξ, of a $(2m+1)$-dimensional Sasakian manifold $\bar{M}$. If M is totally contact umbilical, then the second fundamental form B of M satisfies

$$(4.1) \qquad B(X,Y) = [g(X,Y) - \eta(X)\eta(Y)]\alpha + \eta(X)FY + \eta(Y)FX$$

by (1.7) and (1.11). From (1.1) and (1.6) we see that $\alpha = \frac{1}{n}\mathrm{Tr}B$ $= \frac{n+1}{n}\mu$, where μ denotes the mean curvature vector of M. Therefore, (1.16) and (1.17) imply the following lemma.

Lemma 4.1. Let M be a totally contact umbilical submanifold, tangent to the structure vector field ξ, of a Sasakian manifold $\bar{M}$. Then M is totally contact geodesic if and only if M is minimal.

Theorem 4.1. Let M be a totally contact umbilical non-trivial contact CR submanifold of a Sasakian manifold $\bar{M}$. If $\dim D^{\perp} > 2$, then M is totally contact geodesic in $\bar{M}$.

Proof. First of all, we prove $t\alpha = 0$. From (3.1) we obtain

$$A_{FX}t\alpha = A_{Ft\alpha}X$$

for any $X \in D^{\perp}$ such that $\eta(X) = 0$. From this and (4.1) we have

$$g(t\alpha,X)g(\alpha,FX) = g(X,X)g(\alpha,Ft\alpha),$$

from which

(4.2) $$g(X,X)g(t\alpha,t\alpha) = g(t\alpha,X)g(t\alpha,X).$$

Since dim $D^{\perp} > 2$, we can choose X in such a way that $g(t\alpha,X) = 0$ and hence $t\alpha = 0$.

On the other hand, from (1.11) we find

$$g((\nabla_X t)\alpha,Y) = -g(tD_X\alpha,Y) = g(A_{f\alpha}X,Y) - g(PA_\alpha X,Y)$$

$$= g(X,PY)g(\alpha,\alpha).$$

Thus we have

(4.3) $$g(D_X\alpha,FY) = g(X,PY)g(\alpha,\alpha).$$

Since M is non-trivial, we can put $Y = PX$ in (4.3). Then, since $FP = 0$, we see that $\alpha = 0$ and hence $\mu = 0$. Therefore, our theorem follows from Lemma 4.1.

§5. Examples of contact CR submanifolds

In this section we give some examples of anti-invariant submanifolds, generic submanifolds and contact CR submanifolds of a Sasakian space form.

Example 5.1. Let $S^m(r)$ be an m-dimensional sphere with radius r. We consider an odd-dimensional unit sphere S^{2m+1} in the complex number space C^{m+1} of complex dimension m+1. Then S^{2m+1} admits a Sasakian structure (ϕ,ξ,η,g). Let v be the position vector representing a point of S^{2m+1} in C^{m+1}. Then the structure vector field ξ of S^{2m+1} is given by $\xi = Jv$, where J is the almost complex structure of C^{m+1}. We now consider the orthogonal projection

$$\pi : T_x(C^{m+1}) \longrightarrow T_x(S^{2m+1}),$$

and put $\phi = \pi \cdot J$. Denote by η the 1-form dual to ξ and by g the standard metric tensor field on S^{2m+1}. Then for any vector field X tangent to S^{2m+1}, we have.

(5.1) $$\phi X = JX + \eta(X)v.$$

We then consider the following immersion:

$$S^{m_1}(r_1) \times \cdots \times S^{m_k}(r_k) \longrightarrow S^{n+k}, \quad n+1 = \sum_{i=1}^{k} m_i,$$

where $m_1,\ldots,m_k$ are odd numbers and $r_1^2 + \cdots + r_k^2 = 1$. Here n+k is odd. Let v_i be a point of $S^{m_i}(r_i)$ in $R^{m_i+1} = C^{(m_i+1)/2}$. $S^{m_i}(r_i)$ is a real hypersurface of $C^{(m_i+1)/2}$ with unit normal $r_i^{-1}v_i$. Thus $v = (v_1,\ldots,v_k)$ is a unit vector in $R^{n+k+1} = C^{(n+k+1)/2}$. We restrict the almost complex structure of $C^{(n+k+1)/2}$ to $C^{(m_i+1)/2}$. Then each Jv_i is tangent to $S^{m_i}(r_i)$. Thus Jv is tangent to $M_{m_1,\ldots,m_k} = S^{m_1}(r_1) \times \cdots \times S^{m_k}(r_k)$. We then consider the normal space of $M_{m_1,\ldots,m_k}$ in S^{n+k} which is the orthogonal complement of the 1-dimensional space $<v>$ spanned by v in the space $<v_1,\ldots,v_k>$ spanned by $v_1,\ldots,v_k$. That is,

$$<v> \oplus T_x(M_{m_1,\ldots,m_k})^{\perp} = <v_1,\ldots,v_k> \text{ in } C^{(n+k+1)/2}.$$

Let $w_1,\ldots,w_{k-1}$ be an orthonormal frame for $T_x(M_{m_1,\ldots,m_k})^{\perp}$. Then w_i is given by a linear combination of $v_1,\ldots,v_k$. Thus Jw_i is tangent to $M_{m_1,\ldots,m_k}$, and hence by (5.1), we see that

$$\phi w_i = Jw_i + \eta(w_i)v = Jw_i.$$

Therefore w_i is tangent to $M_{m_1,\ldots,m_k}$ for all $i = 1,\ldots,k-1$. Thus we have

(5.2) $$\phi T_x(M_{m_1,\ldots,m_k})^{\perp} \subset T_x(M_{m_1,\ldots,m_k}).$$

Therefore, $M_{m_1,\ldots,m_k}$ is a generic submanifold of S^{n+k}. $M_{m_1,\ldots,m_k}$ has parallel second fundamental form and flat normal connection (see §5 of Chapter II).

Furthermore, $M_{m_1,\ldots,m_k}$ is a contact CR submanifold of S^{2m+1} $(2m+1 > n+k)$ with parallel second fundamental form and flat normal connection.

Example 5.2. In Example 5.1 we consider the immersion

$$S^{m_1}(r_1) \times \cdots \times S^{m_k}(r_k) \longrightarrow S^{n+k},$$

where $r_i = (m_i/(n+1))^{1/2}$ $(i = 1,\ldots,k)$. Then $M_{m_1,\ldots,m_k}$ is a generic minimal submanifold of S^{n+k}, and hence minimal contact CR submanifold of S^{2m+1} $(2m+1 > n+1)$.

Example 5.3. In Example 5.1, if we put $m_i = 1$ for all $i = 1,\ldots,k$ $(k = n+1)$, then $M_{m_1,\ldots,m_{n+1}}$ is an anti-invariant submanifold of S^{2n+1}.

§6. Flat normal connection

Let M be an $(n+1)$-dimensional contact CR submanifold of a $(2m+1)$-dimensional Sasakian manifold $\bar{M}$. Then we have the following decomposition of the tangent space $T_x(M)$ at each point x of M:

$$T_x(M) = H_x(M) \oplus \{\xi\} \oplus N_x(M),$$

where $H_x(M) = \phi H_x(M)$ and $N_x(M)$ is the orthogonal complement of $H_x(M) \oplus \{\xi\}$ in $T_x(M)$. Then $\phi N_x(M) = FN_x(M) \subset T_x(M)^\perp$. Similarly, we have

$$T_x(M)^\perp = FN_x(M) \oplus N_x(M)^\perp,$$

where $N_x(M)^\perp$ is the orthogonal complement of $FN_x(M)$ in $T_x(M)^\perp$. Then $\phi N_x(N)^\perp = fN_x(M)^\perp = N_x(M)^\perp$.

We take an orthonormal frame $e_1,\ldots,e_{2m+1}$ of $\bar{M}$ such that, restricted to M, $e_1,\ldots,e_{n+1}$ are tangent to M. Then $e_1,\ldots,e_{n+1}$ form an orthonormal frame of M. We can take $e_1,\ldots,e_{n+1}$ such that $e_1,\ldots,e_p$ form an orthonormal frame of $N_x(M)$ and $e_{p+1},\ldots,e_n$ form an orthonormal frame of $H_x(M)$ and $e_{n+1} = \xi$, where $\dim N_x(M) = p$. Moreover, we can take $e_{n+2},\ldots,e_{2m+1}$ of an orthonormal frame of $T_x(M)^\perp$ such that $e_{n+2},\ldots,e_{n+1+p}$ form an orthonormal frame of $FN_x(M)$ and $e_{n+2+p},\ldots,e_{2m+1}$ form an orthonormal frame of $N_x(M)^\perp$. In case of need, we can take $e_{n+2},\ldots,e_{n+1+p}$ such that $e_{n+2} = Fe_1,\ldots,e_{n+1+p} = Fe_p$. Unless otherwise stated, we use the conventions that the ranges of indices are respectively:

$$i,j,k = 1,\ldots,n+1; \quad x,y,z = 1,\ldots,p;$$
$$a,b,c = p+1,\ldots,n; \quad \alpha,\beta,\gamma = n+2,\ldots,n+1+p.$$

Here, we take a $(2m+1)$-dimensional unit sphere S^{2m+1} as an ambient manifold $\bar{M}$. Then we have

Lemma 6.1. If the normal connection of M is flat, then

$$A_{fV} = 0$$

for any vector field V normal to M.

Proof. Let U and V be vector fields normal to M. Since $R^\perp = 0$, equation of Ricci implies that $A_V A_U = A_U A_V$. Thus, from (1.7), we find

(6.1) $$A_V tU = A_U tV.$$

Since $tf = 0$, using (6.1), we see that $A_{fV} tU = 0$ and $A_{fV}\xi = 0$.

Moreover, from (1.12), we have

$$g((\nabla_X f)fV,U) = -g(FA_{fV}X,U) - g(B(X,tfV),U) = g(A_{fV}tU,X) = 0,$$

from which

$$(\nabla_X f)fV = 0.$$

Thus, from (1.10) and (2.9), we have

$$g((\nabla_X f)fV,FY) = -g(f^2V,(\nabla_X F)Y) = -g(A_{fV}X,Y) + g(A_{f^2V}X,PY) = 0.$$

From this and the fact that $A_{fV}A_{f^2V} = A_{f^2V}A_{fV}$, we have

$$\mathrm{Tr}A_{fV}^2 = \mathrm{Tr}A_{f^2V}PA_{fV} = -\mathrm{Tr}A_{fV}PA_{f^2V} = -\mathrm{Tr}A_{f^2V}A_{fV}P$$

$$= -\mathrm{Tr}A_{fV}A_{f^2V}P = -\mathrm{Tr}A_{f^2V}PA_{fV} = -\mathrm{Tr}A_{fV}^2.$$

Consequently, we have $\mathrm{Tr}A_{fV}^2 = 0$ and hence $A_{fV} = 0$.

Lemma 6.2. Let M be an (n+1)-dimensional contact CR submanifold of S^{2m+1} with flat normal connection. If $PA_V = A_V P$ for any vector field V normal to M, then

(6.2) $\quad g(A_U X,A_V Y) = g(X,Y)g(tU,tV) - \sum_i g(A_U tV,e_i)g(A_{Fe_i}X,Y).$

Proof. From the assumption we see that

$$g(A_U PX,tV) = 0,$$

from which

$$g((\nabla_Y A)_U PX, tV) + g(A_U(\nabla_Y P)X, tV) + g(A_U PX, (\nabla_Y t)V) = 0.$$

Thus, from (1.9) and (1.11), we have

$$g((\nabla_Y A)_U PX, tV) - g(X,Y)g(A_U \xi, tV) + \eta(X)g(A_U Y, tV)$$

$$+ g(A_U A_{FX} Y, tV) + g(A_U tB(Y,X), tV) + g(A_U PX, A_{fV} Y)$$

$$- g(A_U PX, PA_V Y) = 0,$$

from which and Lemma 6.1, we find

$$g((\nabla_{PY} A)_U PX, tV) + g(X, PY)g(tU, tU)$$

$$+ g(A_U tV, tB(PY, X)) - g(A_U PX, PA_V PY) = 0.$$

On the other hand, we have

$$g(A_U tV, tB(PY, X)) = - \sum_i g(A_U tV, e_i)g(A_{Fe_i} X, PY),$$

$$- g(A_U PX, PA_V PY) = g(A_U PX, A_V Y).$$

From these equations we find

$$g((\nabla_{PY} A)_U PX, tV) + g(X, PY)g(tU, tV)$$

$$\doteq \sum_i g(A_U tV, e_i)g(A_{Fe_i} X, PY) + g(A_U PX, A_V Y) = 0.$$

Therefore, the Codazzi equation implies

$$g(X,PY)g(tU,tV) - \sum_i g(A_U tV, e_i)g(A_{Fe_i} X, PY) + g(A_U PX, A_V Y) = 0,$$

which then implies

$$(6.3) \quad g(PX,PY)g(tU,tV) - \sum_i g(A_U tV, e_i)g(A_{Fe_i} PX, PY) + g(A_U P^2 X, A_V Y) = 0.$$

On the other hand, we have

$$g(PX,PY)g(tU,tV) = g(X,Y)g(tU,tV) - \eta(X)\eta(Y)g(tU,tV)$$

$$- g(FX,FY)g(tU,tV),$$

$$- \sum_i g(A_U tV, e_i)g(A_{Fe_i} PX, PY) = - \sum_i g(A_U tV, e_i)g(A_{Fe_i} X, Y)$$

$$+ \eta(Y)g(A_U tV, X) + \eta(X)\eta(Y)g(tU,tV) - \sum_i g(A_U tV, e_i)g(A_{Fe_i} X, tFY),$$

$$g(A_U P^2 X, A_V Y) = -g(A_U X, A_V Y) - \eta(Y)g(A_U tV, X) - g(A_U X, A_V tFY).$$

Substituting these equations into (6.3), we find

$$g(X,Y)g(tU,tV) - \sum_i g(A_U tV, e_i)g(A_{Fe_i} X, Y) - g(A_U X, A_V Y)$$

$$- g(FX,FY)g(tU,tV) - \sum_i g(A_U tV, e_i)g(A_{Fe_i} X, tFY)$$

$$- g(A_U X, A_V tFY) = 0.$$

Moreover, we obtain

$$- \sum_{i} g(A_U tV, e_i) g(A_{Fe_i} X, tFY) = g(A_U tV, A_{FY}) + g(FX, FY) g(tU, tV),$$

$$- g(A_U X, A_V tFY) = - g(A_U tV, A_{FY} X).$$

From these equations we find (6.2).

<u>Lemma 6.3.</u> Let M be an (n+1)-dimensional contact CR submanifold of S^{2m+1} with flat normal connection. If the mean curvature vector of M is parallel, and if $PA_V = A_V P$ for any vector field V normal to M, then the square of the length of the second fundamental form of M is constant.

<u>Proof.</u> From Lemma 6.1 the square of the length of the second fundamental form of M is given by $\sum_{\alpha} TrA_{\alpha}^2$, where $A_{\alpha} = A_{e_{\alpha}}$. Using (6.2), we have

$$\sum_{\alpha} TrA_{\alpha}^2 = (n+1)p + \sum_{\alpha,\beta} g(A_{\alpha} te_{\alpha}, te_{\beta}) TrA_{\beta}.$$

Since the normal connection of M is flat, we can take $\{e_{\alpha}\}$ such that $D_X e_{\alpha} = 0$ for each α, because, for any $V \in FN(M)$ we have $D_X V \in FN(M)$ by (1.12) and (6.1). Then we have

$$\nabla_X (\sum_{\alpha} TrA_{\alpha}^2) = \sum_{\alpha,\beta} g((\nabla_X A)_{\alpha} te_{\alpha}, te_{\beta}) TrA_{\beta}$$

$$= \sum_{\alpha,\beta} g((\nabla_{te_{\alpha}} A)_{\beta} te_{\alpha}, X) TrA_{\beta}$$

by using $\nabla_X (te_{\alpha}) = (\nabla_X t) e_{\alpha} = A_{fe_{\alpha}} X - PA_{\alpha} X$ and $Pt = 0$.

On the other hand, using $PA_V = A_V P$, we have, for any $X \in T_x(M)$,

$$\sum_i g((\nabla_{Pe_i} A)_\alpha Pe_i, X) = \sum_i [g((\nabla_{Pe_i} P)A_\alpha e_i, X) + g(P(\nabla_{Pe_i} A)_\alpha e_i, X)$$
$$- g(A_\alpha(\nabla_{Pe_i} P)e_i, X)].$$

Since A_α is symmetric and P is skew-symmetric, using (1.9), we see that

$$\sum_i g((\nabla_{Pe_i} P)A_\alpha e_i, X) = 0 \quad \text{and} \quad \sum_i g(A_\alpha(\nabla_{Pe_i} P)e_i, X) = 0.$$

Therefore, we have

$$\sum_i g((\nabla_{Pe_i} A)_\alpha Pe_i, X) = \sum_i g(P(\nabla_{Pe_i} A)_\alpha e_i, X)$$
$$= -\sum_i g((\nabla_{Pe_i} A)_\alpha e_i, PX) = -\sum_i g((\nabla_{PX} A)_\alpha Pe_i, e_i) = 0,$$

where we have used the Codazzi equation and the fact that $(\nabla_{PX} A)$ is symmetric and P is skew-symmetric.

Since we have $\sum_a (\nabla_{e_a} A)_\alpha e_a = \sum_i (\nabla_{Pe_i} A)_\alpha Pe_i$, the equation above implies

(6.4)
$$\sum_a (\nabla_{e_a} A)_\alpha e_a = 0.$$

Moreover, we see that

(6.5)
$$(\nabla_\xi A)_\alpha \xi = 0.$$

From the assumption the mean curvature vector of M is parallel, and hence we have

$$0 = \sum_i (\nabla_{e_i} A)_\alpha e_i = \sum_a (\nabla_{e_a} A)_\alpha e_a + (\nabla_\xi A)_\alpha \xi + \sum_x (\nabla_{e_x} A)_\alpha e_x$$

$$= \sum_x (\nabla_{e_x} A)_\alpha e_x = \sum_\beta (\nabla_{te_\beta} A)_\alpha te_\beta.$$

Therefore the square of the length of the second fundamental form of M is constant.

From Lemmas 6.1 and 6.3, using (I.1.8) and (II.4.9), we have

Lemma 6.4. Let M be an (n+1)-dimensional contact CR submanifold of S^{2m+1} with flat normal connection. If the mean curvature vector of M is parallel, and if $PA_V = A_V P$ for any vector field V normal to M, then

(6.6) $g(\nabla A, \nabla A) = -(n+1)\sum_\alpha TrA_\alpha^2 + \sum_\alpha (TrA_\alpha)^2$

$$+ \sum_{\alpha,\beta} [Tr(A_\alpha A_\beta)]^2 - \sum_{\alpha,\beta} TrA_\beta TrA_\alpha^2 A_\beta.$$

Lemma 6.5. Under the same assumptions as those of Lemma 6.4, the second fundamental form of M is parallel.

Proof. From (6.2) we obtain

$$TrA_\alpha^2 A_\beta = TrA_\alpha g(e_\alpha, e_\beta) + \sum_\gamma Tr(A_\gamma A_\alpha) g(A_\gamma te_\alpha, te_\beta),$$

$$Tr(A_\alpha A_\beta) = (n+1)g(e_\alpha, e_\beta) + \sum_\gamma TrA_\gamma g(A_\gamma te_\alpha, te_\beta).$$

Thus we have

$$\sum_{\alpha,\beta} [\text{Tr}(A_\alpha A_\beta)]^2 = (n+1)\sum_\alpha \text{Tr}A_\alpha^2 + \sum_{\alpha,\beta,\gamma} \text{Tr}(A_\alpha A_\beta)\text{Tr}A_\gamma g(A_\gamma te_\alpha, te_\beta),$$

$$- \sum_{\alpha,\beta} \text{Tr}A_\beta \text{Tr}A_\alpha^2 A_\beta = - \sum_\alpha (\text{Tr}A_\alpha)^2 - \sum_{\alpha,\beta,\gamma} \text{Tr}(A_\alpha A_\beta)\text{Tr}A_\gamma g(A_\gamma te_\alpha, te_\beta).$$

Substituting these equations into (6.6), we find $g(\nabla A, \nabla A) = 0$, which shows that the second fundamental form of M is parallel.

Theorem 6.1 (Yano-Kon [73]). Let M be an (n+1)-dimensional complete contact CR submanifold of S^{2m+1} with flat normal connection. If the mean curvature vector of M is parallel, and if $PA_V = A_V P$ for any vector field V normal to M, then M is S^{n+1} or

$$S^{m_1}(r_1) \times \cdots \times S^{m_k}(r_k), \quad n+1 = \sum_{i=1}^k m_i, \quad 2 \leq k \leq n+1, \quad \sum_{i=1}^k r_i^2 = 1$$

in some S^{n+1+p}, where $m_1,\ldots,m_k$ are odd numbers.

Proof. We first assume that $F = 0$, that is, M is an invariant submanifold of S^{2m+1}. Then the second fundamental form of M satisfies $PA_V + A_V P = 0$ (see Lemma 1.1). Thus we have $PA_V = 0$, which implies that $A_V = 0$ and hence M is totally geodesic in S^{2m+1}. Therefore M is an S^{n+1} and n+1 is odd.

We next assume that $F \neq 0$. Since the second fundamental form of M is parallel and $R^\perp = 0$, by Theorem II.6.1, the sectional curvature of M is non-negative. On the other hand, from (6.2), we see that $A_V \neq 0$ for any $V \in FN_x(M)$. Thus Lemma 6.1 shows that the first normal space is of dimension p, where $p = \dim N_x(M)$. Therefore, by Theorem II.6.1, Theorem II.6.3 and Example 5.1, we have our assertion.

Corollary 6.1. Let M be an (n+1)-dimensional complete generic submanifold of S^{2m+1} with flat normal connection. If the mean curvature vector of M is parallel, and if $PA_V = A_V P$ for any vector field V normal to M, then M is

$$S^{m_1}(r_1) \times \cdots \times S^{m_k}(r_k), \quad n+1 = \sum_{i=1}^{k} m_i, \quad 2 \le k \le n+1, \quad \sum_{i=1}^{k} r_i^2 = 1,$$

where $m_1,\ldots,m_k$ are odd numbers.

§7. Minimal contact CR submanifolds

Let M be an (n+1)-dimensional contact CR submanifold of S^{2m+1} with flat normal connection. Let V be a vector field normal to M. Then, by Lemma 6.1, $A_{fV} = 0$ so (1.11) implies

$$\nabla_X tV = -PA_V X,$$

when V is parallel in the normal bundle of M. Hence we have

$$\text{div } tV = -\text{TrPA}_V = 0, \quad \text{div}((\text{div } tV)tV) = 0.$$

Consequently, from (I.1.10), we obtain

$$(7.1) \qquad \text{div}(\nabla_{tV} tV) = S(tV,tV) + \frac{1}{2}|L(tV)g|^2 - |\nabla tV|^2,$$

where S denotes the Ricci tensor of M.

In the following, we assume that M is minimal. Then the Ricci tensor S of M is given by

$$S(X,Y) = ng(X,Y) - \sum_{\alpha} g(A_{\alpha}^2 X, Y)$$

because of $A_{fV} = 0$.

On the other hand, we have

$$|\nabla tV|^2 = TrA_V^2 - g(tV,tV) - \sum_i g(FA_V e_i, FA_V e_i)$$

$$= TrA_V^2 - g(tV,tV) - \sum_{\alpha} g(A_{\alpha} tV, A_{\alpha} tV).$$

Therefore, equation (7.1) reduces to

(7.2) $$\qquad div(\nabla_{tV} tV) = (n+1)g(tV,tV) - TrA_V^2 + \frac{1}{2}|L(tV)g|^2.$$

Proposition 7.1. Let M be a compact orientable $(n+1)$-dimensional contact CR submanifold of S^{2m+1} with flat normal connection and with parallel section V in the normal bundle. If M is minimal and if

$$\int_M [TrA_V^2 - (n+1)g(tV,tV)]*1 \leq 0,$$

then tV is an infinitesimal isometry of M and $PA_V = A_V P$.

Proof. For any vector fields X, Y tangent to M, we have

$$(L(tV)g)(X,Y) = g(\nabla_X tV, Y) + g(\nabla_Y tV, X)$$

$$= g((A_V P - PA_V)X, Y),$$

from which we have our assertion.

Since the normal connection of M is flat, we can take a frame $\{e_\alpha\}$ of FN(M) such that $De_\alpha = 0$ for each α. Thus we have

$$\text{div}(\sum_\alpha \nabla_{te_\alpha} te_\alpha) = (n+1)p - \sum_\alpha \text{Tr}A_\alpha^2 + \frac{1}{2}\sum_\alpha |L(te_\alpha)g|^2.$$

From this we obtain

Theorem 7.1. Let M be a compact orientable $(n+1)$-dimensional minimal contact CR submanifold of S^{2m+1} with flat normal connection. Then

$$0 \le \frac{1}{2}\int_M \sum_\alpha |L(te_\alpha)g|^2*1 = \int_M [\sum_\alpha \text{Tr}A_\alpha^2 - (n+1)p]*1.$$

As an application of Theorem 7.1, we have

Theorem 7.2. Let M be a compact orientable $(n+1)$-dimensional minimal contact CR submanifold of S^{2m+1} with flat normal connection. If the square of the length of the second fundamental form of M is $(n+1)p$, then M is

$$S^{m_1}(r_1) \times \cdots \times S^{m_k}(r_k), \quad r_i = (m_i/(n+1))^{1/2} \ (i = 1,\ldots,k),$$

$n+1 = \sum_{i=1}^{k} m_i$, $2 \le i \le n+1$, $\sum_{i=1}^{k} r_i^2 = 1$ in some S^{n+1+p}, where $m_1,\ldots,m_k$ are odd numbers.

Proof. Since $A_{fV} = 0$, the square of the length of the second fundamental form of M is given by $\sum_\alpha \text{Tr}A_\alpha^2$. Thus, from Theorem 7.1, we have $|L(te_\alpha)g| = 0$ for each α and hence $PA_\alpha = A_\alpha P$. On the other hand, from the assumption, M is not totally geodesic. Therefore, our assertion follows from Theorem 6.1.

If M is minimal, the scalar curvature r of M is given by

$$r = n(n+1) - \sum_\alpha \text{Tr} A_\alpha^2 .$$

From this and Theorem 7.2 we have

Theorem 7.3. Let M be a compact orientable $(n+1)$-dimensional minimal contact CR submanifold of S^{2m+1} with flat normal connection. If $r = (n+1)(n-p)$, then M is

$$S^{m_1}(r_1) \times \cdots \times S^{m_k}(r_k), \quad r_i = (m_i/(n+1))^{1/2} \ (i = 1,\ldots,k),$$

$n+1 = \sum_{i=1}^{k} m_i, \ 2 \le i \le n+1, \ \sum_{i=1}^{k} r_i^2 = 1$ in some S^{n+1+p}, where $m_1,\ldots,m_k$ are odd numbers.

Here we prepare the following

Lemma 7.1. Let M be a generic submanifold of a Sasakian manifold $\bar{M}$. Then the immersion is full, that is, there is no totally geodesic submanifold M' of $\bar{M}$ which contains M as a submanifold.

Proof. Let V be the vector field normal to M. If $g(B(X,Y),V) = 0$ for any vector fields X, Y tangent to M, then putting $Y = \xi$, we have $g(FX,V) = 0$. Since M is a generic submanifold of $\bar{M}$, we can take $X = \phi V$. Then we have $g(FX,V) = g(P\phi V,V) = -g(V,V) \ne 0$, which shows that the immersion is full.

We now prove (Yano-Kon [67])

Theorem 7.4. Let M be an $(n+1)$-dimensional complete generic minimal submanifold of S^{2m+1} with parallel second fundamental form. If M is Einstein, then M is

$$S^q(r) \times \cdots \times S^q(r) \text{ (N-times)}, \quad r = (q/(n+1))^{1/2},$$

where q is an odd number and $2m-n = N-1$, $Nq = n+1$.

Proof. From the assumptions and (II.6.1) we have

$$0 = (n+1)\sum_\alpha \mathrm{Tr}A_\alpha^2 - \sum_{\alpha,\beta}(\mathrm{Tr}A_\alpha A_\beta)^2 + \sum_{\alpha,\beta}\mathrm{Tr}[A_\alpha,A_\beta]^2.$$

We now put $T_{\alpha\beta} = \mathrm{Tr}A_\alpha A_\beta$, $T_\alpha = \mathrm{Tr}A_\alpha^2$ and $T = \sum_\alpha T_\alpha$. Since the matrix $(T_{\alpha\beta})$ is symmetric, choosing $\{e_\alpha\}$ suitably, we can diagonalize $(T_{\alpha\beta})$. Diagonalizing $(T_{\alpha\beta})$, we have

$$0 = (n+1)\sum_\alpha \mathrm{Tr}A_\alpha^2 - \sum_\alpha T_\alpha^2 + \sum_{\alpha,\beta}\mathrm{Tr}[A_\alpha,A_\beta]^2.$$

On the other hand, we have

$$\sum_\alpha T_\alpha^2 = \frac{1}{p}T^2 + \frac{1}{p}\sum_{\alpha>\beta}(T_\alpha - T_\beta)^2, \quad p = \dim T_x(M).$$

Consequently, we obtain

$$0 = (n+1)T - \frac{1}{p}T^2 - \frac{1}{p}\sum_{\alpha>\beta}(T_\alpha - T_\beta)^2 + \sum_{\alpha,\beta}\mathrm{Tr}[A_\alpha,A_\beta]^2.$$

On the other hand, the Ricci tensor S of M is given by

$$S(X,Y) = ng(X,Y) - \sum_i g(B(X,e_i),B(Y,e_i)).$$

Putting $X = Y = \xi$ in this equation, we find

$$S(\xi,\xi) = n - \sum_i g(B(\xi,e_i),B(\xi,e_i)) = n - \sum_i g(Fe_i,Fe_i) = n - p.$$

Thus, if M is Einstein, we have

$$S(X,Y) = (n-p)g(X,Y),$$

from which

$$T = \sum_{i,j} g(B(e_i,e_j),B(e_i,e_j)) = - \sum_i S(e_i,e_i) + n(n+1) = (n+1)p.$$

Thus we have

$$0 = - \frac{1}{p} \sum_{\alpha > \beta} (T_\alpha - T_\beta)^2 + \sum_{\alpha,\beta} Tr[A_\alpha,A_\beta]^2.$$

Since we have $\sum_{\alpha > \beta} (T_\alpha - T_\beta)^2 \geq 0$, $\sum_{\alpha,\beta} Tr[A_\alpha,A_\beta]^2 \leq 0$, it follows that

$$T_\alpha = T_\beta \quad \text{for all } \alpha, \beta,$$

$$[A_\alpha,A_\beta] = 0 \quad \text{for all } \alpha, \beta.$$

Therefore, the normal connection of M is flat. Thus, by Theorem II.5.5 and Lemma 7.1, M is

$$S^{p_1}(r_1) \times \cdots \times S^{p_N}(r_N), \quad r_t = (p_t/(n+1))^{1/2} \ (t = 1,\ldots,N)$$

and is of codimension $2m-n = N-1$. Since ξ is tangent to M, we see that $p_1,\ldots,p_N$ are odd and since M is Einstein, we have $p_1 = \cdots = p_N$.

Remark. Since $T = (n+1)p$, we can use Theorem II.6.2 to prove Theorem 7.4.

Chapter IV

CR SUBMANIFOLDS

§1. Submanifolds of Kaehlerian manifolds

Let $\bar{M}$ be a complex m-dimensional (real 2m-dimensional) Kaehlerian manifold with almost complex structure J and with Kaehlerian metric g. Let M be a real n-dimensional Riemannian manifold isometrically immersed in $\bar{M}$. We denote by the same g the Riemannian metric tensor field induced on M from that of $\bar{M}$. The operator of covariant differentiation in $\bar{M}$ (resp. M) will be denoted by $\bar{\nabla}$ (resp. ∇).

For any vector field X tangent to M, we put

$$(1.1) \qquad JX = PX + FX,$$

where PX is the tangential part of JX and FX the normal part of JX. Then P is an endomorphism on the tangent bundle T(M) and F is a normal bundle valued 1-form on the tangent bundle T(M).

For any vector field V normal to M, we put

$$(1.2) \qquad JV = tV + fV,$$

where tV is the tangential part of JV and fV the normal part of JV. For any vector field Y tangent to M, we have, from (1.1), g(JX,Y) = g(PX,Y), which shows that g(PX,Y) is skew-symmetric. Similarly, for any vector field U normal to M, we have, from (1.2), g(JV,U) = g(fV,U), which shows that g(fV,U) is skew-symmetric.

76

From (1.1) and (1.2), we also have

(1.3) $g(FX,V) + g(X,tV) = 0,$

which gives the relation between F and t.

Now, applying J to (1.1) and using (1.1) and (1.2), we find

(1.4) $P^2 = -I - tF,$ $FP + fF = 0.$

Applying J to (1.2) and using (1.1) and (1.2), we find

(1.5) $Pt + tf = 0,$ $f^2 = -I - Ft.$

We define the covariant derivative $\nabla_X P$ of P by
$(\nabla_X P)Y = \nabla_X(PY) - P\nabla_X Y$ and the covariant derivative $\nabla_X F$ of F by
$(\nabla_X F)Y = D_X(FY) - F\nabla_X Y.$ Similarly, we define the covariant derivatives
$\nabla_X t$ of t and $\nabla_X f$ of f by $(\nabla_X t)V = \nabla_X(tV) - tD_X V$ and $(\nabla_X f)V = D_X(fV) -$
$fD_X V,$ respectively. Then, from the Gauss and Weingarten formulas we
have

$$tB(X,Y) + fB(X,Y)$$

$$= (\nabla_X P)Y - A_{FY}X + B(X,PY) + (\nabla_X F)Y.$$

Comparing the tangential and normal parts of the both sides of this
equation, we find

(1.6) $(\nabla_X P)Y = A_{FY}X + tB(X,Y),$

(1.7) $(\nabla_X F)Y = -B(X,PY) + fB(X,Y).$

Similarly, we have

$$-PA_V X - FA_V X$$

$$= (\nabla_X t)V - A_{fV} X + B(X, tV) + (\nabla_X f)V,$$

from which

(1.8) $$(\nabla_X t)V = A_{fV} X - PA_V X,$$

(1.9) $$(\nabla_X f)V = -FA_V X - B(X, tV).$$

Let M be an n-dimensional submanifold of a complex space form $\bar{M}^m(c)$. Then the curvature tensor R of M is given by

$$R(X,Y)Z = \frac{1}{4}c[g(Y,Z)X - g(X,Z)Y + g(JY,Z)JX - g(JX,Z)JY$$

$$+ 2g(X,JY)JZ] + A_{B(Y,Z)}X - A_{B(X,Z)}Y$$

$$+ (\nabla_Y B)(X,Z) - (\nabla_X B)(Y,Z)$$

for any vector fields X, Y and Z tangent to M. Comparing the tangential and normal parts of the both sides of this equation, we have, following equations of Gauss and Codazzi respectively:

(1.10) $$R(X,Y)Z = \frac{1}{4}c[g(Y,Z)X - g(X,Z)Y + g(PY,Z)PX - g(PX,Z)PY$$

$$+ 2g(X,PY)PZ] + A_{B(Y,Z)}X - A_{B(X,Z)}Y,$$

(1.11) $$(\nabla_X B)(Y,Z) - (\nabla_Y B)(X,Z)$$

$$= \frac{1}{4}c[g(PY,Z)FX - g(PX,Z)FY + 2g(X,PY)FZ].$$

Similarly, we have equation of Ricci:

(1.12) $g(R^{\perp}(X,Y)U,V) + g([A_V,A_U]X,Y)$

$= \frac{1}{4}c[g(FY,U)g(FX,V) - g(FX,U)g(FY,V) + 2g(X,PY)g(fU,V)].$

Definition. Let $\bar{M}$ be a Kaehlerian manifold with almost complex structure J. A submanifold M of $\bar{M}$ is called a CR submanifold of $\bar{M}$ if there exists a differentiable distribution $D : x \longrightarrow D_x \subset T_x(M)$ on M satisfying the following conditions:

(i) D is invariant, i.e., $JD_x = D_x$ for each $x \in M$, and

(ii) the complementary orthogonal distribution

$D^{\perp} : x \longrightarrow D_x^{\perp} \subset T_x(M)$ is anti-invariant, i.e., $JD_x^{\perp} \subset T_x(M)^{\perp}$ for each $x \in M$.

In the sequel, we put dim $\bar{M} = 2m$, dim $M = n$, dim $D = h$, dim $D^{\perp} = q$ and codim $M = 2m-n = p$. If $q = 0$, then a CR submanifold M is called an invariant submanifold of $\bar{M}$, and if $h = 0$, then M is called an anti-invariant submanifold of $\bar{M}$. If $p = q$, then a CR submanifold M is called a generic submanifold of $\bar{M}$. If $h > 0$ and $q > 0$, then a CR submanifold M is said to be non-trivial (proper).

Remark. Sometimes, the definitions of CR submanifold, generic submanifold and anti-invariant submanifold (totally real submanifold) are respectively given as follows (cf. Wells [52], [53]).

Let M be a real n-dimensional submanifold of a complex m-dimensional complex manifold $\bar{M}$. We define

$$H_x(M) = T_x(M) \cap JT_x(M),$$

as holomorphic tangent space to M at x. If $\dim_C H_x(M)$ is constant on M, then M is called a CR submanifold. It is well known that

$$\max(n-m,0) \leq \dim_C H_x(M) \leq \frac{n}{2}.$$

If $\dim_C H_x(M) = \max(n-m,0)$ at each $x \in M$, then M is called a generic submanifold. Moreover, if $\dim_C H_x(M) = 0$, then M is called a totally real submanifold.

On the other hand, Chen [13] defined a generic submanifold as follows: If the maximal complex subspace $H_x(M)$ has constant dimension on M and it defines a differentiable distribution on M, then M is called a generic submanifold.

If M is an invariant submanifold of a Kaehlerian manifold $\bar{M}$, F in (1.1) vanishes identically. Moreover, we see that t in (1.2) vanishes identically. Thus we have JX = PX and JV = fV. From (1.6) we see that any invariant submanifold of a Kaehlerian manifold is also a Kaehlerian manifold with respect to the induced structure. From (1.7) and (1.8) we have

Lemma 1.1. Let M be an invariant submanifold of a Kaehlerian manifold $\bar{M}$. Then

(1.13) $B(X,JY) = B(JX,Y) = JB(X,Y),$

(1.14) $JA_V X + A_V JX = 0,$

(1.15) $A_{JV} X = JA_V X.$

From (1.13) we easily obtain

Proposition 1.1. Any invariant submanifold M is a minimal submanifold.

Proposition 1.2. Any invariant submanifold M of a complex space form $\bar{M}(c)$ of constant holomorphic sectional curvature c is totally geodesic if and only if M is of constant holomorphic sectional curvature c.

Proof. Let $\bar{R}$ and R denote the Riemannian curvature tensors of $\bar{M}$ and M respectively. Then (II.2.4) and (1.13) imply

$$R(X,JX,X,JX) = \bar{R}(X,JX,X,JX) - 2g(B(X,X),B(X,X)),$$

which proves our assertion.

Example 1.1. Let $CP^m(c)$ be a complex projective space of complex dimension m and of constant holomorphic sectional curvature c > 0. Any complex projective space CP^n (m > n) is totally geodesic in $CP^m(c)$. Let C^m be a complex m-dimensional number space with holomorphic sectional curvature 0. Any C^n (m > n) is totally geodesic in C^m. The open unit ball D^n is also totally geodesic in D^m (m > n).

Example 1.2. Let $(z^0, z^1, \ldots, z^m)$ be a homogeneous coordinate system in $CP^m(c)$. We put

$$Q^{m-1} = \{(z^0, z^1, \ldots, z^m) \in CP^m(c) : \sum_{i=0}^{m} (z^i)^2 = 0\}.$$

Then Q^{m-1} is complex analitically isometric to the Hermitian symmetric space $SO(m+1)/SO(2) \times SO(m-1)$. Q^{m-1} is called a hyperquadric of $CP^m(c)$. The hyperquadric Q^{m-1} is an Einstein invariant submanifold of $CP^m(c)$.

If M is an anti-invariant submanifold of a Kaehlerian manifold $\bar{M}$, then P in (1.1) vanishes identically and $JX = FX$ for any vector field X tangent to M. Thus we have $2m-n \geq n$, that is, $m \geq n$.

Proposition 1.3. Let M be an n-dimensional anti-invariant submanifold of a complex n-dimensional Kaehlerian manifold $\bar{M}$. Then the normal connection of M is flat if and only if M is flat.

Proof. From (1.6) we have $A_{JY}X = -JB(X,Y)$ because of $JX = FX$ and $JV = tV$. Since $JT_X(M) = T_X(M)^{\perp}$, (I.2.1) and (II.2.7) imply

$$g(R^{\perp}(X,Y)JZ,JW) = g(\bar{R}(X,Y)JZ,JW) - g(A_{JW}A_{JZ}X,Y) + g(A_{JZ}A_{JW}X,Y)$$

$$= g(\bar{R}(X,Y)Z,W) - g(JB(Y,W),JB(X,Z)) + g(JB(X,W),JB(Y,Z))$$

$$= g(R(X,Y)Z,W)$$

for any X, Y, Z and W tangent to M. This proves our assertion.

Theorem 1.1 (Abe [1]). An n-dimensional complete totally geodesic submanifold M of $CP^m(c)$ is either a complex projective space $CP^n(c)$ or a real projective space $RP^n(\frac{1}{4}c)$. If M is an invariant submanifold, then M is given by the natural imbedding of C^{n+1} into C^{m+1}, i.e., $(z^0,\ldots,z^n) \longrightarrow (z^0,\ldots,z^n,0,\ldots,0)$ in C^{m+1}. If M is a real projective space, by taking real and complex homogeneous coordinates properly in M and $CP^m(c)$, respectively, the imbedding of M into $CP^m(c)$ is given as follows. Let $(x^0,\ldots,x^n)$ and $(z^0,\ldots,z^m)$ be the homogeneous coordinates of M and $CP^m(c)$ respectively. Our imbedding is given by the natural imbedding of R^{n+1} into C^{m+1}, i.e., $(x^0,\ldots,x^n) \longrightarrow (x^0,\ldots,x^n,0,\ldots,0)$. In this case, M is an anti-invariant submanifold of $CP^m(c)$ with constant curvature $\frac{1}{4}c$.

This theorem shows that a complete totally geodesic anti-invariant submanifold of a complex projective space is a real projective space. Obviously, R^n is anti-invariant and totally geodesic in C^m ($m \geq n$).

§2. CR submanifolds of Hermitian manifolds

Let $\bar{M}$ be an almost Hermitian manifold with almost complex structure J. A submanifold M of $\bar{M}$ is called a CR submanifold of $\bar{M}$ if there exists a differentiable distribution $D : x \longrightarrow D_x \subset T_x(M)$ on M satisfying the following two conditions:

(i) D is invariant, i.e., $JD_x = D_x$ for each $x \in M$, and

(ii) the complementary orthogonal distribution

$D^\perp : x \longrightarrow D_x^\perp \subset T_x(M)$ is anti-invariant, i.e., $JD_x^\perp \subset T_x(M)^\perp$

for each $x \in M$.

We recall here the notion of CR manifolds (see [19]). Let M be a differentiable manifold and $T(M)^C$ its complexified tangent bundle. A CR structure on M is a complex subbundle H of $T(M)^C$ such that $H_x \cap \bar{H}_x = \{0\}$ and H is involutive, i.e., for complex vector fields X and Y in H, [X,Y] is in H. It is well known that on a CR manifold there exists a (real) distribution D and a field of endomorphism $p : D \longrightarrow D$ such that $p^2 = -I_D$. D is just $\mathrm{Re}(H \oplus \bar{H})$ and $H_x = \{X-\sqrt{-1}pX : X \in D_x\}$. We can now state the following result which justifies the name of CR submanifolds.

Theorem 2.1 (Blair-Chen [8]). Let M be a CR submanifold of a Hermitian manifold $\bar{M}$. If M is non-trivial ($D_x \neq 0$, $D_x \neq T_x(M)$), then M is a CR manifold.

On M we denote by l the projection map of T(M) to D and $l^{\perp}$ the projection to $D^{\perp}$. We define a tensor field p of type $(1,1)$ on M by $p = Jl$. Now on M we define a complex subbundle H by $H_X = \{X - \sqrt{-1}pX :$ $X \in D_X\}$. The first of the following two lemmas is evident, so we give only the proof of the second.

<u>Lemma 2.1.</u> $- p(X - \sqrt{-1}pX) \in H_X$ for every $X \in T_X(M)$.

<u>Lemma 2.2.</u> For vector fields X and Y belonging to D,

$$l^{\perp}([JX,Y] + [X,JY]) = 0.$$

<u>Proof</u>. Since $\bar{M}$ is Hermitian, the Nijenhuis torsion of J vanishes. Therefore

$$0 = -[JX,Y] - [X,JY] + J[X,Y] - J[JX,JY],$$

but $[X,Y]$ and $[JX,JY]$ are tangent to M and hence $J([JX,Y] + [X,JY]) = -[X,Y] + [JX,JY]$ is tangent to M. Therefore, $[JX,Y] + [X,JY]$ has no $D^{\perp}$ component.

<u>Proof of Theorem 2.1.</u> Let X and Y be vector fields belonging to D. Since the Nijenhuis torsion of J vanishes, we have

$$[X - \sqrt{-1}\,X, Y - \sqrt{-1}\,Y] = [X,Y] - [JX,JY] - \sqrt{-1}[JX,Y] - \sqrt{-1}[X,JY]$$

$$= -J[JX,Y] - J[X,JY] - \sqrt{-1}[JX,Y] - \sqrt{-1}[X,JY]$$

$$= -p[JX,Y] - Jl^{\perp}[JX,Y] - p[X,JY] - Jl^{\perp}[X,JY]$$
$$+ \sqrt{-1}p^2[JX,Y] - \sqrt{-1}l^{\perp}[JX,Y] + \sqrt{-1}p^2[X,JY] - \sqrt{-1}l^{\perp}[X,JY]$$

$$= -p([JX,Y] - \sqrt{-1}p[JX,Y]) - p([X,JY] - \sqrt{-1}p[X,JY])$$
$$-Jl^{\perp}([JX,Y] + [X,JY]) - \sqrt{-1}l^{\perp}([JX,Y] + [X,JY]).$$

By Lemma 2.2 the last two terms vanish and By Lemma 2.1 the first two terms belong to H.

§3. Characterization of CR submanifolds

Suppose that M is a CR submanifold of a Kaehlerian manifold $\bar{M}$ and denote by l the projection operator on D_x and by $l^{\perp}$ that on $D_x^{\perp}$. Then we have

$$l + l^{\perp} = I, \quad l^2 = l, \quad l^{\perp 2} = l^{\perp}, \quad l l^{\perp} = l^{\perp} l = 0,$$

I being the identity operator.

From (1.1) we have

$$l^{\perp} P l = 0, \quad F l = 0, \quad P l = P,$$

from which and the second equation of (1.4), we find

$$(3.1) \qquad FP = 0.$$

Thus we have

$$(3.2) \qquad fF = 0.$$

From (1.3) and (3.2) we obtain

$$(3.3) \qquad tf = 0,$$

and consequently, from the first equation of (1.5)

(3.4) $$Pt = 0.$$

Thus, from the first equation of (1.4) we have

(3.5) $$P^3 + P = 0,$$

which shows that P is an f-structure on M and from the second equation of (1.5), we have

(3.6) $$f^3 + f = 0,$$

which shows that f is an f-structure in the normal bundle $T(M)^\perp$.

Conversely, for a submanifold M of a Kaehlerian manifold $\bar{M}$, assume that we have (3.1), i.e., $FP = 0$, then we have (3.2), (3.3), (3.4), (3.5) and (3.6). We now put

(3.7) $$l = -P^2, \qquad l^\perp = I - l.$$

Then we can easily verify that

$$l + l^\perp = I, \quad l^2 = l, \quad l^{\perp 2} = l^\perp, \quad l l^\perp = l^\perp l = 0,$$

which show that l and $l^\perp$ are complementary projection operators and consequently define complementary orthogonal distributions D and $D^\perp$ respectively. From the first equation of (3.7) we have

$$Pl = P.$$

This equation can be written as

$$P t^{\perp} = 0.$$

But $g(PX,Y)$ is skew-symmetric and $g(t^{\perp}X,Y)$ is symmetric and consequently the above equation gives

$$t^{\perp}P = 0,$$

and hence

$$t^{\perp}Pt = 0.$$

From the first equation of (3.7) we have

$$Ft = 0.$$

These equations show that the distribution D is invariant and distribution $D^{\perp}$ is anti-invariant. Thus we have (Yano-Kon [71])

Theorem 3.1. In order for a submanifold M of a Kaehlerian manifold $\bar{M}$ to be a CR submanifold, it is necessary and sufficient that FP = 0.

Theorem 3.2. Let M be a CR submanifold of a Kaehlerian manifold $\bar{M}$. Then P is an f-structure in M and f is an f-structure in the normal bundle of M.

We next give a characterization of CR submanifolds in a complex space form in terms of the curvature tensor of the ambient space.

Let $\bar{R}$ be the curvature tensor of a complex space form $\bar{M}(c)$. Then we have

Theorem 3.3 (Blair-Chen [8]). Let M be a submanifold of a complex space form $\bar{M}(c)$ with $c \neq 0$. Then M is a CR submanifold of $\bar{M}$ if and only if the maximal holomorphic subspace $D_x = T_x(M) \cap JT_x(M)$, $x \in M$, defines a non-trivial differentiable distribution D on M such that

(3.8) $$g(\bar{R}(X,Y)Z,W) = 0$$

for all X, $Y \in D$ and Z, $W \in D^{\perp}$, where $D^{\perp}$ denotes the orthogonal complementary distribution of D in M.

Proof. If M is a CR submanifold of $\bar{M}$, then for any $X \in D$, $JX \in D$ and $g(X,Z) = 0$ for $Z \in D^{\perp}$. Thus we have

$$\bar{R}(X,Y)Z = \frac{1}{2}cg(X,JY)JZ.$$

Since $JZ = FZ \in T(M)^{\perp}$, we have (3.8).

Conversely, since D is non-trivial, suppose that M is not anti-invariant in $\bar{M}$ and $D_x = T_x(M) \cap JT_x(M)$ defines a differentiable distribution D on M. Then D is a holomorphic distribution of dimension ≥ 2. Now, suppose that (3.8) holds for all X, $Y \in D$ and Z, $W \in D^{\perp}$. Then we have

$$g(\bar{R}(JX,X)Z,W) = \frac{1}{2}cg(X,X)g(JZ,W) = 0$$

for all $X \in D$ and Z, $W \in D^{\perp}$. From this we see that $JD_x^{\perp}$ is perpendicular to $D_x^{\perp}$. Since D is holomorphic, $JD_x^{\perp}$ is also perpendicular to D_x. Therefore, $JD_x^{\perp} \subset T_x(M)^{\perp}$. This shows that M is a CR submanifold.

Let us now suppose that $\bar{M}$ is a Hermitian manifold and let Ω be the fundamental 2-form of $\bar{M}$, i.e., $\Omega(X,Y) = g(X,JY)$. $\bar{M}$ is a Kaehlerian manifold if and only if $d\Omega = 0$. However we consider a class of Hermitian manifolds slightly larger than that of Kaehlerian manifolds for which $d\Omega = \Omega \wedge \omega$, ω being a 1-form called the Lee form. When ω is closed we call these manifolds locally conformal symplectic manifolds. They include the well known Hopf manifolds.

Theorem 3.4 (Blair-Chen [8]). Let $\bar{M}$ be a Hermitian manifold with $d\Omega = \Omega \wedge \omega$. Then in order for M to be a CR submanifold it is necessary that $D^{\perp}$ be integrable.

Proof. Let X be a vector field in D and Z, W vector fields in $D^{\perp}$. Then $\Omega(X,Z) = 0$ and $\Omega(Z,W) = 0$. Consequently $\Omega \wedge \omega(X,Z,W) = 0$ and hence

$$0 = 3d\Omega(X,Z,W)$$

$$= X\Omega(Z,W) + Z\Omega(W,X) + W\Omega(X,Z)$$

$$- \Omega([X,Z],W) - \Omega([W,X],Z) - \Omega([Z,W],X)$$

$$= - g([Z,W],JX),$$

but X and hence JX is arbitrary in D and [Z,W] is tangent to M, therefore [Z,W] is in $D^{\perp}$.

§4. Distributions

We first prove

Lemma 4.1. Let M be a CR submanifold of a Kaehlerian manifold $\bar{M}$. Then we have

$$(4.1) \qquad A_{FX}Y = A_{FY}X$$

for any vector fields X and Y in $D^{\perp}$.

Proof. For any X, $Y \in D^{\perp}$ we have $g((\nabla_Z P)X,Y) = g(\nabla_Z(PX),Y) - g(P\nabla_Z X,Y)$, Z being any vector field tangent to M. Therefore, (1.6) implies

$$0 = g((\nabla_Z P)X,Y) = g(A_{FX}Z,Y) + g(tB(Z,X),Y),$$

from which

$$g(A_{FX}Y,Z) = g(A_{FY}X,Z).$$

Thus we have (4.1).

Theorem 4.1. Let M be a CR submanifold of a Kaehlerian manifold $\bar{M}$. Then the distribution $D^{\perp}$ is completely integrable and its maximal integral submanifold $M^{\perp}$ is an anti-invariant submanifold of $\bar{M}$.

Proof. Let X and Y be vector fields in $D^{\perp}$. Then (1.6) and (4.1) imply

$$P[X,Y] = P\nabla_X Y - P\nabla_Y X = -(\nabla_X P)Y + (\nabla_Y P)X = A_{FX}Y - A_{FY}X = 0.$$

Thus the distribution is completely integrable, and we see, from definition, that the maximal integral submanifold $M^\perp$ of $D^\perp$ is an anti-invariant submanifold of $\bar{M}$.

If the distribution D is integrable and moreover if the almost complex structure P induced on each integral submanifold of D is integrable, then we say that f-structure P is <u>partially integrable</u> (see [56], [59]).

<u>Theorem 4.2.</u> Let M be a CR submanifold of a Kaehlerian manifold $\bar{M}$. Then the f-structure P is partially integrable if and only if

$$(4.2) \qquad\qquad B(PX,Y) = B(X,PY)$$

for any vector fields X and Y in D.

$\quad$ <u>Proof</u>. Let X and Y be vector fields in D. Then (1.7) implies

$$F[X,Y] = F\nabla_X Y - F\nabla_Y X = -(\nabla_X F)Y + (\nabla_Y F)X$$

$$= B(X,PY) - B(PX,Y).$$

Thus, D is integrable if and only if (4.2) holds. In this case the integral submanifold M^T of D is an invariant submanifold of $\bar{M}$ and hence M^T is also a Kaehlerian manifold. Thus the almost complex structure induced from P on M^T is integrable. Consequently, P is partially integrable if and only if (4.2) holds.

Proposition 4.1. A necessary and sufficient condition for the integral submanifold $M^\perp$ of $D^\perp$ to be totally geodesic in M is that

$$B(X,Y) \in fT(M)^\perp$$

for all $X \in D^\perp$ and $Y \in D$.

Proof. Let $X, Z \in D^\perp$ and $Y \in D$. Then (1.6) implies that

$$g(P\nabla_X Z,Y) = -g(A_{FZ}X,Y) = -g(B(X,Y),FZ),$$

which proves our assertion.

A CR submanifold M of a Kaehlerian manifold $\tilde{M}$ is said to be <u>mixed totally geodesic</u> if $B(X,Y) = 0$ for each $X \in D$ and $Y \in D^\perp$ (see [7]).

Corollary 4.1. Let M be a mixed totally geodesic CR submanifold of a Kaehlerian manifold $\tilde{M}$. Then, each leaf of anti-invariant distribution $D^\perp$ is totally geodesic in M.

Corollary 4.2. A generic submanifold M of a Kaehlerian manifold $\tilde{M}$ is mixed totally geodesic if and only if each leaf of anti-invariant distribution is totally geodesic in M.

Proposition 4.2. Let M be a CR submanifold of a Kaehlerian manifold $\tilde{M}$. If

$$g(B(X,Y),FZ) = 0 \quad \text{for } X,Y \in D,\ Z \in D^\perp,$$

then M is foliated by complex manifolds such that every leaf is totally geodesic in M.

Proof. From (1.7) we have

$$g(F\nabla_X Y, FZ) = - g(B(X,PY),FZ) = 0,$$

which proves our assertion.

If $B(X,Y) = 0$ for all X, $Y \in D$, then a CR submanifold M is said to be D-totally geodesic (see [7]).

Corollary 4.3. Let M be a CR submanifold of a Kaehlerian manifold $\bar{M}$. If D is totally geodesic, i.e., M is D-totally geodesic, then M is foliated by totally geodesic invariant submanifolds of M.

A CR submanifold M is said to be mixed foliate if it is mixed totally geodesic and $B(PX,Y) = B(X,PY)$ for all X, $Y \in D$ (see [7]).

Lemma 4.2. Let M be a mixed foliate CR submanifold of a Kaehlerian manifold $\bar{M}$. Then we have

(4.3) $$A_V P + P A_V = 0$$

for any vector field V normal to M.

Proof. From the assumption we have $B(X,PY) = B(PX,Y)$ for X, $Y \in D$ and $B(X,Y) = 0$ for $X \in D$, $Y \in D^{\perp}$. Moreover, we see that $PX \in D$ for any vector field X tangent to M. Consequently, we see that $B(X,PY) = B(PX,Y)$ for any vector fields X, Y tangent to M, which proves (4.3).

<u>Proposition 4.3</u>. If M is a mixed foliate non-trivial CR submanifold, i.e., neither an invariant submanifold nor anti-invariant submanifold, of a complex space form $\bar{M}^m(c)$, then we have $c \leq 0$.

<u>Proof</u>. Let X, $Y \in D$ and $Z \in D^{\perp}$. Then we have

$$(\nabla_X B)(Y,Z) - (\nabla_Y B)(X,Z) = B(X,\nabla_Y Z) - B(Y,\nabla_X Z).$$

If we take a vector field V normal to M such that $Z = JV = tV$, we obtain $\nabla_Y Z = -PA_V Y + tD_Y V$. Thus (4.3) implies

$$(\nabla_X B)(Y,Z) - (\nabla_Y B)(X,Z) = B(PY,A_V X) + B(X,A_V PY).$$

Putting $X = PY$ in this equation, and using (1.11), we see that

(4.4)
$$0 \leq 2g(A_V PY, A_V PY) = -\frac{1}{2}cg(PY,PY)g(V,V).$$

This proves our assertion.

<u>Corollary 4.4</u>. Let M be a mixed foliate CR submanifold of a complex space form $\bar{M}^m(c)$. If $c > 0$, then M is an invariant submanifold or an anti-invariant submanifold of $\bar{M}^m(c)$.

§5. Parallel f-structure

Let M be an n-dimensional CR submanifold of a complex m-dimensional Kaehlerian manifold $\tilde{M}$.

If $\nabla_X P = 0$ for any vector field X tangent to M, then the f-structure P is said to be <u>parallel</u>.

Proposition 5.1. Let M be an n-dimensional generic submanifold of a complex m-dimensional Kaehlerian manifold $\tilde{M}$. If the f-structure P on M is parallel, then M is locally a Riemannian direct product $M^T \times M^\perp$, where M^T is a totally geodesic invariant submanifold of $\tilde{M}$ of complex dimension n-m and $M^\perp$ is an anti-invariant submanifold of $\tilde{M}$ of real dimension 2m-n.

Proof. From the assumption and (1.6) we have $JB(X,Y) = tB(X,Y) = -A_{FY}X$. Thus we have $JB(X,PY) = 0$ and hence $B(X,PY) = 0$. On the other hand, from (1.7) we obtain $(\nabla_X F)Y = -B(X,PY) = 0$. Let $Y \in D^\perp$. Then we have $P\nabla_X Y = \nabla_X(PY) - (\nabla_X P)Y = 0$ for any vector field X tangent to M. Therefore, the distribution $D^\perp$ is parallel. Similarly, the distribution D is also parallel. Consequently, M is locally a Riemannian direct product $M^T \times M^\perp$, where M^T is a leaf of D and $M^\perp$ is that of $D^\perp$. By definitions M^T is an invariant submanifold of $\tilde{M}$ and $M^\perp$ is an anti-invariant submanifold of $\tilde{M}$. On the other hand, since $B(X,PY) = 0$ for any vector fields X and Y tangent to M, M^T is totally geodesic in $\tilde{M}$. Thus we have proved Proposition 5.1.

Theorem 5.1. Let M be an n-dimensional complete generic submanifold of a complex m-dimensional, simply connected complete space form $\tilde{M}^m(c)$. If the f-structure P on M is parallel, then M is an m-dimensional anti-invariant submanifold of $\tilde{M}^m(c)$ or, c = 0 and M is $C^{n-m} \times M^{2m-n}$, a submanifold of C^m, where M^{2m-n} is an anti-invariant submanifold of C^m.

Proof. First of all, we have

$$(\nabla_X B)(Y,PZ) = D_X(B(Y,PZ)) - B(\nabla_X Y,PZ) - B(Y,P\nabla_X Z) = 0.$$

Thus (1.11) implies

$$\frac{1}{4}c[g(PY,PY)FX - g(PX,PY)FY] = 0.$$

Therefore, we have $c = 0$ or $P = 0$. If $P = 0$, then M is a real m-dimensional anti-invariant submanifold of $\bar{M}^m(c)$. If $c = 0$, then the ambient manifold $\bar{M}^m(c)$ is the complex number space C^m and our assertion follows from Proposition 5.1.

Proposition 5.2. Let M be an n-dimensional complete mixed foliate non-trivial generic submanifold of a simply connected complete complex space form $\bar{M}^m(c)$. If $c \geq 0$, then $c = 0$ and M is $C^{n-m} \times M^{2m-n}$, a submanifold of C^m, where M^{2m-n} is an anti-invariant submanifold of C^m.

Proof. From Proposition 4.3 we see that $c = 0$ and hence $\bar{M}^m(c) = C^m$. Thus (4.4) implies that $A_V X = 0$ for any $X \in D$. From this and (1.6) we see that P is parallel. Thus Theorem 5.1 proves our assertion.

§6. Totally umbilical submanifolds

We prove

Theorem 6.1 (Bejancu [6]). Let M be a totally umbilical non-trivial CR submanifold of a Kaehlerian manifold $\bar{M}$. If dim $D^\perp > 1$, then M is totally geodesic in $\bar{M}$.

Proof. We first prove that $t\mu = 0$, where μ is the mean curvature vector of M. Since (4.1) holds for each $X \in D^\perp$ we have

(6.1) $$A_{FX}t\mu = A_{Ft\mu}X.$$

Now, M being totally umbilical, we obtain from (6.1)

$$g(X,X)g(Ft\mu,\mu) = g(t\mu,X)g(FX,\mu),$$

from which

(6.2) $$g(X,X)g(t\mu,t\mu) = g(t\mu,X)g(t\mu,X).$$

Since dim $D^\perp > 1$, we can choose X in such a way that we have $g(t\mu,X) = 0$ and hence $t\mu = 0$.

On the other hand, from (1.8) we find

$$g((\nabla_X t)\mu,Y) = -g(tD_X\mu,Y) = g(A_{f\mu}X,Y) - g(PA_\mu X,Y)$$

$$= g(X,Y)g(f\mu,\mu) + g(A_\mu X,PY)$$

$$= g(X,PY)g(\mu,\mu)$$

for any vector fields X and Y tangent to M. Putting Y = PX in this equation, we have

$$g(X,P^2X)g(\mu,\mu) = 0,$$

from which

(6.3) $$g(X,X)g(\mu,\mu) - g(FX,FX)g(\mu,\mu) = 0.$$

Since M is non-trivial, we can choose an X in D such that FX = 0. Then we have $\mu = 0$, and hence M is totally geodesic.

If M is a totally geodesic CR submanifold of a Kaehlerian manifold $\bar{M}$, then the distributions D and $D^{\perp}$ are parallel. Indeed, for any $X \in D$ and for any vector field Z tangent to M, we have

$$F\nabla_Z X = - (\nabla_Z F)X = 0$$

by (1.7). Similarly, for any $Y \in D^{\perp}$, we have from (1.6),

$$P\nabla_Z Y = - (\nabla_Z P)Y = 0.$$

Thus M is locally a Riemannian product of an invariant submanifold and an anti-invariant submanifold. Consequently, we have

Theorem 6.2. Let M be a totally geodesic CR submanifold of a Kaehlerian manifold $\bar{M}$. Then M is locally a Riemannian product of an invariant submanifold and an anti-invariant submanifold of $\bar{M}$.

Corollary 6.1. Let M be a totally umbilical non-trivial CR submanifold of a Kaehlerian manifold $\bar{M}$. If dim $D^{\perp} > 1$, then M is locally a Riemannian direct product of the form $M^T \times M^{\perp}$, where M^T is a totally geodesic invariant submanifold of $\bar{M}$ and $M^{\perp}$ is a totally geodesic anti-invariant submanifold of $\bar{M}$.

§7. Examples of CR submanifolds

In this section we give some examples of anti-invariant submanifolds, generic submanifolds and CR submanifolds of complex space forms.

Example 7.1. Let C^m be the complex number space of complex dimension m. C^m can be identified with the real number space R^{2m}. Let M be a product Riemannian manifold of the form $C^p \times M^q$, where M^q is a real q-dimensional anti-invariant submanifold of $C^q \times C^{p+q}$. Then $C^p \times M^q$ is a generic submanifold of C^{p+q}, and $C^p \times M^q$ is moreover a CR submanifold of C^m, where $m > p+q$.

Example 7.2. Let us consider an immersion:

$$S^{m_1}(r_1) \times \cdots \times S^{m_k}(r_k) \longrightarrow C^{(n+k)/2}, \quad n = \sum_{i=1}^{k} m_i,$$

where $m_1, \ldots, m_k$ are odd numbers. Then n+k is even. We now consider

$$S^{m_i}(r_i) \subset C^{(m_i+1)/2} \quad (i = 1, \ldots, k)$$

and

$$C^{(n+k)/2} = C^{(m_1+1)/2} \times \cdots \times C^{(m_k+1)/2}.$$

Thus each $S^{m_i}(r_i)$ is a real hypersurface of $C^{(m_i+1)/2}$, and $S^{m_1}(r_1) \times \cdots \times S^{m_k}(r_k)$ is a generic submanifold of $C^{(n+k)/2}$, and hence CR submanifold of C^m ($2m > n+k$) with parallel mean curvature vector and flat normal connection. Similarly, we can consider an immersion:

$$S^{m_1}(r_1) \times \cdots \times S^{m_k}(r_k) \times R^p \longrightarrow C^{(n+k)/2} \times C^p \subset C^m$$

where $(n+k)+2p < 2m$. Then the submanifold is a generic submanifold of $C^{(n+k+2p)/2}$ and a CR submanifold of C^m with parallel mean curvature vector and flat normal connection.

In the following we need some results of Riemannian fibre bundles.

Let $\bar{N}$ be a $(2m+1)$-dimensional Sasakian manifold with structure tensors (ϕ,ξ,η,G). We suppose that there is a fibering

$$\bar{\pi} : \bar{N} \longrightarrow \bar{N}/\xi = \bar{M},$$

where $\bar{M}$ denotes the set of orbits of ξ and is a real $2m$-dimensional Kaehlerian manifold.

Remark. For the existence of the above fibration, see Boothby-Wang [10] and Hatakeyama [20].

We denote by (J,g) the Kaehlerian structure of $\bar{M}$. We denote by * the horizontal lift with respect to the connection η. Then we have

(7.1) $(JX)^* = \phi X^*, \qquad G(X^*,Y^*) = g(X,Y)^*$

for any vector fields X and Y on $\bar{M}$. We denote by $\bar{\nabla}'$ (resp. $\bar{\nabla}$) the operator of covariant differentiation with respect to G (resp. g). Then we have

(7.2) $(\bar{\nabla}_X Y)^* = -\phi^2 \bar{\nabla}'_{X^*} Y^* = \bar{\nabla}'_{X^*} Y^* + G(\phi X^*, Y^*)\xi.$

Let N be an (n+1)-dimensional submanifold immersed in $\bar{N}$ and M be an n-dimensional submanifold immersed in $\bar{M}$. In the sequel, we assume that N is tangent to the structure vector field ξ of $\bar{N}$ and there exists a fibration $\pi : N \longrightarrow M$ such that the diagram

$$
\begin{array}{ccc}
N & \xrightarrow{\quad i' \quad} & \bar{N} \\
\pi \downarrow & & \downarrow \bar{\pi} \\
M & \xrightarrow{\quad i \quad} & \bar{M}
\end{array}
$$

(7.3)

commutes and the immersion i' is a diffeomorphism on the fibres.

We denote by the same G and g the induced metric tensor fields of N and M respectively. Let ∇' (resp. ∇) be the operator of covariant differentiation with respect to the induced metric G (resp. g). We denote by α (resp. B) the second fundamental form of the immersion i' (resp. i) and the associated second fundamental form will be denoted by H (resp. A). For any vector fields X and Y on M, the Gauss formulas are given by

$$\bar{\nabla}_X Y = \nabla_X Y + B(X,Y) \quad \text{and} \quad \bar{\nabla}'_{X*} Y* = \nabla'_{X*} Y* + \alpha(X*,Y*).$$

From these equations and (7.2) we have

(7.4) $$(\nabla_X Y)* = -\phi^2 \nabla'_{X*} Y* = \nabla'_{X*} Y* + G(\phi X*, Y*)\xi,$$

(7.5) $$(B(X,Y))* = \alpha(X*,Y*).$$

Let D' and D be the operators of covariant differentiation with respect to the linear connections induced in the normal bundles of N and M respectively. For any tangent vector field X and any normal vector field V of M, we have the Weingarten formulas

$$\bar{\nabla}_X V = -A_V X + D_X V \quad \text{and} \quad \bar{\nabla}'_{X*} V^* = -H_{V*} X^* + D'_{X*} V^*.$$

From these equations and (7.2) we obtain

(7.6) $$(A_V X)^* = - \phi^2 H_{V*} X^* = H_{V*} X^* + G(H_{V*} X^*, \xi)\xi,$$

(7.7) $$(D_X V)^* = D'_{X*} V^*.$$

Let P, F, t and f be operators on M appearing in (1.1) and (1.2). We denote by P', F', t' and f' the operators in N corresponding respectively to P, F, t and f, which are defined by (III.1.1) and (III.1.2). Then we have, from (7.1),

(7.8) $$(PX)^* = P'X^*, \qquad (FX)^* = F'X^*,$$

(7.9) $$(tV)^* = t'V^*, \qquad (fV)^* = f'V^*.$$

From (7.8) and (7.9) we have

Proposition 7.1. (i) N is a contact CR submanifold of $\bar{N}$ if and only if M is a CR submanifold of $\bar{M}$.

(ii) N is a generic submanifold of $\bar{N}$ if and only if M is a generic submanifold of $\bar{M}$.

(iii) N is an anti-invariant submanifold of $\bar{N}$ tangent to ξ if and only if M is an anti-invariant submanifold of $\bar{M}$.

(iv) N is an invariant submanifold of $\bar{N}$ if and only if M is an invariant submanifold of $\bar{M}$.

We now study the relations between covariant differentiations of the second fundamental forms B and α.

First of all, from (7.2), (7.5) and (7.7), we have

$$((\nabla_X B)(Y,Z))^* = (\nabla_{X*}\alpha)(Y^*,Z^*) - G(Y^*,\phi X^*)\alpha(\xi,Z^*)$$

$$- G(Z^*,\phi X^*)\alpha(\xi,Y^*),$$

from which, using (III.1.7) and (7.1), we find

$$(7.10) \quad (\nabla_{X*}\alpha)(Y^*,Z^*) = ((\nabla_X B)(Y,Z) + g(Y,PX)FZ + g(Z,PX)FY)^*.$$

On the other hand, we have

$$(\nabla_{X*}\alpha)(Y^*,\xi) = D'_{X*}(F'Y^*) - F'\nabla'_{X*}Y^* - \alpha(Y^*,P'X^*)$$

$$= (\nabla_{X*}F')Y^* - \alpha(Y^*,P'X^*)$$

$$= f'\alpha(X^*,Y^*) - \alpha(X^*,P'Y^*) - \alpha(Y^*,P'X^*).$$

From this and (7.5) we have

$$(7.11) \quad (\nabla_{X*}\alpha)(Y^*,\xi) = (fB(X,Y) - B(X,PY) - B(Y,PX))^*.$$

Consequently, we obtain

Lemma 7.1. The second fundamental form α of N is parallel if and only if the second fundamental form B of M satisfies the conditions

(7.12) $\qquad (\nabla_X B)(Y,Z) = g(X,PY)FZ + g(X,PZ)FY$

and

(7.13) $\qquad fB(X,Y) = B(X,PY) + B(Y,PX).$

From (1.7) we see that the condition (7.13) is equivalent to

(7.14) $\qquad (\nabla_X F)Y = B(Y,PX).$

Let X and Y be vector fields tangent to M and U and V be vector fields normal to M. Then, from (7.7), we have

$$(D_X D_Y V)^* = D'_{X*} D'_{Y*} V^*, \qquad (D_Y D_X V)^* = D'_{Y*} D'_{X*} V^*.$$

Since $[X,Y]^* = [X^*,Y^*] + 2G(P'X^*,Y^*)\xi$, we find

$$(D_{[X,Y]} V)^* = D'_{[X^*,Y^*]} V^* + 2G(P'X^*,Y^*)D'_\xi V^*.$$

From these equations we see that

(7.15) $\quad (g(R^\perp(X,Y)U,V) + 2g(PX,Y)g(fV,U))^* = G(K^\perp(X^*,Y^*)V^*,U^*),$

where $K^\perp$ denotes the normal curvature tensor of N.

On the other hand, from (II.2.7) and $\tilde{R}'(X^*,\xi)V^* = 0$, we have

$$G(K^{\perp}(X^*,\xi)V^*,U^*) = G([H_{U^*},H_{V^*}]X^*,\xi).$$

Using (III.1.7) we find

$$G([H_{U^*},H_{V^*}]X^*,\xi) = G(H_{U^*}X^*,t'V^*) - G(H_{V^*}X^*,t'U^*)$$

$$= (-g(fA_U X,V) - g(B(X,tU),V))^*.$$

Therefore (1.9) implies

$$(7.16) \qquad G([H_{U^*},H_{V^*}]X^*,\xi) = g((\nabla_X f)U,V)^*,$$

from which

$$(7.17) \qquad G(K^{\perp}(X^*,\xi)V^*,U^*) = g((\nabla_X f)U,V)^*.$$

From (7.15) and (7.16) we have

Lemma 7.2. The normal connection of N is flat if and only if M satisfies the conditions

$$(7.18) \qquad R^{\perp}(X,Y)V = 2g(X,PY)fV$$

and

$$(7.19) \qquad (\nabla_X f)V = 0.$$

<u>Lemma 7.3.</u> For the square of the length of the second fundamental forms A and H, we have

$$(7.20) \qquad G(H,H) = g(A,A) + 2\sum_i g(Fe_i, Fe_i).$$

<u>Proof.</u> Let $\{e_i\}$ be an orthonormal frame of M. Then we have

$$
\begin{aligned}
G(H,H) &= \sum_{i,j} G(\alpha(e_i^*, e_j^*), \alpha(e_i^*, e_j^*)) + 2\sum_i G(\alpha(e_i^*, \xi), \alpha(e_i^*, \xi)) \\
&= \sum_{i,j} g(B(e_i, e_j), B(e_i, e_j)) + 2\sum_i G(F'e_i^*, F'e_i^*) \\
&= g(A,A) + 2\sum_i g(Fe_i, Fe_i),
\end{aligned}
$$

which proves (7.20).

<u>Example 7.3.</u> We consider the immersion i':

$$M_{m_1,\ldots,m_k} \xrightarrow{\hspace{2cm}} S^{n+k}$$

in Example 5.1 of Chapter III. Then we have the following commutative diagram:

$$
\begin{array}{ccc}
M_{m_1,\ldots,m_k} & \xrightarrow{\quad i' \quad} & S^{n+k} \\
\pi \downarrow & & \downarrow \bar{\pi} \\
N_{m_1,\ldots,m_k} & \xrightarrow{\quad i \quad} & CP^{(n+k-1)/2},
\end{array}
$$

where we have put $N_{m_1,\ldots,m_k} = \pi(M_{m_1,\ldots,m_k})$. Then, from

Example III.5.1 and Proposition 7.1, we see that $N_{m_1,\ldots,m_k}$ is a generic submanifold of $CP^{(n+k-1)/2}$. Furthermore, $N_{m_1,\ldots,m_k}$ is a CR submanifold of CP^m ($2m+1 > n+k$). Since the normal connection of $M_{m_1,\ldots,m_k}$ is flat, we see that the normal connection of $N_{m_1,\ldots,m_k}$ satisfies $R^\perp(X,Y) = 2g(X,PY)f$ and $\nabla f = 0$ by virtue of Lemma 7.2. Moreover, the second fundamental form of $N_{m_1,\ldots,m_k}$ satisfies (7.12) and (7.13) because of Lemma 7.1.

Example 7.4. In Example 7.3, if $r_i = (m_i/(n+1))^{1/2}$ ($i = 1,\ldots,k$), then $M_{m_1,\ldots,m_k}$ is minimal and hence, from (III.1.8) and (7.5), we see that $N_{m_1,\ldots,m_k}$ is also minimal.

§8. Semi-flat normal connection

Let M be an n-dimensional CR submanifold of a complex projective space CP^m with constant holomorphic sectional curvature 4. If the curvature tensor $R^\perp$ of the normal bundle of M satisfies

$$(8.1) \qquad R^\perp(X,Y)V = 2g(X,PY)fV$$

for any vector fields X, Y tangent to M and any vector field V normal to M, then the normal connection of M is said to be semi-flat. The justification of this definition is given by Lemma 7.2.

We now consider the following commutative diagram which is a special case of (7.3)

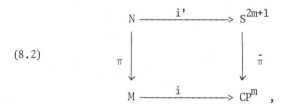

$$(8.2)$$

where N is an (n+1)-dimensional contact CR submanifold of S^{2m+1}. Then we have

Lemma 8.1. Let M be an n-dimensional CR submanifold of CP^m with semi-flat normal connection. Suppose that dim D = h $\geq$ 4 and the f-structure in the normal bundle of M is parallel. If B satisfies (7.12), i.e.,

$$(\nabla_X B)(Y,Z) = g(X,PY)FZ + g(X,PZ)FY,$$

then the second fundamental form α of N of S^{2m+1} is parallel.

Proof. From the assumption and Lemma 7.2 the normal connection of N is flat. On the other hand, by (7.10) and the assumption, $(\nabla_X \alpha)(Y,Z) = 0$ for any vector fields X, Y and Z tangent to N and orthogonal to ξ. From this we have

$$(\nabla_X \nabla_Y \alpha)(Z,W) = G(Z,\phi X)(\nabla_Y \alpha)(\xi,W) + G(W,\phi X)(\nabla_Y \alpha)(Z,\xi),$$

$$(8.3) \qquad (\nabla_Y \nabla_X \alpha)(Z,W) = G(Z,\phi Y)(\nabla_X \alpha)(\xi,W) + G(W,\phi Y)(\nabla_X \alpha)(Z,\xi),$$

$$(\nabla_{[X,Y]}\alpha)(Z,W) = 2G(X,\phi Y)(\nabla_\xi \alpha)(Z,W),$$

because of $G(\nabla'_X Z,\xi) = -G(Z,\phi X)$ and $G([X,Y],\xi) = 2G(X,\phi Y)$ for any vector fields X, Y, Z and W tangent to N and orthogonal to ξ. We denote by K the curvature tensor of N. Since the normal connection of N is flat, we have

$$(K(X,Y)\alpha)(Z,W) = K^{\perp}(X,Y)(\alpha(Z,W)) - \alpha(K(X,Y)Z,W) - \alpha(Z,K(X,Y)W)$$

$$= - \alpha(K(X,Y)Z,W) - \alpha(Z,K(X,Y)W).$$

Thus (8.3) gives

$$(8.4) \quad \alpha(K(X,Y)Z,W) + \alpha(Z,K(X,Y)W)$$

$$= 2G(X,\phi Y)(\nabla_{\xi}\alpha)(Z,W) - G(Z,\phi X)(\nabla_Y\alpha)(\xi,W)$$

$$- G(W,\phi X)(\nabla_Y\alpha)(Z,\xi) + G(Z,\phi Y)(\nabla_X\alpha)(\xi,W)$$

$$+ G(W,\phi Y)(\nabla_X\alpha)(Z,\xi).$$

Using the Gauss equation for N, and putting W = Z in (8.4), we get

$$(8.5) \quad G(Y,Z)\alpha(X,Z) - G(X,Z)\alpha(Y,Z) + \alpha(H_{\alpha(Y,Z)}X,Z) - \alpha(H_{\alpha(X,Z)}Y,Z)$$

$$= G(X,\phi Y)(\nabla_{\xi}\alpha)(Z,Z) - G(Z,\phi X)(\nabla_Y\alpha)(\xi,Z) + G(Z,\phi Y)(\nabla_X\alpha)(\xi,Z).$$

We put $X = \phi Y \in T_x(N) \cap \phi T_x(N)$. Then $Y \in T_x(N) \cap \phi T_x(N)$ and (8.5) becomes

$$(8.6) \quad G(Y,Z)\alpha(\phi Y,Z) - G(\phi Y,Z)\alpha(Y,Z) + \alpha(H_{\alpha(Y,Z)}\phi Y,Z) - \alpha(H_{\alpha(\phi Y,Z)}Y,Z)$$

$$= G(Y,Y)(\nabla_{\xi}\alpha)(Z,Z) + G(Z,Y)(\nabla_Y\alpha)(\xi,Z) + G(Z,\phi Y)(\nabla_{\phi Y}\alpha)(\xi,Z).$$

We notice here that, for any vector field Z tangent to N, $\phi^2 Z$ is also tangent to N and orthogonal to ξ. Thus, replacing Z in (8.6) by $\phi^2 Z$, Z being arbitrary vector tangent to N, we have

(8.7) $\quad G(Y,Z)\alpha(\phi Y,Z) - G(\phi Y,Z)\alpha(Y,Z) - \alpha(H_{\alpha(Y,Z)}\phi Y,\phi^2 Z)$

$$+ \alpha(H_{\alpha(\phi Y,Z)}Y,\phi^2 Z) = G(Y,Y)(\nabla_\xi\alpha)(Z,Z) + G(Z,Y)(\nabla_Y\alpha)(\xi,Z)$$

$$+ G(Z,\phi Y)(\nabla_{\phi Y}\alpha)(\xi,Z),$$

where we have used the fact that FP = 0 and (III.1.7).

Let $\{e_i\}$ be an orthonormal frame of $T_x(N)$ and $\{v_a\}$ be an orthonormal frame of $T_x(N)^\perp$. Since the normal connection of N is flat, we see that $H_a H_b = H_b H_a$ for all a, b. Thus we can choose an orthonormal frame $\{e_i\}$ of $T_x(N)$ such that $H_a e_i = \lambda_i^a e_i$ for any a. Thus if we put $Z = e_k$, (8.7) implies

(8.8) $\quad G(Y,e_k)\alpha(\phi Y,e_k) - G(\phi Y,e_k)\alpha(Y,e_k)$

$$- \sum_{a,i}[\alpha(e_i,\phi^2 e_k)G(e_i,H_a\phi Y)\lambda_k^a G(Y,e_k)$$

$$- \alpha(e_i,\phi^2 e_k)G(e_i,H_a Y)\lambda_k^a G(\phi Y,e_k)]$$

$$= G(Y,Y)(\nabla_\xi\alpha)(e_k,e_k) + G(e_k,Y)(\nabla_Y\alpha)(\xi,e_k)$$

$$+ G(e_k,\phi Y)(\nabla_{\phi Y}\alpha)(\xi,e_k).$$

Since dim $D \geq 4$, we see that $\dim(T_x(N) \cap \phi T_x(N)) \geq 4$ and hence we can choose Y and ϕY in $T_x(N) \cap \phi T_x(N)$ in such a way that Y and ϕY are orthogonal to e_k. Thus (8.8) reduces to

$$(\nabla_\xi\alpha)(e_k,e_k) = 0$$

for all k. Since α is symmetric, we have $(\nabla_\xi\alpha)(X,Y) = 0$ for any X, $Y \in T_x(N)$. Consequently, (7.11) and Lemma 7.1 show that the second fundamental form α of N is parallel.

Lemma 8.2. Let M be an n-dimensional CR submanifold of CP^m. Then we have

$$(8.9) \qquad g(\nabla B, \nabla B) \geq 2hq,$$

where h = dim D and q = dim $D^\perp$, and the equality in (8.9) holds if and only if (7.12) holds.

Proof. We put $T(X,Y,Z) = (\nabla_X B)(Y,Z) + g(Y,PX)FZ + g(Z,PX)FY$. Then T = 0 if and only if (7.12) holds. We compute the square of the length of T. Let $\{e_i\}$ be an orthonormal frame of $T_X(M)$. Then we have

$$g(T,T) = g(\nabla B, \nabla B) + 2hq + 4 \sum_{i,j} g((\nabla_{e_i} B)(Pe_i, e_j), Fe_j).$$

On the other hand, equation of Codazzi implies

$$\sum_{i,j} g((\nabla_{e_i} B)(Pe_i, e_j), Fe_j) = \sum_{i,j} g((\nabla_{e_j} B)(e_i, Pe_i), Fe_j) - hq.$$

Since B is symmetric and P is skew-symmetric, the first term in the right hand side of the equation above vanishes. Consequently, we have

$$g(T,T) = g(\nabla B, \nabla B) - 2hq.$$

From this we have our assertion.

Theorem 8.1. Let M be an n-dimensional complete CR submanifold of CP^m with semi-flat normal connection and $h \geq 4$. If the f-structure f in the normal bundle of M is parallel and if $g(\nabla B, \nabla B) = 2hq$, then M is totally geodesic invariant submanifold $CP^{n/2}$ of CP^m or M is a generic submanifold of $CP^{(n+q)/2}$ in CP^m and is

$$\pi(S^{m_1}(r_1) \times \cdots \times S^{m_k}(r_k)), \quad n+1 = \sum_{i=1}^{k} m_i, \quad \sum_{i=1}^{k} r_i^2 = 1,$$

where $2 \leq k \leq n-3$ and $m_1, \ldots, m_k$ are odd numbers and $q = k-1$.

Proof. First we assume that $q = 0$. Then M is an invariant submanifold of CP^m. From (1.12) we have $[A_V, A_U] = 0$ for any vector fields U and V normal to M. Thus Lemma 1.1 implies

$$0 = A_{JU}A_U - A_U A_{JU} = 2JA_U^2,$$

and hence $A_U = 0$, which shows that M is totally geodesic in CP^m. Thus we see that M is $CP^{n/2}$.

Let us next assume that $q \geq 1$. From Lemmas 8.1 and 8.2 we see that the second fundamental form α of N of S^{2m+1} is parallel. On the other hand, the second fundamental form B of M satisfies (7.14). Thus we have

$$g(B(Y,PX), fV) = g(A_{fV}PX, Y)$$

$$= g((\nabla_X F)Y, fV) = - g(FY, (\nabla_X f)V) = 0$$

for any vector field V normal to M, which means that $A_{fV}PX = 0$ for any vector field X tangent to M and hence $A_{fV}Z = 0$ for any $Z \in D$, where we have used $fF = 0$. Moreover, from (1.9) we have

$$g(FA_{fV}X,U) = -g(A_{fV}tU,X) = -g(B(X,tfV),U) = 0,$$

for any vector field U normal to M, which shows that $A_{fV}Y = 0$ for any $Y \in D^{\perp}$. Consequently, we obtain $A_{fV} = 0$ for any vector field V normal to M. We also have, from (7.6), $H_{f'V*} = 0$. If $A_{FX} = 0$ for some vector X tangent to M, (1.12) implies that $c = 0$ when $q \geq 2$. This is a contradiction. When $q = 1$, if $A_{FX} = 0$, M is totally geodesic in CP^m. This is also a contradiction (see Theorem 1.1). Thus the first normal space of M is of dimension q and hence the first normal space of N is of dimension q. Moreover, the first normal space are parallel by (7.14). Therefore, there is a totally geodesic $(n+1+q)$-dimensional submanifold S^{n+1+q} of S^{2m+1}, and hence $CP^{(n+q)/2}$ of CP^m containing N and M respectively. Then, from the definition, M is a generic submanifold of $CP^{(n+q)/2}$. Now, using Theorem II.6.3, Lemma 7.2, Example III.5.1 and Example 7.3, we have our assertion.

From Theorem 8.1 we have (Yano-Kon [66])

<u>Theorem 8.2.</u> Let M be an n-dimensional complete generic submanifold of CP^m with flat normal connection. If $h \geq 4$ and $g(\nabla B, \nabla B) = 2hp$ (p = codim M), then M is

$$\pi(S^{m_1}(r_1) \times \cdots \times S^{m_k}(r_k)), \quad n+1 = \sum_{i=1}^{k} m_i, \quad \sum_{i=1}^{k} r_i^2 = 1,$$

where $2 \leq k \leq n-3$, $m = (n+k-1)/2$ and $m_1, \ldots, m_k$ are odd numbers.

Theorem 8.3. Let M be an n-dimensional complete minimal CR submanifold of CP^m. Suppose that $g(\nabla B, \nabla B) = 2hq$, $g(A,A) \geq (n+1)(2m-n) - 2q$ and B satisfies (7.13). Then M is a generic submanifold of CP^m and $q = 2m-n$. Moreover, M is

$$\pi(S^{m_1}(r_1) \times \cdots \times S^{m_k}(r_k)), \quad r_i = (m_i/(n+1))^{1/2} \ (i = 1,\ldots,k),$$

where $\sum_{i=1}^{k} m_i = n+1$, $2m-n = k-1$ and $m_1,\ldots,m_k$ are odd numbers.

Proof. From Lemma 7.1 the second fundamental form α of N in S^{2m+1} is parallel. Moreover, we see, from (7.20), that

$$G(H,H) = g(A,A) + 2q \geq (n+1)(2m-n).$$

Thus our theorem follows from Theorem II.6.2.

§9. Normal connection of invariant submanifolds

Let $\tilde{M}$ be a complex $(n+p)$-dimensional Kaehlerian manifold and M a complex n-dimensional invariant submanifold of $\tilde{M}$. In this section, we study invariant submanifolds M satisfying

(9.1) $R^{\perp}(X,Y)V = \rho g(X,JY)JV$

for any vector fields X, Y tangent to M and any vector field V normal to M, ρ being a function on M.

Lemma 9.1. Let M be a complex n-dimensional $(n \geq 2)$ invariant submanifold of a Kaehlerian manifold $\tilde{M}$. If the normal connection of M satisfies the condition (9.1), then ρ is a constant.

Proof. We define $\nabla_X R^{\perp}$ by

$$(\nabla_X R^{\perp})(Y,Z)V = D_X(R^{\perp}(Y,Z)V) - R^{\perp}(\nabla_X Y,Z)V - R^{\perp}(Y,\nabla_X Z)V$$
$$- R^{\perp}(Y,Z)D_X V.$$

Then we can easily prove that

$$(\nabla_X R^{\perp})(Y,Z) + (\nabla_Y R^{\perp})(Z,X) + (\nabla_Z R^{\perp})(X,Y) = 0.$$

On the other hand, by (9.1) we have

$$(\nabla_X R^{\perp})(Y,Z) = (X\rho)g(Y,JZ)J.$$

Therefore, we have

$$(X\rho)g(Y,JZ) + (Y\rho)g(Z,JX) + (Z\rho)g(X,JY) = 0.$$

Putting $Z = JY$ in this equation, we obtain

$$-(X\rho)g(Y,Y) + (Y\rho)g(Y,X) + (JY\rho)g(X,JY) = 0.$$

Then, assuming that X is perpendicular to Y and JY, we find

$$(X\rho)g(Y,Y) = 0,$$

which shows that ρ is constant on M.

Theorem 9.1 (Ishihara [21]). Let M be a complex n-dimensional ($n \geq 2$) invariant submanifold of a complex $(n+p)$-dimensional complex space form $\bar{M}^{n+p}(c)$. If the normal connection of M satisfies the condition (9.1), then either M is totally geodesic or is an Einstein complex hypersurface of $\bar{M}^{n+p}(c)$ with scalar curvature n^2c. The latter case occurs only when $c > 0$.

Proof. From the Ricci equation and (9.1) we have

$$(9.2) \qquad \frac{1}{2}cg(X,JY)g(JV,U) = g(X,JY)g(JV,U) - g([A_V,A_U]X,Y).$$

Putting $U = JV$ in (9.2) and using Lemma 1.1, we have

$$\frac{1}{2}cg(X,JY)g(V,V) = g(X,JY)g(V,V) + 2g(JA_V^2X,Y),$$

or equivalently

$$g(A_V^2X,JY) = \frac{1}{4}(2\rho-c)g(V,V)g(X,JY),$$

from which

$$(9.3) \qquad A_V^2 = \frac{1}{4}(2\rho-c)g(V,V)I,$$

where I denotes the identity transformation. Assuming $2\rho = c$, we find $A_V^2 = 0$, which means that $A_V = 0$, that is, M is totally geodesic.

Next we assume that $2\rho \neq c$ and $p \geq 2$. Let $\{V_1,\ldots,V_p,JV_1,\ldots,JV_p\}$ be an orthonormal frame of $T_x(M)^{\perp}$. From (9.3) and $A_{V_a+V_b}^2 = A_{V_a}^2 + A_{V_a}A_{V_b} + A_{V_b}A_{V_a} + A_{V_b}^2$, a, b = $1,\ldots,p$, we obtain

(9.4) $\qquad A_{V_a} A_{V_b} + A_{V_b} A_{V_a} = 0 \quad$ for $a \neq b$.

On the other hand, from (9.2) we get

(9.5) $\qquad A_{V_a} A_{V_b} - A_{V_b} A_{V_a} = 0.$

Equations (9.4) and (9.5) imply $A_{V_a} A_{V_b} = 0$ for $a \neq b$. Thus, from (9.3) we have

$$0 = A_{V_a} A_{V_b}^2 = \frac{1}{4}(2\rho-c)g(V_b,V_b)A_{V_a},$$

which shows that $A_{V_a} = 0$. Consequently, (9.3) implies that $2\rho = c$. This is a contradiction. Thus we have $p = 1$, that is, M is a complex hypersurface of $\bar{M}$. Moreover, from (1.10) and (9.3) we see that M is an Einstein complex hypersurface. Thus our result follows from the following theorem due to Chern [15] (see also Takahashi [49]).

Theorem 9.2. Let M be a complex n-dimensional $(n \geq 2)$ Einstein hypersurface of a complex space form $\bar{M}^{n+1}(c)$. If $c \leq 0$, M is totally geodesic. If $c > 0$, M is either totally geodesic or the scalar curvature of M is $n^2 c$.

Now, we use the following classification theorem.

Theorem 9.3 (Smyth [44]). The only simply connected complete Einstein complex hypersurfaces M in C^{n+1} (resp. D^{n+1}), $n \geq 2$, are C^n (resp. D^n). The only complete Einstein complex hypersurfaces M in CP^{n+1}, $n \geq 2$, are CP^n or a complex quadric Q^n.

Combining Theorem 9.1 and Theorem 9.3, we have

Theorem 9.4 (Ishihara [21]). If $n \geq 2$, then

(i) CP^n and Q^{m-1} are the only complete invariant submanifolds of CP^m which satisfies the condition (9.1).

(ii) D^n (resp. C^n) is the only simply connected complete invariant submanifold of D^m (resp. C^m) which satisfies the condition (9.1).

If the normal connection of M is flat, then $\rho = 0$, and (9.3) implies

$$g(A_V X, A_V X) = -\frac{1}{4} cg(X,X)g(V,V),$$

from which we see that $c \leq 0$. Therefore, Theorem 9.1 reduces to

Theorem 9.5 (Chen-Ogiue [14], Kon [29], Sakamoto [41]). Let M be an invariant submanifold of a complex space form $\bar{M}^m(c)$. Then the normal connection of M is flat if and only if $c = 0$ and M is totally geodesic.

§10. Parallel mean curvature vector

Let M be an n-dimensional CR submanifold of a complex m-dimensional Kaehlerian manifold $\bar{M}$. Then we have the following decomposition of the tangent space $T_x(M)$ at each point x of M:

$$T_x(M) = D_x \oplus D_x^{\perp}.$$

Similarly, we have

$$T_x(M)^{\perp} = FD_x \oplus N_x,$$

where N_x is the orthogonal complement of $FD_x^{\perp}$ in $T_x(M)^{\perp}$. Thus $JN_x = fN_x = N_x$.

We can take an orthonormal frame $\{e_1,\ldots,e_{2m}\}$ of $\tilde{M}$ such that, restricted to M, $e_1,\ldots,e_n$ are tangent to M. Then $e_1,\ldots,e_n$ form an orthonormal frame of M. We can take $\{e_1,\ldots,e_n\}$ in such a way that $e_1,\ldots,e_{n-q}$ form an orthonormal frame of D_x and $e_{n-q+1},\ldots,e_n$ form an orthonormal frame of $D_x^{\perp}$, where $q = \dim D_x^{\perp}$ and $n-q = h = \dim D_x$. Moreover, we can take $\{e_{n+1},\ldots,e_{2m}\}$ in such a way that $e_{n+1},\ldots,e_{n+q}$ form an orthonormal frame of $FD_x^{\perp}$ and $e_{n+q+1},\ldots,e_{2m}$ form an orthonormal frame of N_x. Unless otherwise stated, we use the conventions that the ranges of indices are respectively:

$$i,j,k = 1,\ldots,n; \quad r,s,t = 1,\ldots,n-q; \quad a,b,c = n-q+1,\ldots,n;$$
$$x,y,z = n+1,\ldots,n+q; \quad \lambda,\mu,\nu = n+q+1,\ldots,2m.$$

Lemma 10.1. Let M be a CR submanifold of CP^m with semi-flat normal connection. If the f-structure f is parallel, then

$$(10.1) \qquad\qquad A_{fV} = 0$$

for any vector field V normal to M, that is, $A_{\lambda} = 0$, where $A_{\lambda} = A_{e_{\lambda}}$.

Proof. Since the f-structure f is parallel, (1.9) implies

$$(10.2) \qquad\qquad A_V tU = A_U tV$$

for any vector fields U and V normal to M. On the other hand, the Ricci equation (1.12) and (8.1) imply

$$(10.3) \qquad g([A_V,A_U]X,Y) = g(FY,U)g(FX,V) - g(FX,U)g(FY,V).$$

Using (1.7), we have

$$0 = g((\nabla_X f)fV, FY) = -g(f^2 V, (\nabla_X F)Y)$$

$$= g(A_{f^2 V}X, PY) - g(A_{fV}X, Y),$$

from which

(10.4) $\qquad g(A_{fV}X, A_{fV}X) = g(A_{f^2 V}X, PA_{fV}X).$

Moreover, we have, from (10.3)

(10.5) $\qquad A_{fV}A_{f^2 V} = A_{f^2 V}A_{fV}.$

From (10.4) and (10.5) we see that $\mathrm{Tr}A_{fV}^2 = 0$ and hence $A_{fV} = 0$ for any vector field V normal to M.

Lemma 10.2. Let M be a CR submanifold of CP^m with semi-flat normal connection and parallel f-structure f. If $PA_V = A_V P$ for any vector field V normal to M, then

(10.6) $\quad g(A_U X, A_V Y) = g(X,Y)g(tU, tV) - g(FX,U)g(FY,V)$

$$- \sum_i g(A_U tV, e_i)g(A_{Fe_i}X, Y).$$

Proof. From the assumption we have $g(A_U PX, tV) = 0$, from which

$$g((\nabla_Y A)_U PX, tV) + g(A_U(\nabla_Y P)X, tV) + g(A_U PX, (\nabla_Y t)V) = 0.$$

Thus, from (1.6), (1.8) and (10.1), we find

$$g((\nabla_{PX}A)_U PX, tV) + g(A_U tB(PY,X), tV) - g(PA_U X, P^2 A_V Y) = 0,$$

from which

$$g((\nabla_{PY}A)_U PX, tV) - \sum_i g(A_U tV, e_i) g(A_{Fe_i} X, PY) + g(PA_U X, A_V Y) = 0.$$

From this and the Codazzi equation (1.11) we have

$$g(PX,PY)g(tU,tV) - \sum_i g(A_U tV, e_i) g(A_{Fe_i} PX, PY) + g(P^2 A_U X, A_V Y) = 0.$$

On the other hand, we have

$$g(PX,PY)g(tU,tV) = g(X,Y)g(tU,tV) - g(FX,FY)g(tU,tV),$$

$$- \sum_i g(A_U tV, e_i) g(A_{Fe_i} PX, PY) = - \sum_i g(A_U tV, e_i) g(A_{Fe_i} X, Y) + g(A_U tV, A_{FY} X),$$

$$g(P^2 A_U X, A_V Y) = - g(A_U X, A_V Y) - g(A_U X, A_{FY} tV).$$

Moreover, from (10.3), we see that

$$g(A_U tV, A_{FY} X) - g(A_U X, A_{FY} tV) = g(tU, tV)g(FX, FY) - g(FX, U)g(FY, V).$$

From these equations we obtain

$$g(X,Y)g(tU,tV) - g(FX,U)g(FY,V)$$

$$- \sum_i g(A_U tV, e_i) g(A_{Fe_i} X, Y) - g(A_U X, A_V Y) = 0,$$

which proves (10.6).

A parallel section U of the normal bundle of M is called an isoperimetric section if $\text{Tr}A_U = \text{constant} \neq 0$ and a minimal section if $\text{Tr}A_U = 0$.

Lemma 10.3. Let M be a CR submanifold of CP^m. For any isoperimetric or minimal section U of the normal bundle of M, we have

$$(10.7) \qquad \sum_j (\nabla_{e_j} A)_U e_j = 0.$$

Proof. For any vector field X tangent to M, we have

$$\sum_j g((\nabla_{e_j} A)_U e_j, X) = \sum_j [g((\nabla_X A)_U e_j, e_j) + g(Fe_j, U)g(PX, e_i)$$

$$- g(FX, U)g(Pe_j, e_j) - 2g(e_j, PX)g(tU, e_j)] = 0$$

because of the Codazzi equation (1.11).

Lemma 10.4. Let M be a CR submanifold of CP^m with semi-flat normal connection and parallel f-structure f. If the mean curvature vector of M is parallel and if $PA_V = A_V P$ for any vector field V normal to M, then the square of the length of the second fundamental form of M is constant.

Proof. From (10.1) and (10.6) the square of the length of the second fundamental form of M is given by

$$\sum_X \text{Tr}A_X^2 = (n-1)q + \sum_{x,y} g(A_x te_x, te_y)\text{Tr}A_y,$$

where $A_x = A_{e_x}$. On the other hand, for any vector field $V \in FD^\perp$, we have $D_X V \in FD^\perp$ because of $\nabla f = 0$. From (1.7), we also have, for any $V \in N$, $D_X V \in N$. Therefore, since $R^\perp(X, Y)V = 0$ for any $V \in FD^\perp$, we can

take an orthonormal frame $\{e_x\}$ of FD such that $De_x = 0$ for each x
(see Proposition II.3.1). Then we see that $\nabla_X(te_x) = -PA_X X$. Since the
mean curvature vector of M is parallel and $PA_V = A_V P$, from the
Codazzi equation (1.11) and (10.2), we find

$$\nabla_X(\sum_x \mathrm{Tr}A_x^2) = \sum_{x,y} g((\nabla_{te_x} A)_y te_x, X) \mathrm{Tr}A_y.$$

On the other hand, using $PA_V = A_V P$ and (1.6), we have

$$\sum_i g((\nabla_{Pe_i} A)_x Pe_i, tV) = 0 \quad \text{and} \quad \sum_i g((\nabla_{Pe_i} A)_x Pe_i, PX) = 0$$

for any vector field V normal to M and any vector field X tangent to
M. Consequently, we have

$$\sum_s (\nabla_{e_s} A)_x e_s = \sum_i (\nabla_{Pe_i} A)_x Pe_i = 0$$

for each x. Since the mean curvature vector of M is parallel, (10.7)
implies

$$0 = \sum_i (\nabla_{e_i} A)_x e_i = \sum_s (\nabla_{e_s} A)_x e_s + \sum_a (\nabla_{e_a} A)_x e_a$$

$$= \sum_a (\nabla_{e_a} A)_x e_a = \sum_y (\nabla_{te_y} A)_x te_y$$

for each x, and hence $\sum_x \mathrm{Tr}A_x^2 = $ constant.

Proposition 10.1. Let M be an n-dimensional CR submanifold of CP^m with
semi-flat normal connection and parallel f-structure f and parallel
mean curvature vector. If $PA_V = A_V P$ for any vector field V normal to
M, then we have $g(\nabla A, \nabla A) = 2(n-q)q$.

Proof. Using (I.2.2), (II.4.9) and (10.1), we have by a straighrforward computation,

$$(10.8) \quad g(\nabla^2 A, A) = \sum_{x,i,j} g((\nabla_{e_i} \nabla_{e_i} A)_x e_j, A_x e_j)$$

$$= (n-3)\sum_x \text{Tr}A_x^2 - \sum_x (\text{Tr}A_x)^2 + 6\sum_x [\text{Tr}(A_x P)^2 - \text{Tr}A_x^2 P^2]$$

$$+ 3\sum_{x,y} [g(A_x te_y, A_x te_y) - g(A_x te_x, A_y te_y)]$$

$$- \frac{1}{2}\sum_{x,y,i} g([A_x, A_y]e_i, [A_x, A_y]e_i) + \sum_{x,y} [3g(A_x te_x, te_y)\text{Tr}A_y$$

$$- (\text{Tr}A_x A_y)^2 + (\text{Tr}A_y)(\text{Tr}A_x^2 A_y)],$$

where we took $\{e_x\}$ such that $De_x = 0$ for each x and used the fact that $(\nabla_X A)_V Y = 0$ for any $V \in N_x$. On the other hand, from (10.3), we have

$$(10.9) \quad \sum_{x,y,i} g([A_x, A_y]e_i, [A_x, A_y]e_i) = 2q(q-1),$$

$$(10.10) \quad \sum_{x,y} [g(A_x te_y, A_x te_y) - g(A_x te_x, A_y te_y)] = q(q-1).$$

From (10.8), (10.9) and (10.10) we have

$$(10.11) \quad g(\nabla^2 A, A) = (n-3)\sum_x \text{Tr}A_x^2 - \sum_x (\text{Tr}A_x)^2 + 3\sum_x |[P, A_x]|^2 + 2q(q-1)$$

$$+ \sum_{x,y} [3g(A_x te_x, te_y)\text{Tr}A_y - (\text{Tr}A_x A_y)^2 + (\text{Tr}A_y)(\text{Tr}A_x^2 A_y)].$$

Since $PA_V = A_V P$, (10.6) implies

$$(10.12) \quad \sum_{x,y} \text{Tr}A_y g(A_x te_x, te_y) = \sum_x \text{Tr}A_x^2 - (n-1)q.$$

On the other hand, Lemma 10.4 implies that $g(\nabla A, \nabla A) = -g(\nabla^2 A, A)$. Therefore, substituting (10.12) into (10.11), we obtain

$$(10.13) \quad g(\nabla A, \nabla A) - 2(n-q)q = \sum_{x,y} (\mathrm{Tr} A_x A_y)^2 - n\sum_x \mathrm{Tr} A_x^2 + \sum_x (\mathrm{Tr} A_x)^2$$
$$- \sum_{x,y} (\mathrm{Tr} A_x)(\mathrm{Tr} A_y^2 A_x) + (n-1)q.$$

Now, using (10.6), we have

$$\sum_{x,y} (\mathrm{Tr} A_x A_y)^2 = (n-1)\sum_x \mathrm{Tr} A_x^2 + \sum_{x,y,z} (\mathrm{Tr} A_z)(\mathrm{Tr} A_x A_y) g(A_x t e_y, t e_z),$$

$$- \sum_{x,y} (\mathrm{Tr} A_x)(\mathrm{Tr} A_y^2 A_x) = - \sum_x (\mathrm{Tr} A_x)^2 + \sum_{x,y} \mathrm{Tr} A_x g(A_x t e_y, t e_y).$$

Substituting these equations into (10.13), we find

$$(10.14) \quad g(\nabla A, \nabla A) - 2(n-q)q = - \sum_x \mathrm{Tr} A_x^2 + \sum_{x,y} \mathrm{Tr} A_x g(A_x t e_y, t e_y) + (n-1)q.$$

From (10.12) and (10.14) we see that $g(\nabla A, \nabla A) = 2(n-q)q$, which proves our assertion.

Here, we notice that $g(\nabla B, \nabla B) = g(\nabla A, \nabla A)$ in general. Moreover, if $PA_V = A_V P$, then we can prove Theorem 7.1 without the assumption $h \geq 4$ (see Lemmas III.7.1, 8.1, 8.2 and 10.1). Therefore, from Theorem 8.1 and Proposition 10.1, we have (Yano-Kon [71])

Theorem 10.1. Let M be an n-dimensional complete CR submanifold of CP^m with semi-flat normal connection and parallel f-structure f and parallel mean curvature vector. If $PA_V = A_V P$ for any vector field V normal to M, then M is a totally geodesic invariant submanifold $CP^{n/2}$ of CP^m or M is a generic submanifold of $CP^{(n+q)/2}$ in CP^m and is

$$\pi(S^{m_1}(r_1) \times \cdots \times S^{m_k}(r_k)), \quad \sum_{i=1}^{k} m_i = n+1, \quad \sum_{i=1}^{k} r_i^2 = 1,$$

where $q = k-1$ and $m_1, \ldots, m_k$ are odd numbers.

Theorem 10.2 (Ki-Pak-Kim [27]). Let M be an n-dimensional complete generic submanifold of CP^m with flat normal connection and parallel mean curvature vector. If $PA_V = A_V P$ for any vector field V normal to M, then M is

$$\pi(S^{m_1}(r_1) \times \cdots \times S^{m_k}(r_k)), \quad \sum_{i=1}^{k} m_i = n+1, \quad \sum_{i=1}^{k} r_i^2 = 1,$$

where $2m-n = k-1$ and $m_1, \ldots, m_k$ are odd numbers.

Theorem 10.3. Let M be an n-dimensional complete minimal CR submanifold of CP^m with semi-flat normal connection and parallel f-structure f. If $PA_V = A_V P$ for any vector field V normal to M, then M is $CP^{n/2}$ or M is a generic submanifold of $CP^{(n+q)/2}$ in CP^m and is

$$\pi(S^{m_1}(r_1) \times \cdots \times S^{m_k}(r_k)), \quad r_i = (m_i/(n+1))^{1/2} \ (i=1,\ldots,k),$$

where $\sum_{i=1}^{k} m_i = n+1$ and $m_1, \ldots, m_k$ are odd numbers.

Theorem 10.4. Let M be an n-dimensional complete minimal generic submanifold of CP^m with flat normal connection. If $PA_V = A_V P$ for any vector field V normal to M, then M is

$$\pi(S^{m_1}(r_1) \times \cdots \times S^{m_k}(r_k)), \quad r_i = (m_i/(n+1))^{1/2} \ (i=1,\ldots,k),$$

where $\sum_{i=1}^{k} m_i = n+1$ and $m_1,\ldots,m_k$ are odd numbers.

We next consider the meaning of the condition $PA_V = A_V P$ in terms of the f-structure.

Let M be a CR submanifold of a Kaehlerian manifold $\bar{M}$. The Nijenhuis tensor of the f-structure P on M is given by

$$N_P(X,Y) = P^2[X,Y] + [PX,PY] - P[PX,Y] - P[X,PY].$$

We consider a tensor field S defined by

$$S(X,Y) = N_P(X,Y) - t[(\nabla_X F)Y - (\nabla_Y F)X].$$

The f-structure P on M is said to be _normal_ if S vanishes identically. We now prove the following

Theorem 10.5. Let M be a CR submanifold of a Kaehlerian manifold $\bar{M}$. Then the f-structure P on M is normal if and only if $A_{FX}P = PA_{FX}$ for any vector field X tangent to M.

Proof. From the definitions we have

$$S(X,Y) = (\nabla_{PX}P)Y - (\nabla_{PY}P)X + P[(\nabla_Y P)X - (\nabla_X P)Y]$$

$$- t[(\nabla_X F)Y - (\nabla_Y F)X].$$

From this and (1.6), (1.7) we have

$$S(X,Y) = (A_{FY}P - PA_{FY})X - (A_{FX}P - PA_{FX})Y.$$

If $A_{FX}P = PA_{FX}$ for any vector field X tangent to M, then $S(X,Y) = 0$. Conversely, suppose that $S(X,Y) = 0$. Let $X \in D^{\perp}$ and $Y \in D$. Then we have

(10.5) $$A_{FX}PY = PA_{FX}Y.$$

Let $Z \in D^{\perp}$. Then we have

$$g(A_{FX}PY,Z) = g(PA_{FX}Y,Z) = 0,$$

from which $A_{FX}Z \in D^{\perp}$ for $Z \in D^{\perp}$. Thus we have

(10.6) $$A_{FX}PZ = PA_{FX}Z, \qquad Z \in D^{\perp}.$$

Consequently, we obtain

$$A_{FX}P = PA_{FX}$$

for any vector field X tangent to M. Thus Theorem 10.5 is proved.

§11. Integral formulas

Let M be an n-dimensional CR submanifold of CP^m with semi-flat normal connection and parallel f-structure f in the normal bundle of M. Suppose that U is a parallel section of the normal bundle of M. Then, from equation of Ricci (1.12) and (10.1), we have $fU = 0$ and hence $U \in FD^\perp$. We also have $\nabla_X tU = -PA_U X$, and hence

$$\text{div } tU = \sum_i g(\nabla_{e_i} tU, e_i) = -\text{TrPA}_U = 0,$$

since A_U is symmetric and P is skew-symmetric. Thus we have, from (I.1.10),

$$(11.1) \qquad \text{div}(\nabla_{tU} tU) = S(tU, tU) + \frac{1}{2}|L(tU)g|^2 - |\nabla tU|^2,$$

where S is the Ricci tensor of M. On the other hand, from (1.10) and (10.1) we have

$$(11.2) \qquad S(tU, tU) = (n-1)g(tU, tU) + \sum_X \text{TrA}_X g(A_X tU, tU) - \sum_X g(A_X^2 tU, tU).$$

Moreover, we have

$$(11.3) \qquad |\nabla tU|^2 = \text{TrA}_U^2 - \sum_X g(A_X^2 tU, tU).$$

From (11.1), (11.2) and (11.3) we have

$$(11.4) \qquad \text{div}(\nabla_{tU} tU) = (n-1)g(tU, tU) + \sum_X \text{TrA}_X g(A_X tU, tU)$$
$$- \text{TrA}_U^2 + \frac{1}{2}|L(tU)g|^2.$$

We now take an orthonormal frame $\{e_x\}$ such that $De_x = 0$ for each x. Then (11.4) implies

(11.5) $\operatorname{div}(\sum_x \nabla_{te_x} te_x) = (n-1)q + \sum_{x,y} \operatorname{Tr} A_x g(A_x te_y, te_y)$

$$- \sum_x \operatorname{Tr} A_x^2 + \frac{1}{2}\sum_x |L(te_x)g|^2.$$

It is easy to show by (10.1) that the right hand side of (11.5) is independent of the choice of an orthonormal frame of $T_x(M)^\perp$. We notice that $|L(tU)g|^2 = |[P, A_U]|^2$.

<u>Proposition 11.1.</u> Let M be an n-dimensional compact orientable CR submanifold of CP^m with semi-flat normal connection and with parallel f-structure f. If U is a parallel section in the normal bundle of M, then

(11.6) $\int_M [(n-1)g(tU,tU) - \operatorname{Tr} A_U^2 + \sum_x \operatorname{Tr} A_x g(A_x tU, tU)]*1 = \frac{1}{2}\int_M |L(tU)g|^2*1.$

If M is a generic submanifold of CP^m, then f = 0 and hence we have

<u>Proposition 11.2.</u> Let M be an n-dimensional compact orientable generic submanifold of CP^m with parallel section U in the normal bundle. Then we have the formula (11.6).

<u>Corollary 11.1.</u> Under the same assumption as that of Proposition 11.1, if M is minimal, we have

(11.7) $\int_M [(n-1)g(tU,tU) - \operatorname{Tr} A_U^2]*1 = \frac{1}{2}\int_M |L(tU)g|^2*1.$

Corollary 11.2. Under the same assumption as that of Proposition 11.2, if M is minimal, then we have the same formula (11.7).

Corollary 11.3. Under the same assumption as that of Proposition 11.1, if

$$\int_M [(n-1)g(tU,tU) - TrA_U^2 + \sum_X TrA_X g(A_X tU,tU)]*1 \geq 0,$$

then tU is an infinitesimal isometry of M and $PA_U = A_U P$. Moreover, if M is minimal and if

$$\int_M [(n-1)g(tU,tU) - TrA_U^2]*1 \geq 0,$$

then we have the same conclusion.

From (11.5) we have

Theorem 11.1. Let M be a compact orientable n-dimensional CR submanifold of CP^m with semi-flat normal connection and parallel f-structure f. Then

$$(11.8) \quad \int_M [(n-1)q - \sum_X TrA_X^2 + \sum_{x,y} TrA_X g(A_X te_y,te_y)]*1 = -\frac{1}{2}\int_M \sum_X |[P,A_X]|^2*1.$$

Theorem 11.2. Let M be a compact orientable n-dimensional minimal CR submanifold of CP^m with semi-flat normal connection and parallel f-structure f. Then

$$(11.9) \quad \int_M [(n-1)q - \sum_X TrA_X^2]*1 = -\frac{1}{2}\int_M \sum_X |[P,A_X]|^2*1.$$

Theorem 11.3. Let M be an n-dimensional compact orientable CR submanifold of CP^m with semi-flat normal connection and parallel f-structure f. If the mean curvature vector of M is parallel, then we have

$$(11.10) \quad 0 \le \int_M [g(\nabla A, \nabla A) - 2(n-q)q + \frac{3}{2}\sum_x |[P, A_x]|^2]*1$$

$$= \int_M [\sum_{x,y} (TrA_x A_y)^2 - n\sum_x TrA_x^2 + \sum_x (TrA_x)^2$$

$$- \sum_{x,y} (TrA_x)(TrA_y^2 A_x) + (n-1)q]*1.$$

Proof. From the assumption we have (10.11). From this and (11.5) we have (11.10).

From Theorems 10.1 and 11.1 we have

Theorem 11.4. Let M be an n-dimensional compact orientable CR submanifold of CP^m with semi-flat normal connection and with parallel f-structure f. If the mean curvature vector of M is parallel and if

$$\int_M [(n-1)q - \sum_x TrA_x^2 + \sum_{x,y} TrA_x g(A_x te_y, te_y)]*1 \ge 0,$$

then M is $CP^{n/2}$, or M is a generic submanifold of $CP^{(n+q)/2}$ in CP^m and is

$$\pi(S^{m_1}(r_1) \times \cdots \times S^{m_k}(r_k)), \quad \sum_{i=1}^{k} m_i = n+1, \quad \sum_{i=1}^{k} r_i^2 = 1,$$

where $q = k-1$ and $m_1, \ldots, m_k$ are odd numbers.

From Theorems 10.1 and 11.3 we have

Theorem 11.5. Let M be an n-dimensional compact orientable CR submanifold of CP^m with semi-flat normal connection and with parallel f-structure f. If the mean curvature vector of M is parallel and if

$$\int_M [\sum_{x,y} (TrA_xA_y)^2 - n\sum_x TrA_x^2 + \sum_x (TrA_x)^2$$
$$- \sum_{x,y} (TrA_x)(TrA_y^2A_x) + (n-1)q]*1 \leq 0,$$

then M is $CP^{n/2}$, or M is a generic submanifold of $CP^{(n+q)/2}$ in CP^m and is

$$\pi(S^{m_1}(r_1) \times \cdots \times S^{m_k}(r_k)), \quad \sum_{i=1}^{k} m_i = n+1, \quad \sum_{i=1}^{k} r_i^2 = 1,$$

where q = k-1 and $m_1,\ldots,m_k$ are odd numbers.

From Theorems 10.3 and 11.2 we have

Theorem 11.6. Let M be an n-dimensional compact orientable minimal CR submanifold of CP^m with semi-flat normal connection and with parallel f-structure f. If

$$\int_M [(n-1)q - \sum_x TrA_x^2]*1 \geq 0,$$

then M is $CP^{n/2}$, or M is a generic submanifold of $CP^{(n+q)/2}$ in CP^m and is

$$\pi(S^{m_1}(r_1) \times \cdots \times S^{m_k}(r_k)), \quad r_i = (m_i/(n+1))^{1/2} \ (i=1,\ldots,k),$$

where $\sum_{i=1}^{k} m_i = n+1$ and $m_1,\ldots,m_k$ are odd numbers.

Especially we have

Theorem 11.7. Let M be an n-dimensional compact orientable minimal CR submanifold of CP^m with semi-flat normal connection and with parallel f-structure f. If $\sum_X \text{Tr} A_X^2 \leq (n-1)q$, then M is $CP^{n/2}$, or M is a generic minimal submanifold of $CP^{(n+q)/2}$ in CP^m and is

$$\pi(S^{m_1}(r_1) \times \cdots \times S^{m_k}(r_k)), \quad r_i = (m_i/(n+1))^{1/2} \ (i=1,\ldots,k),$$

where $\sum_{i=1}^{k} m_i = n+1$ and $m_1,\ldots,m_k$ are odd numbers.

Since the scalar curvature r of M is given by

$$r = (n^2 + 2n - 3p) - \sum_X \text{Tr} A_X^2,$$

we have

Theorem 11.8. Under the same assumption as that of Theorem 11.7, if $r \geq (n+2)(n-q)$, then we have the same conclusion as that of Theorem 11.7.

From Theorem 11.5 and Theorem 11.6 we have the following theorems, respectively.

Theorem 11.9. Let M be an n-dimensional compact orientable generic submanifold of CP^m with flat normal connection. If the mean curvature vector of M is parallel and if

$$\int_M [\sum_{x,y} (\mathrm{Tr}A_x A_y)^2 - n\sum_x \mathrm{Tr}A_x^2 + \sum_x (\mathrm{Tr}A_x)^2$$

$$- \sum_{x,y} (\mathrm{Tr}A_x)(\mathrm{Tr}A_y^2 A_x) + (n-1)q]*1 \leq 0,$$

then M is

$$\pi(S^{m_1}(r_1) \times \cdots \times S^{m_k}(r_k)), \quad \sum_{i=1}^k m_i = n+1, \quad \sum_{i=1}^k r_i^2 = 1,$$

where $2m-n = k-1$ and $m_1, \ldots, m_k$ are odd numbers.

Theorem 11.10. Let M be an n-dimensional compact orientable minimal generic submanifold of CP^m with flat normal connection. If

$$\int_M [(n-1)q - \sum_x \mathrm{Tr}A_x^2]*1 \geq 0,$$

then M is

$$\pi(S^{m_1}(r_1) \times \cdots \times S^{m_k}(r_k)), \quad r_i = (m_i/(n+1))^{1/2} \quad (i=1,\ldots,k),$$

where $\sum_{i=1}^k m_i = n+1$ and $m_1, \ldots, m_k$ are odd numbers.

In the following, we assume that M is an n-dimensional CR submanifold of CP^m with flat normal connection. Then the Ricci equation (1.12) gives

(11.11) $$g([A_{fU}, A_U]PX, X) = 2g(PX, PX)g(fU, fU)$$

for any vector field X tangent to M and any vector field U normal to M. Thus we have

$$(11.12) \qquad \mathrm{Tr} A_{fU} A_U P - \mathrm{Tr} A_U A_{fU} P = 2(n-q) g(fU, fU).$$

If $PA_V = A_V P$ for any vector field V normal to M, then we have $\mathrm{Tr} A_{fU} A_U P = \mathrm{Tr} A_U A_{fU} P$, and hence (11.12) implies that n = q, that is, P = 0 and M is an anti-invariant submanifold of CP^m, or f = 0, that is, M is a generic submanifold of CP^m. Therefore, from Theorems 10.1 and 10.2, we have (Yano-Kon [71])

Theorem 11.11. Let M be an n-dimensional complete CR submanifold of CP^m with flat normal connection and parallel mean curvature vector. If $PA_V = A_V P$ for any vector field V normal to M, then M is

$$\pi(S^1(r_1) \times \cdots \times S^1(r_{n+1})), \qquad \sum_{i=1}^{n+1} r_i^2 = 1$$

in CP^n in CP^m, or M is

$$\pi(S^{m_1}(r_1) \times \cdots \times S^{m_k}(r_k)), \qquad \sum_{i=1}^{k} m_i = n+1, \quad \sum_{i=1}^{k} r_i^2 = 1,$$

where $m_1, \ldots, m_k$ are odd numbers and q = k-1, 2m = n+q.

§12. CR submanifolds of C^m

Let M be an n-dimensional CR submanifold of C^m with flat normal connection and with parallel f-structure f in the normal bundle of M. Then the Ricci equation (1.12) implies

$$(12.1) \qquad A_V A_U = A_U A_V$$

for any vector fields U and V normal to M. Since f is parallel, we have, from (1.7),

$$(12.2) \qquad 0 = g((\nabla_X f)fV, FY) = g(A_{f_V}X, PY) - g(A_{fV}X, Y).$$

From (12.1) and (12.2) we have

$$TrA_{fV}^2 = TrA_{f^2V}PA_{fV} = -TrA_{fV}PA_{f^2V} = -TrA_{f^2V}A_{fV}P$$

$$= -TrA_{fV}A_{f^2V}P = -TrA_{f^2V}PA_{fV} = -TrA_{fV}^2,$$

from which $TrA_{fV}^2 = 0$ and hence

$$(12.3) \qquad\qquad A_{fV} = 0$$

for any vector field V normal to M.

Moreover, we suppose that $PA_V = A_V P$ for any vector field V normal to M. Then, by a method quite similar to that used in the proof of Lemma 10.2, we have

$$(12.4) \quad g((\nabla_{PY}A)_U PX, tV) - \sum_i g(A_U tV, e_i)g(A_{Fe_i}X, PY) + g(PA_U X, A_V Y) = 0.$$

From the Codazzi equation (1.11) and (12.4) we find

$$g(PA_U X, A_V Y) = \sum_i g(A_U tV, e_i)g(A_{Fe_i}X, PY),$$

from which

$$g(A_U X, A_V Y) + g(A_U X, A_{FY} tV)$$

$$= - \sum_i g(A_U tV, e_i) g(A_{Fe_i} X, Y) + g(A_U tV, A_{FY} X).$$

Since $A_U A_{FY} = A_{FY} A_U$, this equation becomes

(12.5) $$g(A_U X, A_V Y) = - \sum_i g(A_U tV, e_i) g(A_{Fe_i} X, Y).$$

Therefore, from (12.3) and (12.5), the square of the length of the second fundamental form of M is given by

(12.6) $$\sum_x \mathrm{Tr} A_x^2 = \sum_{x,y} g(A_x te_x, te_y) \mathrm{Tr} A_y.$$

Since f is parallel, we can take an orthonormal frame $\{e_x\}$ of $FD^\perp$ such that $De_x = 0$ for each x. Now, suppose that the mean curvature vector of M is parallel. Then we have

(12.7) $$\nabla_X (\sum_x \mathrm{Tr} A_x^2) = \sum_{x,y} g((\nabla_X A)_x te_x, te_y) \mathrm{Tr} A_y,$$

where we have used the fact that $\nabla_X te_x = -PA_x X$ and $PA_V = A_V P$. Using the Codazzi equation (1.11), we have, from (12.7)

(12.8) $$\nabla_X (\sum_x \mathrm{Tr} A_x^2) = \sum_{x,y} g((\nabla_{te_x} A)_y te_x, X) \mathrm{Tr} A_y.$$

Since the mean curvature vector of M is parallel, we see that $\sum_x (\nabla_{te_x} A)_y te_x = 0$ (see the proof of Lemma 10.4), and hence $\sum_x \mathrm{Tr} A_x^2$ is a constant.

We next compute the Laplacian of the second fundamental form.

From (II.4.9) we obtain

$$(12.9) \qquad g(\nabla^2 A, A) = \sum_{x,y} [(\mathrm{Tr} A_x)(\mathrm{Tr} A_y^2 A_x) - (\mathrm{Tr} A_x A_y)^2$$

$$+ 2\mathrm{Tr}(A_x A_y)^2 - 2\mathrm{Tr} A_x^2 A_y^2]$$

$$= \sum_{x,y} [(\mathrm{Tr} A_x)(\mathrm{Tr} A_y^2 A_x) - (\mathrm{Tr} A_x A_y)^2].$$

On the other hand, from (12.5), the right hand side of (12.9) vanishes. Consequently, we obtain $g(\nabla^2 A, A) = 0$. Since $g(A,A)$ is constant, we obtain $g(\nabla A, \nabla A) = 0$ and hence the second fundamental form of M is parallel. Therefore, we have

Lemma 12.1. Let M be a CR submanifold of C^m with flat normal connection and with parallel f-structure f. If the mean curvature vector of M is parallel and if $PA_V = A_V P$ for any vector field V normal to M, then the second fundamental form of M is parallel.

From Theorem II.6.1 and Lemma 12.1 we see that the sectional curvature of M is non-negative. Thus Theorem II.5.1 implies the following

Theorem 12.1. Let M be an n-dimensional complete CR submanifold of C^m with flat normal connection and with parallel f-structure f. If the mean curvature vector of M is parallel and if $PA_V = A_V P$ for any vector field V normal to M, then M is a sphere $S^n(r)$, a plane R^n, a pythagorean product of the form

$$S^{p_1}(r_1) \times \cdots \times S^{p_N}(r_N), \quad p_1, \ldots, p_N \geq 1, \ \Sigma p_i = n, \ 1 < N \leq m-n,$$

or

$$S^{p_1}(r_1) \times \cdots \times S^{p_N}(r_N) \times R^p, \quad p_1, \ldots, p_N, p \geq 1, \ \Sigma p_i + p = n, \ 1 < N \leq m-n.$$

Theorem 12.2 (Ki-Pak [26]). Let M be a complete n-dimensional generic submanifold of C^m with flat normal connection and with parallel mean curvature vector. If $PA_V = A_V P$ for any vector field V normal to M, then we have the same conclusion as that of Theorem 12.1.

Chapter V

SUBMANIFOLDS AND RIEMANNIAN FIBRE BUNDLES

§1. Curvature tensors

Let $\bar{N}$ be a $(2m+1)$-dimensional Sasakian manifold with structure tensors (ϕ, ξ, η, G) such that there is a fibering $\bar{\pi} : \bar{N} \longrightarrow \bar{M}$, where $\bar{M}$ is a real $2m$-dimensional Kaehlerian manifold. In the following we use the same notations as those used in §7 of Chapter IV.

We denote by $\bar{R}'$ and $\bar{R}$ the curvature tensors of $\bar{N}$ and $\bar{M}$ respectively. Then we have

Lemma 1.1. The curvature tensors $\bar{R}'$ and $\bar{R}$ satisfy

$$(1.1) \quad (\bar{R}(X,Y)Z)^* = \bar{R}'(X^*,Y^*)Z^* + G(Z^*,\phi Y^*)\phi X^*$$

$$- G(Z^*,\phi X^*)\phi Y^* - 2G(Y^*,\phi X^*)\phi Z^*$$

for any vector fields X, Y and Z on $\bar{M}$.

Proof. From (IV.7.2) we have

$$(\bar{\nabla}_X \bar{\nabla}_Y Z)^* = \bar{\nabla}'_{X^*}(\bar{\nabla}_Y Z)^* + G((\bar{\nabla}_Y Z)^*, \phi X^*)\xi$$

$$= \bar{\nabla}'_{X^*}\bar{\nabla}'_{Y^*}Z^* + G(\bar{\nabla}'_{X^*}Z^*, \phi Y^*)\xi + G(\bar{\nabla}'_{Y^*}Z^*, \phi X^*)\xi$$

$$+ G(Z^*, \phi\bar{\nabla}'_{X^*}Y^*)\xi + G(Z^*, \phi Y^*)\phi X^*.$$

Similarly, we have

$$(\bar{\nabla}_Y\bar{\nabla}_X Z)^* = \bar{\nabla}'_{Y*}\bar{\nabla}'_{X*}Z^* + G(\bar{\nabla}'_{Y*}Z^*,\phi X^*)\xi + G(\bar{\nabla}'_{X*}Z^*,\phi Y^*)\xi$$

$$+ G(Z^*,\phi\bar{\nabla}'_{Y*}X^*)\xi + G(Z^*,\phi X^*)\phi Y^*.$$

Moreover, we have

$$(\bar{\nabla}_{[X,Y]}Z)^* = \bar{\nabla}'_{[X*,Y*]}Z^* + G(Z^*,\phi[X^*,Y^*])\xi + 2G(Y^*,\phi X^*)\phi Z^*.$$

From these equations we have (1.1).

Let $\bar{S}'$ and $\bar{S}$ be the Ricci tensors of $\bar{N}$ and $\bar{M}$ respectively. Then, from (1.1) we have

(1.2) $$\bar{S}(X,Y) = \bar{S}'(X^*,Y^*) + 2G(X^*,Y^*),$$

from which

(1.3) $$\bar{r} = \bar{r}' + 2m,$$

where $\bar{r}'$ and $\bar{r}$ denote the scalar curvatures of $\bar{N}$ and $\bar{M}$ respectively. Moreover, the sectional curvatures of $\bar{N}$ and $\bar{M}$ determined by orthonormal vectors X and Y on $\bar{M}$ satisfy

(1.4) $$\bar{K}(X,Y) = \bar{K}'(X^*,Y^*) + 3G(X^*,\phi Y^*),$$

from which

(1.5) $$\bar{K}(X,JX) = \bar{K}'(X^*,\phi X^*) + 3.$$

Therefore we have

Proposition 1.1. $\bar{N}$ is of constant ϕ-sectional curvature c if and only if $\bar{M}$ is of constant holomorphic sectional curvature (c+3).

Let N be an (n+1)-dimensional submanifold tangent to ξ of $\bar{N}$ and M be an n-dimensuonal submanifold of $\bar{M}$ such that the diagram

$$
\begin{array}{ccc}
N & \xrightarrow{\;\;\;i'\;\;\;} & \bar{N} \\
\pi \downarrow & & \downarrow \bar{\pi} \\
M & \xrightarrow{\;\;\;i\;\;\;} & \bar{M}
\end{array}
$$

(1.6)

commutes (see §7 of Chapter IV).

Let R' and R be the Riemannian curvature tensors of N and M respectively. Then, from (II.2.3) and (1.1) we have

$$(R(X,Y)Z)^* - (A_{B(Y,Z)}X)^* + (A_{B(X,Z)}Y)^* + ((\nabla_X B)(Y,Z))^*$$

$$- ((\nabla_Y B)(X,Z))^* = R'(X^*,Y^*)Z^* - H_{\alpha(Y^*,Z^*)}X^* + H_{\alpha(X^*,Z^*)}Y^*$$

$$+ (\nabla_{X^*}\alpha)(Y^*,Z^*) - (\nabla_{Y^*}\alpha)(X^*,Z^*) + G(Z^*,\phi Y^*)\phi X^* - G(Z^*,\phi X^*)\phi Y^*$$

$$- 2G(Y^*,\phi X^*)\phi Z^*$$

for any vector fields X, Y and Z tangent to M. Taking the tangential part of this equation and using (IV.7.6), we obtain

Lemma 1.2. The Riemannian curvature tensors R' and R satisfy

$$(1.7) \quad (R(X,Y)Z)^* = R'(X^*,Y^*)Z^* + G(H_{F'Y^*}X^*,Z^*)\xi - G(H_{F'X^*}Y^*,Z^*)\xi$$

$$+ G(P'Y^*,Z^*)P'X^* - G(P'X^*,Z^*)P'Y^* - 2G(P'X^*,Y^*)P'Z^*$$

for any vector fields X, Y and Z tangent to M.

From Lemma 1.2 we have

Proposition 1.2. If N is of constant curvature c, then we have

$$(1.8) \quad R(X,Y)Z = c[g(Y,Z)X - g(X,Z)Y]$$

$$+ g(PY,Z)PX - g(PX,Z)PY - 2g(PX,Y)PZ.$$

Let S' and S be the Ricci tensors of N and M respectively. Then, from (1.7) we have

$$(1.9) \qquad S(X,Y) = S'(X^*,Y^*) + 2g(PX,PY).$$

Let $\{e_i\}$ be an orthonormal frame of M. Because of (1.9), the scalar curvature r' of N and the scalar curvature r of M satisfy

$$(1.10) \qquad r = r' + \sum_i g(Pe_i, Pe_i).$$

Since $\sum_i g(Pe_i, Pe_i) = n - \sum_i g(Fe_i, Fe_i)$, we have, from (1.1),

$$(1.11) \qquad r = r' + n - \sum_i g(Fe_i, Fe_i).$$

<u>Proposition 1.3.</u> (1) N and M are anti-invariant submanifolds if and only if $r = r'$.

(2) N and M are invariant submanifolds if and only if $r = r' + n$.

    <u>Proof.</u> From (1.10) we see that $r = r'$ if and only if $Pe_i = 0$ for all i, which means that $P = 0$. Thus we have (1). Similarly, $r = r' + n$ if and only if $F = 0$, from which we have (2).

§2. Mean curvature vectors

    We consider the situation that the diagram (1.6) shows. First of all, we prove

<u>Lemma 2.1.</u> Let μ' and μ be the mean curvature vectors of N and M respectively. Then we have

(2.1) $$\mu^* = \frac{n+1}{n}\,\mu'.$$

    <u>Proof.</u> We take an orthonormal frame $\{e_i\}$ for $T_x(M)$. Then $\{e_i^*, \xi\}$ is an orthonormal frame for $T_y(N)$ ($\pi(y) = x$). Therefore, from (III.1.8) and (IV.7.5) we have

$$\mu^* = \frac{1}{n}(\text{Tr}B)^* = \frac{1}{n}[\sum_i \alpha(e_i^*, e_i^*) + \alpha(\xi, \xi)]$$

$$= \frac{1}{n}\text{Tr}\alpha = \frac{n+1}{n}\,\mu'.$$

Thus we have (2.1).

    From (2.1) we have

<u>Proposition 2.1.</u> N is minimal if and only if M is minimal.

From (IV.7.7) and (2.1) we obtain

$$(2.2) \qquad D'_{X*}\mu' = \frac{n}{n+1}D'_{X*}\mu^* = \frac{n}{n+1}(D_X\mu)^*.$$

Therefore we have

Proposition 2.2. If the mean curvature vector μ' of N is parallel, then the mean curvature vector μ of M is also parallel.

Lemma 2.2. Let N be a submanifold tangent to ξ of a Sasakian manifold $\tilde{N}$. Then we have

$$(2.3) \qquad D'_\xi\mu' = f'\mu'.$$

Proof. Since $\tilde{N}$ is a Sasakian manifold, the second fundamental form α of N satisfies $(\nabla_\xi\alpha)(X,Y) = (\nabla_X\alpha)(\xi,Y)$. Let $\{e_i\}$ be an orthonormal frame of N. Then we have, from (III.1.10),

$$
\begin{aligned}
(n+1)G(D'_\xi\mu',V) &= \sum_i G((\nabla_\xi\alpha)(e_i,e_i),V) = \sum_i G((\nabla_{e_i}\alpha)(\xi,e_i),V) \\
&= \sum_i [G(D'_{e_i}\alpha(\xi,e_i),V) - G(\alpha(\nabla'_{e_i}\xi,e_i),V)] \\
&= \sum_i [G(D'_{e_i}(F'e_i),V) - G(\alpha(P'e_i,e_i),V)] \\
&= \sum_i G((\nabla_{e_i}F')e_i,V) \\
&= \sum_i [-G(\alpha(e_i,P'e_i),V) + f'\alpha(e_i,e_i)] \\
&= (n+1)f'\mu',
\end{aligned}
$$

where V is a vector field normal to N. In the above we have denoted by the same e_i local, orthonormal vector fields on N which extend e_i

of the orthonormal frame $\{e_i\}$ of N, and which are covariant constant with respect to ∇' at $x \in N$. Thus we have (2.3).

If N is a generic submanifold of $\bar{N}$, then $f' = 0$ identically. Thus, from (2.2) and (2.3) we have the following

Proposition 2.3. Let M be a generic submanifold of $\bar{M}$ and N be a generic submanifold of $\bar{N}$. Then the mean curvature vector μ of M is parallel if and only if the mean curvature vector μ' of N is parallel.

From (IV.7.5) we have

Proposition 2.4. If N is totally geodesic in $\bar{N}$, then M is totally geodesic in $\bar{M}$.

Moreover, (III.1.18) and (IV.7.5) imply

Proposition 2.5. Let N be an invariant submanifold of $\bar{N}$ and M be an invariant submanifold of $\bar{M}$. Then N is totally geodesic if and only if M is totally geodesic.

Proposition 2.6. N is totally contact umbilical if and only if M is totally umbilical.

Proof. If M is totally umbilical in $\bar{M}$, then $B(X,Y) = g(X,Y)\mu$ for any vector fields X, Y on M. Thus (IV.7.5) implies that $\alpha(X^*,Y^*) = G(X^*,Y^*)\mu^*$. We have seen that $\alpha(\xi,\xi) = 0$. On the other hand, the horizontal space of π is given by $\{\phi^2 X : X \in T_x(N)\}$. Consequently, if M is totally umbilical, we have

$$\alpha(X,Y) = \mu^*[G(X,Y) - \eta(X)\eta(Y)] + \eta(X)\alpha(Y,\xi) + \eta(Y)\alpha(X,\xi)$$

for any vector fields X and Y on N. Therefore N is totally contact umbilical.

Conversely, if N is totally contact umbilical, we have $\alpha(\phi^2X, \phi^2Y)$ = $G(\phi^2X, \phi^2Y)\beta$, where β is a normal vector to N. From this and (IV.7.5) we see that M is totally umbilical.

Similarly, we have

Proposition 2.7. N is totally contact geodesic if and only if M is totally geodesic.

Example 2.1. Let S^{2m+1} be a unit sphere of dimension $2m+1$ with standard Sasakian structure and let CP^m be a complex projective space of real dimension $2m$ with constant holomorphic sectional curvature 4. A real projective space RP^n of dimension n (n < m) of constant curvature 1 is imbedded in CP^n in CP^m as an anti-invariant and totally geodesic submanifold. We now consider the following commutative diagram:

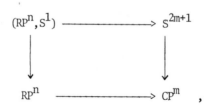

where (RP^n, S^1) denotes a circle bundle over RP^n. Then (RP^n, S^1) is a totally contact geodesic anti-invariant submanifold of S^{2n+1} in S^{2m+1}.

Let M^d be a d-dimensional totally umbilical submanifold of RP^n. Then the circle bundle (M^d, S^1) over M^d is a totally contact umbilical submanifold of S^{2m+1}.

§3. Lengths of the second fundamental forms

Let N and M be submanifolds of $\bar{N}$ and $\bar{M}$ respectively satisfying (1.6). Then, from (IV.7.20) we have

(3.1) $$G(H,H) = g(A,A) + 2n - 2\sum_i g(Pe_i, Pe_i).$$

From (IV.7.20) and (3.1) we have

Proposition 3.1. (1) N and M are invariant submanifolds if and only if $G(H,H) = g(A,A)$.

(2) N and M are anti-invariant submanifolds if and only if $G(H,H) = g(A,A) + 2n$.

We now prove the following theorems:

Theorem 3.1. Let M be an n-dimensional compact orientable minimal submanifold of CP^m. If the scalar curvature r of M satisfies the inequality

$$r \geq n(n+2) - \frac{n+1}{2-1/p} \qquad (p = 2m-n),$$

then M is a totally geodesic complex projective space $CP^{n/2}$.

Proof. Since M is minimal, N is also minimal. Thus the scalar curvature r' of N is given by

(3.2) $$r' = n(n+1) - G(H,H).$$

From (1.11) and (3.2) we have

(3.3) $G(H,H) = n(n+2) - r - \sum_i g(Fe_i, Fe_i) \leq n(n+2) - r.$

From (3.3) and the assumption on r we obtain

(3.4) $G(H,H) \leq \dfrac{n+1}{2-1/p}$.

Therefore Theorem II.6.4 implies that H = 0 or G(H,H) = (n+1)/(2-1/p). If H = 0, then N is totally geodesic in S^{2m+1} and hence M is a totally geodesic complex projective space $CP^{n/2}$. If G(H,H) = (n+1)/(2-1/p), then F = 0 and N is an invariant submanifold of S^{2m+1}. Moreover, from Theorem II.6.5, N is a Veronese surface in S^4 or a Clifford minimal hypersurface in S^{n+2}. But the ambient manifold S^{2m+1} is odd dimensional and any hypersurface of S^{n+2} is not invariant. From these considerations we have our assertion.

<u>Theorem 3.2.</u> Let M be an n-dimensional compact orientable minimal submanifold of CP^m. If

$$g(A,A) \leq \frac{n+3-4p}{2-1/p} \qquad (p = 2m-n),$$

then M is a totally geodesic complex projective space $CP^{n/2}$ or a real hypersurface

$$\pi(S^k((k/(n+1))^{1/2}) \times S^{n+1-k}(((n+1-k)/(n+1))^{1/2})),$$

where k is an odd number and p = 1.

Proof. From (IV.7.20) we have

$$G(H,H) = g(A,A) + 2\sum_i g(Fe_i, Fe_i) \leq g(A,A) + 2p.$$

From this and the assumption we see that $G(H,H) \leq (n+1)/(2-1/p)$. Therefore, by Theorem II.6.4, we see that N is totally geodesic or $G(H,H) = (n+1)/(2-1/p)$. If N is totally geodesic, then M is $CP^{n/2}$. If $G(H,H) = (n+1)/(2-1/p)$, then we have $\sum_i g(Fe_i, Fe_i) = p$, which implies

$$\sum_i g(Fe_i, Fe_i) = \sum_{i,a} g(Fe_i, v_a) g(v_a, Fe_i)$$

$$= \sum_{i,a} g(e_i, tv_a) g(tv_a, e_i)$$

$$= \sum_a g(tv_a, tv_a) = p,$$

where $\{v_a\}$ is an orthonormal frame for $T_x(M)$. On the other hand, we have

$$\sum_a g(tv_a, tv_a) + \sum_a g(fv_a, fv_a) = p.$$

Thus we have $fv_a = 0$ for all a, which means that M is a generic submanifold of CP^m. From this and Theorem II.6.5 we have our assertion.

Chapter VI

HYPERSURFACES

§1. Real hypersurfaces of complex space forms

Let M be a real $(2n-1)$-dimensional hypersurfce of a Kaehlerian manifold $\bar{M}$ of complex dimension n (real dimension 2n). Then M is obviously a generic submanifold of $\bar{M}$. We denote by C a unit normal of M in $\bar{M}$ and put

$$(1.1) \qquad\qquad JC = -U.$$

Then U is a unit vector field on M. For any vector field X tangent to M we have

$$(1.2) \qquad\qquad FX = u(X)C,$$

where u is a 1-form defined to be $u(X) = g(X,U)$. Thus (IV.1.1) can also be written as

$$(1.3) \qquad\qquad JX = PX + u(X)C.$$

Then we have

$$(1.4) \qquad P^2X = -X + u(X)U, \qquad PU = 0, \qquad u(PX) = 0.$$

Thus (P,u) defines an almost contact structure on M (see Tashiro [50]). Moreover we have

$$(1.5) \qquad g(PX,PY) = g(X,Y) - u(X)u(Y).$$

We denote by A the second fundamental form of M in place of A_C. Then the Gauss and Weingarten formulas are respectively given by

$$(1.6) \qquad \bar{\nabla}_X Y = \nabla_X Y + g(AX,Y)C,$$

$$(1.7) \qquad \bar{\nabla}_X C = -AX.$$

Moreover, (IV.1.6) and (IV.1.8) can be respectively written as

$$(1.8) \qquad (\nabla_X P)Y = u(Y)AX - g(AX,Y)U$$

and

$$(1.9) \qquad \nabla_X U = PAX.$$

Let $\bar{M}$ be a complex space form of constant holomorphic sectional curvature 4c and denote it by $\bar{M}^n(c)$. Then we have

$$(1.10) \qquad R(X,Y)Z = c[g(Y,Z)X - g(X,Z)Y + g(PY,Z)PX - g(PX,Z)PY$$
$$+ 2g(X,PY)PZ] + g(AY,Z)AX - g(AX,Z)AY,$$

$$(1.11) \qquad (\nabla_X A)Y - (\nabla_Y A)X = c[u(X)PY - u(Y)PX + 2g(X,PY)U].$$

In particular, we have

$$(1.12) \qquad g((\nabla_X A)U, U) = g((\nabla_U A)X, U).$$

From (1.10) we see that the Ricci tensor S of M is given by

$$(1.13) \qquad S(X,Y) = (2n+1)cg(X,Y) - 3cu(X)u(Y)$$

$$+ Hg(AX,Y) - g(AX,AY),$$

where we have put $H = \text{Tr}A$. Therefore the scalar curvature r of M is given by

$$(1.14) \qquad r = 4(n^2-1)c + H^2 - \text{Tr}A^2.$$

Now, we state some fundamental lemmas for later use. In the following we suppose that $\dim M = 2n-1 \geq 3$, i.e., $n \geq 2$. First of all, from (1.11) we have (cf. [51])

Lemma 1.1. Let M be a real hypersurface of a complex space form $\tilde{M}^n(c)$. If $c \neq 0$, then M is not totally umbilical.

The second fundamental form A of M can be considered as a symmetric $(2n-1, 2n-1)$-matrix. The rank of A at a point x of M is called the type number at x and is denoted by $t(x)$.

Now we assume that the vector U is an eigenvector of A, that is, $AU = \alpha U$. Then (1.9) implies that

$$(\nabla_X A)U = (X\alpha)U + \alpha PAX - APAX,$$

from which it follows that

(1.15) $\qquad g((\nabla_X A)Y,U) = (X\alpha)u(Y) + \alpha g(Y,PAX) - g(Y,APAX).$

By Codazzi equation (1.11) and (1.15) we have

(1.16) $\qquad 2cg(X,PY) = (X\alpha)u(Y) - (Y\alpha)u(X) + g((PA+AP)X,Y)$

$$- 2g(APAX,Y).$$

Putting $X = U$ or $Y = U$ in (1.16), we see that $X\alpha = (U\alpha)u(X)$ and $Y\alpha = (U\alpha)u(Y)$, and hence (1.16) reduces to

(1.17) $\qquad 2cg(X,PY) = \alpha g((PA+AP)X,Y) - 2g(APAX,Y).$

Lemma 1.2. Let M be a real hypersurface of a complex space form $\bar{M}^n(c)$. If $PA + AP = 0$, then $c \leq 0$. Moreover, if $c = 0$, then $t(x) \leq 1$ at all x.

$\qquad$ Proof. Since $PA + AP = 0$, we have $PAU = 0$ and hence $AU = u(AU)U$. This means that the vector U is an eigenvector of A. We now put $\alpha = u(AU)$. Then (1.17) implies that

$$cg(X,PY) = -g(PAX,AY) = g(APX,AY).$$

From this we see that $cg(PX,PX) = -g(APX,APX) \leq 0$. Since the rank of P is $2n-2$ and $n \geq 2$, we must have $c \leq 0$. If $c = 0$, we have $g(APX,APX) = 0$ and hence $APX = -PAX = 0$. Therefore we obtain $AX = \alpha u(X)U$. Thus we have $t(x) \leq 1$ at each point x of M.

Lemma 1.3. Let M be a real hypersurface of a complex space form $\bar{M}^n(c)$ $(c > 0)$. If U is an eigenvector of A, then $\alpha = u(AU)$ is constant.

Proof. Since we have $X\alpha = (U\alpha)u(X)$, we see that $\nabla_X \text{grad}\alpha = (X\beta)U + \beta PAX$, where we have put $\beta = U\alpha$. From this we have

(1.18) $(Y\beta)u(X) - (X\beta)u(Y) = \beta g(PAX,Y) - \beta g(PAY,X)$,

because of the fact that $g(\nabla_X \text{grad}\alpha, Y) = g(\nabla_Y \text{grad}\alpha, X)$. Putting $X = U$ or $Y = U$ in (1.18), we obtain $X\beta = (U\beta)u(X)$ and $Y\beta = (U\beta)u(Y)$. Therefore we have $\beta g((PA+AP)X,Y) = 0$. From this and Lemma 1.2, we have $\beta = 0$ and hence α is constant.

Lemma 1.4. Let M be a real hypersurface of a complex space form $\bar{M}^n(c)$ $(c \neq 0)$. Then $t(x) > 1$ at some point x of M.

Proof. Let us assume that $t(x) \leq 1$ at any point x of M. We can then choose an orthonormal frame field of M for which the second fundamental form of M is diagonal, that is, $Ae_i = 0$, $i = 1,\ldots,2n-2$ and $Ae_{2n-1} = \lambda e_{2n-1}$. Let $M' = \{x \in M : \lambda_x \neq 0\}$. Then M' is an open set of M. In the following our computation is done on M'. First we have

$$g((\nabla_{e_i}A)e_j, e_k) = 0 \quad \text{for } i,j,k = 1,\ldots,2n-2.$$

From this and (1.11) we have

$$u(e_i)g(Pe_j,e_k) - u(e_j)g(Pe_i,e_k) + 2u(e_k)g(e_i,Pe_j) = 0.$$

Putting $j = k$ in this equation, we see that

$$u(e_j)g(e_i,Pe_j) = 0,$$

from which we obtain

$$\sum_{i=1}^{2n-2} u(e_j)g(e_i,Pe_j)g(e_i,Pe_{2n-1})$$

$$= u(e_j)g(Pe_j,Pe_{2n-1}) = -u(e_j)u(e_j)u(e_{2n-1}) = 0.$$

Consequently we see that $u(e_j) = 0$ for $j = 1,\ldots,2n-2$ or $u(e_{2n-1}) = 0$. If $u(e_j) = 0$ for $j = 1,\ldots,2n-2$, then $u(e_{2n-1}) = 1$ and hence $e_{2n-1} = U$. Since we have $g((\nabla_{e_i} A)e_j,U) = 0$ for $i,j = 1,\ldots,2n-2$, (1.11) implies $g(e_i,Pe_j) = 0$. Thus we have

$$\sum_{i,j=1}^{2n-2} g(e_i,Pe_j)g(e_i,Pe_j) = 2n - 2 = 0,$$

which is a contradiction. Next we suppose that $u(e_{2n-1}) = 0$. Then $AU = 0$ and hence $(\nabla_X A)U + APAX = 0$. If $AX \neq 0$, we have $APX = 0$. Thus we have $(\nabla_X A)U = 0$ for any vector field X tangent to M. From this and (1.11) we obtain $g(X,PY) = 0$. This is also a contradiction. Therefore we see that M' is empty, that is, M is totally geodesic. But this contradicts the fact that M is not totally umbilical. Therefore we must have $t(x) > 1$ at some point x of M.

Lemma 1.5. Let M be a real hypersurface of a complex space form $\bar{M}^n(c)$ $(c \neq 0)$. If $PA = AP$, then M has at most three constant principal curvatures.

Proof. From the assumption, we see that U is an eigenvector of A. From this and (1.18) we obtain $\beta g(PAX,Y) = 0$. If $\beta \neq 0$ at some point x of M, then $PAX = 0$ and hence (1.17) implies that $cg(X,PY) = 0$. From this we get $c = 0$. This is a contradiction. Thus we have $\beta = 0$ and hence α is constant. On the other hand, from (1.17) it follows that

$$(1.19) \qquad PA^2X - \alpha PAX - cPX = 0.$$

Using (1.4) and (1.19), we obtain

(1.20) $\qquad A^2X - \alpha AX - cX + cu(X)U = 0.$

Here, we may assume that $Ae_i = \lambda_i e_i$, $i = 1,\ldots,2n-2$ and $Ae_{2n-1} = \alpha e_{2n-1}$, $e_{2n-1} = U$. Then (1.20) implies that at most two λ_i are distinct, which will be denoted by λ and μ. Then $\lambda + \mu = \alpha$ and $\lambda\mu = -c$. Therefore λ and μ are constant. This proves our assertion.

If M is totally η-umbilical, that is, if the second fundamental form A of M is of the form $AX = aX + bu(X)U$ for some scalar functions a and b, then we have $PA = AP$. Therefore Lemma 1.5 implies

Lemma 1.6. Let M be a totally η-umbilical real hypersurface of a complex space form $\bar{M}^n(c)$ ($c \neq 0$). Then M has two constant principal curvatures.

Proof. From the assumption, we see that M has two principal curvatures. From Lemma 1.5 these principal curvatures are constant.

Lemma 1.7. Let M be a real hypersurface of a complex space form $\bar{M}^n(c)$. If $PA + AP = kP$ for some constant $k \neq 0$, then M has at most three constant principal curvatures λ, μ and α. If $\lambda \neq \mu$, then the multiplicities of λ and μ are equal.

Proof. From the assumption the vector U is an eigenvector of A. Therefore (1.17) implies

(1.19) $\qquad 2cg(X,PY) = \alpha kg(PX,Y) - 2g(APAX,Y).$

On the other hand, in the proof of Lemma 1.3 we have already shown that $\beta g((PA+AP)X,Y) = 0$, where $\beta = U\alpha$. Thus $\beta kg(PX,Y) = 0$. Since $k \neq 0$, we obtain $\beta = 0$ and hence α is constant. From the assumption and (1.21) we also have

$$2PA^2X - 2kPAX + \alpha kPX + 2cPX = 0,$$

which implies that

$$(1.22) \quad 2A^2X - 2kAX + (\alpha k+2c)X - 2(\alpha^2+c)u(X)U + \alpha ku(X)U = 0.$$

We denote by λ_i $(i = 1,\ldots,2n-2),\alpha$ the eigenvalues of A. Then (1.22) implies that these eigenvalues satisfy the following quadratic equation

$$2t^2 - 2kt + (\alpha k+2c) = 0.$$

Therefore at most two λ_i are distinct, and hence M has at most three principal curvatures λ, μ and α. Since α, k and c are constant, λ and μ are also constant. If $AX = \lambda X$, then $APX = (k-\lambda)PX = \mu PX$. Therefore the multiplicities of λ and μ are equal to n-1. If $\lambda = \mu$, then $AP = PA$, and therefore $2AP = 2PA = kP$, which implies that $-2AX + 2\alpha u(X)U = -kX + ku(X)U$, that is, we have $AX = \frac{1}{2}kX + \frac{1}{2}(k-2\alpha)u(X)U$. Consequently, M is totally η-umbilical.

Example 1.1. We give examples of real hypersurfaces in a complex projective space CP^n with constant holomorphic sectional curvature 4 (see Takagi [46], [47]).

Let C^{n+1} be the space of (n+1)-tuples of complex numbers $(z_1,\ldots,z_{n+1})$. Put

$$S^{2n+1} = \{(z_1,\ldots,z_{n+1}) \in C^{n+1} : \sum_{j=1}^{n+1}|z_j|^2 = 1\}.$$

For a positive number r we denote by $M_0'(2n,r)$ a hypersurface of S^{2n+1} defined by

(1.23)
$$\sum_{j=1}^{n}|z_j|^2 = r|z_{n+1}|^2, \qquad \sum_{j=1}^{n+1}|z_j|^2 = 1.$$

For an integer m $(2 \leq m \leq n-1)$ and a positive number s, a hypersurface $M'(2n,m,s)$ of S^{2n+1} is defined by

(1.24)
$$\sum_{j=1}^{m}|z_j|^2 = s\sum_{j=m+1}^{n+1}|z_j|^2, \qquad \sum_{j=1}^{n+1}|z_j|^2 = 1.$$

For a number t $(0 < t < 1)$ we denote by $M'(2n,t)$ a hypersurface of S^{2n+1} defined by

(1.25)
$$|\sum_{j=1}^{n+1}z_j^2|^2 = t, \qquad \sum_{j=1}^{n+1}|z_j|^2 = 1.$$

Let π be the natural projection of S^{2n+1} onto CP^n. Then $M_0(2n-1,r) = \pi(M_0'(2n,r))$ is a connected compact real hypersurface of CP^n with two constant principal curvatures. We call $M_0(2n-1,r)$ a geodesic hypersphere of CP^n. Moreover, $M(2n-1,m,s) = \pi(M'(2n,m,s))$ $(n \geq 3)$ and $M(2n-1,t) = \pi(M'(2n,t))$ $(n \geq 2)$ are connected compact real hypersurfaces in CP^n with three constant principal curvatures.

Theorem 1.1 (Takagi [46]). If M is a connected complete real hypersurface in CP^n $(n \geq 2)$ with two constant principal curvatures, then M is a geodesic hypersphere.

Theorem 1.2 (Takagi [47]). If M is a connected complete real hypersurface of CP^n $(n \geq 3)$ with three constant principal curvatures, then M is congruent to some $M(2n-1,m,s)$ or $M(2n-1,t)$.

Real hypersurfaces $M_0(2n-1,r)$, $M(2n-1,m,s)$ and $M(2n-1,t)$ are said to be types A_1, A_2 and B respectively in Takagi [46]. We denote by $\xi_1,\ldots,\xi_j$ the principal curvatures of M in CP^n, and by $m(\xi_1),\ldots,$ $m(\xi_j)$ their multiplicities. Then Takagi gave the following table:

Table 1.1.

	dim M	j	ξ_i	$m(\xi_i)$
A_1	$2n - 1$ $(n \geq 2)$	2	$\xi_1 = \cot\theta$ $\xi_2 = 2\cot^2\theta$	$m(\xi_1) = 2(n-1)$ $m(\xi_2) = 1$
A_2	$2(p+q) - 3$ $(p \geq q \geq 2)$	3	$\xi_1 = \cot\theta$ $\xi_2 = -\tan\theta$ $\xi_3 = 2\cot 2\theta$	$m(\xi_1) = 2(p-1)$ $m(\xi_2) = 2(q-1)$ $m(\xi_3) = 1$
B	$2p - 3$ $(p \geq 3)$	3	$\xi_1 = \cot(\theta-\pi/4)$ $\xi_2 = -\tan(\theta-\pi/4)$ $\xi_3 = 2\cot 2\theta$	$m(\xi_1) = p-2$ $m(\xi_2) = p-2$ $m(\xi_3) = 1$

Let λ, μ and α be principal curvatures of $M(2n-1,m,s)$ or $M(2n-1,t)$ and let $T_\lambda = \{X : AX = \lambda X\}$, $T_\mu = \{X : AX = \mu X\}$. Then $PT_\lambda \subset T_\lambda$ and $PT_\mu \subset T_\mu$ on $M(2n-1,m,s)$, and $PT_\lambda \subset T_\mu$ and $PT_\mu \subset T_\lambda$ on $M(2n-1,t)$ (cf. Takagi [47]). If $PA = AP$, then $PT_\lambda \subset T_\lambda$ and $PT_\mu \subset T_\mu$. Thus by Lemma 1.5 and Theorems 1.1 and 1.2 we obtain

Theorem 1.3 (Okumura [37]). Let M be a connected complete real kypersurface in CP^n $(n \geq 3)$. If $PA = AP$, then M is congruent to some $M_0(2n-1,r)$ or $M(2n-1,m,s)$.

From Lemma 1.6 and Theorem 1.1 we have

Theorem 1.4 (Takagi [46]). If M is a connected complete totally η-umbilical real hypersurface in CP^n ($n \geq 2$), then M is a geodesic hypersphere $M_0(2n-1,r)$.

Furthermore, by Lemma 1.7 and Theorems 1.1 and 1.2 we obtain

Theorem 1.5. Let M be a connected complete real hypersurface in CP^n ($n \geq 3$). If $PA + AP = kP$ for some constant $k \neq 0$, then M is congruent to some $M_0(2n-1,r)$ or $M(2n-1,t)$.

In Theorem 1.5, if $k = 0$, then by Lemma 1.2 there is no real hypersurface in CP^n.

Let M be a real hypersurface of C^n. If $PA = AP$, then U is an eigenvector of A, that is, $AU = \alpha U$. Thus (1.17) implies that

$$\alpha g(APX,Y) = g(APAX,Y),$$

from which we have

$$\alpha g(APX,PX) = g(APX,APX).$$

We now take an orthonormal frame $\{e_i,U\}$ such that $Ae_i = \lambda_i e_i$ ($i=1,\ldots,2n-2$). Then

$$\alpha\lambda_i = \lambda_i^2 \quad (i = 1,\ldots,2n-2).$$

Therefore, if $\alpha = 0$, then $\lambda_i = 0$ for each i. If $\alpha \neq 0$, then $\lambda_i = 0$ or $\lambda_i = \alpha$. Thus we see that M is totally geodesic or totally umbilical or cylindrical. Consequently we have

Theorem 1.6. Let M be a complete real hypersurface of C^n. If PA = AP, then M is R^{2n-1} or $S^{2n-1}(r)$ or $\gamma \times R^{2n-2}$, where γ is a curve in R^2.

§2. Pseudo-Einstein real hypersurfaces

Let M be a real hypersurface of a Kaehlerian manifold $\tilde{M}$. If the Ricci tensor S of M is of the form $S(X,Y) = ag(X,Y) + bu(X)u(Y)$ for some constants a and b, then M is called a pseudo-Einstein real hypersurface of $\tilde{M}$. If b = 0, then M is an Einstein real hypersurface.

Here we first give some examples of pseudo-Einstein real hyper-surfaces of CP^n.

Example 2.1. First of all, any geodesic hypersphere $M_0(2n-1,r)$ is pseudo-Einstein. We next show that M(2n-1,m,(m-1)/(n-m)) and M(2n-1,1/(n-1)) are pseudo-Einstein. From (1.13) and Table 1.1 we see that M(2n-1,m,s) is pseudo-Einstein if and only if

(2.1) $H\cot\theta - \cot^2\theta = -H\tan\theta - \tan^2\theta$.

Since $H = p\cot\theta - (2n-2-p)\tan\theta + 2\cot2\theta$, where p denotes the multiplicity of $\cot\theta$, (2.1) implies that $\sin^2\theta = p/(2n-2)$. On the other hand, a hypersurface M'(2n,m,s) of S^{2n+1} has two principal curvatures $\cot\theta$ and $-\tan\theta$ with multiplicities p+1 and 2n-1-p respectively (cf. Takagi [47]). Thus p = m-2 and

$$M' = S^{2m-1}(\frac{n-1}{m-1}) \times S^{2(n-m)+1}(\frac{n-1}{n-m}),$$

where $(n-1)/(m-1) = \xi_1^2 + 1$ and $(n-1)/(n-m) = \xi_2^2 + 1$. From this and (1.24) we obtain s = (m-1)/(n-m). Thus M(2n-1,m,(m-1)/(n-m)) is pseudo-Einstein and the Ricci tensor S of M(2n-1,m,(m-1)/(n-m)) is of the form $S(X,Y) = ag(X,Y) + bu(X)u(Y)$ for some constants a and b. Next we determine a and b. From (1.13) a is given by $a = (2n+1) + Hcot\theta - cot^2\theta$. Since $sin^2\theta = p/(2n-2)$, $Hcot\theta - cot^2\theta = -1$ and hence $a = 2n$. Moreover, from (1.13) it follows that b is given by $b = -2 + 2Hcot2\theta - 4cot^2 2\theta$. From this we obtain $b = -2$. Thus we have $S(X,Y) = 2ng(X,Y) - 2u(X)u(Y)$.

Furthermore, from (1.13) and Table 1.1 we see that $M(2n-1,t)$ is pseudo-Einstein if and only if

$$(2.2) \quad Hcot(\theta-\pi/4) - cot^2(\theta-\pi/4) = -Htan(\theta-\pi/4) - tan^2(\theta-\pi/4),$$

which, together with

$$H = (n-1)[cot(\theta-\pi/4) - tan(\theta-\pi/4)] + 2cot2\theta,$$

gives $sin^2 2\theta = 1/(n-1)$. On the other hand, from the results of Nomizu [36] and Takagi [47] it follows that a hypersurface $M'(2n,t)$ of S^{2n+1} has four constant principal curvatures $cot(\theta-\pi/4)$, $cot\theta$, $cot(\theta+\pi/4) = -tan(\theta-\pi/4)$ and $cot(\theta+\pi/2)$ with multiplicities n-1, 1, n-1 and 1 respectively, and that t is given by $t = sin^2 2\theta$ (see also Takagi [48]). Consequently we obtain $t = 1/(n-1)$. Thus $M(2n-1,1/(n-1))$ is pseudo-Einstein. Moreover we have $a = 2n$ and $b = 2-4n$, and hence the Ricci tensor S of $M(2n-1,1/(n-1))$ is given by $S(X,Y) = 2ng(X,Y) + (2-4n)u(X)u(Y)$.

Next, in consequence of (2.1), $M(2n-1,m,(m-1)/(n-m))$ is minimal if and only if $sin^2\theta = cos^2\theta$, $sin^2\theta = 1/2$. Since $sin^2\theta = (m-1)/(n-m)$, we have $m = (n+1)/2$. Thus $M(2n-1,(n+1)/2,1)$ is a pseudo-Einstein minimal real hypersurface in CP^n. In this case, n must be odd.

If we suppose that $M(2n-1,1/(n-1))$ is minimal, (2.2) implies that $\cot^2(\theta-\pi/4) = \tan^2(\theta-\pi/4)$. From this we have $\sin 2\theta = 0$. This is a contradiction to the fact that $\sin^2 2\theta = 1/(n-1)$. Therefore $M(2n-1, 1/(n-1))$ is not minimal.

A geodesic hypersphere $M_0(2n-1,r)$ is minimal if and only if $H = (2n-2)\cot\theta + 2\cot 2\theta = 0$, i.e., $\cos^2\theta = 1/2n$. Then we have (see Takagi [46])

$$M_0' = S^{2n-1}(\frac{2n}{2n-1}) \times S^1(2n),$$

where $2n/(2n-1) = \xi_1^2 + 1$ and $2n = 1/\xi_1^2 + 1$. Thus from (1.23) we have $r = 2n-1$. Therefore a geodesic hypersphere $M_0(2n-1,2n-1)$ is minimal. For a constant a of $M_0(2n-1,r)$ we obtain $a = 2n + (2n-2)\cot^2\theta$ by using (1.13). Thus we have $a > 2n$, and also $b = -2n$.

From these considerations we see that $M_0(2n-1,r)$, $M(2n-1,m, (m-1)/(n-m))$ and $M(2n-1,1/(n-1))$ are not Einstein.

Let M be a connected real hypersurface of a complex space form $\bar{M}^n(c)$ $(n \geq 3)$. We can choose a local field of orthonormal frames $e_1,\ldots,e_{2n-1},e_{2n}$ in $\bar{M}^n(c)$ in such a way that, restricted to M, $e_1,\ldots,e_{2n-1}$ are tangent to M, and $e_{2n-1} = U$, $e_{2n} = Je_{2n-1} = C$. Then for a suitable choice of $e_1,\ldots,e_{2n-2}$, the second fundamental form A is represented by a matrix form

$$(2.3) \qquad A = \begin{pmatrix} \lambda_1 & & & & h_1 \\ & \ddots & & 0 & \vdots \\ & & \ddots & & \vdots \\ & & & \ddots & \vdots \\ 0 & & & \ddots & \vdots \\ & & & & \lambda_{2n-2} & h_{2n-2} \\ h_1 & \cdots\cdots & & h_{2n-2} & \alpha \end{pmatrix},$$

where we have put $h_i = g(Ae_i, U)$, $i = 1, \ldots, 2n-2$, and $\alpha = g(AU, U)$.

In the following we assume that M is a pseudo-Einstein real hypersurface of $\bar{M}^n(c)$. Then (1.13) reduces to

$$(2.4) \qquad ag(X,Y) + bu(X)u(Y)$$

$$= (2n+1)cg(X,Y) - 3cu(X)u(Y) + Hg(AX,Y) - g(AX,AY).$$

From (2.3) and (2.4) we have the following equations:

$$g(Ae_i, Ae_j) = 0 \quad \text{for } i \neq j, \quad i,j = 1, \ldots, 2n-2,$$

$$Hg(Ae_i, U) - g(Ae_i, AU) = 0 \quad \text{for } i = 1, \ldots, 2n-2.$$

From these equations we obtain

$$(2.5) \qquad h_i h_j = 0, \quad i \neq j, \ i,j = 1, \ldots, 2n-2,$$

$$(2.6) \qquad h_i (H - \lambda_i - \alpha) = 0, \quad i = 1, \ldots, 2n-2.$$

Equations (2.5) show that at most one h_i does not vanish. Thus we can assume that $h_i = 0$ for $i = 2, \ldots, 2n-2$. Moreover, using (2.4) we obtain the following equations:

$$(2.7) \qquad a = (2n+1)c + H\lambda_i - \lambda_i^2, \quad i = 1, \ldots, 2n-2,$$

$$(2.8) \qquad a = (2n+1)c + H\lambda_1 - \lambda_1^2 - h_1^2,$$

$$(2.9) \qquad a = (2n-2)c - b + H\alpha - \alpha^2 - h_1^2.$$

Lemma 2.1. Let M be a connected pseudo-Einstein real hypersurface of CP^n. Then $h_1 = 0$.

Proof. Suppose that $H = \lambda_1 + \alpha$. Then (2.8) and (2.9) imply $b = -3$. Therefore (2.4) can be written as

(2.10) $ag(X,Y) = (2n+1)g(X,Y) + Hg(AX,Y) - g(AX,AY).$

Here we take a new local frame of orthonormal vectors $e_1, \ldots, e_{2n-1}$ of M for which the second fundamental form A can be represented by a diagonal matrix form, i.e., $Ae_i = \beta_i e_i$ $(i = 1, \ldots, 2n-1)$. Then (2.10) implies

(2.11) $\beta_i^2 - H\beta_i + a - (2n+1) = 0.$

Therefore each principal curvature β_i satisfies the quadratic equation

(2.12) $t^2 - Ht + a - (2n+1) = 0.$

Thus at most two principal curvatures can be distinct at each point. Let us denote them by λ and μ with $\lambda \geq \mu$. Since M is not totally umbilical, we may suppose that $\lambda \neq \mu$ at some point. Then from (2.12) we see that

(2.13) $H = \lambda + \mu, \qquad \lambda\mu = a - (2n+1).$

Let p be the multiplicity of λ. Then we have $H = p\lambda + (2n-1-p)\mu$. Combining this with (2.13) gives

(2.14) $(p-1)\lambda + (2n-2-p)\mu = 0.$

Suppose a > (2n+1). Then the second equation of (2.13) shows that λ and μ have the same sign at some point. Therefore (2.14) implies that p = 1 and n = 3/2, which is a contradiction. If a < (2n+1) and $\lambda = \mu$ at some point, then we have $(2n-2)\lambda^2 = a - (2n+1) < 0$ by (2.12). This is also a contradiction. Hence M has exactly two distinct principal curvatures $\lambda > \mu$ at each point. Thus we obtain 1 < p < 2n-2 from (2.14), and

$$\lambda^2 = - \frac{(2n-2-p)(a-2n-1)}{(p-1)} , \qquad \mu^2 = - \frac{(p-1)(a-2n-1)}{(2n-2-p)} ,$$

from (2.13) and (2.14). Therefore the two principal curvatures λ and μ are constant. Then we must have p = 1 (see Lemma 3.3 of Takagi [46]) or p = 2n-2. This is also a contradiction. Next we assume that a = (2n+1). Then the product of two principal curvatures is zero, and (2.12) shows that $\lambda^2 - H\lambda = 0$, from which $(p-1)\lambda^2 = 0$. This gives $t(x) \leq 1$ at each point. This contradicts Lemma 1.4. Consequently, we obtain $H \neq \lambda_1 + \alpha$. Thus (2.16) implies that $h_1 = 0$.

From Lemma 2.1 we see that the vector U is an eigenvector of A, i.e., $AU = \alpha U$. Therefore from (2.4) the principal curvatures λ_i satisfy

(2.15) $\lambda_i^2 - H\lambda_i + a - (2n+1) = 0, \quad i = 1,\ldots,2n-2.$

Thus each λ_i satisfies the quadratic equation (2.12). Therefore at most two λ_i can be distinct. Let us denote them by λ and μ with $\lambda \geq \mu$. Consequently M has at most three principal curvatures λ, μ and α. In Lemma 1.3 we have already seen that α is constant.

Theorem 2.1 (Kon [30]). Let M be a connected pseudo-Einstein real hypersurface of CP^n (n $\geq$ 3). Then M has at most three constant principal curvatures.

Proof. First of all, (2.4) gives

(2.16) $a = (2n-2) - b + H\alpha - \alpha^2.$

If $\alpha \neq 0$, then H is constant by (2.16), and (2.15) implies that λ and μ are constant. Next we suppose that $\alpha = 0$. Then we have $H = p\lambda + (2n-2-p)\mu$, where p denotes the multiplicity of λ.

Let $a > (2n+1)$. If $\lambda \neq \mu$ at some point x of M, then from $H = \lambda+\mu$, we get $(p-1)\lambda + (2n-3-p)\mu = 0$. Since $\lambda\mu = a - (2n+1) > 0$, we conclude that $p = 1$ and $2n-3 = p$ and hence $n = 2$. This is a contradiction to the assumption $n \geq 3$. Thus we must have $\lambda = \mu$ at each point. Then (2.15) implies that $(2n-3)\lambda^2 = a - (2n+1)$ showing that λ is a constant.

Suppose that $a < (2n+1)$. If $\lambda = \mu$ at some point, then we have $(2n-3)\lambda^2 = a - (2n+1) < 0$ by (2.15). This is a contradiction. Therefore $\lambda \neq \mu$ at each point. Thus, from (2.12) we obtain $H = p\lambda + (2n-2-p)\mu = \lambda + \mu$ and $\lambda\mu = a - (2n+1)$ from which

$$\lambda^2 = - \frac{(2n-3-p)(a-2n-1)}{(p-1)}, \qquad \mu^2 = - \frac{(p-1)(a-2n-1)}{(2n-3-p)} .$$

Consequently, the principal curvatures λ and μ are constant.

Next we assume that $a = (2n+1)$. In this case the product of two principal curvatures is zero. Thus, if $\lambda \neq 0$, then $H = p\lambda$, and (2.15) implies $(p-1)\lambda^2 = 0$. Hence $p = 1$, and $t(x) \leq 1$ at each point. This is a contradiction by Lemma 1.4. Consequently M has at most three constant principal curvatures.

From Theorems 1.1, 1.2 and 2.1 we have (Kon [30])

Theorem 2.2. If M is a connected complete pseudo-Einstein real hyper-surface of CP^n ($n \geq 3$), then M is congruent to some geodesic hypersphere $M_0(2n-1,r)$ or $M(2n-1,m,(m-1)/(n-m))$ or $M(2n-1,1/(n-1))$.

Theorem 2.3. If M is a connected complete pseudo-Einstein real minimal hypersurface of CP^n ($n \geq 3$), then M is congruent to $M_0(2n-1,2n-1)$ or $M(2n-1,(n+1)/2,1)$. In the latter case, n is odd.

Theorem 2.4. Let M be a connected complete real hypersurface of CP^n ($n \geq 3$). Then M is not Einstein.

§3. Generic minimal submanifolds

In this section we first prove

Theorem 3.1 (Kon [33]). Let M be a compact orientable n-dimensional generic minimal submanifold of $CP^{(n+p)/2}$. If the Ricci tensor S of M satisfies $S(X,X) \geq (n-1)g(X,X) + 2g(PX,PX)$, then M is a real projective space RP^n ($p = n$), or M is the pseudo-Einstein real hypersurface $\pi(S^m(r) \times S^m(r))$ ($m = (n+1)/2$, $r = (1/2)^{1/2}$) of $CP^{(n+1)/2}$ ($p = 1$).

We use the following lemma to prove our theorem.

Lemma 3.1. Let M be a generic submanifold of $CP^{(n+p)/2}$. If the second fundamental form A of M is parallel, then M is anti-invariant in $CP^{(n+p)/2}$.

Proof. Since $\nabla A = 0$, the Codazzi equation implies that $g(X,PY)g(tV,tV) = 0$ for any vector fields X, Y tangent to M and any vector field V normal to M. Thus we have $g(X,PY) = 0$ and hence $P = 0$. Therefore, M is anti-invariant in $CP^{(n+p)/2}$.

Let $\{v_a\}$ be an orthonormal frame for $T_x(M)$. Then Proposition II.4.2 implies

Lemma 3.2. Let M be an n-dimensional generic minimal submanifold of $CP^{(n+p)/2}$. Then

$$-g(\nabla^2 A, A) = \sum_{a,b} (TrA_a A_b)^2 + \sum_{a,b} |[A_a, A_b]|^2 - (n-3)\sum_a TrA_a^2$$
$$- 3\sum_a |[P, A_a]|^2 - 4\sum_{a,b} [g(A_a tv_b, A_a tv_b) - g(A_a tv_a, A_b tv_b)].$$

Proof of Theorem 3.1. The Ricci tensor S of M is given by

$$S(X,Y) = (n-1)g(X,Y) + 3g(PX,PY) - \sum_a g(A_a^2 X, Y).$$

In accordance with the assumption on the Ricci tensor S, we see that $g(PX,PX) \geq \sum_a g(A_a X, A_a X) \geq 0$. Since $PtV = 0$ for any vector field V normal to M, we have

(3.1) $\qquad\qquad A_a tV = 0 \qquad$ for each a.

Moreover, we have

(3.2) $\qquad\qquad \sum_a TrA_a^2 \leq n - p.$

If $n = p$, then (3.2) shows that M is totally geodesic in $CP^{(n+p)/2}$ and hence M is the real projective space RP^n.

In the following we assume that $n \neq p$. Let $\lambda_1^a, \ldots, \lambda_n^a$ be the eigenvalues of A_a. Then

$$\sum_b |[A_a, A_b]|^2 = \sum_{b \neq a, i, j} (h_{ij}^b)^2 (\lambda_i^a - \lambda_j^a)^2 \leq 4 \sum_{b \neq a, i, j} (h_{ij}^b)^2 (\lambda_j^a)^2,$$

where we have put $A_b = (h_{ij}^b)$. On the other hand, by the assumption on the Ricci tensor S of M, we find

$$\sum_{b \neq a, i} (h_{ij}^b)^2 \leq g(Pe_j, Pe_j) - (\lambda_j^a)^2 \leq 1 - (\lambda_j^a)^2$$

for each j, where e_j is the eigenvector corresponding to λ_j^a. Thus we have

$$\sum_b |[A_a, A_b]|^2 \leq 4 TrA_a^2 - 4 TrA_a^4.$$

From (3.1) we see that rank $A_a \leq n-p$ for each a. Since A_a is symmetric, it follows that $(TrA_a^2)^2 \leq (n-p) TrA_a^4$, and hence

$$(3.3) \qquad \sum_b |[A_a, A_b]|^2 \leq 4 TrA_a^2 - \frac{4}{n-p}(TrA_a^2)^2 \qquad \text{for each a.}$$

From (3.1) we see that $A_a tv_b = 0$ for all a and b. Thus, equation of Lemma 3.2 implies with (3.3) that

$$(3.4) \quad - g(\nabla^2 A, A) + (p-3) \sum_a TrA_a^2 + 3 \sum_a |[P, A_a]|^2$$

$$\leq \sum_{a,b} (TrA_a A_b)^2 - \frac{4}{n-p} \sum_a (TrA_a^2)^2 - (n-p-4) \sum_a TrA_a^2.$$

On the other hand, the (p,p)-matrix $(TrA_a A_b)$ is symmetric. Thus, it can be diagonalized by a suitable choice of a frame $\{v_a\}$ at each point of M so that $\sum_{a,b} (TrA_a A_b)^2 = \sum_a (TrA_a^2)^2$. We also have $\sum_a (TrA_a^2)^2 \leq (\sum_a TrA_a^2)^2$.
Suppose now that $n-p-4 \geq 0$. Then (3.4) becomes

$$- g(\nabla^2 A, A) + (p-3)\sum_a \text{Tr}A_a^2 + 3\sum_a |[P, A_a]|^2$$

$$\leq \frac{n-p-4}{n-p}[\sum_a \text{Tr}A_a^2 - (n-p)](\sum_b \text{Tr}A_b^2).$$

Since M is compact orientable, we obtain

(3.5) $\qquad \int_M [g(\nabla A, \nabla A) + (p-3)\sum_a \text{Tr}A_a^2 + 3\sum_a |[P, A_a]|^2] *1$

$$\leq \frac{n-p-4}{n-p} \int_M [\sum_a \text{Tr}A_a^2 - (n-p)](\sum_b \text{Tr}A_b^2) *1.$$

Since we assume that n-p-4 $\geq$ 0, (3.2) implies that the right hand side of (3.5) is non-positive. If p $\geq$ 3, then $\nabla A = 0$, that is, the second fundamental form A of M is parallel. This contradicts Lemma 3.1 and n $\neq$ p. If p = 2, then (IV.8.9) implies

$$g(\nabla A, \nabla A) + (p-3)\sum_a \text{Tr}A_a^2 = g(\nabla A, \nabla A) - \sum_a \text{Tr}A_a^2$$

$$\geq g(\nabla A, \nabla A) - (n-2) = g(\nabla A, \nabla A) - 2(n-2)2 + 3(n-2) \geq 0.$$

To prove the inequality part of this, we used (3.2). Hence we have n = 2 = p. This is a contradiction. If p = 1, then (IV.8.9) implies

$$g(\nabla A, \nabla A) - 2\sum_a \text{Tr}A_a^2 \geq g(\nabla A, \nabla A) - 2(n-1) \geq 0.$$

Therefore, (3.5) shows that $g(\nabla A, \nabla A) = 2(n-1)$, PA = AP, and we also have $S(X,X) = (n-1)g(X,X) + 2g(PX,PX)$, that is, M is a pseudo-Einstein real minimal hypersurface of $CP^{(n+1)/2}$. Moreover, we obtain $\text{Tr}A^2 = n-1$. Hence Theorem IV.10.4 and Example 2.1 show that M is $\pi(S^m(r) \times S^m(r))$ (m = (n+1)/2, r = $(1/2)^{1/2}$).

In the next place, we suppose that n-p-4 < 0. Then n-4 < p < n.

Since n+p is even, it follows that $p = n-2$. From (3.1) and the fact that $\nabla_X Jv_a = -PA_a X + JD_X v_a$, we find

$$g((\nabla_X A)_a Y, Jv_a) = g((\nabla_X A)_a Jv_a, Y) = g(A_a PA_a X, Y).$$

Therefore, the Codazzi equation implies that $g(A_a PA_a X, Y) = g(PX, Y)$. Putting $Y = PX$, we get

$$g(A_a PA_a X, PX) = g(PX, PX).$$

Since $p = n-2$, the holomorphic subspace $PT_X(M)$ is spanned by X and PX, where X is a unit vector in $PT_X(M)$ such that $A_a X = \lambda X$. We can take such a vector X by (3.1). From the minimality of M, we see that $A_a PX = -\lambda PX$. We then have

$$g(A_a PA_a X, PX) = -\lambda^2 g(PX, PX) = g(PX, PX),$$

from which $\lambda = 0$ and hence $g(PX, PX) = 0$. This is a contradiction. From these considerations we have our theorem.

Next we prove

Theorem 3.2 (Yano-Kon [74]). Let M be an n-dimensional compact orientable generic minimal submanifold of $CP^{(n+p)/2}$ with flat normal connection. If the minimum of the sectional curvature of M is $(n-p)/n(n-1)$, then $p = 1$ and M is the geodesic minimal hypersphere

$$\pi(S^n(r_1) \times S^1(r_2)), \quad r_1 = (n/(n+1))^{1/2}, \quad r_2 = (1/(n+1))^{1/2},$$

or $p = n$ and M is the flat anti-invariant submanifold

$$\pi(S^1(r_1) \times \cdots \times S^1(r_{n+1})), \quad r_1 = \cdots = r_{n+1} = (1/(n+1))^{1/2}.$$

Proof. From (IV.11.5) we have

(3.6) $\text{div}(\sum_a \nabla_{Jv_a} Jv_a) = (n-1)p - \sum_a \text{Tr}A_a^2 + \frac{1}{2}\sum_a |[P,A_a]|^2,$

where $\{v_a\}$ denotes an orthonormal frame for $T_x(M)$ such that $Dv_a = 0$ for each a. On the other hand, using (II.4.1), by a straightforward computation, we obtain

(3.7) $g(\nabla^2 A,A) = \sum_{a,i,j} g((R(e_j,e_i)A_a)e_j,A_a e_i)$

$$+ \frac{3}{2}\sum_a |[P,A_a]|^2 - 3\sum_a \text{Tr}A_a^2 + 3(p-1)p,$$

where $\{e_i\}$ is an orthonormal frame of M.

Since M is compact orientable, (3.6) and (3.7) imply

$$\int_M [g(\nabla A,\nabla A) - 2(n-p)p]*1$$

$$= \int_M [(n-p)p - \sum_{a,i,j} g((R(e_j,e_i)A_a)e_j,A_a e_i)]*1.$$

On the other hand, we have $g(\nabla A,\nabla A) - 2(n-p)p \geq 0$ by (IV.8.9). Thus the left hand side of this equation is non-negative. Here we choose $\{e_i\}$ such that $A_a e_i = \lambda_i^a e_i$ $(i = 1,\ldots,n)$. Then

$$\sum_{i,j} g((R(e_j,e_i)A_a)e_j,A_a e_i) = \frac{1}{2}\sum_{i,j} (\lambda_j^a - \lambda_i^a)^2 K_{ij},$$

where K_{ij} denotes the sectional curvature of M with respect to the section spanned by e_i and e_j. By the assumption, we have $K_{ij} \geq (n-p)/n(n-1)$ and hence

$$\sum_{i,j} g((R(e_j,e_i)A_a)e_j,A_a e_i) \geq \frac{n-p}{2n(n-1)}\sum_{i,j} (\lambda_j^a - \lambda_i^a)^2 = \frac{n-p}{n-1} \text{Tr}A_a^2.$$

Therefore we have, using (3.6),

$$0 \leq \int_M [g(\nabla A, \nabla A) - 2(n-p)p]*1 \leq \frac{n-p}{n-1} \int_M [(n-1)p - \sum_a \mathrm{Tr} A_a^2]*1$$

$$= -\frac{n-p}{2(n-1)} \int_M \sum_a |[P, A_a]|^2 *1.$$

From this we see that $g(\nabla A, \nabla A) = 2(n-p)p$. Moreover, we have $n = p$ or $(n-1)p = \sum_a \mathrm{Tr} A_a^2$ and $PA_a = A_a P$ for all a. If $n = p$, then M is an anti-invariant submanifold and hence $P = 0$. Any anti-invariant submanifold with $n = p$ and flat normal connection is flat by Proposition IV.1.3. Thus the Gauss equation of M implies that $\sum_a \mathrm{Tr} A_a^2 = n(n-1)$. Consequently, Theorem IV.7.3 implies that M is

$$\pi(S^1(r_1) \times \cdots \times S^1(r_{n+1})), \quad r_1 = \cdots = r_{n+1} = (1/(n+1))^{1/2},$$

or

$$\pi(S^{m_1}(r_1) \times S^{m_2}(r_2)), \quad r_i = (m_i/(n+1))^{1/2} \ (i = 1,2),$$

where $m_1 + m_2 = n+1$. On the other hand, if m_1, $m_2 > 2$, then the sectional curvature of M takes value 0 for some plane section. But, if $m_1 = 1$ or $m_2 = 1$, the sectional curvature K_{ij} of M satisfies $K_{ij} \geq 1/n$. Thus M is a geodesic hypersphere. From these we have our theorem.

Since $1/n \geq (n-p)/n(n-1)$, Theorem 3.2 implies the following theorems.

Theorem 3.3 (Yano-Kon [70]). Let M be an n-dimensional compact orientable generic minimal submanifold of $CP^{(n+p)/2}$ with flat normal connection. If the minimum of the sectional curvature of M is $1/n$, then $p = 1$ and M is the geodesic hypersphere

$$\pi(S^n(r_1) \times S^1(r_2)), \quad r_1 = (n/(n+1))^{1/2}, \quad r_2 = (1/(n+1))^{1/2}.$$

Theorem 3.4 (Kon [32]). Let M be a compact orientable real minimal hypersurface of $CP^{(n+1)/2}$. If the minimum of the sectional curvature of M is $1/n$, then M is the geodesic hypersphere

$$\pi(S^n(r_1) \times S^1(r_2)), \quad r_1 = (n/(n+1))^{1/2}, \quad r_2 = (1/(n+1))^{1/2}.$$

§4. Semidefinite second fundamental form

Let M be an n-dimensional generic submanifold of $CP^{(n+p)/2}$. If each vector V normal to M satisfies $g(A_V X, X) \geq 0$ or $g(A_V X, X) \leq 0$ for any vector X tangent to M, then the second fundamental form A of M is said to be semidefinite.

Theorem 4.1 (Yano-Kon [68]). Let M be a compact orientable n-dimensional generic submanifold of $CP^{(n+p)/2}$ with flat normal connection such that the second fundamental form is semidefinite. If $\sum_a TrA_a^2 \leq (n-1)p$, then $p = 1$ and M is the geodesic hypersphere $\pi(S^n(r) \times S^1(r))$, $r = (1/2)^{1/2}$, of $CP^{(n+1)/2}$.

Proof. From (IV.11.8) we have

$$\int_M [(n-1)p - \sum_a TrA_a^2 + \sum_{a,b} TrA_a g(A_a Jv_b, Jv_b)]*1 = -\frac{1}{2}\int_M \sum_a |[P,A_a]|^2 *1.$$

From the assumptions we see that the left hand side of this equation is non-negative. Thus we obtain

(4.1) $$\sum_a \mathrm{Tr}A_a^2 = (n-1)p,$$

(4.2) $$PA_a = A_aP \quad \text{for any } a,$$

(4.3) $$\mathrm{Tr}A_a g(A_aJv_b,Jv_b) = 0 \quad \text{for any } a, b.$$

Suppose that $\mathrm{Tr}A_a = 0$ for some a. Since the second fundamental form is semidefinite, we see that $A_a = 0$. On the other hand, the equation of Codazzi is given by

$$(\nabla_X A)_V Y - (\nabla_Y A)_V X = -g(X,JV)PY + g(JV,Y)PX - 2g(X,PY)JV.$$

Putting $V = v_a$ and $X = JV$ in this equation, we obtain $g(JV,JV)PY = 0$. Thus we have $P = 0$ and hence M is anti-invariant and $\sum_b g(A_aJv_b,Jv_b) = \mathrm{Tr}A_a$ for any a. Therefore $\mathrm{Tr}A_a g(A_aJv_b,Jv_b) = 0$ implies that $\mathrm{Tr}A_a = 0$ for all a, and hence M is totally geodesic. This contradicts the fact that $\sum_a \mathrm{Tr}A_a^2 = (n-1)p$. Consequently, we must have $\mathrm{Tr}A_a \neq 0$ for all a and then $g(A_aJv_b,Jv_b) = 0$ for any a and b. Let V be a unit vector normal to M. We take an orthonormal frame $\{V_a\}$ of $T_x(M)$ such that $V = V_1$. Then we obtain

$$\sum_d g(A_aJV_d,JV_d) = \sum_{b,c,d} g(V_d,v_b)g(V_d,v_c)g(A_aJv_b,Jv_c)$$

$$= \sum_b g(A_aJv_b,Jv_b) = 0.$$

From this we see that $g(A_aJV,JV) = 0$ for any unit vector V normal to M. Since A_a is symmetric, we obtain $g(A_aJv_b,Jv_c) = 0$ for any a, b and c by putting $V = (v_a+v_c)/2^{1/2}$. We now use the following equation of Ricci

$$g(R^{\perp}(X,Y)U,V) + g([A_V,A_U]X,Y) = g(FY,U)g(FX,V) - g(FX,U)g(FY,V).$$

Putting $V = v_a$, $U = v_b$, $X = Jv_a$ and $Y = Jv_b$ in this equation, and using $R^{\perp} = 0$, we have $g(v_a,v_a)g(v_b,v_b) - g(v_a,v_b)^2 = 0$. Therefore we obtain $p = 1$, that is, M is a real hypersurface of $CP^{(n+1)/2}$. Since $PA = AP$, we see that $U = -JC$ is an eigenvector, where C is a unit normal of M. From $g(AJC,JC) = 0$ we obtain $AU = 0$ and hence (1.20) implies that $A^2X = X - u(X)U$. From this, since A is semidefinite, we obtain for a suitable basis $e_1,\ldots,e_{n-1},e_n=U$, $Ae_i = -e_i$ or $Ae_i = e_i$ for $i = 1,\ldots,n-1$. Therefore M has two constant principal curvatures and hence M is a geodesic hypersphere (cf. Theorem 1.4). From Table 1.1 we see that $\xi_1 = \pm 1$, $\xi_2 = 0$ and hence $r = 1$ by (1.23). Therefore $M = M_0(n,1)$, that is, M = $\pi(S^n(r) \times S^1(r))$, $r = (1/2)^{1/2}$ (see Example 2.1).

From Theorem 4.1 we have

Theorem 4.2 (Yano-Kon [68]). Let M be a compact orientable real hypersurface of $CP^{(n+1)/2}$ such that the second fundamental form of M is semidefinite. If $\text{Tr}A^2 \leq n-1$, then M is the geodesic hypersphere $\pi(S^n(r) \times S^1(r))$, $r = (1/2)^{1/2}$.

Theorem 4.3 (Yano-Kon [68]). Let M be a compact orientable n-dimensional generic submanifold of $CP^{(n+p)/2}$ with flat normal connection. If the mean curvature vector of M is parallel and $\Sigma(\text{Tr}A_a)^2 \leq (n-1)^2p$, then $p = 1$ and M is the geodesic hypersphere $\pi(S^n(r) \times S^1(r))$, $r = (1/2)^{1/2}$, of $CP^{(n+1)/2}$.

Proof. From (IV.11.8) and (IV.11.9) we have

$$\int_M [g(\nabla A, \nabla A) - 2(n-p)p + 3\sum_a |[P, A_a]|^2] * 1$$

$$= \int_M [\sum_{a,b} (\text{Tr} A_a A_b)^2 - \sum_{a,b} (\text{Tr} A_a)(\text{Tr} A_b^2 A_a) - (n-3)\sum_a \text{Tr} A_a^2$$

$$+ \sum_a (\text{Tr} A_a)^2 - 3\sum_{a,b} \text{Tr} A_a g(A_a J v_b, J v_b) - 2(n-1)p] * 1.$$

For any a and for some b, we put $K_a X = A_a X + (\text{Tr} A_a g(J v_b, X) J v_b)/(n-1)$. Since K_a is symmetric, we see that

$$n \text{Tr} K_a^2 \geq (\text{Tr} K_a)^2,$$

from which

$$(\text{Tr} A_a)^2 \leq (n-1)\text{Tr} A_a^2 + 2\text{Tr} A_a g(A_a J v_b, J v_b)$$

for any a and b. Thus we obtain

$$\sum_a (\text{Tr} A_a)^2 \leq (n-1)\sum_a \text{Tr} A_a^2 + 2\sum_a \text{Tr} A_a g(A_a J v_b, J v_b).$$

Therefore we see that

$$\int_M [g(\nabla A, \nabla A) - 2(n-p)p + 3\sum_a |[P, A_a]|^2] * 1$$

$$\leq \int_M [\sum_{a,b} (\text{Tr} A_a A_b)^2 - \sum_{a,b} (\text{Tr} A_a)(\text{Tr} A_b^2 A_a) + \frac{2}{n-1}(\sum_a (\text{Tr} A_a)^2 - (n-1)^2 p)$$

$$- \frac{n+3}{n-1}\sum_{a,b} \text{Tr} A_a g(A_a J v_b, J v_b)] * 1.$$

On the other hand, we have $g(\nabla A, \nabla A) \geq 2(n-p)p$ by (IV.8.9) and hence the left hand side of this inequality is non-negative. Moreover, from the assumption we see that the right hand side of this inequality is non-positive. Consequently, we have $\Sigma_a (\mathrm{Tr}A_a)^2 = (n-1)^2 p$, $(\mathrm{Tr}A_a A_b)^2 =$ $(\mathrm{Tr}A_a)(\mathrm{Tr}A_b^2 A_a)$ and $\mathrm{Tr}A_a g(A_a J v_b, J v_b) = 0$ for any a and b. Moreover, we have $PA_a = A_a P$ for any a. By a method similar to that used in the proof of Theorem 4.1, we can prove our theorem.

Theorem 4.4 (Okumura [39]). Let M be a compact orientable real hyper-surface of $CP^{(n+1)/2}$ with constant mean curvature such that the second fundamental form is semidefinite. If $(\mathrm{Tr}A)^2 \leq (n-1)^2$, then M is $\pi(S^n(r) \times S^1(r))$, $r = (1/2)^{1/2}$.

§5. Hypersurfaces of S^{2n+1}

Let M be a hypersurface of a Sasakian manifold $\bar{M}$. In the following we suppose that M is tangent to the structure vector field ξ of $\bar{M}$. We denote by C the unit normal of M in $\bar{M}$. For any vector field X tangent to M, we have

$$\phi X = PX + u(X)C, \qquad u(X)C = FX,$$

where we have put

$$\phi C = -U, \qquad u(X) = g(U,X).$$

Then we find

$$P^2 X = -X + u(X)U + \eta(X)\xi,$$

and

$$PU = 0, \qquad u(\xi) = 0, \qquad u(U) = 1.$$

We denote the second fundamental form of M by A in place of A_C to simplify the notation. Then the Gauss and Weingarten formulas are given respectively by

$$\bar{\nabla}_X Y = \nabla_X Y + g(AX,Y)C \quad \text{and} \quad \bar{\nabla}_X C = -AX.$$

We also have

$$\nabla_X U = PAX,$$

$$(\nabla_X P)Y = \eta(Y)X + u(Y)AX - g(X,Y)\xi - g(AX,Y)U.$$

If the second fundamental form A of M is of the form

$$AX = a[X - \eta(X)\xi] + bu(X)U + \eta(X)U + u(X)\xi$$

for any vector field X tangent to M, a and b being functions, then M is called a pseudo-umbilical hypersurface of $\bar{M}$. The notion of pseudo-umbilical hypersurfaces of Sasakian manifolds corresponds to that of η-umbilical real hypersurfaces of Kaehlerian manifolds. That is, from (IV.7.6), we have

Theorem 5.1. Let $\bar{M}$ be a Sasakian manifold and M be a hypersurface of $\bar{M}$ tangent to ξ, and $\bar{N}$ be a Kaehlerian manifold and N be a real hypersurface of $\bar{N}$ such that the diagram

$$
\begin{array}{ccc}
M & \xrightarrow{\quad i \quad} & \bar{M} \\
\pi \downarrow & & \downarrow \bar{\pi} \\
N & \xrightarrow{\quad i' \quad} & \bar{N}
\end{array}
$$

commutes and the immersion i is a diffeomorphism on the fibres. Then M is pseudo-umbilical if and only if N is η-umbilical.

Let M be a pseudo-umbilical hypersurface of a Sasakian space form $\bar{M}^{2n+1}(c)$. Then we have

$$(\nabla_Y A)X = (Ya)[X - \eta(X)\xi] + (Yb)u(X)U + a[-g(PY,X)\xi - \eta(X)PY]$$

$$+ b[g(PAY,X)U + u(X)PAY] + g(PY,X)U + \eta(X)PAY + g(PAY,X)\xi + u(X)PY.$$

From this and equation of Codazzi we find

$$\frac{1}{4}(c+3)[g(PY,Z)u(X) - g(PX,Z)u(Y) - 2g(PX,Y)u(Z)]$$

$$= (Xa)[g(Y,Z) - \eta(Y)\eta(Z)] - (Ya)[g(X,Z) - \eta(X)\eta(Z)] + (Xb)u(Y)u(Z)$$

$$- (Yb)u(X)u(Z) + a[2g(PY,X)\eta(Z) - \eta(Y)g(PX,Z) + \eta(X)g(PY,Z)]$$

$$+ b[g(PAX,Y)u(Z) - g(PAY,X)u(Z) + g(PAX,Z)u(Y) - g(PAY,Z)u(X)]$$

$$+ \eta(Y)g(PAX,Z) - \eta(X)g(PAY,Z) + \eta(Z)g(PAX,Y) - \eta(Z)g(PAY,X).$$

Putting Y = U in this equation, we obtain

$$[ab + \frac{1}{4}(c+3)]g(PX,Z) = -u(Z)X(a+b) + (Ub)u(X)u(Z)$$

$$+ (Ua)[g(X,Z) - \eta(X)\eta(Z)].$$

Moreover, putting Z = U in this equation, we find X(a+b) = u(X)U(a+b), from which

$$[ab + \frac{1}{4}(c+3)]g(PX,Z) = (Ua)[g(X,Z) - \eta(X)\eta(Z)] - (Ua)u(X)u(Z).$$

Since P is skew-symmetric, we have

$$[ab + \frac{1}{4}(c+3)]g(PX,Z) = 0.$$

If $n \geq 2$, then we have $ab = -(c+3)/4$. Suppose that the ambient manifold $\bar{M}^{2n+1}(c)$ is S^{2n+1}. Then $ab = -1$. Since $g(AU,U) = a+b$, we obtain

$$X(a+b) = g((\nabla_X A)U,U) = (U(a+b))u(X).$$

We put $\beta = U(a+b)$. Then we have

$$XY(a+b) = (X\beta)u(Y) + \beta ag(PX,Y) + \beta u(\nabla_X Y),$$

$$YX(a+b) = (Y\beta)u(X) + \beta ag(PY,X) + \beta u(\nabla_Y X),$$

$$[X,Y](a+b) = \beta u([X,Y]).$$

Since $R(X,Y)(a+b) = 0$, we have

$$0 = (X\beta)u(Y) - (Y\beta)u(X) + 2\beta ag(PX,Y).$$

Since $n > 2$ and $a \neq 0$, we have $\beta = 0$ and hence $X(a+b) = 0$. Therefore $a+b$ is constant. From this and $ab = -1$, a and b are both constant. On the other hand, A is represented in the following matrix form, for an orthonormal frame $e_1, \ldots, e_{2n}$ such that $e_{2n-1} = U$ and $e_{2n} = \xi$,

$$A = \begin{pmatrix} a & & & & & \\ & \ddots & 0 & & 0 & 0 \\ & & \ddots & & & \\ 0 & & \ddots & & & \\ & & & a & & \\ \hline 0 & & & 0 & a+b & 1 \\ \hline 0 & & & & 1 & 0 \end{pmatrix} \cdot$$

We consider the matrix $\begin{pmatrix} a+b & 1 \\ 1 & 0 \end{pmatrix}$. Then the eigenvalue λ of this matrix satisfies $\lambda^2 - (a+b)\lambda - 1 = 0$. Since $ab = -1$, we have $\lambda = a$ or $\lambda = b$. Therefore, the principal curvatures of M are a and b. The multiplicity of a is 2n-1 and that of b is 1. Consequently we have

<u>Lemma 5.1</u>. Let M be a pseudo-umbilical hypersurface of S^{2n+1} ($n \geq 2$). Then M has two constant principal curvatures with multiplicities 2n-1 and 1 respectively.

From Lemma 5.1 and a well known theorem (cf. [40]) we have

<u>Theorem 5.2</u>. Let M be a compact orientable pseudo-umbilical hypersurface of S^{2n+1} ($n \geq 2$). Then M is

$$S^{2n-1}(r_1) \times S^1(r_2), \quad r_1^2 + r_2^2 = 1.$$

Next we consider a pseudo-Einstein hypersurface of S^{2n+1}. Let M be a hypersurface, tangent to the structure vector field ξ, of S^{2n+1}. If the Ricci tensor S of M satisfies

(5.1) $\qquad S(\phi^2 X, \phi^2 Y) = ag(\phi^2 X, \phi^2 Y) + bu(\phi^2 X)u(\phi^2 Y)$

for any vector fields X and Y tangent to M, a and b being constant, then M is called a <u>pseudo-Einstein hypersurface</u> of S^{2n+1}. Equation (5.1) is equivalent to

(5.2) $\quad S(X,Y) = a[g(X,Y) - \eta(X)\eta(Y)] + bu(X)u(Y)$

$$+ \eta(X)S(\xi,Y) + \eta(Y)S(\xi,X) - \eta(X)\eta(Y)S(\xi,\xi).$$

We notice here that $S(\xi,\xi) = 2n-2$.

On the other hand, the Ricci tensor S of M is given by

(5.3) $\quad\quad\quad S(X,Y) = (2n-1)g(X,Y) + Hg(AX,Y) - g(AX,AY),$

H denoting the mean curvature of M, i.e., $H = TrA$.

From (5.2) and (5.3) we have

(5.4) $\quad a[g(X,Y) - \eta(X)\eta(Y)] + bu(X)u(Y) + \eta(X)S(\xi,Y) + \eta(Y)S(\xi,X)$

$\quad\quad\quad - \eta(X)\eta(Y)S(\xi,\xi) = (2n-1)g(X,Y) + Hg(AX,Y) - g(AX,AY).$

In the following, we assume that $n \geq 3$. We can choose a local field of orthonormal frames $e_1,\ldots,e_{2n-1},e_{2n},e_{2n+1}$ in S^{2n+1} in such a way that, restricted to M, $e_1,\ldots,e_{2n}$ are tangent to M and $e_{2n-1} = \xi$, $e_{2n} = U$, $e_{2n+1} = \phi e_{2n} = C$. Then, if we choose $e_1,\ldots,e_{2n-2}$ suitably, A is represented by a matrix form

(5.5) $\quad A =$

$$A = \left(\begin{array}{cccc|c|c}
\lambda_1 & & & \mathbf{0} & & h_1 \\
& \cdot & & & & \cdot \\
& & \cdot & & 0 & \cdot \\
\mathbf{0} & & & \cdot & & \cdot \\
& & & \lambda_{2n-2} & & h_{2n-2} \\
\hline
& 0 & & & 0 & 1 \\
\hline
h_1 & \cdot \quad \cdot \quad \cdot & \cdot h_{2n-2} & & 1 & \alpha
\end{array}\right) ,$$

where we have put $h_i = g(AU,e_i)$, $i = 1,\ldots,2n-2$, $\alpha = g(AU,U)$. Then we have

$$h_ih_j = 0, \quad i \neq j, \quad i,j = 1,\ldots,2n-2,$$

$$h_i(H - \lambda_i - \alpha) = 0, \quad i = 1,\ldots,2n-2.$$

Therefore, we can assume that $h_i = 0$ for $i = 2, \ldots, 2n-2$. Thus we have

(5.6) $\qquad\qquad\qquad h_1 (H - \lambda_1 - \alpha) = 0.$

We now suppose that $H = \lambda_1 + \alpha$. Then (5.4) and (5.5) imply that $b = -1$. Thus, for any vector fields X, Y tangent to M such that $\eta(X) = 0$, $\eta(Y) = 0$, we have

(5.7) $\quad ag(X,Y) - u(X)u(Y) = (2n-1)g(X,Y) + Hg(AX,Y) - g(AX,AY).$

We now take a new local field of orthonormal frames $e_1, \ldots, e_{2n}$ of M such that $e_{2n} = \xi$ for which A is represented by a matrix form

(5.8) $\qquad A =$
$$
\begin{pmatrix}
\beta_1 & & & & u_1 \\
& \ddots & & 0 & \vdots \\
& & \ddots & & \vdots \\
0 & & & \beta_{2n-1} & u_{2n-1} \\
\hline
u_1 & \cdots & u_{2n-1} & & 0
\end{pmatrix}
,
$$

where $u_i = g(A\xi, e_i) = u(e_i)$, $i = 1, \ldots, 2n-1$. From (5.7) and (5.8) we have

(5.9) $\qquad\qquad a = (2n-1) + H\beta_i - \beta_i^2, \quad i = 1, \ldots, 2n-1.$

Therefore, each β_i satisfies the quadratic equation

(5.10) $\qquad\qquad\qquad t^2 - Ht + a - (2n-1) = 0.$

We put

$$(5.11) \qquad L = \begin{pmatrix} \beta_1 & & & & 0 \\ & \cdot & & & \\ & & \cdot & & \\ & & & \cdot & \\ 0 & & & & \beta_{2n-1} \end{pmatrix} .$$

We now prepare some lemmas.

<u>Lemma 5.2</u>. If $\beta_1 = \cdots = \beta_{2n-1} = \beta$ at every point of M, then M is totally contact umbilical.

<u>Lemma 5.3</u>. If $AU = \alpha U + \xi$, then α is a constant.

<u>Lemma 5.4</u>. rank L > 1 at some point of M.

For the proof of these lemmas, see §2 of Chapter VI. From (5.10) we see that at most two λ_i can be distinct at each point of M. Let us denote them by λ and μ. We denote by p the multiplicity of λ. Then the multiplicity of μ is 2n-1-p.

<u>Lemma 5.5</u>. Let $H = \lambda_1 + \alpha$. If λ and μ are constant, $\lambda \neq \mu$, and if $p \geq 2$, $2n-1-p \geq 2$, then $\lambda\mu > 0$ or $h_1 = 0$.

<u>Proof</u>. Let $\{e_a\}$ be orthonormal vector fields such that $Ae_a = \lambda e_a + u(e_a)\xi$, $\{e_r\}$ orthonormal vector fields such that $Ae_r = \mu e_r + u(e_r)\xi$ and $\{e_a, e_r\}$ a local field of orthonormal frames for L. The indices a, b, c and r, s, t run the ranges $\{1,\ldots,p\}$ and $\{p+1,\ldots,2n-1\}$ respectively. Then, by a straightforward computation, we find (see [67])

$$(\mu^2 - \lambda\mu + 2)g(Pe_a, e_r) = 0.$$

If $e_r = U$, then $AU = \mu U + \xi$. Then, from the definition of h_1, we have

$h_1 = 0$. If $e_r \neq U$, then we can prove that $g(e_s, Pe_r) = 0$ for all s. From this we see that $g(Pe_a, e_r) = -g(e_a, Pe_r) \neq 0$ for some a. Consequently, we obtain $\mu^2 - \lambda\mu + 2 = 0$. Thus we have $\lambda\mu = \mu^2 + 2 > 0$.

Lemma 5.6. Let M be a pseudo-Einstein hypersurface of S^{2n+1} $(n \geq 3)$. Then we have $h_1 = 0$.

Proof. We assume that $H = \lambda_1 + \alpha$. Consider λ and μ in Lemma 5.5. If $\lambda = \mu$ at any point of M, then Lemma 5.2 shows that M is totally contact umbilical. But we can prove that there is no totally contact umbilical hypersurface of S^{2n+1} (see [67]). Therefore $\lambda \neq \mu$ at some point. Thus we have

(5.12) $\qquad H = \lambda + \mu, \qquad \lambda\mu = a - (2n-1)$.

Since $H = p\lambda + (2n-1-p)\mu$, (5.12) implies that

(5.13) $\qquad (p-1)\lambda + (2n-2-p)\mu = 0$.

Suppose that $a > (2n-1)$. Then the second equation of (5.12) shows that λ and μ have the same sign. Therefore (5.13) implies that $p = 1$ and $n = 3/2$. This is a contradiction. Let $a < (2n-1)$. If $\lambda = \mu$ at some point of M, then we have $(2n-2)\lambda^2 = a - (2n-1) < 0$ by (5.9). This is a contradiction. Hence $\lambda \neq \mu$ at each point. Thus (5.13) implies that $1 < p < 2n-2$. From (5.12) and (5.13) we see that λ and μ are constant. Thus Lemma 5.5 implies that $\lambda\mu > 0$ or $h_1 = 0$. If $\lambda\mu > 0$, this contradicts the fact that $\lambda\mu = a - (2n-1) < 0$. We now assume that $a = (2n-1)$. Then $\lambda\mu = 0$. This gives rank $L \leq 1$. This is a contradiction by Lemma 5.4. Consequently, we see that $H \neq \lambda_1 + \alpha$ and hence $h_1 = 0$ by (5.6).

Theorem 5.3. Let M be a pseudo-Einstein hypersurface of S^{2n+1} $(n \geq 3)$. Then M has two constant principal curvatures or four constant principal curvatures.

Proof. Since $h_1 = 0$, we have from (5.5)

(5.14) $\qquad a = (2n-1) + H\lambda_i - \lambda_i^2, \quad i = 1,\ldots,2n-2,$

(5.15) $\qquad a+b = (2n-2) + H\alpha - \alpha^2.$

On the other hand, by Lemma 5.3, α is a constant. If $\alpha \neq 0$, then H is constant by (5.15). From (5.14) we see that at most two λ_i are distinct and so we denote them by λ and μ. Since H is constant, λ and μ are constant by (5.14).

We next assume that $\alpha = 0$. Then we have $H = p\lambda + (2n-2-p)\mu$, where p denotes the multiplicity of λ.

Suppose that $a > (2n-1)$. If $\lambda \neq \mu$ at some point, then from $H = \lambda + \mu$, we have $(p-1)\lambda + (2n-3-p)\mu = 0$. Since $\lambda\mu = a - (2n-1) > 0$, λ and μ have the same sign and hence $p = 1$ and $n = 4/2 = 2$. This is a contradiction. Thus we must have $\lambda = \mu$ at each point. Thus (5.14) implies that $(2n-3)\lambda^2 = a - (2n-1)$, and hence λ is constant. Suppose that $a < (2n-1)$. If $\lambda = \mu$ at some point, then $(2n-3)\lambda^2 = a - (2n-1) < 0$. This is a contradiction and hence $\lambda \neq \mu$ at each point. Thus we have $H = p\lambda + (2n-2-p)\mu = \lambda + \mu$ and $\lambda\mu = a - (2n-1)$. Consequently, λ and μ are constant. We next assume that $a = (2n-1)$. Then $\lambda\mu = 0$. Thus if $\lambda \neq 0$, then $H = p\lambda$ and hence (5.14) implies that $(p-1)\lambda^2 = 0$. Thus we have $p = 1$. We assume that $Ae_i = 0$, $i = 1,\ldots,2n-3$, $Ae_{2n-2} = \lambda e_{2n-2}$. On the other hand, we have $AU = \alpha U + \xi$. Thus we have

$$g((\nabla_{e_i} A)e_j, U) = -g(e_j, Pe_i), \quad i,j = 1,\ldots,2n-3.$$

Hence the equation of Codazzi implies that $g(e_j, Pe_i) = 0$. Since $n \geq 3$, we can take e_j and e_i such that $g(e_j, Pe_i) \neq 0$. This is a contradiction. Therefore $a \neq (2n-1)$.

We now consider the matrix $\begin{bmatrix} 0 & 1 \\ 1 & \alpha \end{bmatrix}$. Then the eigenvalues of this matrix satisfy the quadratic equation

$$(5.16) \qquad\qquad t^2 - \alpha t - 1 = 0.$$

Let $\lambda = \mu$. Then we have

$$g((\nabla_{e_i} A)e_j, U) = -\lambda^2 g(e_j, Pe_i) + \alpha\lambda g(e_j, Pe_i) + g(e_j, Pe_i).$$

From the equation of Codazzi we have

$$(5.17) \qquad\qquad (\lambda^2 - \alpha\lambda - 1)g(e_j, Pe_i) = 0.$$

Therefore we have $\lambda^2 - \alpha\lambda - 1 = 0$ and hence λ satisfies (5.16). Thus M has two constant principal curvatures. Let $\lambda \neq \mu$. We take an orthonormal frame $\{e_a, e_r, U, \xi\}$ such that $Ae_a = \lambda e_a$, $Ae_r = \mu e_r$, where $a,b,c = 1,\ldots,p$; $r,s,t = p+1,\ldots,2n-2$. Then we have

$$g((\nabla_{e_r} A)e_a, U) = \alpha\mu g(e_a, Pe_r) + g(e_a, Pe_r) - \lambda\mu g(e_a, Pe_r),$$

$$g((\nabla_{e_a} A)e_r, U) = \alpha\lambda g(e_r, Pe_a) + g(e_r, Pe_a) - \lambda\mu g(e_r, Pe_a).$$

From these equations and equation of Codazzi we have

(5.18) $\qquad (\alpha\lambda + \alpha\mu + 2 - 2\lambda\mu)g(e_r, Pe_a) = 0.$

If $g(e_r, Pe_a) \neq 0$ for some r and a, then we have

(5.19) $\qquad \alpha\lambda + \alpha\mu + 2 - 2\lambda\mu = 0.$

If λ or μ satisfies (5.16), then $\lambda^2 - \alpha\lambda - 1 = 0$ or $\mu^2 - \alpha\mu - 1 = 0$.
Let $\lambda^2 - \alpha\lambda - 1 = 0$. Then (5.19) implies that $(\alpha-2\lambda)(\mu-\lambda) = 0$. Since
$\lambda \neq \mu$, we have $\lambda = \alpha/2$. Thus we have $\alpha^2/4 - \alpha^2/2 - 1 = 0$ and hence
$-\alpha^2/4 = 1$. This is a contradiction. Consequently, λ and μ do not satisfy
(5.16). Thus M has four constant principal curvatures.

If $g(e_r, Pe_a) = 0$ for all r and a, then we have $p \geq 2$ and
$(2n-2-p) \geq 2$. In this case, by the method similar to that used to obtain
(5.17), we have $\lambda^2 - \alpha\lambda - 1 = 0$ and $\mu^2 - \alpha\mu - 1 = 0$. Therefore λ and μ
satisfy (5.16). Moreover, we see that p and $(2n-2-p)$ are even. Thus the
multiplicities of λ and μ are p+1 and 2n-1-p respectively and hence
they are odd. Consequently, M has two constant principal curvatures.
This proves our theorem.

From Examples 1.1 and 2.1 we see that $M_0'(2n,r)$ is always a pseudo-
Einstein hypersurface of S^{2n+1} and $M'(2n,m,s)$ is pseudo-Einstein if
$s = (m-1)/(n-m)$. Then the Ricci tensor S of $M'(2n,m,(m-1)/(n-m))$ is
given by

$$S(X,Y) = (2n-2)[g(X,Y) - \eta(X)\eta(Y)]$$

$$+ \eta(X)S(\xi,Y) + \eta(Y)S(\xi,X) - \eta(X)\eta(Y)S(\xi,\xi),$$

that is, $a = 2n-2$ and $b = 0$. Furthermore $M'(2n,t)$ is pseudo-Einstein if t = 1/(n-1) and the Ricci tensor S of M'(2n,1/(n-1)) is given by

$$S(X,Y) = (2n-2)[g(X,Y) - \eta(X)\eta(Y)] + (4-4n)u(X)u(Y)$$

$$+ \eta(X)S(\xi,Y) + \eta(Y)S(\xi,X) - \eta(X)\eta(Y)S(\xi,\xi),$$

that is, a = 2n-2 and b = 4-4n.

Moreover, M'(2n,1/(n-1)) is not minimal and $M_0'(2n,2n-1)$, M'(2n,(n+1)/2,1) are minimal in S^{2n+1}.

Theorem 5.4 (Yano-Kon [67]). If M is a complete pseudo-Einstein hypersurafce of S^{2n+1} (n $\geq$ 3), then M is congruent to some $M_0'(2n,r)$ or to some M'(2n,m,(m-1)/(n-m)) or to M'(2n,1/(n-1)).

Proof. From Theorem 5.3 we see that M has two or four constant principal curvatures. If M has two constant principal curvatures, then M is $M_0'(2n,r)$ or M'(2n,m,s) (cf. [40]). Since M is pseudo-Einstein, M is $M_0'(2n,r)$ or M'(2n,m,(m-1)/(n-m)). If M has four constant principal curvatures, one of the principal curvatures has multiplicity 1. Therefore, by a theorem of [48], M is M'(2n,t). Since M is pseudo-Einstein, M is congruent to M'(2n,1/(n-1)).

Theorem 5.5 (Yano-Kon [67]). If M is a complete pseudo-Einstein minimal hypersurface of S^{2n+1} (n $\geq$ 3), then M is congruent to $M_0'(2n,2n-1)$ or to M'(2n,(n+1)/2,1). In the latter case, n is odd.

From the results of §1 of Chapter V we have

Theorem 5.6. Let M be a hypersurface of S^{2n+1} tangent to ξ and N be a real hypersurface of CP^n such that the diagram

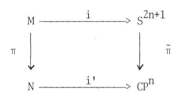

commutes and i is a diffeomorphism on the fibres. Then M is pseudo-Einstein hypersurface of S^{2n+1} if and only if N is a pseudo-Einstein real hypersurface of CP^n.

§6. (f,g,u,v,λ)-structure

Let S^{2n+1} be a $(2n+1)$-dimensional unit sphere with standard Sasakian structure (ϕ,ξ,η,g) and M be a 2n-dimensional hypersurface isometrically immersed in S^{2n+1}. We denote by the same g as that of S^{2n+1} the induced metric tensor field of M. We also denote by C a unit normal of M in S^{2n+1}.

For any vector field X tangent to M we put

$$\phi X = fX + u(X)C, \qquad \xi = V + \lambda C, \qquad \phi C = -U,$$

$$v(X) = \eta(X), \qquad \lambda = \eta(C) = g(\xi,C),$$

where f is a tensor field of type $(1,1)$, u, v 1-forms, U, V vector fields and λ a scalar function on M. Then they satisfy

$$f^2X = -X + u(X)U + v(X)V, \quad u(fX) = \lambda v(X), \quad v(fX) = -\lambda u(X),$$

$$fU = -\lambda V, \quad fV = \lambda U, \quad u(V) = 0, \quad v(U) = 0, u(U) = 1 - \lambda^2,$$

$$v(V) = 1 - \lambda^2.$$

Moreover, we have

$$g(U,X) = u(X), \quad g(V,X) = v(X), \quad g(fX,Y) = -g(X,fY),$$

$$g(fX,fY) = g(X,Y) - u(X)u(Y) - v(X)v(Y).$$

In other words, M has the so-called (f,g,u,v,λ)-structure (Yano-Okumura [75]).

If we consider a 2n-dimensional unit sphere S^{2n} as a totally geodesic hypersurface of S^{2n+1}, then S^{2n} has an (f,g,u,v,λ)-structure.

It might be interesting to study hypersurfaces of S^{2n+1} by means of (f,g,u,v,λ)-structure (see Blair-Ludden-Yano [9], Kon [30], Nakagawa-Yokote [35], Yamaguchi [54] and Yano-Ishihara [62]).

In the following we state some results for such hypersurfaces.

Theorem 6.1 (Kon [30]). Let M be a complete hypersurface of S^{2n+1} (n $\geq$ 2). If fA = Af, then M is congruent to $S^{2n}(\alpha^2+1)$, $\alpha = v(AV)/(1-\lambda^2)$, or to $S^{2p+1}(r_1) \times S^{2q+1}(r_2)$, p+q = n-1.

Theorem 6.2 (Nakagawa-Yokote [35]). Let M be a complete hypersurface of S^{2n+1} $(n \geq 3)$ with constant scalar curvature. If $fA + Af = kf$, k being a function, then one of the following two assertions (a) and (b) is true:

(a) M is congruent to one of the following spaces:

    (1) the great sphere S^{2n},

    (2) the small sphere $S^{2n}(r)$,

    (3) the product manifold $S^{2n-1}(r_1) \times S^1(r_2)$,

    (4) the product manifold $S^n(r_1) \times S^n(r_2)$,

(b) M has exactly four distinct constant principal curvatures of multiplicities n-1, n-1, 1 and 1 respectively.

The hypersurface appearing in (b) of Theorem 6.2 is determined by a theorem of Takagi [48] (see also Example 1.1 of Chapter VI), that is, the hypersurface is M'(2n,t).

In Theorem 6.2, if M is compact orientable, we have the same conclusion without the assumption that the scalar curvature of M is constant.

Let S^{2m} be a 2m-dimensional unit sphere with (f,g,u,v,λ)-structure. We next consider an n-dimensional submanifold M of S^{2m} (Yano-Kon [64]).

Theorem 6.3. Let M be a complete submanifold of S^{2m}. If M is tangent to the vector field U, then M is a sphere of radius 1.

If fX is tangent to M for all vectors X tangent to M, then M is called an <u>invariant submanifold</u> of S^{2m}.

Theorem 6.4. Let M be an n-dimensional complete invariant submanifold of S^{2m} with $\lambda \neq 0$ almost everywhere on M. If M is minimal, then M is an even dimensional sphere of radius 1.

Theorem 6.5. Let M be an n-dimensional submanifold of S^{2m} normal to the vector field U. If $\lambda = 0$, then M lies on a great hypersphere orthogonal to U. If $\lambda \neq 0$, then M lies on a small hypersphere orthogonal to U.

If $T_x(M) \perp fT_x(M)$ for all $x \in M$, then M is called an <u>anti-invariant submanifold</u> of S^{2m}.

Theorem 6.6. Let M be an n-dimensional anti-invariant submanifold of S^{2m}. If $\lambda = 0$ on M, then M is an anti-invariant submanifold of a great hypersphere S^{2m-1} in S^{2m} orthogonal to U with respect to the induced Sasakian structure on S^{2m-1}.

Theorem 6.7. Let M be an n-dimensional submanifold of S^{2m} normal to the vector field V. If $\lambda = 0$ on M, then M is an anti-invariant submanifold of a great hypersphere S^{2m-1} orthogonal to U in S^{2m} with respect to the induced Sasakian structure on S^{2m-1}.

BIBLIOGRAPHY

[1] K. Abe, Applications of Riccati type differential equation to Rie-mannian manifolds with totally geodesic distribution, Tôhoku Math. J., 25 (1973), 425-444.

[2] A. Bejancu, CR submanifolds of a Kaehler manifold I, Proc. Amer. Math. Soc., 69 (1978), 135-142.

[3] ____, On integrability conditions on a CR submanifold, An.st. Univ. "Al. I. Cuza" Iasi, 24 (1978), 21-24.

[4] ____, CR submanifolds of a Kaehler manifold II, Trans. Amer. Math. Soc., 250 (1979), 333-345.

[5] ____, Normal CR-submanifolds of a Kaehler manifold, An. st. Univ. "Al. I. Cuza" Iasi, 26 (1980), 123-132.

[6] ____, Umbilical CR-submanifolds of a Kaehler manifold, Rendiconti di Mat., (3) 15 serie VI (1980), 431-446.

[7] A. Bejancu, M. Kon and K. Yano, CR-submanifolds of a complex space form, J. Differential Geometry, 16 (1981), 137-145.

[8] D. E. Blair and B. Y. Chen, On CR-submanifolds of Hermitian mani-folds, Israel J. Math., 34 (1979), 353-363.

[9] D. E. Blair, G. D. Ludden and K. Yano, Hypersurfaces of an odd-dimensional sphere, J. Differential Geometry, 5 (1971), 479-486.

[10] W. Boothby and H. C. Wang, On contact manifolds, Ann. of Math., 68 (1958), 721-734.

[11] B. Y. Chen, Geometry of submanifolds, Marcel Dekker, Inc., New York, 1973.

[12] ____, On CR-submanifolds of a Kaehler manifold, to appear.

[13] ____, Differential geometry of real submanifolds in a Kaehler manifold, to appear.

[14] B. Y. Chen and K. Ogiue, Some extrinsic results for Kaehler submanifolds, Tamkang J. Math., 4 (1973), 207-213.

[15] S. S. Chern, Einstein hypersurfaces in a Kaehler manifold of constant holomorphic curvature, J. Differential Geometry, 1 (1967), 21-31.

[16] S. S. Chern, M. do Carmo and S. Kobayashi, Minimal submanifolds with second fundamental form of constant length, Functional analysis and related fields, Springer, (1970), 59-75.

[17] J. Erbacher, Reduction of the codimension of an isometric immersion, J. Differential Geometry, 5 (1971), 333-340.

[18] _____, Isometric immersions of constant mean curvature and triviality of the normal connection, Nagoya Math. J., 45 (1971), 139-165.

[19] S. Greenfield, Cauchy-Riemann equations in several variables, Ann. Scuola Norm. Sup. Pisa, 22 (1968), 275-314.

[20] Y. Hatakeyama, Some notes on differentiable manifolds with almost contact structures, Tôhoku Math. J., 15 (1963), 176-181.

[21] I. Ishihara, Kaehler submanifolds satisfying a certain condition on normal connection, Atti della Accademia Nazionale dei Lincei, LXII (1977), 30-35.

[22] I. Ishihara and M. Kon, Contact totally umbilical submanifolds of a Sasakian space form, Annali di Mat., 114 (1977), 351-364.

[23] S. Ishihara, Normal structure f satisfying $f^3 + f = 0$, Kōdai Math. Sem. Rep., 18 (1966), 36-47.

[24] S. Ishihara and M. Konishi, Differential geometry of fibred spaces, Study Group of Differential Geometry, Japan, 1973.

[25] K. Kenmotsu, Some remarks on minimal submanifolds, Tôhoku Math. J., 22 (1970), 240-248.

[26] U-Hang Ki and J. S. Pak, Generic submanifolds of an even-dimensional Euclidean space, J. Differential Geometry, 16 (1981), 293-303.

[27] U-Hang Ki, J. S. Pak and Y. H. Kim, Generic submanifolds of complex projective spaces with parallel mean curvature vector, Kodai Math. J., 4 (1981), 137-155.

[28] S. Kobayashi and K. Nomizu, Foundations of differential geometry, Vol. I and II, Wiley Interscience, 1963 and 1969.

[29] M. Kon, Kaehler immersions with trivial normal connection, TRU Math., 9 (1973), 29-33.

[30] _____, On hypersurfaces immersed in S^{2n+1}, Ann. Fac. Aci. de Kinshasa, 4 (1978), 1-24.

[31] _____, Pseudo-Einstein real hypersurfaces in complex space forms, J. Differential Geometry, 14 (1979), 339-354.

[32] _____, Real minimal hypersurfaces in a complex projective space, Proc. Amer. Math. Soc., 79 (1980), 285-288.

[33] _____, Generic minimal submanifolds of a complex projective space, Bull. London Math. Soc., 12 (1980), 355-357.

[34] H. B. Lawson Jr., Rigidity theorems in rank-1 symmetric spaces, J. Differential Geometry, 4 (1970), 349-357.

[35] H. Nakagawa and I. Yokote, Compact hypersurfaces in an odd dimensional sphere, Kōdai Math. Sem. Rep., 25 (1973), 225-245.

[36] K. Nomizu, Some results in E. Cartan's theory of isoparametric families of hypersurfaces, Bull. Amer. Math. Soc., 79 (1973), 1184-1188.

[37] M. Okumura, On some real hypersurfaces of a complex projective space, Trans. Amer. Math. Soc., 212 (1975), 355-364.

[38] _____, Compact real hypersurfaces of a complex projective space, J. Differential Geometry, 12 (1977), 595-598.

[39] _____, Compact real hypersurfaces with constant mean curvature of a complex projective space, J. Differential Geometry, 13 (1978), 43-50.

[40] P. J. Ryan, Homogeneity and some curvature conditions for hypersurfaces, Tôhoku Math. J., 21 (1969), 363-388.

[41] K. Sakamoto, Complex submanifolds with certain conditions, Kōdai Math. Sem. Rep., 27 (1976), 334-344.

[42] S. Sasaki, Almost contact manifolds, Lecture Notes, Tôhoku Univ., 1965.

[43] J. Simons, Minimal varieties in riemannian manifolds, Ann. of Math., 88 (1968), 62-105.

[44] B. Smyth, Differential geometry of complex hypersurfaces, Ann. of Math., 85 (1967), 247-266.

[45] R. E. Stong, The rank of an f-structure, Kōdai Math. Sem. Rep., 29 (1977), 207-209.

[46] R. Takagi, Real hypersurfaces in a complex projective space with constant principal curvatures, J. Math. Soc. Japan, 27 (1975), 43-53.

[47] ____, Real hypersurfaces in a complex projective space with constant principal curvatures II, J. Math. Soc. Japan, 27 (1975), 507-516.

[48] ____, A class of hypersurfaces with constant principal curvatures in a sphere, J. Differential Geometry, 11 (1976), 225-233.

[49] T. Takahashi, Hypersurface with parallel Ricci tensor in a space of constant holomorphic sectional curvature, J. Math. Soc. Japan, 19 (1967), 199-204.

[50] Y. Tashiro, On contact structure of hypersurfaces in complex manifolds, I, Tôhoku Math. J., 15 (1963), 62-78.

[51] Y. Tashiro and S. Tachibana, On Fubinian and C-Fubinian manifolds, Kōdai Math. Sem. Rep., 15 (1963), 176-183.

[52] R. O. Wells, Jr., Compact real submanifolds of a complex manifold with nondegenerate holomorphic tangent bundles, Math. Ann., 179 (1969), 123-129.

[53] ____, Function theory on differentiable manifolds, Contribution to analysis, Academic Press, (1974), 407-441.

[54] S. Yamaguchi, On hypersurfaces in Sasakian manifolds, Kōdai Math. Sem. Rep., 21 (1969), 64-72.

[55] K. Yano, On harmonic and Killing vector fields, Ann. of Math., 55 (1952), 38-45.

[56] ____, On a structure defined by a tensor field f of type $(1,1)$ satisfying $f^3 + f = 0$, Tensor N. S., 14 (1963), 99-109.

[57] ____, Differential geometry on complex and almost complex spaces, Pergamon Press, New York, 1965.

[58] K. Yano, Integral formulas in Riemannian geometry, Marcel Dekker Inc., New York, 1970.

[59] K. Yano and S. Ishihara, On integrability conditions of a structure f satisfying $f^3 + f = 0$, Quart. J. Math., 15 (1964), 217-222.

[60] ____, Fibred spaces with invariant Riemannian metric, Kōdai Math. Sem. Rep., 19 (1967), 317-360.

[61] ____, Submanifolds with parallel mean curvature vector, J. Differential Geometry, 6 (1971), 95-118.

[62] ____, Notes on hypersurfaces of an odd-dimensional sphere, Kōdai Math. Sem. Rep., 24 (1972), 422-429.

[63] K. Yano and M. Kon, Anti-invariant submanifolds, Marcel Dekker Inc., New York, 1976.

[64] ____, Submanifolds of an even-dimensional sphere, Geometriae Dedicata, 6 (1977), 131-139.

[65] ____, CR-sous-variétés d'un espace projectif complexe, C. R. Acad. Sci. Paris, 288 (1979), 515-517.

[66] ____, Generic submanifolds, Annali di Mat., 123 (1980), 59-92.

[67] ____, Generic submanifolds of Sasakian manifolds, Kodai Math. J., 3 (1980), 163-196.

[68] ____, Generic submanifolds with semidefinite second fundamental form of a complex projective space, Kyungpook Math. J., 20 (1980), 47-51.

[69] ____, Differential geometry of CR-submanifolds, Geometriae Dedicata, 10 (1981), 369-391.

[70] ____, Generic minimal submanifolds with flat normal connection, E. B. Christoffel, Aachen Birkhäuser Verlag, Basel, (1981), 592-599.

[71] ____, CR submanifolds of a complex projective space, J. Differential Geometry, 16 (1981), 431-444.

[72] ____, On some minimal submanifolds of an odd dimensional sphere with flat normal connection, Tensor N. S., 36 (1982), 175-179.

[73] K. Yano and M. Kon, Contact CR submanifolds, Kodai Math. J., 5 (1982), 238-252.

[74] _____, Generic minimal submanifolds with flat normal connection II, to appear.

[75] K. Yano and M. Okumura, on (f,g,u,v,λ)-structure, Kōdai Math. Sem. Rep., 22 (1970), 401-423.

AUTHOR INDEX

Progress in Mathematics
Edited by J. Coates and S. Helgason

Progress in Physics
Edited by A. Jaffe and D. Ruelle

- A collection of research-oriented monographs, reports, notes arising from lectures or seminars
- Quickly published concurrent with research
- Easily accessible through international distribution facilities
- Reasonably priced
- Reporting research developments combining original results with an expository treatment of the particular subject area
- A contribution to the international scientific community: for colleagues and for graduate students who are seeking current information and directions in their graduate and post-graduate work.

Manuscripts

Manuscripts should be no less than 100 and preferably no more than 500 pages in length.

They are reproduced by a photographic process and therefore must be typed with extreme care. Symbols not on the typewriter should be inserted by hand in indelible black ink. Corrections to the typescript should be made by pasting in the new text or painting out errors with white correction fluid.

The typescript is reduced slightly (75%) in size during reproduction; best results will not be obtained unless the text on any one page is kept within the overall limit of 6x9½ in (16x24 cm). On request, the publisher will supply special paper with the typing area outlined.

Manuscripts should be sent to the editors or directly to:
Birkhäuser Boston, Inc., P.O. Box 2007, Cambridge,
Massachusetts 02139

PROGRESS IN MATHEMATICS
Already published

PROGRESS IN PHYSICS

Already published